WE ARE VOTING REPUBLICAN YEAR RIGHT DOWN THE LINE. N UNGLERS AND WASTERS FOR

"D" LABORER

FAVNRFN IAP

Democrat

Defeat

NO! NO
WE DON

WANT STRONG
ARY FORCES
PROTECTION!

REPUBLIC

Invasion

Watkins Fiddle

World Burn

Watk

Stand in Korean Crisis Shocks U

Vatkins Extreme Isolationist

JK 1976
PG4 US
Electioneering
Propaganda Campaign

"It would be a BIASED CRITIC, indeed who uld withhold from Mr. Truman full credit for bold decision made by him in the Korean

the House, the only bleat came from
antonio who st adheres to the
T POINT OF VI CARES FAR LESS
UR CONSTITU OR AN OAK
A FALL no one
to line u THE
and
as
he
V

"Cong
elled t
was
Bridg
Pres
re
s

MSCLES IN'

r to Electi

en

to Electi

POLITICAL
DYNAMITING

POLITICAL DYNAMITING

FRANK H. JONAS

EDITOR

UNIVERSITY OF UTAH PRESS
SALT LAKE CITY, UTAH

LIBRARY OF CONGRESS CATALOG CARD NUMBER 74-131378
STANDARD BOOK NUMBER 0-87480-071-4
©1970 BY THE UNIVERSITY OF UTAH
PRINTED IN THE UNITED STATES OF AMERICA

Walter E. Quigley
In Memoriam

PREFACE

THE members of a panel came together in San Diego in March 1963 on the occasion of the annual meeting of the Western Political Science Association to present their papers on political slander in selected election campaigns in some Western states. Before they met, the importance of two aspects other than a description of campaign strategy and tactics had become evident. These aspects were questions of definition and problems concerning what to do about ethically improving political campaigns.

Because the phrase "political dynamiting" had not come into either academic or general usage, it was decided to entitle the panel "Political Slander in Election Campaigns." There had been considerable discussion about whether to use the word "slander" in the panel's title or the originally proposed title, "political dynamiting."

Bruce Felknor, chairman of the panel, had dealt directly for many years with the problem of political behavior in election campaigns as executive director of the Fair Campaign Practices Committee with headquarters in New York City. He stated in his introductory remarks that

> dynamiting is a more explicit title than slander. . . . Slander is inexact, for the most troublesome matter in our area is hard to deal with exactly because it is *not* slander or libel. Defamation is too general. Innuendo is too limited. Character assassination is only older, no more scholarly nor more precise per se. You could say the destruction of political careers by sudden strategically timed publication of carefully researched, damaging, difficult-to-answer charges based upon selected excerpts from the truth.

The term "smear" was avoided for what seemed to be obvious reasons. Objection had been made to the word "slander" because it is a legal term and the panel was to deal with political behavior and campaign materials which were not illegal. Felknor had hit upon the essence of the meaning of "political dynamiting" when he used the words, "selected excerpts from the truth." True, these selections usually appeared in print at a well-timed moment of the campaign, but the publication need not have been a roorback, an entirely false report. The purpose of the dynamiting, which could be a well-timed single shot in the form of a "bomb" or a series of small explosions by party hirelings, campaign managers, public relations counsels, or separate but well-coordinated campaigns by political groups, was to blast a man out of public office or out of politics during a campaign. "Political dynamiting" properly refers to "political research" in a candidate's past life and public record and then the use of these materials as propaganda, usually in the form of the printed page, to achieve this purpose. What is important, therefore, is the form in which the researched materials appear in public, and what is even more important is the manner of delivery or release of the printed materials to the public.

On the panel as in this book, I have examined—then briefly, now in considerable detail—"The Political Dynamiter and His Art" by reviewing the work of Walter E. Quigley. For more than fifty years Quigley was on the "dynamiting trail," not only in campaigns in his adopted state of Minnesota, but also in many other states in the campaigns of many famous politicians.

Although Quigley worked as a political researcher and writer in nearly every way a person or public relations counsel is used today in a political campaign, his specialty was a "single shot" in the form of a four- or six-page newspaper. His genius was revealed in the propaganda devices he employed: large banner and subheadlines in black, boldface type; bold and regular type alternated in the story, reminiscent of the Hearst style; carefully selected, truthful statements from the written record of a candidate's previous utterances and actions, rendered with the twist and turn which could make almost any person appear a scoundrel; and especially the cartoon, usually a crude caricature of a man; and finally, repetition. Repetition is not only the mother of learning but is also one of the very few "principles" of propaganda.

Quigley asserted that, in his experience, "people like rough and tumble campaigns." He said that the only way to begin to combat "dynamiting" is to dynamite back, adding as an afterthought, "if one has the ammunition." In political dynamiting—indeed, in any political campaign—the important elements are a theme, a blueprint, strategy and tactics, timing, and pacing. One should not empty his arsenal of tactics on any one day or too early in a campaign; he should always leave something for the next day.

Keeping the newspaper secret until the moment of its appearance, Quigley would use the regular mails to have copies placed on the same day in every mailbox in the state. The result would be a propaganda missile which would strike the electorate like a bombshell and take the entire population into its range of explosive fire, demoralizing the ranks of his client's opponents.

Quigley was a pioneer in the development of mass appeal and mass distribution of political propaganda in campaigns. He not only aroused fear, hate, and doubt in the minds of the voters, but he also caused politicians to fear him. In several campaigns, he was paid by a candidate to stay out so that his opponent could not employ him. Although Quigley's methods were generally disapproved and those who hired him and those who were victimized by his talented efforts would privately damn him, he was generally considered honest; that is, once bought, he stayed bought. He exercised a peculiar power. Calloused by many years of abuse, Quigley was willing to "take it" as well as "dish it out." He would go anywhere, working either side of the political fence, and dare to call a spade a spade. Insensitive to personal attacks, immune from the law, he feared no one. And he never failed to extract a high fee from his clients.

Some observers have noted that the writers have examined only those campaigns in which the Republicans were the dynamiters and the Democrats the victims. They have suggested that the editor should have found a balance in the choice of campaigns. This view, however, does not take into consideration the nature of campaigns in the postwar period.

The period after World War II, especially 1950 to 1954, was a time when hard-hitting campaigns were prevalent not only in the Western states but in the rest of the nation as well. This fact has been recognized by analysts and observers. One analyst, Gerald Edwin Hansen, has written, in "The Conservative Movement in Utah after World War II":

> The elections of 1950, 1952 and 1954 were probably the most bitter in Utah history, and probably the lowest experienced in Utah history. Never had the use of invective, name calling, guilt by association, misquotating, using material out of context and open prevarication, been practiced to such a degree as it was in those elections. To a large extent this was also true of the nation.

One must look at the conditions in each state during this period. Briefly, the situation in Utah was that the Republicans had not held the governorship for twenty-four years, one senatorship for thirty years, and the other for eighteen years. This meant, in the case of the governorship, that the Republicans had little or no patronage in the state capitol. They were desperate men.

In the cases of Arizona and California the Democrats held advantages of a two-to-one or a three-to-two registration. In Arizona, the prestige party was the Democratic party, although a large migration of Republicans from the Midwest was displacing the Democrats, especially in Maricopa County. Also in 1958, the Republicans had to consider seriously a Democratic tide which swept the West and in part the nation. Their first advantage was a colorful incumbent as their nominee, Barry Goldwater. Their second advantage was a Democratic party torn by intraparty conflicts and internecine warfare. Still, the historically Democratic majority in the state and the tide of Democratic popularity were considered heavy Democratic advantages and were compensated for by a well planned and unusually hard-hitting campaign. Fortunately, Goldwater had a comparatively inept candidate as his opponent. Luck was with him and the Republicans in 1958, but victory at the polls was not guaranteed and not secured without hard work and a heavy propaganda bombardment of the electorate. After all, Goldwater was the only Republican in the West to win or retain a senate seat in 1958. Elbert D. Thomas, on the other hand, was the only Democratic member of the congressional delegation from Utah to lose his seat in 1950. It would appear that Goldwater would not have won nor Thomas have lost without the heavy use of propaganda.

Those who would read partisanship on the part of the writers are cautioned to observe closely that the Republicans have been praised for their handiwork. The sole criterion by which propaganda should be judged is success or failure. The Republicans succeeded in Utah and Arizona. They failed in California and Montana. I have tried to give Republican propagandists and political campaign managers in Utah and Arizona credit for their efficient development of a campaign blueprint. Time and again I have criticized their Democratic counterparts for ineptness and lack of preparation. Propaganda campaigns were approached scientifically and were efficiently executed. The fact that some propaganda-supported nominees won and others lost does not make propaganda less scientific. Actually, in a democracy, the losers should not be eliminated from evaluation of political campaigns; they are a necessary and integral part of the political system. They, as much as the winners, make the system work and thereby make democracy work. That the kinds of campaigns described in these pages have the effect of destroying democracy or of making it less than it can and should be, should be a warning to those who are concerned deeply with the survival and continuation of the system. When it was suggested to a group of newspapermen that this kind of exposure and the resultant moral judgments, implied if not directly stated, might serve as a deterrent to questionable political behavior in political campaigns, one newspaperman scoffed; he said that no one would be influenced in this way by reading the history of individual political campaign behavior. If the stakes are high, if the going is rough, if victory is barely in sight or defeat imminent, the politician will hit as hard as he must to win or to overcome an opponent's advantage. A politician generally does not give up in campaigns nor does he refrain from using a campaign technique because of any possible moral consequences or, rather, moral interpretations of his actions. Usually he will use the technique regardless of any future moral consideration.

The bibliography included in this volume is neither complete nor exhaustive. Brought together here are those titles dealing directly with the subject matter and a few titles of general interest to the student of campaign techniques. Actually, the materials dealing directly with political dynamiting are very few in number. The writers used mainly the literature of the time, fugitive materials and newspaper reports; they gained much of their knowledge from personal involvement and close observation and from interviews and correspondence with the principals involved in the campaigns. One purpose of this symposium is to establish some writings in the field of political campaign techniques. It is hoped that this effort might be a beginning for additional studies in this field.

One great problem is that of quantifying, if at all possible, the effectiveness of political techniques in election campaigns. Many techniques are used in a single campaign. Which ones produced success for a candidate? What did the losing candidate fail to do that he might have done to gain success? Winners would prefer not to recall some of the methods used in their campaigns; losers, unless perhaps they have future ambitions, prefer not to recall anything at all about a losing campaign. After the heat and flash of the moment details are soon lost and forgotten. Perhaps only a few impressions remain. Libraries have only begun to accumulate fugitive materials.

The writers are grateful for the help they have received from political analysts, journalists, party officials and workers, public office holders, university colleagues, librarians, and many others.

They are especially grateful to Professor Ellsworth Weaver, editor of the *Western Political Quarterly,* for permission to use materials from the election articles which have appeared biennially in the *Quarterly* since 1948. They also wish to thank Mrs. Elizabeth Dalgliesh, the capable copy editor of the *Western Political Quarterly*, for her service in that capacity on this volume. Her advice and efforts in solving editorial problems are highly valued and very much appreciated.

The writers are also appreciative of the publication of this book by the University of Utah Press; they wish to thank the director, Richard Thurman, and his capable and cooperative staff.

CONTENTS

THE ART OF
POLITICAL
DYNAMITING
AND THE ARTIST

L ATE in the 1950 election campaign in Utah the Republicans hit the people
of the state with a four-page newspaper entitled the *United States Senate
News*, which introduced something new in the form of political publicity into
Utah politics. Printed in Minneapolis, this guided missile, held secret until the
moment of its issue and launched in an extremely efficient manner, struck the
electorate like a bombshell, exploding in every direction at once and taking in
the entire population within its range of explosive fire.

Citizens generally were startled and shocked, some even stunned, although
they already had become morally calloused about anything that might have
come from anywhere because of the incessant and unrelenting propaganda
bombardment that had characterized the most scurrilous campaign in Utah
since the almost forgotten days of the bitter Mormon and anti-Mormon struggles for economic and political position. Republicans understandably were delighted with the further demoralization wrought in the ranks of the Democratic
party by this propaganda invasion from outside the state.

The paper dealt almost exclusively with the candidacy of incumbent
Democratic Senator Elbert D. Thomas, who was trying for his fourth term. Its
contents were designed solely to pin on him the label of communist. In reality,
Republican party strategists intended with this scatological sheet, as some citizens referred to it, to put a clincher on their overall plan to create doubt and
fear in the mind of the voter, and thereby finally to frighten him out of his easy
chair and to the polls on election day.

The *United States Senate News* was the culmination of a Republican campaign based on the single charge of communism against its Democratic opposition. The whole attack was concentrated on Senator Thomas, but it was hoped
that the two incumbent Democratic congressional representatives would be
dragged down with him. Jeremiah Stokes, a former Salt Lake attorney, had
kept a dossier on Thomas even before the 1944 campaign. He sent his materials
to Utah in the form of a thirty-nine-page, photostated article, which was reproduced by the Republicans and used throughout the state. Speakers held up the

photostats and "eyebrows would be lifted and murmurs would roll over the audience."[1] In addition, a broadside, eleven by seventeen inches, was widely distributed. This document alleged that "U.S. Senator Elbert Thomas . . . presided at the Communist war chest, money-raising campaign dinner of the *New Masses* magazine on January 22, 1945, at the Hotel Commodore, New York City." This scurrilous sheet had been issued from the headquarters of Gerald L. K. Smith and Stanley Swift and was distributed in Utah from the apartment of Marilyn R. Allen, their counterpart in the Beehive State. It further alleged that Thomas shared the cochairmanship of the meeting with Paul Robeson. The truth was that Thomas never presided at any Communist function; neither he nor Robeson attended the dinner in question. Of this handbill, Thomas said that it was "the most false, defamatory, insidious, dishonest and hateful attack upon a man's good name and character I have ever seen . . . such a low effort of muckraking servility as to be unbelievable."[2]

But this was merely preliminary. The *coup de grâce* was the *Senate News* itself, the work of Walter E. Quigley of Minneapolis, who made a career of what he himself graphically and accurately called "political dynamiting."[3] Unlike other experts in public relations who usually undertook to manage an entire campaign, Quigley relied mainly upon a single devastating explosion. He was an expert who was called in for this one function. The technique employs the printed page in the form of a newspaper, with dynamite-laden, banner headlines, cartoon caricatures, yellow journalistic make-up, and a slanted presentation of meticulously researched quotations on the published statements and the voting record of the victim of the attack. Such was the *United States Senate News* which was placed in every mailbox in the state.

The Democratic party leaders, who were caught off guard by this event, countered by doing a "research" job on Walter Quigley. They discovered a disbarred lawyer who had a record of association with some questionable elements in his legal practice and political activities in Minnesota. They tried to capitalize on this record and the fact that the paper had come from outside the state. Photostats of this record were sent to Drew Pearson who obliged with this broadcasted commentary:

> Utah Republicans have hired a professional mud-slinger to smear the name of a very fine Senator . . . Elbert D. Thomas of Utah. This paid smear artist is Walter Quigley of Minneapolis, who is now branding Senator Thomas a Communist. Quigley was twice disbarred from practicing law in Minnesota . . . was kicked out as Secretary of the Minneapolis Athletic Commission, but despite this he was hired by [Utah] Republicans.[4]

This attack on Quigley was senseless. It was aimed at the man himself; it neither answered nor countercharged what he had written and published. Indeed, Republican hirelings in the nation's capital, working together full time and uninterruptedly for a solid month, had made significant contributions to the Quigley paper's contents and had had the final word on the make-up. Moreover, Quigley himself gave the best answer to this kind of attack: he merely cited the Pearson broadcast to pinpoint the accuracy of the content in his papers. He wrote later:

> Not only have I never had a libel or slander suit started or threatened, but I have never had the accuracy of anything I ever wrote challenged. I have taken a lot of abuse, even Drew Pearson, during the Thomas campaign, taking after me on a national hookup. But that got me new clients, for they figured I must be good to warrant that attention.[5]

The attack on Quigley was also futile, since it was launched against a man who was neither running for office nor personally responsible for the kind of campaign the Republicans waged in that election year. What has amazed some observers in later years is that the Democrats had absolutely no ammunition in their arsenal to meet the Republican onslaught, although they had had some notice that it would come, if not in this precise form, then in another. It is equally amazing that the Democrats turned their fire on Quigley, who, although a competent hatchet man, was merely a hireling. Why did they not attack the person responsible for the blueprint of the campaign and for paying Quigley's retainer and fees—Guy Gabrielson, chairman of the National Republican Committee, and his staff? Senator Arthur V. Watkins and the members of his Washington staff? Pratt Kesler, Utah State Republican chairman; George Hanson, national committeeman from Utah; and even the Republican senatorial candidate, Wallace F. Bennett, who participated in the major councils which considered and adopted the plan?

What the Democrats learned later was that they had been called upon to deal on the spur of the moment with the polished workmanship of a master craftsman in the art of political publicity, a man who had been on the "dynamiting trail" for almost fifty years and who had prepared some one hundred and fifty similar campaign papers for clients in several states, many with distinguished names.

In fact, the Democrats subsequently could have learned some important lessons in the art of political dynamiting. Indeed, the only effective defense against this kind of propaganda is an offensive prepared in advance for possible use during a campaign. Later Quigley commented on how to meet his own style of propaganda. He did not think that the "quiet way" could offset his type of attack. It had been his experience that "people like rough and tumble campaigns."[6] The only way even to begin to combat "dynamiting" is to dynamite back—"if one has the ammunition." He further observed that he had been fortunate, too, in having clients who were not too vulnerable, except on big issues.

Quigley delighted in recalling the names of his many clients, not only to indicate his expertness, but also to demonstrate his detachment from personal considerations in his work by revealing the range of his clients' political views and affiliations. Referring specifically to his torpedoing of former United States Senators Thomas of Utah and Burton K. Wheeler of Montana, he stated simply that "there was nothing personal in this." Calling attention to the list of his clients on his stationery, he said: "If you will note some of my clients on this stationery you will see I have represented some great liberals and dissenters." At the very top of the list he placed Charles A. Lindbergh, Sr., of Minnesota, and stated parenthetically in his letter, "my former law partner." In another letter, he stated: "Incidentally, I have issued them [campaign papers] for Republicans, Democrats, Farmer-Laborites, Progressives [La Follette] and Independents [George Norris]. So I know them all, probably more so than any person in the nation." On his letterhead he listed such familiar names as Sen. Hiram Johnson of California, Sen. Lynn Frazier of North Dakota, Gov. Charles W. Bryan of Nebraska, Gov. Alfred Smith of New York, Thomas V. Sullivan of Illinois, Sen. James Murray of Montana, Judge Leif Erickson of Montana, Hobart A. Atkins of Tennessee, and Sen. A. V. Watkins of Utah. As groups or committees he listed various labor unions, the National Republican Committee of Washington, and the Utah State Republican Committee. From Minnesota he listed Gov. Floyd B. Olson, Sen. Thomas D. Schall, Sen. Ernest Lundeen, Rep. Harold Knutson, Rep. Harold Hagen, Sen. Joseph H. Ball, Sen. E. F. Ladd, and various party and political group leaders such as Tom Davis, Roy Dunn, A. C. Townley, and M. W. Thatcher. Quigley claimed that 95 percent of his clients were successful at the polls.[7]

Quigley's early career in frontier politics, which began in the then great Northwest, was varied and colorful. While still in high school in 1905 in East Grand Forks, North Dakota, where he was born February 4, 1890, he was on the staff of the Grand Forks *Plaindealer-Press*, a Democratic daily, and after that he worked on a score of papers in several states. His father, Hugh Quigley, born in Canada of Irish parents, was chief of police and a Democrat. His mother was Philmena Ducharme, a French Canadian. Quigley recorded in his unpublished autobiographical manuscript that his "Dad's role depended upon the election of a friendly mayor each biennial election, so our family was a hotbed of politics. From the age of eight until fifteen," he wrote, "I peddled literature, prepared halls for meetings, ran errands for candidates, and nailed posters." Young Quigley, also a Democrat, drifted into police reporting and soon took to the "dynamiting trail" in the "whirlpool of northwestern politics."

At twenty-two he was chairman of the Polk County Democratic organization and president of the Wilson-Ringdal Club and he was up "on the political campaign question so thoroughly that the 'old heads' in politics had little to fear but what the county will show good results."[8]

Quigley quit his job as a reporter and went to work for John Burke, a handsome and articulate Irish-Catholic politician. In a state largely Norwegian-Lutheran east of the Missouri and Russian-German-Lutheran on the western slope, Burke was elected governor three times. With little money, Burke could not afford an experienced publicity man, so Quigley traveled with him. Quigley revealed that he and Burke

> simply raised hell with the "Old Gang," which was vulnerable. No autos and loudspeakers then. We would ride local freights or passenger trains on branch lines or be driven by horses of friendly persons or livery barns. No busses then, either, but my job was to go to the local paper and offer to write a story. County editors are lazy or overworked and, in most cases, they printed my diatribes against the "Gang."[9]

Quigley attended Carleton College for one year and the University of North Dakota law school; he was admitted to the North Dakota bar in 1912. Soon afterwards he went to California for health reasons.

> While in Visalia [California], Hiram Johnson . . . wanted a publicity man, so Whitmore [Charles A. Whitmore, editor and publisher, *Visalia Delta*] "loaned" me to him for six weeks and we tramped around California. Johnson was fighting the Southern Pacific Railroad, which previously had pretty much dominated California politics. He was a rough, tough speaker whom the people liked and admired.[10]

After three months in California, where he served on two newspaper staffs and was admitted to the bar, he returned to Grand Forks and formed a partnership with H. A. Bronson. There followed several legal associations until his disbarment in 1926 and again in 1939. Apparently his law practice brought him only difficulties, but his legal experience undoubtedly gave him the training which enabled him to avoid libel suits in his publicity work.

In 1916 Quigley became an organizer for the Nonpartisan Political League of North Dakota. Except for some skirmishes in North Dakota in 1917, nearly all his League activities were in Nebraska during the two following years; there he had some harrowing and harassing experiences which taught him much about people and propaganda. He took considerable abuse, but "the peppery little Irishman," as he became known, "learned how to take care of himself."[11]

In 1926 Quigley became the notorious author of a round robin which advocated that the Farmer-Labor party identify itself with the Democratic party in the 1926 and 1928 elections. He was charged by the opponents of this movement with being in the employ of the Republicans. He stated categorically that he was paid by the Democrats, and he rationalized his position by pointing to the fact that the Farmer-Labor party did combine with the Democratic party in 1944, a fact which placed him in the role of a prophet vindicated by results. When this prophet role was suggested to him, he began to sign his letters "Eli, the Propheteer."

From 1924 until 1936 Quigley was closely identified with Farmer-Labor party politics and politicians, and in this period he established his reputation as an expert political propagandist and the "bad boy of Minnesota politics," a person to be feared. Subsequently he branched out into other states, particularly with his specialty, the "dynamiting" newspaper—a commodity for which he was still seeking buyers until his death on January 5, 1962. This newspaper technique would seem to have been his own contribution to the art of political propaganda.

A few representative papers will illustrate this technique. For this purpose one "anti"-paper, one "pro"-paper, and two papers with mixed contents have been selected; a few others will be mentioned which contain a different content or emphasis. The Utah paper, however, will be examined in detail in the chapter entitled "The Murder of a Reputation."

In 1946 former Senator Burton K. Wheeler, who had been in the Senate since 1923, was opposed in the primaries for renomination on the Democratic ticket by Leif Erickson. In this election Quigley was hired by A. F. Whitney, president of the Brotherhood of Railroad Trainmen, to do a "hatchet job" on Wheeler, who had been known as a liberal in American politics, but who, prior to the outbreak of World War II, had become widely known as an isolationist. Quigley went to work on him in his characteristic style, on this occasion with a six-page "newspaper" entitled the *Montana News.* Part of the paper contained propaganda favorable to Erickson, while Quigley associated Wheeler with Germany, Hitler, and the Nazis. Because Wheeler allegedly had opposed the American military program, Quigley sought to have the voter believe that Wheeler was unpatriotic and guilty of treason and sabotage. He also made Wheeler appear to be a self-seeking politician who had voted himself a pay raise. One front-page story, just right of center and above the fold, was headlined: "Wheeler Voted SELF Pension During War." On the other side was a similar story headlined, "Wheeler Voted Self Gasoline During War." These two stories, though in single columns, had three lines in boldface type, and were positioned on each side of a cartoon drawing of Leif Erickson which was captioned, "Presenting a Distinguished Montanan." Quigley delighted in characterizing a politician as a selfish person who votes favors for himself, especially in times of war and depression.

With some understanding of Montana politics, Quigley pictured Wheeler as

Presenting A Distinguished Montanan

LEIF ERICKSON

MONTANA

IT'S A PLEASURE TO SHAKE HANDS WITH A FAIR MAN.

APPOINTED BY PRESIDENTS ROOSEVELT AND TRUMAN AS RAIL-LABOR-DISPUTE MEDIATOR; HE HAS SERVED 18 MONTHS IN THIS IMPORTANT WORK. BROTHERHOODS NOMINATED HIM FOR THIS WORK BECAUSE OF HIS FAIRNESS TO LABOR.

NO LONG-TIME WAITING FOR US, BABY! NOT WITH ERICKSON ON OUR SIDE!

A STEP CLOSER TO MY DEGREE.

SPENT MOST OF 15 YEARS WORKING ON MONTANA RANCH AND FARMS. WORKED WAY THROUGH COLLEGE AND UNIVERSITY AS TEACHER, COOK, TAXI DRIVER, WAITER, SALESMAN; WON SCHOLARSHIPS EVEN UNDER RIGID SCHEDULE.

ERICKSON WANTS DIRECT LOANS FOR G.I.'S AT 3%, FLOOR UNDER FARM PRICES FOR 10 YEARS TO HEAD OFF DEPRESSION; INSISTS ON MISSOURI VALLEY AUTHORITY TO DEVELOP MONTANA POWER AND WATER SUPPLY.

Leader to [
Montana F[
Increase Ir

HAS WIDE EXPERIENCE
WAS ELECTED TO STATE
YEARS OF AGE; HELPED [
WATER AND IRRIGATION
THAT HIS ABILITY IS [
FOR DEVELOPMENT TO
AND INDUSTRIAL FUTUR[
A GREAT U. S. SENATOR F

Wheeler Voted
Self Pension
During War

Would Get $4,000
A Year For Life
From Taxpayers

During the darkest days of the war (Jan. 19, 1942), Senator Wheeler voted himself a pension of about $4,000 a year for life on retirement from the Senate, a bill which was passed by a vote of 42-24 on that day. It previously had passed the House.

However, this pensioning of senators and representatives created such a revulsion thruout the nation that later Congress was forced to repeal the law, since virtually every man who had voted for it was under fire from the people of his or her state.

The bill was known as H.B. 3487 and came up for debate on January 19, 1942.

SENATOR HARRY BYRD OF VIRGINIA, ALWAYS AN ADVOCATE OF ECONOMY IN GOVERNMENT AND A DEMOCRAT, SAID, "I

---

a tool of the Anaconda Copper Company—known in Montana politics as "The Company"—a devouring ogre. At the same time he placed Wheeler in opposition to the people, mainly the farmers, the laborers, and the veterans. In addition, he blamed Wheeler for everything he could name which was contrary to the interests of Montana's people. This dynamite-laden paper, paid for by Democrats against a Democrat, was in the same class as the Utah paper paid for by Republicans against Democratic Senator Thomas.

In the Montana paper Wheeler was charged with having "criticized and attacked Soviet Russia, even though hundreds of thousands of Russians were

UNRRA IS COMPOSED OF MANY NATIONS TO FEED THE MILLIONS STARVING IN EUROPE AND ASIA. WHEELER VOTED AGAINST UNRRA, WHICH MEANS HE WAS WILLING TO LET MILLIONS OF WOMEN AND CHILDREN STARVE TO DEATH.

dying on the eastern front, killing off hundreds of thousands of Germans, so the Nazis were able to kill less Americans." In 1950, four years after Wheeler was condemned for having criticized the Russians, Thomas was condemned for having praised them. Thomas should have come up for election in 1946 and Wheeler in 1950; maybe both then would have remained in the Senate for another term.

In this paper there were two sets of eight cartoons each. One set listed the themes against Wheeler. He was pro-German, pro-*America First*, anti-United States preparedness, anti-Roosevelt, anti-Lend-Lease, and anti-UNRRA. In another vein, Quigley cited Wheeler's sending out one million franked postcards in behalf of *America First*.

As a device in depicting Wheeler as pro-German, he used the testimonial, in this case against a person instead of for him; he quoted the former United States ambassador to Germany, William E. Dodd, who allegedly said in 1934 that Wheeler "advocated German domination of all Europe." He used the same technique when he reproduced Henry Stimson's and General George Marshall's reported descriptions of Wheeler's franked postcard mailing as "near treason" and "sabotage."

In calling attention to Wheeler's selfishness and lack of concern for humanity, Quigley really stacked the cards. In a cartoon showing a raggedly dressed mother with a baby in tattered wraps in her arms and a little urchin sitting close by, Wheeler's vote against UNRRA was supposed to have meant that he "was

willing to let millions of women and children starve to death." Then, with stark contrast, in another cartoon in which the reference was to his having voted for a pension for himself, Wheeler was surrounded by moneybags marked with dollar signs; he was represented as saying, "Now, if I get that pension, all my children will be rich too!" Quigley concluded that while millions of children were starving to death, Senator Wheeler was "fixing" to see that his own children would be rich.

Other revelations in Wheeler's record were also intended to make Wheeler appear selfish and grasping. He was supposed to have received five hundred to eight hundred dollars for each speech he made in behalf of *America First*. His wife, the paper pointed out, was treasurer of the *America First* committee's Washington branch, and his son reportedly was California chairman. Then came the association with Nazism. The declaration was made—without documentation—that some Nazi-minded men and organizations helped finance *America First*. By implication, the idea that the Nazis paid Wheeler and the immediate members of his family huge sums of money for "selling the United States down the river" was planted in the minds of the readers.

Although the Montana primary was in 1946 and the war—at least the "battle"—had come and gone, not one single reference was made to any alleged actions or statements by Wheeler in Congress or elsewhere at any time after the war officially began on December 7, 1941. Wheeler apparently honestly believed that President Roosevelt had been leading the United States into war by his policies. Wheeler made the same mistake as those who believe that the nation is not at war until Congress formally so declares. He and others apparently failed to realize that the United States was at war long before Pearl Harbor. The exact date could have been that of either the presidential order to fire on any German submarine or the Lend-Lease agreement with England.

Perhaps the most devastating article Quigley ever wrote for a client about his political opponent was the one in this paper headed, "Wheeler Made Many Bad Predictions: Said U.S. Could Never Be Attacked." Then followed a long list of quotations, in this instance, with complete citations, dates, and sources. The quotations were alternated with commentary which stacked the cards against Wheeler and directed attention to Wheeler's opponent, Erickson.

Quigley rarely quoted from the Bible, but on this occasion he did so: "Where there is no vision, the people perish." Then followed the statements: "Wheeler did not seem to care if the allies lost the war"; "No one has attacked us and no one is going to attack us"; "I do not think we are in any emergency"; "The Japanese Navy could never come over to the U.S. and do any harm"; and finally, "It [Lend-Lease] will plow under every fourth American boy" which was probably the quotation most frequently used against Wheeler in 1941 and then in 1946. Another devastating phrase used against him was that he "did not care if Hitler won." But Quigley carefully avoided making direct charges against Wheeler as he slowly pulled the cloak of Nazism over him. Quigley wrote in his paper that "less than two months before Pearl Harbor, Wheeler gave an interview to the *N.Y. Times Magazine* in which he *practically* said he did not care if Hitler won, and in the same interview Wheeler again *seemed* to care little if Hitler won."[12] He drew these unwarranted conclusions from Wheeler's only quoted statement that "of course we are going to have to make adjustments whoever wins."

In his Montana paper, Quigley quoted from various German-language papers, including the *Voelkischer Beobachter*, the *Deutsche Allgemeine Zeitung*, and the *Deutscher Wekruf*, to the effect that they all "liked the line Wheeler carried on before and during the war. . . ." In one long lead paragraph he mentioned many of these papers with the words Nazis, Lord Haw-Haw, German Bund, Joseph Goebbels, Hitler, and Fritz Kuhn, and placed Wheeler in this company, as if it were natural for him to be there.

Quigley did not know the German language. Nowhere did he give precise citations or references or any indication that these quotations had been translated from the original German by or for him or drawn from an American newspaper text. In two quotations from Hitler he gave the dates but not the name of the newspaper or other source. If any Wheeler supporter had cared enough to check all the quotations from the original German sources for accuracy and reliability, the election would have been over before he could have been well started on his task. After the election, who cared? According to Quigley's paper, the *Beobachter* on March 13, 1941, reported Wheeler's fight against President Roosevelt's Supreme Court reorganization plan. This fight, between Americans, with many Woodrow Wilson Democrats on the Republican side, was news, and every foreign newspaper with a correspondent on American soil would have reported it. The mere fact that Wheeler's name was mentioned in a German newspaper—all newspapers in Germany after the advent of Hitler were Hitler or pro-Nazi newspapers—was enough to condemn him by association. With a slight but practiced twist and turn, Quigley caused each reported quotation or paraphrase to appear to be a friendly tap by Hitler on Wheeler's shoulder. Quigley recalled repeatedly that he liked "to campaign against a man who has written a book or has several hundred votes in Congress or a legislature." He observed that "no matter how sincere he may be, one can take a couple of dozen of these votes or paragraphs from speeches or a book and *crucify* him."[13]

When questioned about his sources for the quotations and statements he used to make Wheeler appear to be a Nazi, Quigley replied that he had found "Senator Wheeler's envelopes in the *New York Times* and *Herald-Tribune* morgues and also in two or three morgues in Washington," but he was not sure, he added, "in just which one he found the translation from the German papers."[14] Actually, Quigley also used German-language newspapers printed in the United States for German readers.

After this lengthy application of the either/or dialectic, which was amplified by long feature stories about Wheeler's evil behavior and Erickson's virtuous conduct and pure thoughts—stories studded, particularly in Wheeler's case, with sententious quotations from his voting record in Congress and his public speeches—Wheeler emerged as a "heel" while Erickson appeared on the clear horizon as a "hero." At least this was what the voters were supposed to see and then think; the contents of this paper, both in picture and word, were aimed at the lowest possible intellectual level. But Quigley knew his people—the masses, and particularly the farmers—for he had worked several years among this group when he was an organizer for the Nonpartisan Political League of North Dakota. Although he worked in this capacity mainly in Nebraska and Minnesota, this episode in his life must be recalled as a factor in the making of a political dynamiter. The farmers in the Farmers Union and the workers in the Mine, Mill and Smelter Union defeated Senator Wheeler in 1946. These groups, associated with the Democratic party, apparently held the balance in Montana politics.

In the second set of cartoons, Wheeler's Democratic primary opponent was depicted as precocious, Roosevelt's friend, a pioneer in bringing electricity to Montana farms, profarmer, and pro-Montana shippers who wanted lower freight rates. While Wheeler was a "bitter opponent of President Roosevelt," Erickson was "a sincere friend and supporter of FDR." While Wheeler was the tool of the Power Trust and Anaconda Copper Mining concern, depicted by two big, double-chinned, fat figures in the cartoon whispering to Wheeler who has his cupped hand to his ear, Erickson "was a pioneer in bringing electricity to Montana farms." While Wheeler opposed a Missouri Valley Authority to make Montana great through power, electricity, irrigation, and reclamation, Erickson, as a farmer himself, was shown seated on a farm tractor in the act of pulling a plough. While Wheeler "was against the Pettengill Bill to correct freight rates so Montana farmers and business could compete with the rest of the nation," Erickson was "for a freight rate structure to help all Montana shippers." And finally, the voters had the choice between an "old man, bitter, opinionated, who has been at the public trough most of his life," or a "young, vigorous, progressive, fair man who will help solve the grave problems of the future."

According to Quigley, he took his copy and cartoons to Helena and went over them with Leif Erickson, who defeated Wheeler 49,419 to 44,513 in the primary. Quigley stated that he prepared all copy in Minneapolis, "taking a steno to the public library and reading and analyzing every vote of Wheeler's from March 4, 1923 to 1946."[15]

The paper was printed in Lewistown, Montana; the CIO distributed it by hand in Butte and Great Falls while in the rest of the state it was delivered by mail to all the boxholders. Quigley said he was paid four thousand dollars for several weeks' work. According to his estimates, in 1946 the total cost, including printing and distribution for covering a state the size of Montana, would have been between ten and twelve thousand dollars.

Quigley cited the *Montana News* as an example of the effectiveness of his efforts. Wheeler, he said, was "considered unbeatable"; he had won in 1940 by a vote of 176,000 to 63,000. He lost in the 1946 Democratic primary to Leif Erickson by about five thousand votes. At the age of thirty-two, Erickson had become a Montana State Supreme Court judge. Quigley thought he was "a very high-class guy and a good speaker," who was backed by most of the labor organizations. Quigley further observed that the conservatives in the Democratic party, "sore about Wheeler's primary defeat, voted for Ecton, the GOP nominee, in November."[16] Later he stated that Erickson had written "to a North Dakota man that my paper was 'decisive.' "

Quigley had little to say about the final outcome of the 1946 senatorial election in Montana. Ecton, the GOP nominee, defeated Erickson by a narrow margin. Quigley thought that Ecton proved to be "one of the weakest senators" he had ever known. Six years later, Mike Mansfield defeated Ecton handily in a successful Republican presidential election year.

When it was suggested to Quigley that the Communists were in the 1946 campaign against Wheeler, and that he himself had used his technique against the Communists in the 1936 and 1938 Minnesota campaigns, he replied that he did not know this fact about the Montana elections until the writer had called it to his attention. Quigley also headlined a two-column boxed story in the *Montana News* as follows: "G. L. K. Smith's America Firsters Endorse Senator Wheeler." However, in his Utah *United States Senate News* he ignored completely the fact that Gerald L. K. Smith had "endorsed" Wallace F. Bennett, the Republican nominee who opposed and defeated incumbent Senator Elbert D. Thomas. It is doubtful if this knowledge, had he possessed it, would have made any difference in his actions. He loved his work, but he was also very interested in the four thousand dollar payment for his services.

Erickson affirmed that the *Montana News* was effective on his behalf in the primary.[17] Apparently there was no such paper in the fall election. The *Montana News* apparently did not particularly surprise the Montana voters. Similar publications had been used in Montana campaigns for many years—perhaps because practically all of the daily newspapers were then owned by the Anaconda Company. The situation has changed since then; the Anaconda Company has now disposed of its newspapers in Montana. Of interest to the discussion of Quigley's identification of Wheeler with "The Company" was the fact that during the period of the Anaconda-controlled press and political domination Wheeler appeared as the Company's enemy and not as its friend or tool. Wheeler once said: "If you ever see my picture on the front page of the Company Press you'll know I've sold out."[18] What had changed in Wheeler's career or in Montana politics to make possible Quigley's identification of Wheeler with the Company was not explained by Quigley; he simply made the identification by association and exploited the unpopularity of the Company with the Montana voters. For example, Quigley captioned the cartoon showing Erickson sitting on a tractor, "Erickson works for a Missouri Valley Authority to make Montana great through power, electricity, irrigation and reclamation. *Wheeler is against MVA, so is Anaconda Copper Mining and so is the power trust.*"

Although no paper comparable to the *Montana News* has since appeared in Montana, the 1946 campaign was not the last vicious one, nor had Quigley made his last appearance in this state. The campaign against United States Senator James E. Murray in 1954 was probably even worse from the standpoint of the smear technique. Murray's opposition issued a twenty-four-page pamphlet entitled *Senator Murray and the Red Web over Congress.* The front cover showed a spider with a man's face hovering over the nation's capitol. The spider was in brilliant red and a hammer and sickle was highlighted on its body. The caption on the bottom of the page read: "The Story of Communist Infiltration of Your U.S. Congress From Official Records and Communist Documents." The narrative, truncated and garbled, which attempted to identify Murray with communism by association, was very similar to that employed by Quigley in his *United States Senate News* against Senator Thomas. Indeed, it would seem that the producers of the material against Senator Murray literally had copied Quigley's style. Although this pamphlet was the principal document used in the 1954 election in Montana, which placed the technique in the category of political dynamiting, the same ideas were used on various radio broadcasts and in newspaper advertisements.

Quigley worked in behalf of Senator Murray in the 1948 senatorial campaign by doing research for the senator's son, Charles. He listed him as a client on his letterhead. Quigley mentioned the Murray campaign frequently in his correspondence. He said he prepared materials for Murray, although he did not specify what materials; he said the CIO paid him. Senator Murray, precisely like Senator Thomas, whom Quigley helped to destroy in 1950, was a 100 percent supporter of New Deal measures, a leading congressional spokesman for labor, and a sponsor of a series of national health-insurance bills. Also he was active in the fight to prevent the passage of the Taft-Hartley bill and later campaigned strongly for its repeal.

Strangely, then, Quigley prepared materials for Murray to combat the kind of propaganda he himself had so effectively prepared *against* Senator Thomas. In the 1950 campaign the identification of Thomas with the CIO was a major factor in the Utah senator's defeat. In the 1948 Montana campaign the CIO hired and paid Quigley. While Senator Thomas lost, Senator Murray was returned to the Senate.

Although Quigley claimed he had blanketed a whole state with a propaganda piece before 1930, the *Minnesota Leader* he prepared in that year appeared to have been his first really successful dynamiting "newspaper," the first extensive use of the technique which was to make him unique among public relations men in politics. It was in this year that Quigley had his greatest success in Minnesota politics; this was in the fight for the senatorial nomination which had the state on edge for months.

The categories of appeals and charges in the *Minnesota Leader* were somewhat different from those in the papers on Thomas and Wheeler, in which Quigley's main objectives were to associate Thomas with communism and Wheeler with Nazism. The *Leader* was produced on behalf of Thomas Schall, blind United States senator, who was seeking the Republican primary nomination and his second term, and was directed against Theodore Christianson, three times the governor of Minnesota (1925-1931), who had raised his sights to take in Washington. Quigley had three main objectives in preparing this paper: to make his client, a Republican, acceptable to the farmer, labor, and veteran groups; to destroy his client's opponent by not letting him or the people forget the alleged scandals which had emerged during his six years in the statehouse; and, finally, to incite racial, nationalistic, and religious groups to hate their governor. These groups included the Catholics, Lutherans, Jews, Irish, Swedish, Germans, Norwegians, and even the Yankees.

Quigley observed that *"many persons vote on their dislikes and prejudices. They would rather vote,"* he said, *"against somebody on a dislike than to ballot for somebody on a fundamental issue."*[19]

In trying to win the farmers for Schall, he adopted the title the *Minnesota Leader*, plagiarizing from the publication of the Nonpartisan League, an action for which, he admitted afterwards, he had "caught hell."[20] According to Quigley's own account:

> The Minnesota Nonpartisan League, which once had 67,000 paid up $16 members . . . had been kept alive by a handful of men and women, the state executive committee. It had a very high value in politics, since it was the "Bible" of so many thousands when the fight was hot. Davis and I were given the mailing list by a majority of the executive committee who backed Schall. The list was old and only about seventy percent alive when we used it. I hired some twenty-five gals in 1930 and we addressed by hand all the list for Schall and it appealed to the Farmer-Laborites to vote for Schall as one who favored labor and the farmers, and it worked. I went to Farmer-Laborites asking that they vote for a GOP, Schall, and they did, by the thousands, and Schall beat the three-

time governor, Theodore Christianson, in the GOP primary in June 1930 by a 94,000 plurality.[21]

The front page bore endorsements of Schall by political and labor leaders. On the left side Quigley reproduced a letter from William E. Borah and on the right side one from William E. Green. These endorsements were referred to repeatedly throughout the paper and were intended to hit both the labor and the farm vote. Two other endorsements were interesting; these were from Theodore Roosevelt and Charles A. Lindbergh, both deceased at the time. Asked if he had a written endorsement on hand from Lindbergh and Roosevelt as documentary evidence, Quigley answered: "Schall supported Ted Roosevelt in 1912 as a Bull Mooser and served with Charles A. Lindbergh, Sr., in Congress from 1914 to 1917."[22] Who was there alive who would say that these two well-known men had not endorsed Schall? The banner headline read: "Progressive Republicans Endorse Schall"; and the three-column, three-line subhead read: "Senator Borah, Harold Knutson, Federation of Labor, Senator Nye, Others, Favor Blind Senator's Wonderful Record at Washington."

In the center of the page, under a sympathetic picture of "the most famous blindman in the world," and his German police dog, Lux, appeared a long list of additional endorsements, the names of persons who "can testify" that the ex-serviceman, the farmer, and the worker "have no more loyal friend in Washington." Lavish use was made of Schall's blindness throughout the paper.

Quigley did not use the cartoon in the *Leader* to the extent he did in the papers on Thomas and Wheeler, but he did reproduce one pro-Schall and three small anti-Christianson cartoons. In one cartoon Schall was represented as a knight with shield and sword. Christianson, on the other hand, was identified with the scandals of his administration. These were fine line drawings and one had to look closely to make out what they represented. In half of the cartoon space the scandals were listed which were pinned on Christianson's administration. Each scandal was named and represented by a drawing: the Cochran-Nelson Gold Note swindle by a man's fat face and a top hat on his head and a pile of moneybags; the Fur Farms case by a small fur-bearing animal with slanted eyes; the two hundred bank failures by a building with a huge hole in one side, which suggested that the job had been done by expert safe-crackers; and the scandal in the treasurer's office by a pile of coins. Two other scandals were merely names, the Foshag collapse and the Diamond Motor Parts.

Christianson's name was brought into these scandals by the usual propaganda technique of pointing out his association with the "criminals." For example, a letter he had written to the president of the Minnesota Conservation Company, wishing the enterprise "every success and hope that it . . . may mean

WHICH?

an additional source of profit and development for Northern Minnesota," was construed as an endorsement for the later actions of the officers of the company, referred to by Quigley as "smooth-tongued salesmen" who had "swindled the public out of hundreds of thousands of dollars," and who, as a result of these actions, had been "indicted by a federal grand jury."

In all these scandals it appeared that the governor had been victimized by some of the men he had trusted and appointed to state office, and who apparently had "let him down," a not unusual occurrence in politics. Actually this paper did not develop in detail each of the scandals—they had received wide press coverage and were still fresh in the voters' memories. Some point was made of the bank failures and of Christianson's alleged refusal to extradite a

Minneapolis banker to Montana where he had been indicted for having made false reports to the state banking commission. One whole page was intended to demonstrate that Schall had fought against chain stores and that chain stores were financing Christianson's campaign, a revelation which was "rallying the independent merchants to the support of Senator Schall."

An appeal to religious groups in behalf of Schall was made by caricaturing Christianson's attitude toward parochial schools. In one cartoon, the figure of a man, labeled "Senor Ted," was depicted in a striding posture with his eyelids almost closed and his mouth turned down. He held a hammer in his hand. He was attired in Mexican garb, with bell-bottom pants and a sash around his waist. In the background were some skeletons of buildings with boards nailed on the doors. These buildings were labeled "parochial school" and "private school." Christianson had advocated that public schools stop teaching the German language and that they not accept grades from private schools.

Years later, in commenting on this cartoon, Quigley said that it "was devastating." He added:

> Minnesota has many Lutheran schools, hundreds of Catholic parochial schools and probably 15 Jewish schools. I intended to appeal to those elements. I can recall on the June night in 1930 when returns were coming in that returns from German, Irish, and Jewish neighborhoods were 10 to 1 for Schall. *People like to vote 'mad'–to hell with fundamentals*–and that is what happened in the GOP primary.[23]

Early in his career Christianson had owned a newspaper called the *Dawson Sentinel*. Besides a long commentary, Quigley had reproduced a facsimile of some devastating quotations taken from this paper whose editorial masthead carried the name of Theodore Christianson, editor. These are a few of the quotations attributed to Schall's opponent and published by him more than a decade before that 1930 election year: "If the German people want food why don't they go down to the bottom of the sea and get it?"; "Pfaender, Lundeen, Van Lear, La Follette, Benedict Arnold, Kaiser Wilhelm and Judas Iscariot. . . . Their words and works speak for them."; "Some of the most outspoken traitors in Lac Qui Parle county are among the Norwegians, Swedes, the Irish and the Yankees." On the other hand Schall was made to appear a great humanitarian: "[The] Governor wanted the German people to starve while Schall made [a] speech to feed women and babies in [the] Fatherland"; and Schall was quoted as having said, "We will be doing our duty as God would have us do it. We can not let prayers for help go up and close our ears against them."

Quigley related that he spent several weeks in the Minnesota State Historical Society archives and read every editorial which Governor Christianson had written in his newspaper between the years 1914 and 1923. He then concluded,

DO YOU WANT THIS?

"The results of my research show that the most vulnerable candidate for office is a newspaperman who writes his own editorial columns."[24] He issued six hundred thousand copies of his special edition of the *Minnesota Leader*. The reception, he noted, was so "enthusiastic" he had an additional one hundred thousand papers printed.

Schall was on the Senate Committee on Post Offices and Post Roads with a veto vote on postmasterships. Quigley assigned men with automobiles to every county to distribute this paper, and these men were loyally assisted in this task by the postmasters. In most cities and towns the papers for every post office patron were left with this official who personally bought the stamps for distribution. In this manner virtually every voter in the state was reached. When the voters saw the reproductions of Christianson's editorials against their institutions, the effect was ruinous to their governor's candidacy. The German voters overwhelmed the governor.

After the primary election in 1930, Quigley continued to produce publicity for Schall and for Floyd Olson, the Farmer-Labor Democratic candidate for governor. He prepared mostly radio speeches which appealed to the farmers in northern and western Minnesota. Olson won handily but Schall's fate hung in the balance until after election day. Behind 50,000 in the early returns from the cities, he finally won over his Democratic opponent by 11,608 votes when the tallies from the northern precincts came in more than 40 to 1 for the blind senator.

An interesting commentary on Quigley's efforts to portray Schall to the voters as a great "progressive senator" was the fact, later reported by Quigley, that when the New Deal assumed power Schall immediately took the lead in fighting every objective of the Roosevelt administration; he kept up a violent and bitter attack on the president and his advisers until the day of his death.

Quigley continued working for Governor Olson in his campaign for reelection in 1932, a presidential election year. He related that soon after Franklin D. Roosevelt visited Minnesota, the Republicans held their state convention and unanimously drafted Earle Brown to run for governor. That night Governor Olson came to Quigley's home perturbed over the endorsement, since Brown had received favorable publicity in the state press for years and almost equaled Olson's county attorney vote when he ran for sheriff. Quigley told Olson he thought Brown would be easy to beat, observing: "Here we are in 1932 with everybody having difficulties paying taxes and making ends meet." He then said:

> Brown, through inheritance, is director of a chain bank; he is a millionaire; a heavy stockholder in the railroad; he owns a herd of Belgium horses worth $125,000, and last year paid only $118.00 in taxes on that herd; he has millions of dollars in cash, bonds and stocks, and only paid $150 in money and credit taxes. *He can be pictured to the voters of this state as a millionaire tax-dodger* and I think will be an easy man to defeat.[25]

Instead of Olson's attacking Brown in the general election, it was decided that the tax-dodging theme should be introduced in the Republican primary. A few days later Franklin Ellsworth, former Republican congressman from the Minnesota Second District, filed as Brown's Republican opponent and Quigley assumed charge of his headquarters at the Rogers Hotel. Quigley was spending Farmer-Labor money in a Republican primary.

Quigley had photographs made of the assessor's records on Brown's horses. Olson obtained a statement of Brown's checking account from the First National Bank of Minneapolis which showed an average daily cash balance for five years of $260,000. A cartoon was drawn, the upper half depicting Brown's horses as prize winners at the International Livestock Show at Chicago and prancing with blue ribbons, the lower half showing old, decrepit, spavined horses with the assessor standing in the yard. This cartoon was posted in many places throughout Minnesota.

Quigley gathered information on the taxes paid by many leading supporters of Brown, including insurance company executives, bankers, and a newspaper owner. These data were compiled and printed, in newspaper form, and hundreds of thousands of the newspapers were distributed throughout Minnesota during the Republican primary. Tom Davis, chief radio speaker for Ellsworth, also publicized these facts and figures about tax dodging. As was expected, Brown defeated Ellsworth, but Brown's candidacy was ruined.

What then happened in the general election illustrated a second requirement in planning a political campaign—having sufficient ammunition in an arsenal of tactics and techniques to be used in any eventuality.

Quigley stated afterwards that:

> The general campaign developed into a mess concerning the morals of the candidates for governor. While I was going through Courthouse files, I found some rather pertinent legal records. There was no intention of using them until I learned that some Republicans had employed women to ring doorbells, ostensibly as cosmetics saleswomen, but actually to spread rumors about Governor Olson. I took photographs of certain documents to Claude McKenzie, Republican National Committeeman, and told him that I proposed to print a half million newspapers containing these photographs. I said to McKenzie: "We have no desire to make a campaign of personalities, and if you will withdraw the women and others, we will not do so. But, if these workers are not recalled within twenty-four hours, I am going to flood the state with papers containing these documents."[26]

McKenzie denied that the doorbell ringers were under his supervision. Quigley felt satisfied that he had the power to recall them and convinced him that the Democrats would retaliate. The matter was then arranged and the scandalmongering was stopped officially.

The 1932 platform was mild, containing none of the public ownership planks of the Nonpartisan League. Olson proposed that "the income tax must be a replacement tax but it must be more than that." He said: "It must shift the burden of taxes from those who cannot, to those who can bear the burden. Taxation must be levied to prevent the concentration of wealth and remove economic inequalities." Olson also advocated that the price of basic farm commodities be fixed by national legislation.

Early in the campaign Olson announced his support of Roosevelt for president, and from that moment on, the candidacies of the two were linked; Roosevelt-Olson clubs were formed all over the state. Farmer-Labor propaganda sought to link Brown with Herbert Hoover's campaign for reelection, and, although Brown sought to avoid the tie-up, he inevitably suffered from the relationship with the national leader of his party. Quigley had put his oar into this part of the campaign, also. He wrote a letter to the members of the Women's Farmer-Labor Club instructing them as follows:

> Place a loud-voiced man at each meeting . . . addressed by Earle Brown. When Mr. Brown begins, it is suggested that you have your man stand up and in a loud voice say: "Mr. Brown, are you supporting President Hoover for re-election?" He will undoubtedly say yes. Then have your man say, "That's all I wanted to know," put on his hat, and walk out.

This incident in Quigley's career is related in his autobiography, but it was also confirmed by Arthur Naftalin, Minnesota state commissioner of administration. He characterized Quigley as a free-lance journalist who, prior to 1932, had wandered in and out of the Farmer-Labor movement. Naftalin had met Quigley; although he never knew him very well, he said that his reputation among those who knew him was of "unconditional venality." Naftalin and others referred to the dynamiting specialist as "poison-pen Quigley." In his few encounters with Quigley, Naftalin was "always impressed with what seemed to be an open, almost winning, friendliness." He said that "at first I found it difficult to deny his sincerity, and it took some time to appreciate fully his true character." Naftalin also added: "As I think about him and your analysis [the writer's] of his work, I believe you have discovered a true genius of his type."[27]

Although Quigley considered his participation in the 1930 Minnesota campaign his most exciting political adventure as a political dynamiter, and certainly the *Minnesota Leader*, which he believed elected Schall, was his masterpiece in the art of political dynamiting up to that time, he pointed to the record he made in the 1938 Minnesota election as the best evidence of the effectiveness of his method. In this year he was employed by Roy Dunn, state Republican chairman, to prepare a separate paper on each of forty-one Farmer-Labor candidates for the Minnesota House of Representatives; thirty-four of them were defeated at the polls, and the legislature in that year went overwhelmingly conservative. In these papers Quigley claimed that after the Communist United Front had been instituted by Soviet Russia in 1935, the Farmer-Labor party had become infiltrated with American Communists, most of them from outside the state and many of them Jews, about whom, surprisingly, he did not hesitate to speak his mind. Not only had they infiltrated the Farmer-Labor party, but they had worked their way into positions of influence and sometimes of control in the CIO, the Workers Alliance, the Board of Regents of the University of Minnesota, and high state offices.

Most surprising to an observer who was not a part of the political situation in Minnesota in the late thirties is the complete frankness with which Quigley exploited the apparently more than latent anti-Semitism prevalent in that area. In a paper prepared to blast the Farmer-Laborite speaker of the Minnesota House of Representatives, he headlined his lead story: "City Editor Manager Barker Campaign." In the three-line, three-column, heavy type subheadline, he referred to Anthon Jacobs as the "power behind the political throne in the speakership battle," and listed Jacobs' sins, one of which was the allegation that he was against the "Father Coughlin program." In the lead he then described Jacobs as the "Jewish editor of the Minnesota State News," and then, before launching on a list of documented citations on Barker's voting record, he mentioned the words "Jew" or "Jewish" five times.

In some of the other papers he prepared for the Republicans in the 1938 campaign, he named the Jews who had associated themselves with the Farmer-Labor party or had attached themselves to its officeholders or office seekers. For example: "Sherman Dryer, young Jewish radical, and Steve Adams, Communist member of the farmer-labor state central committee, are real powers behind the throne in the county with largest vote"; "a motion made by Sam Bellman, Jewish member of the Legislature"; and "Ruben Latz, Jewish delegate." He repeated the phrase, "Sherman Dryer, the young radical Jew," at least four times in one story, throwing in the phrase, "Walter Frank, radical CIO organizer." In one paper he reproduced a photograph of Jacobs which was designed to emphasize so-called Jewish features and captioned it "Art Jacobs Tells George W. Olson." Quigley wrote that Nordstrom, his intended victim, was "twice part of the machine managed by Jewish editor, A. N. Jacobs of Minneapolis," and in another similar paper he pointed out that "Jacobs was so forward in his activities (as private secretary to Barker and dispenser of patronage) that members of the Jewish race believed he was prejudicing the public against the Jews and expressed the opinion that he should not be in such a powerful position for the good of their race."

Quigley did not use the word "Communist" directly or frequently in his papers; he was careful not to do so. He did use the word "radical" often and associated the Jews he mentioned with the Communists who, he alleged in other accounts, took over the control of the Farmer-Labor party. In reflecting on his activities in this period Quigley said:

> The Jewish issue was an important factor. It was charged that a nationality or creed with only one percent of the vote controlled ninety-eight percent of the power and authority. Though Minnesota is known as a Swede state, her biggest voting nationality is of German descent and Benson fared badly where they predominated.[28]

Although not personally anti-Semitic, he was anti-Communistic. His opposition to Communist sympathizers and fellow travelers was consistent throughout his life. However, if he found that Jews were pro-Communist or members of the Communist party, he did not hesitate to use the fact that they were Jews to blast away at American Communists. He did not stop to point out, however, that the pro-Communist Jews no longer practiced Judaism, and that the associations he evoked by his simple, yet very clever, journalistic prose were not fair to practicing Jews and to the Jews who were not involved in infiltrating bourgeois organizations and spreading the Communist doctrine. Indeed, Quigley practiced the art of the political propagandist in not explaining everything and never going on the defensive; he provided only enough detail to damage his opponent or help his client.

Apparently the only instance of a boomerang on Quigley, as a result of what he wrote about the Jews or Communists in Minnesota during the New Deal period, came twenty years later when a group of four CBS technicians rolled up to his house to interview him for a nationally televised program. The interview with Arthur Morse was based on the article, "The Art of Political Dynamiting."[29] Quigley related that Morse, "being a Jew, tried to make much of what the writer of this 'masterpiece' [as Quigley called it], wrote about my bringing the Jewish matter to the forefront in 1938, as I shushed most of that down."[30] If there had been any reactions in 1938 to Quigley's writing about the Jews, none seemed to have been published. Not one of the many persons around Quigley in that period who was interviewed even commented on this phase of his work.

Quigley was a Catholic. Indeed, many of the organizers and early leaders of the Nonpartisan League, formerly Socialists, or liberals as they became known just prior to the Rooseveltian era, were Catholics. In fact, A. C. Townley, a Catholic and a principal founder of the movement and its acknowledged titular leader, became an extreme anti-Communist before his death. Quigley's bitter attitude toward the Communists had been simmering for a decade, and when he had the chance to vent his anger through the medium of his favorite propaganda technique, he took full advantage of it. However, he did not hesitate to exploit latent American anti-Semitism when it was to his advantage to do so on behalf of his clients. After all, the men who hired him, party organization chairmen, campaign managers, and candidates, invariably checked his materials and approved his finished product. Although he boasted that he always insisted on a free rein in his propaganda efforts, he did not always have it. He prepared his newspapers and then *sold* them to his clients. These clients alone must assume the moral and ethical responsibility for what finally appeared in print and was used as a campaign weapon. Quigley, in no instance, disseminated more than his clients would buy, and the material could hardly circulate more than what his clients thought they could "get away with" or what the electorate would be willing to receive.

After the 1938 elections, Roy Dunn, the Republican Rules Committee chairman in the Minnesota House of Representatives, hired Quigley as a "synopsis clerk" in the house. During the previous election when he had worked for Dunn, who was in charge of the campaign to elect a conservative house, Quigley had simultaneously worked for the state Democratic party. At the same time, and without Dunn's knowledge, he was digging up campaign material against Harold Stassen to be used by the Farmer-Labor group. Stassen's friends reportedly were angry. They recalled that in past sessions Quigley had been identified with the opposition.[31] Consequently he lost his job.

Quigley had indeed prepared a sixteen-page pamphlet in an attempt to discredit Stassen.[32] Reportedly Stassen, the lawyer, helped to organize and then represented an organization of 126 truckers for the specific purpose of denying dividends to the Farmer Produce. Stassen's scheme, according to Quigley's research of the 828 pages of sworn testimony before the United States Department of Agriculture, would have destroyed the four Minnesota livestock coops which served more than 170,000 farmers.

This pamphlet was written in behalf of Governor Elmer A. Benson, who was seeking reelection. He had been appointed United States senator in January 1936 by Governor Floyd Olson to fill the seat left vacant by the death of Senator Thomas D. Schall. When Olson died seven months later, Benson became the gubernatorial candidate on the Farmer-Labor ticket and was elected.

However, during his term Benson had drawn the support of the Communists whom Quigley was blasting in the 1938 campaign in order to discredit the Farmer-Labor candidates for the state legislature. According to Orell Leen, an attorney who had taken the "heat" off Quigley for his many hard-hitting campaigning papers by allowing his name to be printed as the responsible party,

Quigley wrote the Stassen pamphlet *before* "he broke openly with the Commie gang backing Benson and with Benson himself."[33]

The dynamite charge attributed to Quigley, which helped greatly to "destroy" Benson for reelection in 1938, was the reproduction of a photograph showing Benson leading a parade in New York City on August 7, 1936. He sat in the rear seat of an open car with a person who was not named in the caption. Apparently a New York newspaper initially published the photograph with the statement that "a detail of communists ran beside the governor's car and offered three cheers at every street corner." The last sentence read: "Speaking from the same platform with Benson was Charles Krumbein, State Secretary of the Communist Party." There was only one figure beside the car, shown from the waist up with his left arm resting on the top of the door. He was leaning forward as if he were running. He wore a white World War I overseas cap like those worn by officers of American veterans organizations. On the cap appeared the words, "Young Communist League." The cap, and especially the position of the arm, indicated that the figure was superimposed on the original picture. Quigley thought it was a superimposed picture, but said that he had nothing to do with its production or distribution.

Benson, the Farmer-Laborite, was defeated by Stassen, the Republican; neither forgave Quigley. His apparent duplicity in this election would seem to give the lie to the opinion held by some Minnesota politicians that he was generally honest and loyal in his relations with the man who hired him, at least for the duration of the employment. Tom Davis, whom Floyd Olson defeated for the Farmer-Labor gubernatorial nomination in 1924, late in his life, when he was retired and living in Phoenix, Arizona, observed that:

> Walter E. Quigley was a "Hessian" and for sale to the highest bidder, but one thing I can say about him is that he will stay bought. He is not a double-crosser. He is a brilliant writer and a brilliant man and if he had gone along the straight road he could have gone very far. I hold no brief for him but as I have often said in political campaigns, "He is my SOB," although he never crossed me in anything he was asked to do.

Davis said he never interested himself in Quigley's activities unless "I wanted to beat some Senator or Representative who deserved to be beaten."[34] Davis, in his private career, after he ceased to be in politics, was a conservative Democrat.

It would be only fair, perhaps, to let Quigley himself describe his actions in the 1938 Minnesota elections. Almost twenty years later he wrote:

> You ask about my "double-dealing" in 1938 in the Stassen-Elmer Benson fight for governor. I had been friendly with Benson and supported him in 1936 and intended to in 1938. However, his secretary, Roger Rutchick was an extreme Red, so much so, that in 1938 midsummer the *Saturday Evening Post* wrote him up. He brought in Clarence

Hathaway, editor of the *Daily Worker*; Lillian Schutz was planted in the lieutenant-governor's office; and scores of Reds from the East came in to work for Benson. If you remember, Benson later became chairman of Henry Wallace's campaign for President working with the Commies. When I protested to Benson and warned him, he virtually told me to go to hell, so I quit the Farmer-Labor party then and went to Roy Dunn, GOP national committeeman and chairman of the [Minnesota] House Rules Committee for years, and offered my services to help defeat Benson and more radical members of the House which had ruled the 1937 session. I put out a series of papers, 41 in all, in 41 districts. We defeated 34 of the 41, and, if I had had a couple of weeks more, we would have wiped every one of them out. Again no apologies. I had a decisive part in stopping some of the most dangerous influences this state has ever known and *I am proud of it—even if it did seem like double-dealing off the deck. Dunn employed me to put out these papers.* [35]

According to his own account, Quigley had started fighting the Commies in 1924 and never had stopped. He said:

I suppose I have written 30 speeches for United States senators and representatives and governors against them, many given over networks. My antipathy is not from what I have read but from what I have seen over the years. *They are dangerous and disciplined and smart. Anybody that underrates them, even at their low ebb of today, is ignorant of their methods.* [36]

After 1938, Quigley stated, he continued working for Dunn, the man who under pressure had fired him, until about 1951. He described Dunn as "a man of great integrity and a real conservative," from whom "I never had the scratch of a pen . . . though I spent tens of thousands of dollars he gathered to keep control of the House and National Committeemanship." [37] Writing in April 1957, Quigley added that Dunn's "faction has split this session and he is rather disgruntled, but he is still a power."

Quigley spent much of 1940 to 1942 in El Paso and California for his health. In 1943 he accepted a job on the St. Paul morning *Pioneer Press*; as he related later, "I hired out April 1 for three weeks to help at the last end of the legislative session and stayed three years, leaving January 1, 1946, to reopen my own office and get into Montana and other campaigns." [38] Actually he was fired from his newspaper job, an event which apparently reoccurred frequently in his life but which never seemed to trouble him. It seemed that he wanted to leave some jobs in any event and took the occasion of his departure to tell some persons precisely what he thought of them. He never once expressed any rancor over being fired. Had he thought he had been dealt with unfairly, he would have sought and patiently waited for revenge, as he had done in the cases of several politicians, notably Senator Joseph H. Ball and Senator Hubert Humphrey.

In 1948, after doing research for Senator Murray's campaign, Quigley was hired by United States Senator Joseph H. Ball to put out a pro-paper for him in his campaign for reelection. Apparently Quigley did not enjoy preparing an exclusively affirmative paper. He was always at his best when he "blasted" an opponent. Quigley himself remarked: "Only when it was agreed with the candidate, like Senator Ball, that the paper was entirely 'pro,' was it 'pro.' *Usually, I then believed, and still do, that 'heat' is what people like.*"[39] Ball himself has commented on Quigley's preference for a "heated" campaign:

> He was a bit unhappy doing a positive job for me, but did it very well. He would have preferred to axe my opponent. Unfortunately, the results in 1948 not only in my own case but in others and nationally, indicate that *positive, constructive campaigning is nowhere near as effective as a good hatchet or smear job. I was on the receiving end of what proved to be a very effective hatchet job by the AFL-CIO in 1948. Guess people still prefer to vote against rather than for.* Quigley's activities in my campaign were confined to writing and distributing the *United States Senate News* (Minnesota edition). I don't think it did any harm, and probably did some good, but obviously not enough.[40]

Quigley and Ball had been newspaper cronies, but in a by-lined article in 1938 Ball had ripped into Quigley in a manner that would have done credit to the master himself. Quigley never forgot this affront, and in 1947, in an article for the *Railroad Trainman*, he tore into Ball in his own typical style.[41] The principal reproach was that Ball sat comfortably in Washington, drawing ten thousand dollars a year and paying his wife five thousand dollars, while fifteen million young Americans faced death. Further, Quigley asserted, Ball had called veterans organizations "gimme" outfits and had tried to kill a bill raising disability pay for veterans. He wrote:

> Ball never saw a buddy get his guts blown out by a shell, never rode a plane with flack bursting all around and death riding on every mile traveled, never sailed a ship where torpedoes whizzed into the sides and blew the sailors and burning oil over the ocean surface; no, Ball was rolling along in luxury while 15,000,000 American young men and women faced death to preserve him and his kind in safety.[42]

While Ball voted a four-billion-dollar loan to Great Britain and virtually repealed the excess profits tax and gave billions back to giant corporations, "he went all out against the wounded and married veterans." Quigley wrote these lines and many more like them with inspired animus to get even with Ball. But soon Quigley, once a poker-playing crony of Ball's, then a bitter enemy, would be working shoulder to shoulder with the man with whom he had sworn "to get even."

In 1948 the public relations director for the Minnesota State Federation of Labor received orders from the Washington headquarters to defeat Ball because of his support of the Taft-Hartley Act. At this juncture Quigley walked into the AFL office loaded with his typical research material from the *Congressional*

Record on Ball; according to Quigley, the AFL bought it from him. In the meantime, Hubert Humphrey became the nominee of the Democratic Farmer-Labor party for United States senator.

Quigley wrote as if he had had some kind of agreement with Humphrey and that they had subsequently disagreed. He stated that Ball paid him well to get him away from Humphrey to prepare a six-page "newspaper," whose front pages he banner headlined, "Sen. Ball Had Leading Part in Passing Fair Labor Law." Quigley tried to soften the antilabor attack on his client by giving the "Taft-Hartley Statute" credit for having "Stopped Disastrous Nation Wide Strikes" and by accusing Ball's AFL opponent of wanting to "Go Back to Trouble and Woe" by repealing this fine law. He then listed the number of strikes the act had prevented and the number which had brought grief because they had not been prevented by this act.

In the second lead story, the great sums of money which had been brought to Minnesota to benefit the farmers were listed—four hundred million dollars in 1948 and four hundred million dollars in 1949 to electrify the farms of Minnesota and the nation. Readers might conceivably forget to read the last three words in this sentence, "and the nation," and receive the impression that these huge sums were spent in Minnesota alone. In all his other papers in which he attacked the opponent of a client who had a legislative record, he invariably recited huge sums to characterize him as wasteful with the taxpayers' money, and in cases where the sums were not large, he would publish a long list of smaller sums and then add them up to make a large total. In his attacks on an opponent, he never explained in detail why the money was appropriated, but in the pro-Ball paper he was careful to do so, making a special effort to reach the farmers.

Most interesting in the Ball paper was a long article on Ball's wife who worked in his office. In 1947, when Quigley attacked Ball in the *Trainman* magazine article, he referred to Mrs. Ball as a five-thousand-dollar addition to the payroll. In 1948 in his pro-Ball paper he headlined: "People Get Service from [his] Wife, Administrative Assistant to Senator"; "When Office was Swamped, . . . She Brought Order Out of Chaos"; and she was a "Skilled, Loyal Worker." In his attacks on his client's opponents, Quigley would surely have pointed out that a relative on the public payroll was a sign of a man's selfishness, of his feathering his own nest, and therefore a waste of the taxpayers' money.

In the pro-Ball paper Quigley attempted to shift the attention of the voter to some of the senator's assets and to some of his voting record with which the voters might be in agreement generally, including some liberal measures. Ball had introduced the bill to eliminate the poll tax and he "opposed OPA [Office of Price Administration] with its black markets and scarceties and thousands of rules and regulations often enforced by people drunk with power." He had secured passage of two veterans bills, supported federal aid to education, retained the tax on oleomargarine, lent aid to the Taft-Ellender-Wagner housing bill, was behind the income tax cut, and he was a friend of the farmer. Finally, he had helped plan the United Nations organization. Actually Ball apparently lacked a personal record actively supporting all the measures listed which, if he had been responsible for them, would have appealed to Minnesota voters. In this case the actions of Congress generally were cited and Ball's name linked to this collective record by his individual vote. Congress' record appeared in the headlines and story leads; Ball's individual vote or support followed, usually a few paragraphs down the column.

Throughout the Ball paper, Quigley relied chiefly on testimonials, reproducing whole pages of favorable newspaper clippings and letters of endorsement from varied sources, which included the Grace Lutheran Church, the Salvation Army, Cecil B. DeMille Productions, Inc., the Furniture Exposition Mart, and the Minnesota Dairy Industry Committee. These were accompanied by a long article containing a list of favorable comments on what Senator Ball had done for improvements in the state.

In this paper Quigley also used the plain-folks device. In one photo Ball is shown at home playing chess with his wife and three children, and in another he is shown with his wife in his office going over a big stack of mail she has just brought in to him. Every attempt was made also to tie him in with the party ticket headed nationally by Thomas Dewey and in the state by Luther W. Youngdahl. But Quigley was not a complete failure in this campaign; across the way the Democrats prepared a propaganda piece based largely on some of the same material used in his attempt to rescue Senator Ball from impending defeat. Quigley probably knew what was coming, too, for in "Warning to Voters" he tried to prepare them for "last minute . . . speeches, pamphlets, labor newspapers, and other means of spreading lies, too late to answer," which would be issued by a "few dozen union bosses in Minnesota" who had raised tens of thousands of dollars to move heaven and earth to try to defeat Senator Ball. Such a propaganda piece based on defamatory falsehoods and tossed late into the campaign has been defined as a roorback. Some years later Quigley defined a roorback as "the usual political trick purposely timed for the final days or hours before election so there will be no chance to answer the charges or set the record straight."[43]

Indeed, labor did issue its four-page, letter-size paper in the final week of the campaign. This small paper, which discussed the issues briefly and then listed ninety-seven of Ball's votes in Congress, was sent throughout the state. It served as a roorback not only because of its late issue, but mainly because Ball could not remember his speeches and, when he was questioned, his own votes. Ball's position was hopeless; there was no time to prepare any answers or any countercharges. Moreover, Ball simply was no match for the mentally agile Humphrey, whom Quigley characterized as a "top-notch campaigner, probably the best in the United States today."[44] What emerged from this campaign was the hatred and respect the two men, Quigley and Humphrey, had for each other.

Quigley's relationship with Humphrey was never made clear either by Quigley or Humphrey. Quigley said that "in 1948 I had intended to work with Hubert Humphrey and did research on Ball with that in mind."[45] Humphrey, on the other hand, wrote that "there was no fight with Quigley," and that he "never had any kind of relationship with him."[46] Humphrey stated that he did not hire Quigley at any time during his campaign. Indeed, he said that Quigley had been a frequent campaigner against him, having been hired by his opposition in two mayoralty races and in two Senate contests. Humphrey was aware, however, that elements of the labor movement had hired Quigley. This could only have been the AFL, which was working in Humphrey's behalf. However, Humphrey said that he did not use Quigley's material or contribute a dime to his support. Technically this was true. According to Quigley, the AFL used the material and paid him. Somewhat evasively Humphrey asserted that Quigley was never supported by any of his volunteer committees. There was no record that Quigley had ever been supported by any "volunteer committee" in any campaign. Generally, no one except the persons who hired and dealt with him knew he was in the campaign. This was especially true in Quigley's campaigns outside Minnesota. In this state he was entirely too well known to escape observation. Humphrey stated that Quigley was a man who sold his services to whoever would buy them, and "I would hesitate to place any credence at all in what he said."

According to Arthur Naftalin, Quigley, when he was writing for the *Dispatch*, had professed great enthusiasm for Hubert Humphrey, then mayor of Minneapolis. Naftalin recalled observing Quigley at one convention, probably in 1944, moved to tears by a Humphrey speech. His next recollection of Quigley was his editing a "scandal" sheet in Humphrey's 1947 mayoralty campaign. Naftalin thought this was a totally dishonest and indecent attack on Humphrey, the obvious work of a person who had absolutely no sense of integrity either as a journalist or as a political operator.[47]

Hubert Humphrey was no less severe in his opinion of Quigley, who, he said, was "not known for being the most scrupulous and ethical in his campaign abilities and conduct . . . there is no doubt that he had ability, and . . . in practically every campaign [he] has been used to doing some hard hitting; in fact, smear attacks on certain candidates."[48]

In return, Quigley stated emphatically that "Humphrey's word is no good; he is undependable. But he is the most brilliant campaigner; he is unbeatable. He is a fast thinker on his feet. You have to give the devil his due. If you don't recognize your opponents' abilities, you can't beat them. You can't ignore your enemies." In another sentence, Quigley compared Humphrey to the former United States senator from Minnesota, Magnus Johnson, whom Thomas Schall defeated in 1924—"his word was not worth a damn."[49]

In 1954, Quigley wrote about the brilliant campaigning of Humphrey and then predicted that he would be a strong candidate for president or vice-president in 1956 or 1960.[50] Early in 1960 he wrote that "we may have some fun on Humphrey. Will let you know. He is another 'unbeatable' who could be beaten, but I admire the guy; he is a neighbor of my daughter at Waverly and she poured at a fund-raising drive for him last week. However, Old Eli has to eat and where the money comes from is unimportant."[51]

Perhaps "Old Eli" did get in the last punch; he claimed that his efforts helped to defeat Humphrey in the West Virginia presidential primary in 1960. Kennedy's victory in this primary practically assured him the Democratic presidential nomination.

Quigley issued a few other pro-papers without heat. He issued such papers for Minnesota Congressmen Harold Knutson and Harold C. Hagen over a period of years. He had formed, apparently, a close personal attachment with these men. Representative Hagen was first sent to Congress from Minnesota's Ninth District in 1942 as a Farmer-Labor member—the last congressman to be elected by that party. Two years later, when the party held a joint convention with the Democrats, Hagen cast his lot with the GOP and was elected four times as a Republican. He was defeated by Coya Knutson in 1954 by 2,400 votes although he ran 40,000 votes ahead of the GOP ticket. Quigley's score in five elections working for Hagen was four wins and one loss. The latter Quigley attributed to Secretary of Agriculture Ezra Taft Benson and to the low price of eggs. Although his campaign material was geared to the field of agriculture, apparently Hagen's weakness, not even Quigley could overcome the thesis that in the face of stark reality, propaganda is either not needed or it is less effective when it is employed in the attempt to redirect the mental images created by realities. If political defeat or victory can be attributed to the personality of a single individual, regardless of his own presence or actions in a campaign, Hagen's defeat can be attributed to the negative influence of Secretary Benson in Minnesota.

Quigley made some interesting observations on propaganda in his last pro-paper for Hagen. He said: "Hagen always conducts a clean, high level campaign. It may be noted that this newspaper contains no gossip, hearsay, rumors or personal attack on Hagen's opponent."[52]

Quigley, however, did prepare and plant news releases which tore into Hagen's opponent, Coya Knutson. Also, little stories were started which fitted into a pattern that seemed to follow the route of her campaigners. At one place the story was to the effect that Coya Knutson stopped at a roadside restaurant and "Boy! Did she tell stories!"—and the gossip would give an exhibition of the type of story. At Detroit Lakes, she attended a church dinner; the next day a story was circulated widely that one of the waitresses had "smelled her breath and Coya Knutson just reeked of liquor." In this case, reportedly the minister himself called the Ladies Aid together and put a stop to the stories emanating from that particular church.[53] The problem for the managers of the candidate who is attacked in this manner is to choose between the alternatives of answering or ignoring such charges.

In some cases Knutson's campaigners fought back; in others they did not answer at all in order to avoid giving stories any further publicity. During the campaign, Knutson's headquarters received anonymous letters referring to "Poison-Pen Quigley." The letter indicated that he was present in the District, that he was a disbarred lawyer, and that he received something like fifteen thousand dollars for a "successful" campaign. After the campaign, in Washington, Hagen's payroll records were checked; Quigley was listed on his congressional payroll, with a Minneapolis address.

In 1956, Hagen's campaign was much more bitter than in the past years. Reportedly a few outright lies were established. For example, the AFL-CIO voting record of congressmen and senators from 1946 to 1956 was quoted to demonstrate that Coya Knutson was absent from 74 to 80 percent of the roll-call votes. No attempt was made to explain that she was not in Congress during this whole period. She was also charged with allowing persons on her payroll to reside in Minnesota and Wisconsin, but it was apparent the device was used to elicit an answer and start an argument with charges and countercharges. This release, issued two weeks before the elections, was carried by the four daily newspapers in the Ninth District. In this case there was time for Knutson, who waited until the final week, to answer the charge on radio and television and to wind up her campaign successfully.

Quigley's function of preparing and planting news releases in the Hagen campaign was one in which he had also developed a high proficiency. In Hagen's district he worked apparently with friendly newspapers. The four dailies, the *Crookston Times*, the *Bemidji Pioneer*, the *Fergus Falls Journal*, and the *Moorhead Daily News*, were not friendly to Congresswoman Knutson.

The *Moorhead Daily News* seemed to have had a policy of printing both sides of a controversy, that is, it printed the original stories, but not the subsequent answers. Editorially, however, it was friendly to Hagen. The edition which published the charge against Knutson was mailed throughout the county, but the answer was not.

It was easy for Quigley to plant his stories. The arrangements were principally made by Hagen, since he knew personally every newsman in the district and had had almost every one on his payroll in Washington for at least a week or two. Quigley could not remember, upon inquiry, if he had "planted" the stories of the charges against Knutson, but he did say he had written releases for Hagen and sent them to the wire services, the AP, UP, and INS, to the big dailies in Minnesota, and to all the weeklies in the fifteen counties in the Ninth District.

Congresswoman Knutson's success in the 1954 campaign makes it difficult to measure the harm Quigley's technique did. Perhaps it was not so harmful as one might at first suspect. After all, she defeated Hagen in spite of Quigley's efforts against her. Her manager in 1954, however, did say that "answering the type of operation engaged in by Walter Quigley required serious thought and consideration before making any move." It was his "own personal conviction that 'political dynamiting' in the more sophisticated sense has the greatest effect on the personal demoralization of the opposition and the sad feature that issues, votes and facts are lost sight of completely in the general picture."[54]

Hagen died in 1957, and with his death Quigley lost a long-time client and close friend. It was Hagen who had supplied him with the *Congressional Record* and other documents he used in his research. Apparently, on some occasions Hagen had also been influential, or at least helpful, in keeping the Bureau of Internal Revenue away from Quigley's doorstep. Quigley's own reticence in talking about how, and by whom, he was paid may have been due more to the fear of the Bureau audit of his income tax returns than to his statement that he wanted to protect his clients.

Quigley worked personally with Harold Knutson, Minnesota congressman, in about eight campaigns. Knutson, who owned a newspaper in Wadena, Minnesota, "was tough to get papers out for as he would change them considerably," but when Magnus Johnson ran against Knutson in 1934, Quigley dug up Magnus' record in the Minnesota state senate, and Knutson, himself a newspaperman, "knew what to do with it." "Fortunately," Quigley added, "I have always had clients who were not vulnerable, except on big issues."[55] Quigley also had clients who were "responsive." This is actually the key to a satisfactory relationship between a public relations man and a political candidate; many a politician has been defeated because of this lack of responsiveness. The campaign manager's dream of an ideal candidate is one who can take the material or data prepared for him and then "know what to do with it."

Political dynamiting was not Quigley's only activity as a public relations man in politics. He prepared and planted news releases, wrote pamphlets and broadsides, ghosted speeches, books, and entries for the *Congressional Record*, and lobbied in the Minnesota legislature and the Congress of the United States. For nearly fifty years he served clients as a researcher and writer in almost every way known to the trade. He blueprinted and managed campaigns, and, on occasion, he was a frequent and sometimes constant companion of a politician on the road. In addition, he wrote articles for trade journals and nationally known periodicals.

In 1941 the *Saturday Evening Post* published his article on Charles A. Lindbergh entitled "Like Father, Like Son."[56] He tried in this piece to explain "how Lindbergh gets that way." Quigley and Lindbergh's father were associated in the same law office from 1922 to May 1924 when the elder Lindbergh died, at a moment when he was campaigning for the Farmer-Labor gubernatorial nomination. In December 1923 Lindbergh had assigned the rights to his book, *Your Country at War*, to Quigley, who wrote the introduction to the 1934 edition, a reprinting. A comment by Quigley on Lindbergh, Jr., would seem worth recording.

In 1923 when Lindbergh, Sr., was campaigning to secure the Farmer-Labor senatorial nomination in a special election to fill the vacancy caused by the death of Senator Knute Nelson, Quigley and the son "threw campaign literature from the air," as they circled in the flyer's plane over Redwood Falls.[57] Quigley did not maintain that this was the first time campaign literature had been thrown from the air, but no candidate had a more famous flyer, as it turned out, performing this kind of service for him. In this election the younger Lindbergh was called back from Lincoln, Nebraska, where he was studying aviation, to fly his father to the meetings which Quigley had scheduled, thereby attracting bigger crowds and getting to more localities. Actually the elder Lindbergh rode with his son only once. The plane was a two-seater, so usually Quigley or a staff member of Lindbergh's headquarters rode to the next town to make arrangements for the meeting. Lindbergh and others would follow in a Model T Ford, a "jalopy." Traveling in the Model T introduced conversations with farmers in the field or by a roadside and at open-air meetings as a characteristic method of electioneering.

Although at the time Quigley mentioned Lindbergh as his "law partner," Lindbergh was only an "associate" in Quigley's office. Lindbergh suffered defeat in the 1917 Republican primary when he tried for the Minnesota gubernatorial nomination in 1918 with the endorsements of the Farmers Nonpartisan

Political League and union labor. Quigley prepared a campaign pamphlet for him which he described to the voters as follows:

> This pamphlet contains a brief history of Minnesota's leading economist and statesman. We ask you to read it all the way through. It contains astounding facts, and answers charges made by the profiteers against the man most feared by them. When you read these facts you will ask for a Farmer-Labor ballot and vote for Charles A. Lindbergh for Governor—The Religious Lie is answered Herein.

The issue of the "Religious Lie" affords the student of politics an excellent study in campaign technique, especially in the use of a roorback.

During his last term in Congress, Lindbergh had introduced a House resolution to investigate the controversy between the Free Press Defense League and the Roman Catholic church and had made speeches in Congress supporting his resolution. In his book, Lindbergh devoted several pages to this controversy.[58]

Judge McGee, a Catholic, called the attention of the leaders of the St. Paul diocese to this part of the book and to Lindbergh's remarks in the *Congressional Record*. The *Catholic Bulletin*, in its last issue before the primary, called upon the Catholics to defeat the League candidate. Priests, on the Sunday before election, devoted part or all of their sermons to Lindbergh. Quigley's excellent pamphlet in Lindbergh's behalf failed to prevail in the face of this roorback; there was not time before election day to counter the tide of opinion developed by the Catholic priests. Thousands of votes were affected and Lindbergh lost the primary, 199,000 to 150,000. At League headquarters, when it became certain that he was defeated, Lindbergh merely shrugged his shoulders and said:

> I was trying to clear up a controversy and get politics and religion separated, but it looks like I only mixed them up. The people will one day wake up and refuse to be divided by the bankers. They split the workers and producers by using race, religion, nationality or any other possible device which will prevent the voters from knowing that the real issue in America is the control of finance by a few.[59]

Quigley gave the impression that his services were greatly in demand. He asserted that "when a campaign is over it is a closed incident and I am lining up work for future elections. . . . I am a professional political writer and take only clients that I elect."[60] In 1952 a wealthy New York Jew received a letter from Quigley offering his services and stating in effect that he was prepared to do a job either for or against any candidate in whom the New Yorker and his associates might be interested. Quigley had heard that this man was "spending large sums" in political campaigns; later, he remembered only vaguely that he had written to Arthur Goldstein of New York City. Goldstein, who did not answer his letter, remembered only vaguely that he had received an inquiry from Quigley. This incident indicates Quigley's completely impersonal approach in soliciting business and toward his clients. He accepted clients with money on the line; he rejected possible clients with uncertain financial resources; he talked about a "good year" and a "decent retainer." Businessmen and professional men serve both Democrats and Republicans, so do doctors and lawyers; why should not he do so? To him, as to others in the public relations field, his occupation was a source of legitimate pride. In any campaign, he worked for money and he was out to win.

In his relations with his clients he liked to work directly with one man, preferably the candidate himself or a single manager with responsibility and authority. He did not like to work with a committee. He demanded a free hand, but it was obvious that he did not always get it. Frequently there was disagreement among campaign managers over the copy and contents of his papers.

Sometimes "his stuff" was not even used by a candidate. But he never went without payment for his work or services, though at times he had difficulty getting all his money. Quigley himself explained what happened to plans for his work in the six senatorial elections in which he was hired to work his hocus-pocus.

> In 1950 I was hired by Guy Gabrielson, National GOP Chairman, through Ab Herman, executive director, to check the records of six U.S. senators. They did not use my dope against Sen. Pat McCarran of Nevada, figuring he was more valuable as chairman of the judiciary committee and anti-Roosevelt and Truman, so we let him alone. But I had a real record on Sen. Glen Taylor of Idaho. I also catalogued records of Elmer Thomas of Oklahoma, Dennis Chavez of New Mexico. I did some work for Gen. Pat Hurley down there, but he would not use the stuff, although he could have plastered the state for $5,000. Instead he fought with me and his publicity manager and later spent a couple of hundred thousand in a contest for the Senate. A millionaire named Williams was the GOP candidate against Magnuson [Warren Magnuson, United States senator from the state of Washington], and did not want that type of campaign, though I had a fine dossier on Magnuson. As a result Williams was handily beaten. The Oklahoma stuff was used effectively and Thomas lost—my stuff on Glen Taylor was devastating and was used again in later campaigns.[61]

Apparently, in 1950 Quigley's typical "newspaper" was issued only in the Utah campaign.

He had clients with whom he formed friendships and personal attachments. These were candidates for public office in Minnesota with whom he worked closely during an entire campaign—men like Tom Davis, a successful attorney but always an unsuccessful candidate; Governor Floyd Olson, deceased; and Congressmen Harold Knutson and Harold Hagen. He stated: "I was on the road with Floyd Olson in four campaigns, for eleven months. He was like a brother, as was Rep. Hagen."[62]

Quigley did not feel hostility toward those he attacked; on the other hand, he felt that he performed a public service in many cases, as in the attacks on Thomas and Wheeler.

When I read these Communist publications and Senator Thomas' book, *The Four Fears*, I became convinced that he was, and I think unconsciously, the one man of high standing selected by the Communists when they wanted a respectable front. Unwittingly he served their cause and was of great value to the sly boys working under orders from abroad. . . . I also call attention to the Montana paper which helped defeat Senator B. K. Wheeler for his speeches for America First which to me were decidedly fascist. I was happy to help defeat Wheeler for what I believe was his aid to fascism and Hitler and just as glad to defeat Senator Elbert Thomas for a similar type of aid to Stalin and Communism.[63]

Nevertheless, he said that both were "good Senators." He was interested principally in the technique.

He preferred not to have his paper appear in the last days of the campaign, for he felt that it had more effect if it lay about the house so that people could pick it up from time to time and look at it. In this respect the printed page, he claimed, is far superior to radio and TV whose message is evanescent. "I am not one of those who believes in last minute work in campaigns. I think more of them are won or lost six months to a year before election and I have pounded my prospective clients for 35 years to get them to do their work early."[64]

Quigley usually warned his readers to beware of roorbacks—of what the opposition would do after reading his papers—which he obviously feared. He probably learned this lesson from his experience with the roorback which crushed Lindbergh in the 1918 Republican primary. And in 1948, a roorback soundly defeated Senator Joseph H. Ball. But generally, after examining Quigley's "newspapers," it would seem that the warning to his readers that the opposition would use smear tactics to answer his facts was a better description of what followed in Quigley's own papers than of what followed as a reaction from the opposition.

His propaganda had a degree of accuracy seldom found in comparable publications, and this made replies more difficult. From a man with thirty years' experience in political public relations work in Minnesota came the observation that:

Quig knows the value of absolute accuracy in the material he uses. Never, to my knowledge, has he been caught in the meshes of libel or successfully challenged. He can be utterly ruthless and make the most respected individual appear to be a downright scalawag, but there never is anything upon which a libel pleading can be based.[65]

Not everyone agrees that the technique is as effective as Quigley thought. Roy Dunn, the Minnesota Republican state chairman who had employed Quigley to produce papers against Farmer-Labor members of the legislature in the 1938 campaign which saw the defeat of thirty-four out of forty-one, was asked about their effectiveness. Dunn answered: "As is frequently the case in instances such as this, claims of accomplishment are presented which are impossible for anyone to substantiate. It is my opinion that the success of any political campaign is the net result of a combination of circumstances and activity."[66] But another experienced observer in Minnesota stated: "Had not the Quigley papers been distributed the F.-L. men all may have been elected." The same observer said that Quigley's statewide paper in the 1930 Minnesota campaign "tipped the state over in a week," leading to the nomination of Schall by a 94,000 plurality.[67] A public relations man corroborated this view: "I believe that had it not been for Quigley's sheet, Christianson would have taken the nomination from incumbent Senator Schall."[68]

To support his claim for the effectiveness of his papers, Quigley pointed to some "unbeatable" men who have been "roundly defeated" by the "right kind of propaganda," properly cartooned, headed, and edited, which all the voters received in their mailboxes. He then cited Wheeler's record in 1940, when he won overwhelmingly by 177,000 votes to 63,000, and added: "Yet we beat him in the primary [1946]." "Senator Elbert Thomas," he continued, "had won three elections with handsome majorities, yet lost by 21,229 [1950] in spite of an array of talent sent to Utah to try to save him," and "Theodore Christianson was elected Governor of Minnesota in 1928 by 230,000 plurality, yet we licked him in 1930, just two years later, by 94,000 majority in his own GOP primary."[69] Other observers, however, would have considered these candidates very vulnerable and, in fact, ideal setups for Quigley's dynamiting propaganda technique.

All three "victims" named by Quigley had been in public office a long time and had accumulated many enemies. All three had a published record of statements on highly controversial policies or issues. In each case Quigley resurrected the past. He dug up statements which were no longer relevant to a candidate's fitness for office and distorted them so that they would arouse fear, doubt, and anger in the voter. In Wheeler's case, he recalled the anger of the anti-Nazi and interventionists generally of the pre-World War II era; in Thomas', he reproduced gestures of good will originally intended to secure peaceful relations between the United States and Russia; and in Christianson's case he resurrected his extravagant anti-German statements made during World War I and his statement that the public schools should not accept credits from parochial schools. In 1946, the propagandist took full advantage of Pearl Harbor in discrediting Wheeler's isolationist position, and in 1950 he exploited fully the cold war in discrediting Thomas' conception of world citizenship.

These candidates were indeed vulnerable; they were perfect targets for Quigley's dynamiting charges.

Neither Wheeler nor Thomas attributed much influence to Quigley's paper in bringing about their defeats. Wheeler said he had only a faint "recollection of Walter Quigley and any part he played in the primary campaign against me."[70] Wheeler himself attributed his defeat to the Brotherhood of Railroad Trainmen, to the Mine, Mill, and Smelter Workers Union, to Jewish money and the Jewish press, and to his opposition to President Roosevelt on the court issue and on the question of the president's policy of "getting the United States into war." Thomas credited his defeat in 1950 principally to the American Medical Association and the Mormon church.[71] The fact that these two former senators discounted the effect of Quigley's activities should not be construed as a basic weakness of this study. Actually, Thomas and Wheeler did not want to admit the effectiveness of Quigley's efforts. To do so would have lent credence to Quigley's claim for effectiveness and only resulted in an even more unpleasant situation to the losers and their families.

Quigley had many and frequent brushes with the law, especially in his early career, as an organizer for the Farmers Nonpartisan League and as an attorney for bootleggers in Minneapolis. In Nebraska, where he sought League membership during World War I, he was jailed and threatened with tar and feathers. League leaders opposed United States entry into World War I; he was challenged constantly by the superpatriots of that time, not for his personal views but for the positions and statements associated with the League's leaders in North Dakota and Minnesota.

In Minnesota he was disbarred not for representing bootleggers precisely, but for fleecing them. His actions were mainly in attempting to get bootleggers charged with violation of the liquor laws transferred from one court, where the judge had the practice of sentencing the guilty ones to prison, to the court of another judge who limited his sentences to fines. Quigley once observed, undoubtedly with some exaggeration, that almost every other establishment in downtown Minneapolis was a speak-easy or a liquor "joint."

Only once, however, did he have a brush with the law over his dynamiting efforts, and on this occasion, though pursued by local gendarmes in the state of Tennessee and by a posse of FBI agents outside the state, he managed to escape their claws until the wind had blown over after the election date, and then the constabularies of these governmental units lost interest in him. However, the point of transgression involved in his Tennessee escapade is of interest both to political dynamiters and to students of their trade.

The Brotherhood of Railroad Trainmen hired Quigley and Tom Davis to help defeat the so-called "Jennings bill," introduced by Representative John

Jennings of Knoxville, Tennessee. This was a "railroad bill" which provided that any person who sued a railroad must bring the action in the county or in the federal district where the accident happened. The bill narrowly passed in the House but was killed in the Senate. Quigley described Jennings as a "mouthy, arrogant guy, and probably the only man I ever fought whom I personally disliked, and I was glad to help defeat him." This was in August 1948.

In the following election, Quigley issued *The 2nd District Congressional Gazette*, in which he attacked Jennings. In issuing this newspaper, Quigley ran afoul of a federal law which provided that literature dealing with election of national officials must have the notation "Prepared, paid for, and circulated by, and the name and address." Quigley had ascertained that no state law existed on this subject. Representative Jennings had the counsel of the House Elections Committee summon Quigley, but Al Whitney, the Trainmen president, whose legal aid bureau had financed the paper, telephoned Attorney General Tom Clark, and the matter was disposed of in five minutes. Quigley admitted, however, that he could have been indicted. After this experience, Quigley placed the information to identify a responsible person in every paper he issued regardless of the existence of a state law. In this instance, he had unintentionally violated the law; he did not let that happen again.

In any event, Quigley was a pioneer in the development of mass appeal and mass distribution of propaganda in political campaigns. Moreover, as a public relations man in politics, Quigley exercised a peculiar power. Whatever originality has been pointed out in his political campaigning may have been due to his own unusual talents and techniques. His ability was not only to arouse fear in the minds of the voters; he caused the politicians to fear him—so much so that they were willing to hire him or pay him a fee so that an opposing candidate could not use his services. His position among politicians in Minnesota brought forth from Governor Floyd Olson the reported statement: "We have to have him on our side for it will be too expensive to fight him."[72] Quigley himself related that when Governor Olson intended to run for the Senate in 1936 against Senator Schall, he was placed in an awkward position; he had directed campaigns for both of them. He then arranged that each should get him several thousand dollars so that he could spend six months in California and stay out of it. Both Schall and Olson died before there was any reason for this arrangement to take effect.[73]

Quigley's power resulted also from his willingness to go anywhere for a fee and to write the things about a candidate that *no one else dared to write*. This willingness was evident at every turn of his career. As a reflection on his successful efforts in the Schall-Christianson senatorial campaign in 1930 in Minnesota, he said: "*My paper wrapped it all up in one package. Nobody else seemed to dare to call it as it was.*"[74] As an expert in attacking a candidate, in dynamiting him out of office, he was called in frequently when "heat" was needed. His employment was a part of a blueprint which called for a hard-hitting campaign. He combined his talents and techniques to construct a propaganda bomb which he had learned how to detonate to cover a whole state at the right moment to bring devastation and destruction in the ranks of his clients' opposition. It is doubtful if Quigley and his "newspaper" would fall into the usual classifications of propagandists and of propaganda. For this reason the term "political dynamiter" and the phrase "political dynamiting" have been created to describe him and his handiwork in the field of the public relations man in politics.

NOTES

1. *Ephraim Enterprise* (Utah), August 18, 1950.

2. *Salt Lake Tribune*, October 10, 1950.

3. This phrase was derived initially from the last paragraph of Quigley's first letter to this writer in answer to an inquiry about his work and the part he played in the 1950 Utah elections campaign: "Am sending the extra papers as they may be of some value to students who want to take up the career of political 'dynamiting' or research. Up to several years ago I had this field to myself in the U.S., but in the last two campaigns this plan has been followed by others in various states." Letter from Walter E. Quigley to the author, April 4, 1951. Correspondence from Quigley will hereafter be cited by the date.

4. Broadcast, October 29, 1950.

5. Letter, March 3, 1957.

6. Letter, March 3, 1957. Italics supplied.

7. Letter, April 4, 1951.

8. News story headed, "Boy Heads Committee," *Minneapolis Dispatch*, September 27, 1912.

9. Letter, March 3, 1957.

10. Letter, April 9, 1957.

11. An excellent account of the League is given by Robert L. Morlan, *Political Prairie Fire: The Nonpartisan League, 1915-1922* (Minneapolis: University of Minnesota Press, 1955). Morlan mentions Quigley twice in connection with an episode in which Quigley defected from the League.

12. Italics supplied.

13. Letter, April 16, 1957. Italics supplied.

14. Letter, April 29, 1957.

15. *Ibid.*

16. Letter, April 9, 1957.

17. Letter from Leif Erickson to author, June 26, 1962.

18. Joseph K. Howard, "The Decline and Fall of Burton K. Wheeler," *Harper's Magazine*, 194 (March 1947), 227. Cited by Thomas Payne in "Under the Copper Dome: Politics in Montana," Frank H. Jonas (ed.), *Western Politics* (Salt Lake City: University of Utah Press, 1961), p. 190. Payne's account, covering the period from 1940 to 1960, provides an excellent summary of the role of the Anaconda Company in Montana politics.

19. Letter, April 16, 1957. Italics supplied.

20. Interview with Walter Quigley, April 4, 1957.

21. Letter, April 16, 1957.

22. Interview with Quigley, April 4, 1957.

23. Letter, April 16, 1957. Italics supplied.

24. *Ibid.*

25. *Ibid.* Italics supplied.

26. Walter E. Quigley, "The Evolution of a Radical," unpublished autobiography in the possession of Frank H. Jonas.

27. Letter from Arthur Naftalin, commissioner of administration, state of Minnesota, to author, May 28, 1957. Naftalin subsequently was elected mayor of Minneapolis. His Master's thesis was on the history of the Farmer-Labor party.

28. Letter, April 9, 1957.

29. Frank H. Jonas, "The Art of Political Dynamiting," *Western Political Quarterly*, 10 (June 1957), 374 ff.

30. Letter, October 21, 1958.

31. *Pioneer Press* (St. Paul, Minnesota), January 16, 1939. This story of apparent duplicity was on one of the photostats in the dossier the Utah Democrats compiled to discredit Quigley.

32. The title of the pamphlet explains its purpose. "Mr. Farmer, Read How the U.S. Government Foiled Scheme to Destroy Livestock Cooperatives and the Part that the Republican Candidate for Governor Played in Behalf of the Schemers."

33. Letter from Orell Leen to author, March 2, 1957.

34. Letter from Tom Davis to author, April 5, 1957. Davis, an attorney, played a "power behind the throne" role in the Farmer-Labor party and on occasion was a candidate. He was never elected to office, although he could poll about seventy-five thousand votes and could swing about that number to anyone he supported. Davis gave Quigley free office space for twelve years. Quigley said:
> I would give Davis an outline and he would revamp the material to suit his fiery temperament. Tom was a devastating campaigner and his radio talks were eagerly awaited by thousands. He was introduced at a Schall meeting by T. J. Caton who called him "the best loved and most hated man in the state."

Quigley, "The Evolution of a Radical."

35. Letter, March 3, 1957. Italics supplied.

36. Letter, April 23, 1957. Italics supplied.

37. When Quigley was negotiating for a retainer from former Senator Claude Pepper of Florida, he wrote: I neglected to tell him that I have handled hundreds of thousands of dollars; I go all the way with him." Letter, November 27, 1959.

38. Letter, April 9, 1957.

39. Letter, April 16, 1957. Italics supplied.

40. Letter from Joseph H. Ball to author, March 24, 1957. Italics supplied.

41. Walter E. Quigley, "Minnesota's Senator Ball," *The Railroad Trainman*, 66 (February 1947), 38. Ball accounted for Quigley's earlier attack on him by saying that "Walt was an honest scoundrel who worked strictly for dough hence the earlier hatchet job on yours truly." Letter from Ball to author, March 24, 1957.

42. *Ibid.*

43. Letter, March 3, 1957.

44. Letter, April 9, 1957.

45. Letter, March 3, 1957.

46. Letter from Hubert H. Humphrey to author, July 2, 1962.

47. Letter from Naftalin to author, May 28, 1957.

48. Letter from Hubert H. Humphrey to author, March 10, 1955.

49. Interview with Quigley, April 4, 1957; letter, April 9, 1957.

50. Letter, November 16, 1954.

51. Letter, April 3, 1960.

52. Interview with Quigley, April 4, 1957; letter, April 9, 1957.

53. Letter from William Kjeldahl to author, April 4, 1953.

54. Letter from Humphrey to author, July 2, 1962.

55. Interview with Quigley, April 4, 1957.

56. June 21, 1941, pp. 37-44.

57. *Ibid.*, p. 42.

58. Charles A. Lindbergh, Sr., *Your Country at War and What Happens to You After a War* (Philadelphia: Dorrance and Company, Inc., 1917), pp. 180-81.

59. Reported by Walter E. Quigley, letter, March 5, 1957.

60. Letter, April 9, 1951.

61. Letter, April 9, 1957.

62. Letter, April 23, 1957.

63. Letter, April 4, 1951.

64. Letter, March 3, 1957.

65. Letter from Orell Leen to author, April 3, 1957.

66. Letter from Roy Dunn to author, March 21, 1957.

67. Letter from Leen to author, March 2, 1957. Leen was the "front" for the papers; the notice, required by law, read "prepared and issued and circulated by Orell Leen." This notice is required by law in most states. Quigley described Leen's part in the papers by saying, "he took the heat." Leen was also the "front" for the 1930 Schall papers.

68. Letter, April 1, 1957. Writer's name withheld by request.

69. See *Reports* of State Canvassing Board, General Elections, 1924, 1926, 1928, compiled by Miles Holm, secretary of state, Minnesota.

70. Letter from Burton K. Wheeler to author, April 8, 1957.

71. See Frank H. Jonas, "The 1950 Elections in Utah," *Western Political Quarterly*, 4 (1951), 86-87.

72. Letter, April 16, 1957.

73. Letter, April 23, 1957.

74. *Ibid.* Italics supplied.

SETTING THE STAGE
FOR THE
POLITICAL DYNAMITER

I N the 1950 elections in Utah, Walter Quigley, the veteran political dynamiter from North Dakota and Minnesota, served as a single-shot artist. His
unique form of propaganda, the *United States Senate News*, carefully guarded,
was brought secretly and silently into the state. Two hundred thousand papers
were wrapped in bundles to be dropped into the Salt Lake City post office,
from where they would be sent to the various post offices in the state. Then the
papers would be dropped into the mailbox of each individual addressee.

All of these arrangements had been made long before this guided propaganda missile was launched in mid-October. Postelection analysis was to reveal
that the bomb had been constructed as much by the Utah Republicans and
their other hirelings as by Quigley. However, the idea was Quigley's; so was the
format; so was the yellow-journalism-style make-up; and so were the cartoons.
Undoubtedly the most characteristic feature, the method of delivery and distribution, shrouded in secrecy, was Quigley's.

Certainly the effectiveness of the *United States Senate News* cannot be estimated with very much accuracy without reference to the events which had set
the stage for its climactic appearance. But it can be partially measured statisti-
cally by the fact that all other Democrats and the Democratic party won at the
polls while Senator Elbert D. Thomas, against whom it was aimed, lost a major
office. A long succession of events, and the entrance of many lesser characters,
all with propaganda blasts, effectively set the stage for the political dynamiter
and his masterpiece.

Thomas had secured his first senatorial nomination in a surprising and
somewhat spectacular turn of events in the 1932 party convention, when he
defeated the incumbent Reed Smoot, an apostle of the Mormon church and a
veteran of thirty years in the United States Senate; Thomas received 56.7 percent of the vote (116,889 to 86,046). Six years later he defeated Franklin S.
Harris, president of Brigham Young University, with 55.8 percent (102,353 to
81,071). In 1944, he shot ahead of another popular Mormon leader, educator,
and businessman, Adam S. Bennion, with 59.1 percent (148,748 to 99,532).

This record must be kept in mind in evaluating the Republican blueprint in 1950 and Thomas' own attitude on entering the campaign for reelection. The Republicans felt that they could not defeat him with a traditional campaign. Though his friends say he was scared, Thomas himself appeared to be very confident, a fact which accounted in great measure for his poorly prepared campaign and for his failure to foresee what he was in for with the whole Republican party officialdom of that year as his opposition. When he learned that Wallace F. Bennett, a Salt Lake City businessman, had been elected president of the National Association of Manufacturers (NAM), he remarked at once that Bennett would be his opponent in 1950. His mistake was in not realizing that he would also run against Republican Senator Arthur V. Watkins (who was *not* up for reelection) and his two aides, Richard Cardall and James McKinney; against Guy Gabrielson, national Republican committee chairman and his aide, Ab Herman; and finally, against a whole array of local Utah political woodcutters who had been preparing to chop him to pieces.

The Republicans adopted a theme which was almost foolproof at the time. This theme, communism, was presented and developed as an issue; it was in reality a "conditioner of the mind." When a theme of this kind is used by a political party in an election campaign, it could be harmful to cry "wolf" unless it can name the wolf, describe him, and print his picture. In the 1950 Utah senatorial election, the Democratic nominee himself, incumbent Senator Elbert D. Thomas, was named as the "wolf"; he had a record of appearances before Soviet-Russian front organizations and associations with Soviet representatives and American fellow travelers and Communist sympathizers.

The Utah voters had not been educated to discern the distinction between an issue and "a conditioner of the mind." Most important, however, for the use of communism as a propaganda theme was the fact that it was timely. Its timeliness would prevent it from boomeranging, a constant fear of political propagandists who use hard-hitting strategies and smear tactics.

United States Senator Joseph McCarthy had launched his attack on February 9, 1950, in Wheeling, West Virginia, on the Department of State as being a haven for members of the Communist party. The next day McCarthy appeared in Denver, where the 205 "Communists" became 205 "bad security risks." On the following day, in a speech at Salt Lake City, the 205 of Wheeling and Denver had changed to "57 card-carrying Communists." McCarthyism had come early in 1950 to Utah, a perfect backdrop for scare scenes in the forthcoming senatorial election.

Late in June of that election year the Korean War broke out. The news from Korea on the front pages of the daily press became a constant flow of free, unsolicited propaganda for the Republicans. Korea gave credence to communism as the campaign theme. McCarthyism and Korea provided a windfall of unexpected good fortune which the Republicans exploited in perfecting their dynamiting plans to oust Senator Thomas from office. In estimating the effectiveness of the techniques used in a political campaign, how much credit should be given to such fortuitous, unanticipated variables?

That the Republican single-theme, single-purpose campaign was effective is seen in the fact that Thomas was defeated by 21,299 votes. Bennett, the winner, received 54.2 percent of the votes cast for United States senator. This was highlighted by the fact that the other Democrats on the ticket were returned to office. Representative Walter K. Granger won a sixth term in the First Congressional District by a margin of 2,293 votes, or 51.08 percent of the 106,029 cast for this office. Reva Beck Bosone, Utah's first woman in Congress, running for a second term in the Second District, emerged victorious by a margin of 10,748 or 53.38 percent of the 157,818 ballots cast. Approximately 75 percent of the electorate went to the polls.[1]

An array of local dynamiters concentrated on associating Thomas with a "socialistic," Democratic administration in Washington. With Korea and McCarthyism as backdrops, Walter Quigley could then concentrate on posing Thomas on the stage with Soviet-front organizations and Communist spokesmen and sympathizers. The label of communism was pinned on Thomas in a long series of dynamiting charges prior to the issue of the *United States Senate News* which wrapped up the Republican campaign against him.

Early in the election year the Republicans decided to concentrate entirely on the senatorial race. They attacked Thomas on three grounds—his record in Congress (he has done nothing for Utah or he has not been a "Utah" senator), his old age, and his alleged association with communistic elements.

Thomas was sixty-seven when the charge of old age was made against him. Actually, he was not in the best of health: an embolism finally took his life early in 1953. He could have served his party well by retirement, and, presumably, another strong Democrat could have won in 1950. Although a Republican tide had developed east of the Mississippi and the Rockies, it had not yet hit Utah. Without the communism theme, and therefore minus the services of Quigley and of Watkins' senatorial staff and a crew of local hatchetmen, the Republicans would have found it difficult to win.

In any event, Thomas' age and the charge that he was a "national" instead of a "Utah" senator were soon lost in the mainstream of the Republicans' successful attempts, in the minds of the voters at least, to associate him with communism and Soviet Russia. The significance of the 1950 Utah senatorial election lies in the fact that the campaign was carried out exactly as it had been blueprinted: the intention from the very beginning was to make it hard hitting and heated. The Republicans had one goal, the defeat of Elbert D. Thomas, and they were not deterred from it by any moral or religious inhibitions. At least one of their principal dynamiters openly operated on the basis that in politics there is no morality. To assume this position in domestic political campaigns, especially in Utah—which someone at the 1952 Republican nominating convention in an unguarded and highly charged, emotional moment referred to as "the Christian State"—was in a way quite new. The planners of this campaign had to commit themselves implicitly, if not overtly, to disregard ethics in order to achieve success.

In most cases, even with blueprints which call for hard-hitting tactics and the employment of political hatchetmen, a political campaign will begin with the recognition of a set of rules and regulations for political behavior. Many opposing nominees, in recent times, have signed the no-smear pledge of the Fair Campaign Practices Committee. As the campaign proceeds, however, especially as it reaches the final stages, nominees become doubtful and even fearful of the outcome. Desire for high office and anxiety at the moment it seems to be within their grasp, or desperation when it appears to be slipping away, will erode lifelong ethical rules and behavior patterns and lead candidates to resort to techniques which they had promised themselves and others that they would not use—techniques which appear to be the only alternatives to bring them victory at the polls. However, the chief characteristic of the Republican campaign in 1950 was that the party leaders began it with the willingness to use any tactics to blast Thomas from public office. The whole purpose was not to elect a United States senator, but to defeat one. Exigencies during the campaign, or desperate need in its final stages, did not determine the choice of weapons. The decisions were made before the campaign got under way.

After the election, Pratt Kesler, Republican state chairman, revealed his party's plan, stating that a definite program and strategy must be decided at the beginning of any campaign. He knew, he said, Mr. Thomas' record to some extent, that he was wide open for criticism on his softness toward communism and Communists. Kesler also cited Thomas' record on the La Follette Committee (actually a subcommittee of the Senate Labor and Education Committee) which in 1940 investigated the methods used by business and its pressure groups to sabotage labor unions. Kesler claimed that Thomas had made a vicious attack upon American business. "Our program," Kesler said, "was to attack him on his record and put him on the defensive to begin with and to keep him there at all times, which we were able to do."

Kesler said it was planned that a vigorous campaign conducted against Thomas would also result in the defeat of the two Democratic congressional candidates. The Republicans thought that the electorate would see that it would not make sense to elect one person to the Senate who would be absolutely opposed to the policies of two opponents in the House. After the fireworks had died down, he admitted that the electorate had not seen it that way nor had it given much thought to the result.[2]

Representatives Granger and Bosone, however, would not fall under the same fire as Thomas. Granger, the Republicans concluded, had been a non-entity in Congress since he was first elected (1940), and a person who does nothing while in office is hard to attack. The Republicans' reasoning with reference to Congresswoman Bosone was that she had not been in office long enough (two years) to establish much of a record, and moreover, they claimed, she had reversed her position on almost every issue.

Thomas, from this standpoint, would cooperate unwittingly but admirably with the Republicans; he had never been known to reverse himself on any issue, and, as expected, he went down in 1950 as a result of the pounding he received from the Republicans without once reversing himself or even without once making some attempt to adjust himself to the changed times and conditions between the 1944 and 1950 elections. No politician can be continuously successful in American politics without either at least a modicum of ruthlessness or some degree of flexibility. Thomas could be neither flexible nor ruthless, and without these qualities he was an easy prey for the Republicans.

Kesler observed that the Republicans' greatest advantage was a nominee, Wallace F. Bennett, who had never held a public office, and, therefore, who had done much less to account for than Granger and Bosone. For these reasons Bennett was difficult for the Democrats to attack. Representative Granger brought a roar from his party's state nominating convention when he referred to Bennett as a man who spoke out in glittering generalities such as faith and freedom, and who was "against sin," but this did not make it any easier for the Democrats to attack Bennett or to speak for Thomas.

The Democrats were not without their strategy. They planned to attack Senator Watkins, particularly for his views on United States foreign policy, and then to pin the label of the National Association of Manufacturers on Bennett. Though the Democrats attacked Bennett on his public utterances, they were forced actually to attack his private record, and about all they had available was his presidency of the NAM. However, hardly anyone, at least in Utah, would construe any statement coming from any official of this organization as traitorous and unpatriotic. In reality, "big business" and the NAM never did have generally in Utah the unfavorable connotations attributed to them in other parts of the nation.

Bennett claimed that he was not "smearing" his opponent, but he did not hesitate to accuse Thomas of "political bribery" and of "buying votes." He claimed that Thomas was guilty on both counts by promising "free medicine, larger assistance checks, bigger farm subsidies, and better pay, all the while pretending that this money comes from someone else who wasn't entitled to it in the first place."[3]

In September the Democrats issued a mimeographed, four-page "fact sheet" on the NAM which hardly anyone would read except a few zealous party workers. But Thomas' words against the NAM could hardly match Bennett's against him. Claiming that his opponent spoke for the NAM, Thomas was credited with saying that the NAM's tax proposals would shift the cost of government to the wage earner and let the big corporations go scot-free. In answer to the Democrats, Pratt Kesler claimed that "the NAM is neither a candidate nor a factor in the present election,"[4] and he called Thomas' attack against it a "vicious smear campaign." True, the NAM was not a candidate, but neither was the Communist party, the Soviet Union, nor the Communist-front organizations with which the Republicans tried to link Thomas.

Bennett denied he was running on the "NAM's record but rather on his own record as a Utah businessman whose companies provided 300 jobs and have a reputation for fine labor relations."[5] In this statement, in which Bennett was divorcing himself from the NAM, he was tying Thomas in with Communist-infiltrated organizations and at the same time trying to project some liberal views, apparently in an effort to take some wind out of the Democrats' sails. He said he favored "extension of federal pensions, social security and minimum wages to all citizens." He claimed he was in favor of the "price supports, soil conservation, cooperatives, and the development of public power."[6]

The exchange of views on the NAM revealed the difference in tone and temper in the use of language by each side to interpret the position and views of the other. Generally the Republican interpretation of what Thomas and the Democrats had said about Bennett and the Republicans, with a few exceptions, was far more vitriolic and vituperative than what Thomas and the Democrats had said in the first place. The Republicans had blueprinted a slugging campaign, and they never once ceased their slugging; indeed, they increased both the number and the power of the blows as they paced the race.

On July 18, 1950, the Democrats placed an advertisement in the Salt Lake City dailies entitled: "Watkins Fiddles While World Burns! Stand in Korean Crisis Shocks Utah and Nation." Quotations then followed from Frank R. Kent, Elmer Davis, the *Salt Lake Tribune*, and *Newsweek* citing Watkins' stand against current American foreign policy and calling him an extreme isolationist and associating him with Vito Marcantonio. Some friends of Watkins' later defended his record in another full-page ad which began: "Thou Hypocrite, first cast the beam out of thine own eye. . . ."[7] 'We deplore dishonesty in politics' say

---

Watkins Fiddles While World Burns!

Stand in Korean Crisis Shocks Utah and Nation

Watkins Extreme Isolationist

"It would be a BIASED CRITIC, indeed who would withhold from Mr. Truman full credit for the bold decision made by him in the Korean crisis . . .'

"In the House, the only bleat came from Marcantonio who strictly adheres to the SOVIET POINT OF VIEW and CARES FAR LESS FOR OUR CONSTITUTION THAN FOR AN OAK LEAF IN A FALL BREEZE. Naturally, no one wanted to line up with this CREATURE OF THE KREMLIN, and the chorus of Presidential approval was non-partisan and overwhelming almost to the point of unanimity . . .

"THERE WERE A COUPLE OF EXTREME ISO-LATIONIST SENATORS (WATKINS, R.) UTAH, KEM (R.) MISSOURI), who cried that the President had 'violated the constitution' . . .

"Our prestige everywhere would have been devastated. Our leadership in the fight for freedom would have become a joke.

"Had we remained supine in face of the Korean challenge practically everything would have gone down the drain . . .

"Vastly more powerful than the Soviet nation, we would have been bluffed and bullied into craven acquiescence of an utterly intolerable situation."

Frank R. Kent, Columnist, July 1950

Watkins Opposes Action

"Congressional leaders of both parties were called to the White House this morning. There was no disagreement among them. Senator Bridges said he approved completely of the President's action. So did other men who were recently among the President's sharpest critics: Sen. Knowland, who called on all Americans to give the President united support; Sen. Hickenlooper, who said that we have to keep faith with peoples under our protection; Congressman Judd, who said we were following the only possible course.

"ONLY THREE MEN OBJECTED—CONGRESS-MAN MARCANTONIO, THAT STEADY FOLLOW-ER OF THE COMMUNIST LINE; and SENATORS KEM AND WATKINS, REPUBLICANS. They all said the President was arrogating to himself the power to declare war without the consent of Congress. Mr. Marcantonio, who is a smart fellow, undoubtedly realized that if the President had waited for Congress to approve his action, Korea could have gone down the drain while they debated; AS FOR SENATORS KEM AND WATKINS, IT IS CHARITABLE TO ASSUME THAT THEY DON'T UNDERSTAND."

Elmer Davis, Broadcast, June 27, 1950

"Isolationist, Divisionists Conspicuous But Scarcer"

"If the RED RUSSIANS ever get a foothold in this country it will be due to the conduct of LEGISLATORS who put PERSONAL PROSPECTS and PARTISAN PREJUDICE above the safety and welfare of the country which has honored them."

Editorial, Salt Lake Tribune, July 4, 1950

"Senator Arthur V. Watkins questioned the whole policy of sending military assistance to nations threatened by communist aggression. He said it represents a false reliance on arms."

Newsweek, July 10, 1950

DOES WATKINS SPEAK FOR UTAH REPUBLICAN CANDIDATES?

Paid Political Advertisement by Dan B. Shields, Salt Lake City, Utah

the Mis-Dealers—but do they? Read their smears. . . . Then read the Truth."
Watkins himself stated that he had seen a number of pieces of literature directed against Thomas and his alleged Communist leanings. He claimed that the Republican party was not responsible for them in any way, which was true.[8] The Republican party did not originate these documents; they copied them and then used them as propaganda pieces.

Senator Thomas and the Democratic leadership in the state publicly announced that they would stand on the record. Watkins reasserted that he was the one who had good reason to ask for an investigation. He was not a candidate, and yet, he said, he was smeared from one end of the state to the other by Senator Thomas, Grant MacFarlane (the Democratic state chairman), and the Democrats generally. He claimed that Thomas deliberately misrepresented his voting record on the Marshall Plan and on all measures restricting the Communists. He asserted further that from day to day in the "Battle Corner" of the *Salt Lake Tribune* Grant MacFarlane went all out in his denunciation and had accused him of nearly everything short of treason to his country, had said that he was 100 percent negative, and had said that he had been against all legislation for the last several years. Watkins stated that the smear campaign against him started before he arrived home following the recess of Congress, beginning soon after the Korean outbreak of hostilities.

Watkins had prepared a full-page newspaper advertisement against Thomas. For some reason the Republican officials objected to its release so early in the campaign and refused to finance it. But Watkins financed it himself and the ad was published. He was not to be pulled off the stage by either Democrats or Republicans; he reappeared occasionally during the campaign and frequently in the closing weeks with speeches and releases repeating the charges of Thomas' associations with Communist-front organizations.

Actually, it seemed that the Republican strategists did not want Watkins around during the campaign; he was quite vulnerable. Obviously, they would not want to be placed in the position of *defending* Watkins or anyone else. They were going to carry the battle to the opposition. They did not want to provide the Democrats with a target. Although some Republicans considered Watkins' presence in Utah a burden rather than an asset, nevertheless it was he who provided the workmen, Richard Cardall and James McKinney, to edit and prepare for final delivery Quigley's *United States Senate News*. Moreover, the Democratic smear against Watkins, as he himself indicated, provided the Republicans with an excuse for their smear against Thomas. Watkins appeared to be a political dynamiter at heart; indeed, at the Democratic state nominating convention it was Representative Walter K. Granger and not Senator Thomas who publicly called him that "little smear artist." Granger's speech received a thunderous ovation from his fellow Democrats. Unfortunately for Thomas and the Democrats, the campaign and party tacticians did not see fit to exploit this display of Granger's own dynamiting talent.

After their first blast against Watkins, the Democrats seemed to forget about him. This event illustrated the difference in skill between the Republicans and Democrats in the use of political propaganda. The Democrats' blast was badly timed; it came too early in the campaign; it was directed against the wrong man—one who was not even a candidate; and above all, it was not followed up. The Democrats had not learned the very lesson that the Republicans were applying at the moment under the Democrats' noses. Once having taken the offensive, the political dynamiter must continue to follow up with both small and large charges, timing his blasts intelligently, relentlessly, and with a strong desire to win. The dynamiter must never be deterred from his goal, nor must he let himself be thrown off his pace by counterattacks, particularly on moral grounds. He must serve his client twenty-four hours a day, every day, until the last voter has emerged from the ballot booth.

It is a peculiar trait of all political dynamiters and smear artists that they warn the voter to be aware of explosive charges and smear tactics against their own clients. Most calls for clean campaigns by candidates and most warnings against dirty ones are generally merely techniques designed to serve the purpose of the candidates who issue them. Whatever may be the truth about who was the original instigator, the Democrats made several fatal errors in propaganda technique. First, they attacked a man who was not running for office, incumbent Senator Arthur V. Watkins. Wallace Bennett, the Republican nominee, had never had any personal or public association with Watkins; though they were members of the same church, their paths had not crossed previously either politically, economically, or socially. Also, Watkins was not a dark, sinister person, nor was he sufficiently mean and nasty to give the charges credence. He just was not bad enough as a target for the Democratic offensive.

After the Democrats lost the offensive they momentarily had with their blast against Watkins, they regained it only once again when Bennett, rather late in the campaign, began to answer the charges that he and business were opposed to every social measure enacted by Congress since 1933. Thomas' staff produced brightly colored fact sheets which graphically informed the voter of the significant part the federal government had played in the state's prosperity. If Thomas could be blamed by the Republicans for the plight of a few economic enterprises—for example, mining, fur-raising, and poultry distribution, and even for the discouraging international situation—he could certainly claim credit for what had been accomplished by the federal government, through financial aid and subsidy, in and for Utah during the preceding eighteen years.

But Thomas himself was of little help to his party's strategy; he could not dramatically present what had been prepared for him. He found it difficult to point to any tangible handiwork of his own with any degree of effectiveness. Nor was he able to identify himself with the payrolls, purchasing power, and prosperity of the postwar era.

Belatedly, and therefore desperately, Thomas publicly associated himself with government achievements in the state. When he did so, however, he appeared to be boasting. Sometimes he seemed cynical; then he appeared to be hurt. He referred to himself as "little Elbert"; he would say, for example, "but it was *little Elbert* who did it." Even some of his closest friends would wince at this personal reference. At this point, Thomas revealed a major weakness as a politician. He had failed to lay carefully a personally oriented organizational groundwork for the 1950 campaign. Above all, he had failed to develop a group of persons who could authoritatively and effectively speak for him or who could use some hard-hitting tactics on his behalf to counter the blows of the Republicans. This was especially true at a late date in the campaign when Watkins claimed that he was "smeared" worse than Thomas. Although this statement was not true, it went completely unchallenged.

Thomas did have a small inner circle made up of some university professors and a few businessmen. By 1950, two or three of the original small group which started with him in 1932 had either died or had withdrawn due to appointment to federal office. In 1950, George Hatch, a radio station executive, was added to the group. Hatch was an excellent organizer, publicity man, and fund-raiser, but he was not given the chance to display his abilities and resources. In fine, Thomas was not a responsive candidate, and after the election, Hatch complained bitterly about this aspect of Thomas' political personality. Thomas failed to recognize the persons who could really have helped him in a hard-hitting and heated campaign which moved fast and furiously.

Nor had Thomas developed a staff in Washington which could serve him either in preparing for or in executing a hurly-burly campaign. He liked to have "nice" persons around him whose presence would result in a "nice" atmosphere. He wanted his office company to be congenial, pleasant, and apparently silently and smilingly cooperative. The staff was neither politically minded nor politically active. Nor did he encourage his staff or his appointees to engage in local Utah politics in his behalf. He changed secretaries rather frequently and would not allow anyone to make a career of this position. A former secretary, who was closer to the senator at the time than any other person who served on his staff, observed: "I believe Senator Thomas left too much to the immature judgment of a young and inexperienced staff during the war."[9] Indeed, he left too much to the immature judgment of a young and inexperienced campaign staff in 1950. His friends did not desert him; they just did not know how to help him, and he did not seem to know how to solicit their assistance or use what was proffered.

Thomas had not frequently appeared in Utah to talk to party organization personnel; he had neglected particularly the persons who did the legwork at the district level. Political observers who made preelection surveys and visits in the counties of the state, talking to political leaders and party officials, stated that three-fourths of the Democratic county chairmen were not "sold" on their senatorial candidate. Thomas' campaign manager put the figure even higher. Republican county chairmen, while skeptical in many cases about their candidate's ability to win, did not dislike him, and as the campaign progressed they put forth greater efforts in his behalf, undoubtedly sensing the coming victory.

Thomas considered himself a *national* senator and not a United States senator from Utah. He devoted his time and energy to his committee work; he did not consider himself a legman or a "job-getter" for Utah citizens, lobbyists, or interest groups. He had offended many key persons in the Democratic party by his apparent lack of concern for their personal problems. He did appoint a few close supporters to high office, but he was not known to be concerned with party conflicts over lesser offices, such as postmasterships. In such cases he either followed the advice of someone else or he acted on the basis of insufficient knowledge due to an earlier lack of concern. When he did recommend the appointment of the University of Utah law professor, Willis Ritter, to the District Court Bench, he antagonized many prominent Democrats. Ritter had been his campaign manager in 1944 and one of the small group of his first and early supporters in 1932. Ritter was professionally capable but generally personally unpopular with those who had dealt with him during the war while he was in the regional Office of Price Administration. Republican Senator Watkins, upon instigation of both Democrats and Republicans, forced extended hearings on the case and managed to delay the appointment so that much unfavorable publicity came to Thomas, who stubbornly stuck to his guns.[10]

This listing of Thomas' shortcomings as a politician, and particularly as an organizer and campaigner, is certainly a part of the stage setting. The Republicans took full advantage of these weaknesses.

Thomas based his hopes for reelection on three political factors: labor, agriculture, and education. The efforts in his behalf may be analyzed briefly for their effectiveness.

Businessmen generally hated Senator Thomas for his labor policies, in spite of what he had done for some single groups of business interest. It was admitted by some business leaders that he had helped them, especially during the war period, but that they hated him for his support of organized labor and legislation in its behalf. While unequivocally supporting labor, Thomas' efforts were constantly directed toward negotiation, discussion, and reconciliation in labor and management relations.

There is no evidence that labor deserted Thomas and the Democratic party. Thomas had received labor's complete organizational endorsement. Carbon and Tooele counties, with large worker groups, stayed with him. He did lose the larger industrial counties of Utah, Salt Lake, and Weber, but observers agreed that this was owing to the large late registration, which was thought to have represented Republican and independent votes. Labor in Utah had not yet developed the exceptionally efficient methods of getting its members registered and then to the polls that it displayed in the 1958 elections. In 1950, however, most labor districts voted for Thomas. He received the unqualified support of Utah labor's Joint Legislative Committee made up of representatives from the AFL, CIO, RRB, IAM, and UMW, with Karl S. Little, general secretary-treasurer of the Brotherhood of Railway and Steamship Clerks as coordinator.[11] He also received favorable endorsements from William Green, president, American Federation of Labor; Harry See, national legislative representative, Brotherhood of Railroad Trainmen; David Dubinsky; and other national labor leaders.[12]

In a postelection editorial on November 9, 1950, headed "Two-Party System Emerges Triumphant," "Labor Leaders, 'Fair Deal' Take a Beating," the *Salt Lake Tribune* observed that "undoubtedly the complaints that Mr. Thomas was subservient to union bosses and spent little of his crowded time on behalf of Utah affairs had more to do with his defeat than the shallow charges of fraternizing with reds." The metal industry "sickness" no doubt played a part.

The Utah Education Association, identified frequently as one of the most powerful pressure groups in the state, favored Senator Thomas. It considered candidates on the basis of their records. Bennett had no record. If incumbent Arthur V. Watkins had been a candidate, he would have received the UEA endorsement. The UEA worked principally by means of the telephone through district, regional, and institutional organizations. Some of these released written endorsements over the names of individual teachers. During the campaign and at the UEA state convention, Thomas debated the issue of federal aid to education with Bennett. Thomas was on sure ground, liked the subject, and acquitted himself well, while Bennett, with the cards stacked against him, tried to indicate that he was *not* opposed to education. This was the only time the two nominees came face to face during the campaign. Had the Democrats sensed the possibilities of this technique in behalf of their nominee, they could have pressed it to advantage, especially if they could have picked the subject.

Bennett was an able speaker, but he would have lacked the precise information on almost any public policy or issue that Thomas had accumulated as a political science professor and then as a United States senator for eighteen years.

Officially agriculture lined up against Thomas. The executive secretary of the Farm Bureau, Frank G. Shelley, was a Republican, but its president, John H. Schenk, was nominally a Democrat. Schenk, however, opposed Thomas and was one of the leaders in the Democrats for Bennett movement in Cache County, Utah's largest dairy area. The board of directors of the Farm Bureau, in an unusual and perhaps questionable procedure, passed resolutions opposing Thomas, Bosone, and Granger, but not against the Democratic party. This action was not popular among all farm leaders although Schenk was subsequently reelected president of the organization at its 1951 state convention. It is doubtful if the Bureau as an organization had any grounds other than political to oppose Thomas so openly and so strongly. In any event, Thomas failed to hold agricultural interests officially.

The L.D.S. church daily newspaper, the *Deseret News*, gave undue publicity during the campaign to the Washington release of Senator Styles Bridges' strong attack on the Farmers Union as pro-Communist. Arthur Gaeth, a radio commentator who was cited by Bridges as having brought communism to the Farmers Union, began a series of radio broadcasts which were continued throughout the 1950 campaign; he associated himself with Thomas, giving talks in his behalf and attacking some of his opponents. Although Gaeth later claimed that his relationship with the union had been explained satisfactorily and the attitude of the church favorably changed, the original newspaper story had done its part in discrediting the Thomas campaign.[13] The Farmers Union denied categorically that it was "red" or "Communist" dominated and quoted its principles and record as evidence.

One Farm Bureau official, who later became its state president, made statements in outlying localities that he had proof that Thomas and Granger were communistic. According to Granger,[14] he also sent out letters under the Farm Bureau name to all its members calling for "our [Granger, Bosone, and Thomas] defeat because we were only interested in the *communistic dominated* Farmers Union." After the campaign, for using the phrase "communistic dominated," the Farmers Union brought the Bureau into Federal District Court where the union won a twenty-seven-thousand-dollar damage suit for libel per se.

Allan B. Kline, president, American Farm Bureau Federation, visited Utah on at least two occasions giving numerous press interviews and public addresses.[15] The Bureau did not leave a stone unturned to defeat the Democrats and to discredit Thomas and Granger. Its political advantages were similar to those of labor unions; it had an established organization and a built-in apparatus to disseminate its propaganda.

Undoubtedly the most vigorous pressure-group attack on Thomas was by the medical groups. These organized especially for the campaign and put some of their most popular spokesmen on the air.

Thomas, in 1949, had sponsored S.B. 1679, the "National Health Insurance and Public Health Act." The health bill represented a plank in the 1948 Democratic platform; the party was committed to its consideration as a legislative measure. Thomas was a loyal party man and a key administrative spokesman on social legislation. Thomas also believed firmly in government by petition. He and his committee were obligated to accept the petition of those who wanted this measure and to consider it thoughtfully and honestly; this is what they were doing; this was democracy in action.

The American Medical Association engaged the San Francisco public relations firm, Campaigns, Inc., to fight pending legislation in Congress. The fight was waged in several states against candidates for reelection to Congress.[16] The doctors waged a full-fledged campaign in Utah against Senator Thomas, who, as chairman of the important Senate Committee on Education and Labor which handled approximately 80 percent of all the social legislation to come before the Senate, came into their direct line of fire.

According to federal law, the American Medical Association, along with other similar associations, could not legally participate directly in a political campaign involving a senator,[17] but mainly for propaganda reasons in order to obscure the role played by the hired public relations firm which blueprinted the campaign and the American Medical Association which financed it, a local doctors' committee was organized, entitled the Utah Healing Arts Committee. This included in its membership representatives of the following professions: physicians and surgeons, dentists, osteopathic physicians, naturopathic physicians, chiropractors, chiropodists, optometrists, registered nurses, doctors' receptionists, pharmacists, wholesale pharmacists, allied traveling druggists, hospital management, and other professional personnel.

Letters were sent to members of the various professions asking them to rally to the cause. The letter began:

Dear Doctor [and others to whom the letter was addressed],

Lenin, the all-powerful dictator of Communist Russia before Stalin, and the father of Communism as we know it today, said, and I quote, "The keystone in the arch of the socialized state is Socialized Medicine."

In America -

We don't like Communism!

We don't like Socialism!
We don't like Compulsion in any Form!
We don't like Regimentation or Governmental Domination of our Profession!

In America -

We Do Love Liberty and the Right of Free Enterprise!

After stating the purpose of the organization as an effort to preserve American health through the maintenance of free enterprise and the preservation of the American way of life, the letter stated the opposition of the doctors to "political medicine" and to any senator or congressman who is in favor of "Socialized Medicine" or "Compulsory Health Insurance"; the doctors concluded by vowing to do everything in their power to defeat them and to elect senators and congressmen who will fight "to preserve America's priceless heritage."[18]

The doctors linked their campaign to anti-communistic propaganda by some devious reasoning, which can be paraphrased as follows: since 1917 the American people have been often reminded that our most dangerous enemy was the Union of Soviet Socialist Republics; to start people on the road to socialism, according to Lenin, who was quoted on this point, one must first introduce a program of socialized medicine. On April 25, 1949, during the Eighty-first Congress, Senator Thomas introduced a bill in Congress entitled the "National Health Insurance and Public Health Act." The bill was cosponsored by Senators Murray, Wagner, Pepper, Chavez, McGrath, Taylor, and Humphrey. The bill would have enabled the government to collect a compulsory tax, control the money, determine the services, set the rates, maintain the records, control the doctors, dentists, nurses, druggists, and hospitals, and direct the participation of patients in the program. The doctors concluded this reasoning by alleging, *since Soviet Russia had a national medical system controlled by the state, any plan suggested in the United States having any of its features would be labeled communistic.*

The most effective method used by the doctors to carry on their campaign was a personal interview with each patient who came to the office—the receptionist, nurse, and doctor telling of the evils of the program and the people who were sponsoring it. When a patient left the office he carried with him a mental picture of the horror which would be created by a program of socialized medicine and some literature, if he would read it, which would keep this image alive.

Furthermore, monthly statements mailed to patients included printed literature on the subject. Some cartoons were very cleverly done. One showed a man drinking from a big bottle labeled "Free Medicine" while at the same time his pocket was being picked. The caption read, "The Government Can Give You Nothing It Doesn't Take From You First—Free Medicine Is No Exception." Other captions read, "There Is No Guarantee That You Will Receive Adequate Health Care Under the Proposed Socialized Medical Plan"; "Under the proposed socialized medicine plan private consultation with your doctor might become a thing of the past"; "Socialized medicine in foreign countries had added fifteen or more days to the length of illness"; "TAXES take 15 weeks of YOUR Pay Every Year, Do you want to give UNCLE SAM six weeks more Pay for 'Free Medicine'?" Letters which attempted to clarify the problem were sent to patients.

The letter, prepared by the political propagandists from California, Cleone Baxter and Clem Whitaker, read:

> Dear Friend:
>
> I feel it my duty as one of your physicians to write you and inform you concerning one of the vital issues involved in the coming election of November 7th. This matter is of great importance to you as a taxpayer and citizen because it involves the future health and medical care of yourself and your family.
>
> *Our present senator, Elbert D. Thomas, has sponsored in Congress a system of Government Medicine under which you would be taxed for your medical bills and your physician would become an employee of the Government.* This would mean that the Doctors would be directed by a great army of politicians and bureaucrats and you and your family would be forced to be attended to and treated by a Doctor chosen for you by the Government.
>
> Naturally this would lead to a deterioration in the quality of medical care. At the same time the nature and details of your illnesses would be known to a lot of government snoopers and bureaucrats. We do not want such a system of political medicine imposed on the American people.
>
> Under our system of free enterprise the practice of medicine in the United States has achieved a degree of quality higher than that in any other nation. To change it now into a system of government or political medicine would be a calamity that we all would regret. All proposals in favor of a Government System of Medicine are but a part of a broad program of Socialism which is prevalent in other countries and with which we as Americans want nothing to do.
>
> *Wallace F. Bennett, Senator Thomas' opponent, is in favor of maintaining the present system of medicine which is admitted everywhere to be the best in the world.* Mr. Bennett is also opposed to other socialistic proposals which have been advocated by Senator Thomas, such as the Brannan Farm Plan, Federal Aid to Education, etc. In the light of these facts I would deem it a personal favor if you would vote on Election Day for Wallace F. Bennett for Senator, which means a vote in favor of our present system of free enterprise in the United States.
>
> Very sincerely yours,
[signature]

Pamphlets amplified the theme that "The Voluntary Way is the American Way." Articles and editorials were furnished the papers throughout the state and were published almost without exception. Advertisements were placed with these papers pinpointing the greatness of American medicine. Instructions were given on how to scratch a ballot in favor of Bennett. Lecture series were sponsored by the group. Doctors took to the airwaves. The Mormon Tabernacle and the Mormon Tabernacle Choir were lent to the association to make their state convention for that year more attractive.

Probably the most ambitious personal campaign against "socialized medicine" was waged by Selvoy J. Boyer. Traditionally a Democrat and a delegate to the 1950 Democratic state convention, Boyer gave four hundred speeches against Thomas between March 1 and November 7, 1950. During one thirty-day period, on leave from his Republican political appointment to an office in the State Department of Engineering, he gave fifty addresses. His audiences ranged from fifty to fifteen hundred listeners.

The campaign waged by the medical and allied groups continued to gain momentum. Thomas attempted to meet their arguments by denying that medical insurance was socialistic, but in the heat of a political campaign, there is no forum in which to approach a problem with an explanation about committee techniques, parliamentary procedure, hearings, and extensive and comparatively calm discussions.[19] The opportunity to educate the public and to air a current problem was lost by both parties and the medical groups. The Democrats failed or refused to exploit the many individual resentments against the medical profession. The proposed bill did contain a number of challenging provisions. When approached as to why he had sponsored the bill or supported it as chairman of the Senate Committee on Labor and Public Welfare, Thomas would merely say that it was a great problem and ought to be discussed thoroughly and openly. This was his approach in politics, which accounted greatly for his shortcomings as a campaigner.

Were the medical pressure groups effective? Was their campaign against Thomas successful? One doctor expressed an opinion, probably held by many others of his profession, that "it was the primary and perhaps the real reason for Thomas' defeat."[20]

Businessmen, also, took an open and active part in the Utah elections, using the Republican party as a medium through which to express their interests and opinions. Senator-elect Bennett, in an address to the Utah State Automobile Dealers Association, stated that "the most significant factor emerging from the 1950 political campaign was the reassumption of political leadership by business leaders."[21]

Business firms carried on extensive indoctrination programs, using the films, publications, and training programs of the Middle West Service Company, Chicago, Illinois, through the services of the Utah Industrial Relations Council of Utah. Firm heads visited each employee the day before election or called the employees together in groups. While the instructions were only to vote, little doubt was left in the mind of the employee as to how his employer wished him to vote. One bank sent enclosures with its November first statements urging persons to vote on November seventh and to tune in on the company's politically slanted radio broadcasts three times a week.

The Democrats for Bennett movement was initiated and sponsored by a group of bankers and businessmen in Logan, Utah. Many members were employees in the rather extensive economic holdings of the Bennett family. Others had been generally opposed to the New Deal since its inception and had hated Thomas since before he became senator in 1933, but particularly since 1946 when it was felt he did not extend himself to save the Bushnell military hospital in Brigham City where some prominent Logan businessmen had invested heavily in real estate development.[22] However, it did seem interesting that Utah's Democratic delegation in Congress, of which Thomas had been the senior member since 1940, and before that perhaps the most influential member,[23] was not credited for having brought Bushnell Hospital to Utah in the first place. On the contrary, everything was done in propaganda to minimize Thomas' role in bringing federal installations to Utah, usually by not mentioning his efforts.

Women entered the 1950 campaign in a unique manner and for an unusual reason. Ora Lewis, candidate for mayor in Logan, Utah, 1949, told the story in a personal letter she sent to her friends.

> Two days prior to election, Senator Thomas was guest speaker at a meeting held in the Tabernacle, sponsored by the Extension Division of the Utah State Agricultural College and Cache County, honoring the first voters. The candidates were invited to attend this meeting as special guests and I was honored to do so—at least until the Senator spoke. He had full knowledge of the campaign in progress and of my candidacy, but in a premeditated manner he mentioned women's suffrage and then made this statement, and I quote—"The people of this nation are not yet ready for petticoat government."

Subsequently a round-robin letter over the signature of the president, Leah Merrill, denouncing the senator, went to every chapter of the Utah Federation of Business and Professional Women's Clubs.[24]

The effect of the attitude of the press in Utah cannot be discounted in the 1950 election. The Utah Press Association listed fifty-eight weekly newspapers. No labor paper was included in this group. At least one weekly, *The News* (Republican), published in Utah county was not listed by the association. No New Deal paper existed among those listed, with the possible exception of the *Salt Lake Times*, whose Democratic slant always seemed to fall somewhat short of New or Fair Dealism. By far the majority of the publishers were Republican. The few others were conservative Democrats who followed either the Republican or L.D.S. church line, or both—usually both—or who did not express their personal political views editorially because of the monopoly their papers had in an area dominated by business advertisers. Only one publisher was known to like Senator Thomas personally.

While some of the Utah daily and weekly press did not openly oppose Senator Thomas in their editorial columns, not a single paper, with the exception of the local labor publications and possibly the weekly *Salt Lake Times*, made any statements in his behalf or in behalf of the Democratic program.[25] The daily *Logan Herald-Journal* and the weekly *Ephraim Enterprise* published extremely strong editorials against him which revealed the intense feelings of the writers and publishers.

The *Logan Herald-Journal*, under the editorship of Gunnar Rasmussen, claimed at one time that it was the only "liberal" paper in Utah. On October 26, 1946, Ray Nelson, columnist and editorial writer, had said of Thomas: "His astonishing memory for details, his vast experience as a political scientist, and his record of achievement as a statesman, qualify Dr. Thomas as one of the foremost public affairs experts in the world." On August 19, 1950, under a new editor, Robert Martin, with Nelson still on the staff, this same paper said: "He [Thomas] is part and parcel of a national administration that has corrupted itself and threatens to corrupt our country," and "He has been among those who presided over the degeneration of the once-great Democratic party into a machine of five-percenting politicians, socialist planners, unprincipled labor leaders, and demagogues."

The publisher of the *Ephraim Enterprise* and the *Manti Messenger*, Ross Cox, a devout Mormon with strong opinions, and a nominal Democrat who had once supported Thomas, wrote an "Open Letter to Senator Elbert D. Thomas" (October 13, 1950) which was reprinted and circulated by the Republican state headquarters. He chided Thomas about the New Deal philosophy of scarcity, with allusions to his socialism, and his old age. This editorial summed up many of the resentments and much of the bitterness which, although suppressed by the Democrats, were harbored by persons to whom the New Deal policies and activities were anathema and which were finding release during this campaign.

The opposition of another portion of the Utah press to Thomas personally was indicated by his receiving the well-known silent treatment (censorship or negative propaganda), or by his being ignored when his achievements or activities might have been editorialized or featured. For example, Drew Pearson's favorable comparison of the arch political rivals, Elbert D. Thomas and J. Reuben Clark, was deleted by the *Salt Lake Telegram*, which had regularly published the column. Pearson called attention to the "radicalism" of Clark in his early years when he pioneered in United States foreign policy. Clark was criticized, Pearson said, for being a radical because he wrote a document proposing a revision of the Monroe Doctrine whereby other Pan-American nations would join us in upholding it. This theory was now generally accepted, but at that earlier time, Reuben Clark and his "bolshevist" views were compared to a "waft of red hot air out of the Kremlin." In speaking of Thomas, Pearson said that

> another Mormon in Washington has been pioneering in U.S. foreign policy. Last year Sen. Elbert Thomas of Utah introduced a resolution creating a United Nations policy force not subject to Soviet veto, but obedient to a majority vote in the UN Assembly. When first introduced, Thomas' resolution was considered revolutionary; that idea is now the official policy of the state department, and is being vigorously opposed by Moscow. Today in Utah, this same senator who pioneered foreign policy ahead of his time is now facing a desperate reelection battle, with the absurd charge being made that he is a Communist. And politics being what it is, the man who is working hardest to defeat him is the other Mormon leader, who also put forward revolutionary ideas ahead of his time—80-year-old Reuben Clark.[26]

But on the whole, the three leading dailies, with large state circulation, the *Salt Lake Tribune*, the *Salt Lake Telegram*, and the *Deseret News*, bent over backwards—and succeeded—in giving equal space and comparable location in their papers to the political candidates and their news releases.[27] The newspapers on occasion refused to accept advertisements that went beyond a standard of good taste. The Democratic campaign managers had no complaint to make of the press in the handling of their releases.

During the campaign, the only departure from the posture of neutrality which all the papers assumed was taken by the *Deseret News*, the L.D.S. church newspaper. On Friday, November third, the paper ran a picture three columns by seven inches of President David O. McKay greeting Mr. Allan Kline, president of the American Farm Bureau Federation. This story was given the top spot on the local page, and carried the by-line of Clarence Barker, assistant church editor. Prominent in the story were accounts of Mr. Kline's meeting with the presidency of the church, followed by his denunciation of governmental controls and advocacy of a "regulated free enterprise." The reader could only draw one conclusion—Mr. Kline, who had been sent into Utah by the Republicans, and his program, enjoyed the approval of the Mormon church.

The *Deseret News* was particularly clear in its daily editorials and in its weekly Mormon church section to emphasize its doctrine of free agency, its support of free enterprise and capitalism, and its opposition to governmental action. Socialism was the opposite of free agency and free enterprise. National Health Insurance was socialistic. Thomas supported National Health Insurance; therefore, Thomas, by suggestion, was a Socialist, and perhaps by association, a

Communist. Generally, that Thomas was a "Socialist" was simply taken for granted and seldom suggested as a question.

Most of the press had a way of siding with the Republican nominee, however, by editorials supporting what he stood for, which hurt his opponent by imputing to him the opposite. In spite of all statistics, there was no question in 1950 as to what candidate the press generally was supporting in the election. That it was Bennett, the businessman, would have been evident to even the most casual observer.

On January 4, 1951, soon after the campaign, the *Salt Lake Tribune*, published an AP Wirephoto, which showed Vice-President Alben Barkley, a Democrat, in the act of congratulating newly elected Senator Bennett. If you looked closely you could see that there was something phony about it, although the caption read, "After taking the oath of office, Sen. Wallace F. Bennett (R., Utah) receives the congratulations of Vice President Alben Barkley, right. In the center is Sen. Francis Case (R., S.D.)."

The original photograph showed the vice-president congratulating the victorious Democratic senator from Missouri, Thomas D. Hennings. In the published photo Senator Hennings stood on the right of Senator Bennett. The *Tribune* artist had cut off Senator Hennings' picture and darkened out that part of his right arm which reached across Bennett and Case. What was in the mind of the editor who ordered the picture distorted in this manner? Did the reproduction indicate the slant of the newspaper in the recent campaign? If so, it gives credence to the charge made by Senator Thomas that he had received biased press treatment.

Observers of the 1950 election campaign noted an increased interest on the part of the Mormon church in politics. The general authorities of the church were, in the main, Republicans, who had opposed overtly or covertly all Democratic proposals and candidates since 1932. Although its influence was apparent, it had not controlled politics. In 1950 the situation was different. In contrast to Thomas, whose identification with the New Deal and with labor made him objectionable in conservative church circles, Wallace Bennett was a most attractive candidate. The *Deseret News* had followed Bennett's career as president of the NAM with interest and approbation, giving very full coverage which prepared the voters to accept him as a political candidate. It was inevitable that the enthusiasm for Bennett should find expression at the various levels of the church. The speeches at the April and October conferences of the church, particularly the former, were interpreted as favoring the Republican cause. Members of the church sometimes quoted Bennett's speeches in church classes; Thomas appears never to have been quoted. Thomas had offended Mormon leaders when he failed to consult any of them in 1932 about his intended candi-

Unretouched photo in the *Deseret News* of January 6, 1951.

Retouched photo in the *Salt Lake Tribune* of January 4, 1951.

Original photo retouched by *Tribune* artist.

dacy for the senatorship, and he continued to bypass the church during his entire tenure in office. Thomas had a meticulous regard for the separation of church and state in politics.

The Mormon church openly entered the 1950 campaign late—or was dragged into it through a peculiar set of circumstances. An unofficial agency of the church, never formally approved but unquestionably having the tacit approval of the "brethren" (church authorities), issued a document which was to have a telling effect on the outcome of the campaign. The organization was the Salt Lake County L.D.S. Law Observance and Enforcement Committee, consisting of twenty-six members, one each from the twenty-six stakes in Salt Lake County, which released a list of endorsements of candidates shortly before the final election.[28] The names of seventeen Democrats, among them Thomas and Bosone, were "scratched," while only two Republicans were "blacklisted."[29] Accompanying the list was a letter stating the objectives of the committee as being the checking and reporting of law enforcement in Salt Lake in five areas: "saloons" open on Sundays, taverns selling liquor to minors, gambling, prostitution, and horse racing.[30] The letter urged the Saints to go to the polls as American citizens, to vote on the basis of principle only, and to seek the counsel of their bishops if they wished further advice as to candidates. The list and letter were sent to stake presidents and state committee members. Although only forty copies were prepared by the committee for distribution, one member allowed copies to be made and circulated widely, even beyond the borders of Salt Lake County.

Many persons immediately questioned the action of the committee in endorsing the Republican candidates for United States senator and congressman and scratching their opponents. Previously, before the primary, the same committee had issued a list of candidates it had approved for election. It failed to list Thomas and Bosone, while it listed Bennett. It also failed on this occasion to list Mrs. Ivy Baker Priest, Republican congressional candidate, and state Senator Rue L. Clegg, who was challenging Bennett in the primary for the Republican nomination. In each case, the committee was supposed to have based its decision on the results of a questionnaire which had purportedly been sent to candidates. The electorate was never informed as to the specific questions put to the candidates or as to the answers received from them.

Democratic managers carried their protest to the church general authorities and to President George Albert Smith, who, upon solicitation, issued a retraction. Other church authorities refused to commit themselves publicly and waited almost two days to print the retraction in the *Deseret News* (November 3, 1950). The *Salt Lake Tribune* and *Telegram* had published it immediately upon its release on the morning of November second.

While the Democrats charged church interference in politics, the Republicans claimed the whole affair was a Democratic "trick"; they alleged that Mormon church endorsement of a candidate would accrue to the benefit of his rival.[31] The general authorities of the church asserted that "the Church had nothing to do with the letter in any way, shape or form. . . ." How would its official spokesmen explain the statement of one of the stake presidents that "we were instructed that the thinking of Elbert D. Thomas was not in conformity with the teachings of our faith"?[32] A leading Democrat, a former state senator, and a church official, said that

> the defeat of Senator Thomas in this county [Weber] . . . may be chargeable to several factors. In my opinion of first importance was the attitude of the Church against him. The letter from the L.D.S. Law Observance and Enforcement Committee was circulated in this county. Whether they received instructions or not I do not know, but from contacts, [I do know that] a large majority of church officials here were rabidly opposed to him.[33]

Senator Thomas, Ivy Baker Priest, and Rue L. Clegg claimed that they had not received the letter which had omitted their names from the list of approved candidates–nor had they ever received the original questionnaire regarding their stand on vice conditions in Salt Lake County. Clegg observed:

> The ballot [issued before the primary] is somewhat self-explanatory. As you will note, the names of those they were opposing were not scratched out; they were just left out. In my opinion, most of the ballot was mere subterfuge. The whole mention was centered around the nomination of a United States senator; however, there were some others besides myself who were discriminated against. You will note the statement at the head of the ballot says the candidates "will uphold the standards of the Church in regards to pending legislation on liquor by the drink, horse racing, etc." The ballot is a misrepresentation on its face for the reason that there is *no* pending legislation on either sale by the drink or horse racing. It was dishonest to submit these two subjects when they are of absolutely no concern to the office of United States senator nor any of the other offices except to the legislative and law enforcement officers. Without mentioning names, there was one man on our ticket they endorsed who I think fills that description and there was one endorsed on the Democratic ticket whom I heard not more than two weeks before the election profaning and calling the presidency of the Mormon Church fascists.[34]

Representative Walter K. Granger stated unequivocally that "the letter of the Law Enforcement Committee of the Church was a stunning blow for us Democrats and Thomas never got over it."[35]

The character of the L.D.S. church campaign to get Thomas out of office placed it within the framework of political dynamiting. The unique character of this type of political dynamiting was that it was done by a religious functionary who in his own mind was carrying out the wishes of those who had hired him, a religious body.

Two propaganda pieces which preceded the infamous *United States Senate News* merit additional detailed treatment at this point. The first was a thirty-nine page article by Jeremiah Stokes which he sent to various Utah Republicans, including Marilyn R. Allen and Governor J. Bracken Lee, who allegedly turned the material over to the Republican state committee.

Allen was a spinster from Georgia, in her fifties or sixties, whose headquarters became the center for the distribution of literature prepared by the various known extremely right-wing groups. These were invariably anti-Negro and anti-Semitic, and sometimes anti-Catholic. In international relations they were anti-UN, anti-foreign soil. Historically, they were the most extreme isolationists. They stumped for Christ and country, and the cross and the flag were their symbols. One of these groups was headed by Gerald L. K. Smith and Stanley Swift, who came to Utah during the campaign and held meetings in Salt Lake City. Swift later related in California that he had visited with Governor Lee.

Jeremiah Stokes was a former Salt Lake City attorney who in 1950 resided in Chicago. His article, which he had been preparing for a decade, documented all of Senator Thomas' alleged connections with Communists, fellow travelers, and Communist-front organizations. All that he established factually was that Thomas had lent his name to numerous pro-Soviet organizations as a sponsor for some of their activities. He made much of the article Thomas wrote for the *New Masses*, although he did not examine for his readers what Thomas had written. He also relied heavily on the praise the *Daily Worker* had given Thomas on the occasion of some of his utterances, which in each instance were very guarded and could be taken as evasive answers to leading questions, just as easily as they were interpreted as endorsement of Soviet interests.

Stokes' importance lay in the fact that he had been gathering the material Quigley and Senator Watkins used in the *United States Senate News* for almost ten years. Some of the lawyers who served Wallace F. Bennett as speakers in 1950 had shared office space with Stokes or had had their offices in the same building. The venom poured out on Thomas had been gathered and prepared before the Republicans hired Quigley, whose poisoned pen was the weapon needed to turn it into a tremendous political campaign blitz weapon. Most of the material in the Stokes article and photostats were included in the *United States Senate News*; an analysis of the latter, substantially an analysis of the former, will be made in detail in the following chapter.

Allen had also published considerably during this period; periodically she issued a mimeographed letter.[36] During the campaign she called the United States Census Bureau and its census enumerating "communistic." She also said that "Admiral Chester W. Nimitz, who was Chief of our Naval Forces in the Pacific during World War II, does dishonor to his American uniform when he joins with the United Nations (which is absolutely run and controlled by Communists), and when he pleads their cause instead of the strictly American cause." Thomas noted this quotation and took strong exception to it. Nimitz, on a lecture tour, spoke in Salt Lake City during the campaign.

In a letter dated October 6, 1950, prepared in his Chicago office, 642 Dearborn Street, Stokes wrote to "Dear Marilyn" as follows:

> You can undoubtedly get to see copies of the *New Masses* at the City Library, or maybe at the library at the U. of U. . . . And should such sources not prove fruitful, write to L. W. Jeffrey, Executive Secretary of the National Republican Senatorial Committee, 428 Senate Office Building, Washington, who will undoubtedly verify the photostats from the files of the Library of Congress. I sent Mr. Jeffrey copies the same as I sent you. I am amazed that the photostats I sent you would be questioned. . . . This is the same horseplay I met with in '44. At that time . . . I couldn't get anyone with the guts to use them. You did a good job on Thomas and I know the material I sent you is invulnerable. I am glad the governor is taking an active part in the campaign and I am hoping he is using the material we have prepared. I know he put it into the hands of the State Republican Committee. More power to you and best regards from us both.
>
> [Signed]
> Jeremiah

As the campaign progressed, a reaction set in against this company of extremists, Allen, Smith, Stokes, and Swift. Responsible Republicans sensed this possible reaction and tried to keep free from this group. None, however, repudiated Allen, Smith, et al., openly and publicly; secretly and silently they seemed to acquiesce to their objectives and arguments. Both groups had the same objective–the defeat of Thomas. Their methods differed in degree if not in kind. Marilyn R. Allen appeared at the Republican headquarters. Some of her printed materials were kept and distributed from this point, and a few top Republicans did correspond with her. The Republican party organizations remained free from her group and denied publicly and emphatically that they had anything to do with the materials produced and distributed by it. According to Republican officials, the party became involved with this group despite its desire to stay clear. No Republican in that year appeared to be very discriminating in his choice of associates and their materials as long as they all contributed to the total propaganda effect, and to the missiles which were coming down on the heads of Senator Thomas and other Democratic nominees. They were imbued with one sole purpose, to knock Senator Elbert D. Thomas out of public office.

The second propaganda item which was to floor Thomas for the count of nine before Quigley's bomb reached the state was a single sheet in black and white, eleven by seventeen inches. Across the top, in white letters blocked out by solid black ink, were two lines: "Senator Elbert Thomas Presides at Communist Meeting." Five inches below appeared the words, "Presides at Communist Banquet." The repetition of these words throughout the written material became the gimmick, so well-known to professional propagandists. Below the two identical phrases was the paragraph:

> Sometime back The New Masses decided that it wanted to expand its propaganda activities which required that a large sum of money be raised. The committee to raise the money . . . decided to turn to a sympathetic member of the United States Senate for one to preside at this dinner. Believe it or not, the invitation went to Senator Elbert Thomas of Utah and, worse still, he accepted. *He did it and he cannot deny it.* Expert observers were not surprised because Stalin's weekly magazine noted above (The New Masses) had on various occasions carried articles written by Senator Thomas.[37] The committee knew where the Utah Senator's sympathies were before they invited him to preside at their Communist war chest, money-raising dinner.

Then came a surprisingly good photograph of Thomas on the left side of the circular, with the caption, "U.S. Senator Elbert Thomas of Utah who presided at the Communist war chest, money-raising campaign dinner of The New Masses magazine on January 22, 1945, at the Hotel Commodore, New York City." On the right side opposite Thomas was a picture of Paul Robeson in a typical Hitler speaking pose, mouth open and both hands upraised, and who, the caption read, is "Considered one of the most dangerous Communists in America, who acted as Chairman of the Communist money-raising committee and served as Co-Chairman with Senator Thomas at the banquet mentioned above." Between the pictures were two columns of names of "the Communists and their sympathizers who served on the committee that invited Senator Thomas to *preside at the Communist money-raising campaign* affair. Many of those named . . . are now [1950] either in prison or indicted for their un-American activities." The names of some noted American writers followed: Louis Adamic, William Rose Benét, Van Wyck Brooks, Theodore Dreiser, Lion Feuchtwanger, Dorothy Canfield Fisher, Cary McWilliams, Dr. Thomas Mann, Donald Ogden Stewart, and others.

Below this were listed the questions which were put to Mr. Thomas (the title "senator" was suddenly dropped).

> 1. Why did you preside at the Communist banquet?
> 2. If you knew it was a Communist banquet why did you accept?
> 3. If you did not know it was a Communist banquet, how can you expect American citizens to trust your intelligence in a critical hour like this?
> 4. Why do you not apologize to the citizens of Utah and America for *presiding* at a Communist money-raising campaign dinner?
> 5. How can you expect to deserve the votes of Utah citizens when you help to make respectable such notorious Red revolutionists as Paul Robeson?

SENATOR ELBERT THOMAS
Presides at Communist Meeting

All patriotic voters in Utah should know that Senator Elbert Thomas has forfeited the confidence of good Americans by the loose and limp manner in which he has fraternized with America's worst enemies. It is no longer a secret that in the Headquarters Office of the American Communist Party Senator Elbert Thomas has been considered a friend of the Marxist program in America along with such men as Glen Taylor (Senator Glen Taylor of Idaho, running mate of Henry Wallace) and Congressman Marcantonio of New York who never fails to support legislation supported by the American Communist Party.

Expert observers in Washington, D. C. have been stunned and shocked as they have observed Elbert Thomas playing ball with the Red propagandists of the U.S.A. The American Anti-Communist League which works in cooperation with over 100 organizations fighting Communism in America is of the opinion that there are thousands of innocent voters in Utah who do not realize that their senior Senator has been dining and associating and speaking with the most vicious and ruthless Communist propagandists in the nation.

The purpose of this circular is to cite one scandalous example which is only a sample of the hundreds of such contacts that have been developed by Mr. Thomas.

PRESIDES AT COMMUNIST BANQUET

Sometime back The New Masses (official weekly organ of the Communist Party in America whose Editors are all members of the Communist Party) decided that it wanted to expand its propaganda activities which required that a large sum of money be raised. The committee to raise the money was headed by the notorious Black Red, Paul Robeson. Under the leadership of Paul Robeson and the special Committee, they decided to turn to a sympathetic member of the United States Senate for one to preside at this dinner. Believe it or not, the invitation went to Senator Elbert Thomas of Utah and, worse still, he accepted. He did it and he cannot deny it. Expert observers were not surprised because Stalin's weekly magazine noted above (The New Masses) had on various occasions carried articles written by Senator Thomas. The committee knew where the Utah Senator's sympathies were before they invited him to preside at their Communist war chest, money-raising dinner.

U. S. SENATOR ELBERT THOMAS

of Utah who presided at the Communist war chest, money-raising campaign dinner of The New Masses magazine on January 22, 1945 at the Hotel Commodore, New York City.

Below are the names of the Communists and their sympathizers who served on the committee that invited Senator Thomas to preside at the Communist money-raising campaign affair.

Many of those named below are now either in prison or indicted for their un-American activities.

Louis Adamic
Milton Avery
William Rose Benet
Mary McLeod
  Bethune
Arnold Blanch
Peter Blume
Dorothy Brewster
Alexander Brook
Van Wyck Brooks
Henrietta Buckmaster
David Burliuk
Edward Chodorov
Nicolai Cikovsky
Aaron Copland
Adolf Dehn
Dean Dixon
Muriel Draper
Theodore Dreiser
Philip Evergood
Lion Feuchtwanger
Frederick V. Field
Dorothy Canfield
  Fisher
Daniel R. Fitzpatrick
Rev. Stephen H.
  Fritchman
Hugo Gellert
Chaim Gross
Robert Gwathmey
Minna Harkavy
Joseph Hirsch
Lena Horne
Leo Huberman
Langston Hughes
George Jessel
Crockett Johnson
Bernard Karfiol
Rockwell Kent
Dr. John A. Kingsbury
Moise Kisling

Canada Lee
Ray Lev
Ring Lardner, Jr.
Alain Locke
Robert Morss Lovett
Louis Lozowick
Cary McWilliams
Fritz Mahler
Albert Maltz
Heinrich Mann
Dr. Thomas Mann
Fletcher Martin
Ruth McKenney
Rev. William Howard
  Melish
Lewis Merrill
Lewis Milestone
Waldo Peirce
Arthur Upham Pope
Carl Randau
Prof. Walter Rautenstrauch
Gardner Rea
Vivian Rivkin
Robert Rossen
Hazel Scott
Vincent Sherman
Elie Siegmeister
John Sloan
Moses Soyer
Raphael Soyer
Prof. Bernhard Stern
Donald Ogden
  Stewart
Prof. Dirk J. Struik
Ilona Ralf Sues
Genevieve Taggard
Dalton Trumbo
Frank Tuttle
Eda Lou Walton
Max Weber
Dame May Whitty
Doxey Wilkerson

PAUL ROBESON

Considered one of the most dangerous Communists in America, who acted as Chairman of the Communist money-raising committee and served as Co-Chairman with Senator Thomas at the banquet mentioned above.

QUESTIONS WHICH MR. THOMAS MUST ANSWER

1. Why did you preside at the Communist banquet?

2. If you knew it was a Communist banquet why did you accept?

3. If you did not know it was a Communist banquet, how can you expect American citizens to trust your intelligence in a critical hour like this?

4. Why do you not apologize to the citizens of Utah and America for presiding at a Communist money-raising campaign dinner?

5. How can you expect to deserve the votes of Utah citizens when you help to make respectable such notorious Red revolutionists as Paul Robeson?

This circular has been prepared by the American Anti-Communist League, St. Louis, Missouri. This circular is being distributed by the Utah Anti-Communist League. Additional copies may be obtained by addressing requests to either of the following addresses: American Anti-Communist League, P. O. Box 1031, St. Louis 1, Missouri OR Miss Marilyn R. Allen (Utah Anti-Communist League) P. O. Box 2243, Salt Lake City, Utah.

1-5 of these circulars will be sent Free to any individual who requests them, enclosing stamps for postage. For a packet of more than 5 circulars they may be had at the following rates: 100 - $2.00; 50 - $1.00; 25 - $.50; 10 - $.25.

IMPORTANT NOTE: Senator Elbert Thomas has no right to ask for the confidence of the American people or the votes of the Utah people as long as he fails to explain his intimate and scandalous association with Communists.

The circular then stated it was prepared by the American Anti-Communist League, St. Louis, Missouri, and distributed by the Utah Anti-Communist League. Addresses where copies could be secured were given, with Miss Marilyn R. Allen's as that of the Utah Anti-Communist League. One could buy fifty copies for a dollar. The last two lines were prefaced by the phrase, "Important Note," in capital letters. "Senator Thomas," the lines read, "has no right to ask for the confidence of the American people or the votes of the Utah people as long as he fails to explain his intimate and scandalous association with Communists."

The gimmick in this sheet is the line, "Senator Elbert Thomas presides at Communist meeting." This was repeated again and again. Actually Senator Thomas did *not* preside at this or any other Communist meeting. He was undoubtedly invited to do so and tentatively accepted. He informed the committee later that he would not be present. Paul Robeson also did not attend the banquet. The people who prepared the circular knew these facts when they had it published; those who distributed it also knew without a doubt.

One Republican party strategist and a candidate for the Republican convention primary senatorial nomination in 1950 wrote to a key party worker on October 6, 1950 as follows:

> Find enclosed my check for $1.00 for which will you please send fifty (50) copies of the enclosed circular to J. Leonard Love, 1735 Yalecrest Avenue, Salt Lake City.

In a postscript the writer of this letter, who in his speeches had suggested that Thomas was a socialist and then, through guilt by association, that he was a Communist, added in postscript: "I understand Thomas did not attend the banquet. But regardless of that he did accept the title as chairman."

After the election, this writer stated that although he did say that Thomas had socialist leanings, he never said he was a Communist nor had he heard of any other Republican of any standing who made such a statement. The writer did admit that Thomas' socialist leanings tied him up with certain Communist beliefs to the extent that some people did mistake him for a Communist. He had stated in speeches during the campaign that Senator Thomas had called himself the leading New Dealer, and that he was right. He added that what Thomas doesn't want you to see is that the term "New Deal" is just another name for the kind of socialism which already has wrecked four former world powers and which now threatens America. Thomas' detractor was equating the New Deal and socialism. Others in the Republican propaganda factory, in the meantime, were busily preparing the equation, socialism equals communism.

Miss Allen produced and published a pamphlet of her own, under her own name, entitled, "Let's 'Can' Senator Thomas." She reproduced two principal photostats which were held up before audiences by Republicans. Exhibit A was a copy of the invitation to the *New Masses* awards dinner. Paul Robeson and Senator Elbert D. Thomas were listed as "Co-Chairmen of the Dinner Committee." Exhibit B was a copy of the front cover of the *New Masses* for August 1943. Senator Thomas' book on Jefferson, *Thomas Jefferson: World Citizen*, published in 1942, was listed along with three other titles under the heading, "Thomas Jefferson: 200 Years."[38] The book was really a simple, innocuous piece of writing, which brought out, if anything, Thomas' philosophy of life, or better still, his approach to political and human relations.

The entire Allen brochure was based on the Stokes material. The full flavor of her writings can be caught only by reading them. Important phrases (important to her) and substantives were capitalized, in the style of yellow-journalism editorials. There was no relief from the hard-hitting repetition of what she wanted to drive home; in fact, when one had finished reading a page of an article she had written, nothing stood out in relief, nothing remained with the reader except the impression that the writer was terribly angry. Her writing was like a train that always runs at the same high speed without ever slowing down at stations. Her pen just seemed to run right off the page.

The Republican propagandists emulated her approach and style. They were angry, and they wanted the voters to become angry; they wanted them to have fears and to harbor doubts, and they wanted them to go to the polls in this mood.

Although the exact number of copies of the "Senator Elbert Thomas Presides at Communist Meeting" broadside was not ascertained and the Republican state and county headquarters denied distributing it, the number was sufficient to evoke an indignant reaction from Thomas and the Democrats and an equally indignant counterblast from the Republicans. This episode of righteous defense and exchange of Biblical quotations was significant as a prelude to the worst which was yet to come, the shattering explosion of the *United States Senate News* which was detonated by the Republicans with the technical assistance of a master in political dynamiting, Walter Quigley. Both sides, by their display of righteous indignation over the Anti-Communist League broadside, had wrung their moral consciences dry. The Democrats were too numb already to react offensively to the Quigley bombshell, which took in everybody in Utah in its range of fire; they ran for shelter, and stayed there, weary, confused, and uncertain. The Republicans had become so calloused by their year-long campaign to pin the label of Communist on Senator Thomas and by a long series of dynamiting charges branding Thomas as a socialist and fellow traveler that they could not see the moral magnitude of the final explosion. Each succeeding charge became larger and larger in the sense that each explosion was seen and heard by more voters at a single time. The difference between the next to last charge and the final blast was not great; the difference between the first few rifle shots made at cottage meetings by individual speakers and the last explosion which hit the entire populace at once was tremendous. Imperceptibly, the public had become morally paralyzed by a crescendo of propaganda outpourings in meetings, through the mails, and over the air. Apparently, the public simply had become morally apathetic.

NOTES

1. The figure in 1948 was also 75 percent, compared with the national average of 52 percent. In 1946, the previous nonpresidential year, Utah's average was 55 percent, compared to the national average of 38 percent.

2. Letter from Pratt Kesler to author, January 4, 1951. Kesler credited Representative Bosone's victory to some Republican women who had supported her for a number of years only because she was a woman. Granger, he said, was elected because of the heavy labor union vote in Ogden city and Weber County. Granger, in truth, was behind everywhere else, except in Carbon County, a traditional stronghold of the Democratic party and the United Mine Workers Union.

3. *Deseret News*, August 28, 1950.

4. *Salt Lake Tribune*, November 1, 1950.

5. *Ibid.*, October 10, 1950.

6. *Ibid.*, October 29, 1950, and *Deseret News*, October 29, 1950.

7. *Salt Lake Tribune*, October 27, 1950.

8. This position was announced in an advertisement in the *Salt Lake Tribune* on October 11, 1950.

9. Letter, October 26, 1955. Writer's name withheld by request.

10. For the position of Watkins, see U.S., *Congressional Record*, 81st Cong., 2nd Sess., 96 (June 29, 1950), 9580-90.

11. Letters from the labor leaders mentioned to Elbert D. Thomas, February 20, 22, and 24, 1950. See O. N. Malmquist, "Labor Poses 50 Utah Vote Battle," *Salt Lake Tribune*, March 5, 1950.

12. Letters, August 6, 1959, February 2, and July 17, 1950. See the *United Mine Workers Journal*, 61 (June 15, 1950), 5. Also, the article by Senator Elbert D. Thomas, "An Era of Decision of Civil Liberties," *The Advance* (Amalgamated Clothing Workers of America), 36 (September 1, 1950), 31. Of interest was the Republican-inspired political advertisement signed by D. D. Cox, a member of the CIO, which appeared in all of the newspapers of the state on November third and damaged the campaign of Senator Thomas. The advertisement usually appeared two columns wide and five inches long. An eye catcher on any page, it contained only the five words, "The CIO Endorses Senator Thomas," in bold, black type. In

1950, the CIO and AFL had not yet amalgamated, and the CIO was identified as the radical wing of labor. The strikes and labor difficulties in Utah in the period prior to the 1950 elections were attributed to the CIO. Thomas did have the endorsement of labor generally and of most unions, but to associate him with the local conditions which brought on strikes in Utah would seem far fetched. This advertisement is cited here as a typical example of the very brief spot announcement used at the time. It was repeated frequently and had widespread coverage.

13. *Deseret News*, October 29, 1950.

14. Former Representative Granger related later somewhat wryly:
They [the Farm Bureau] later attacked me because I was a co-sponsor of a bill that would have done away with the tremendous surpluses that our present Secretary of Agriculture [Benson] is moaning about. It would have done away with the present farm subsidies as suggested by Secretary Brannan. The sheepmen now have the same identical bill which is not now socialistic. I included wool in my bill and had two or three perishables also. It was introduced as an experiment to solve the agricultural surpluses and the tremendous rents for storage of the same. *They linked Thomas with this bill, though he had nothing to do with it and it never reached the Senate for him to express an opinion.* I had done many things to assist those very men but they ignored them and viciously attacked me and Thomas.
Letter from Walter K. Granger to Rulon Garfield, April 12, 1956.

15. *Salt Lake Tribune*, August 9, 12, and October 24, 1950; *Deseret News*, October 29, and November 2, 4, 1950.

16. A description of the public relations firm of Campaigns, Inc., headed by Clem Whitaker and Leon Baxter, may be found in Stanley Kelly, *Professional Public Relations and Political Power* (Baltimore: John Hopkins Press, 1956). An exhaustive and scholarly study of the American Medical Association may be found in David R. Hyde and Payson Wolff, "The American Medical Association: Power, Purpose, and Politics in Organized Medicine," *Yale Law Journal*, 63 (May 7, 1954), 937-1022.

17. *U.S. Code*, Title 18, Section 610; see also Section 608 and Title 26, Section 501c.

18. This letter was signed by a member of the committee, preferably someone who was a personal friend of the addressee. The enclosed application form was in three parts; the first concerned contribution; another told the committee whether or not to use the applicant's name; and the final part was an estimate on how many votes could be secured "for the American Cause." Two blanks provided for the applicant's name and address.

19. Thomas viewed the campaign as a teaching process rather than the practice of the art of selecting and distorting the facts to win votes. Thomas was a teacher at heart and disclaimed the tactics of those who completely abandoned scientific objectivity. In one instance, Thomas was invited to speak to a political science class on the campus of the University of Utah on a subject in international relations. Planted there was a physician who was not a student, who repeatedly brought up the subject of socialized medicine. The chairman of the group tried unsuccessfully to silence him by referring to courteous behavior. Finally, Thomas really answered him in very strong language. The chairman recalled later that had Thomas campaigned as vigorously and lucidly as he did in that class, the Republicans would have had a much more difficult task to defeat him.

20. Rulon Garfield, "An Approach to the Politics of Elbert D. Thomas" (M.A. thesis, University of Utah, 1956), p. 24.

21. *Deseret News*, December 27, 1950. See also his speech before the 55th Annual Congress of American Industry, *Salt Lake Telegram*, December 7, 1950.

22. The hospital was subsequently transferred to the Bureau of Indian Affairs and converted to a Navajo Training School.

23. Actually, Senator William H. King (1917-1941) was the senior member from 1933 to 1941, but he was anti-New Deal and in the last few years in office he talked, acted, and voted like a Republican. See Frank H. Jonas, "Utah: Sagebrush Democracy," in Thomas Donnelly (ed.), *Rocky Mountain Politics* (Albuquerque: University of New Mexico Press, 1940), p. 46.

24. One trained observer from the campus of Utah State University who was at the meeting has remembered the contrast between the statement by Senator Thomas and the quotation taken out of context and used by Ora Lewis. He said that Senator Thomas was speaking to young citizens about the development of voting rights, and referred to the growth of woman suffrage in Utah and Wyoming, and eventually the national campaign culminating in the adoption of the Nineteenth Amendment to the United States Constitution. He spoke of the extremes taken by those who felt that the participation by women would purify political life and those who feared that women would completely dominate the political process. He added that we do not have and will not have petticoat government.

25. The daily newspapers were the *Salt Lake Tribune* (morning), and the *Salt Lake Telegram* (evening), owned and controlled by the Kearns estate, founded by former U.S. Senator Thomas Kearns; the *Deseret News* (evening), owned and controlled by the Mormon church; the *Ogden Standard-Examiner*; the *Logan Herald-Journal*; and the *Provo Herald*. The *Tribune* and *Telegram*, with mining interests and Catholic backgrounds, the *Deseret News*, with big business interests, and the *Examiner*, were Republican. The Logan and Provo papers were owned by out-of-state interests. In former years both had Democratic editors but recently the Logan paper had become Republican and the Provo paper was reportedly noncommittal. However, the Provo paper's staff consisted mainly of individual Republicans.

The *Intermountain Labor American* was the leading Utah labor paper, published by a group of labor leaders. The *Utah Labor Broadcast* was published by the AFL of Utah. The *Beacon* was a labor-management publication. In addition, a trades journal was published in Ogden. The *Progressive Opinion* of Salt Lake City and the *Wyoming Labor Journal*, formerly circulated among coal miners in Carbon County, had ceased publication.

26. *Post Register* (Idaho Falls, Idaho), November 3, 1950.

27. A student in the Department of Journalism at the University of Utah made a study of the space allotted to the candidates by the three Salt Lake City newspapers. His conclusions were based on the examination of clippings for the last two weeks of the campaign. Although two of the three papers (in Salt Lake City) devoted somewhat more space to Republican candidates than to Democratic, none may be said to have been biased from this standpoint. There was a very obvious effort in all cases to maintain the outward signs of impartiality. The *Tribune* followed the policy of playing the stories of rival candidates for congressional posts on the second section or split page, of making coverage of equal length, and of allowing to each an identically sized headline. The *Telegram* followed suit in this respect, while the *Deseret News* ordinarily ran coverage of rival candidates on their local page side-by-side under a two-column head and a two-column introductory lead; the difference between the Republican and Democratic coverage represented only .016 of the combined coverage, while the *Telegram* difference of four inches out of a combined 360 was even less, .011. The *Deseret News* gave the Republicans 26 inches more than the Democrats, a difference of .050 percent of the total.

28. A stake is a geographical administrative unit of the L.D.S. church comparable to a Catholic diocese.

29. One of them was the county prosecuting attorney, Edward M. Morrissey, a Catholic. Morrissey attributed his defeat at the polls to this action and his supporters interpreted it as an act of religious discrimination. The other Republican, Richard S. Allen, candidate for the legislature, was informed, upon inquiry, that his being scratched had been a mistake.

30. This "letter" carried the address of 38 North State Street, Salt Lake City, an L.D.S. church property and the residence of Colonel Elmer Thomas, Republican chairman of the committee, who was an employee of the church. When Colonel Thomas was interrogated about his infamous missile he stated simply that Elbert D. Thomas was *not* a Communist but that he had been in office for twenty years (actually eighteen) and that "we had to get him out." He reiterated that his committee had the "blessings of the brethren." As a member of the state legislature, having been asked to run for that office, his function was to report the voting records of legislative members—particularly high officeholders, bishops, and stake presidents—to the authorities. He made his reports to Apostle Spencer Kimball. He said that what the brethren were for, he was for; that what they were against, he was against; it was as simple as all that.

31. This allegation had its roots in recent Utah political history. In the 1930's, when the Democrats were high in the saddle, the party officials claimed that the L.D.S. church endorsement of their rivals helped their own candidates. See Jonas, "Utah Sagebrush Democracy," p. 34.

32. Letter from J. Angus Christensen, president, Palmyra Stake, to author, January 3, 1951.

33. Letter, December 18, 1950, name of writer withheld by request.

34. Letter from Rue L. Clegg to author, November 24, 1950.

35. Letter from Walter K. Granger to Rulon Garfield, April 12, 1955.

36. Marilyn R. Allen published many pamphlets as well as the book, *Alien Minorities and Mongolization* (Boston: Meador Publishing Co., 1949).

37. According to other assertions, even by the senator's enemies, there had been only *one* article.

38. *Titan of Freedom* by Robert Minor; *Marxism is Democracy* by A. Landy; *Mr. Jefferson's Plow* by Louis Lerman.

THE MURDER
OF A REPUTATION

W HILE speaking briefly but heatedly in behalf of his candidacy for the
Democratic senatorial nomination at the party's 1962 state organizing
convention, Calvin Rampton, now Utah's governor, suddenly whipped out and
held up before the somewhat surprised delegates an unfolded copy of the
United States Senate News. Although many of the older delegates remembered
Walter Eli Quigley's notorious propaganda missile from the 1950 senatorial
campaign, only a few could recall its contents and construction. Moreover, a
whole new generation of delegates was in the audience. Had they been able to
examine the paper at close range, they would have seen the details of the consummate Quigley style and skill in the field of political dynamiting. Although
Quigley continued until his death in 1962 to solicit business from clients and to
do work for them, he never again equaled his performance in the 1950 Utah
campaign. In truth he was never offered a comparable opportunity to demonstrate his consummate craftsmanship.

The four-page Republican "newspaper," or "scurrilous sheet" as the
Democrats called it, had the masthead of *United States Senate News* (Utah Edition). The front page blared forth like a typical Hearst editorial page, with boldface headlines and boldface letters alternating with larger-than-ordinary regular
newspaper type. Although the banner headline, "Thomas Philosophy Wins Red
Approval," struck the keynote for the numerous stories to follow, which were
designed to associate Senator Elbert D. Thomas with communism and Communists, it was the large cartoon on the front page and seven smaller ones on the
third page which carried the leitmotif and introduced the various refrains of the
"Thomas and the Commies" song.

The front page cartoon, entitled "The Puppet!" showed Thomas dangling
from sets of strings, which were fastened to small oblong-shaped blocks of
wood labeled "votes." These were held by four men whose grossly caricatured
faces represented factions labeled ILO (for the International Labor Office),
pink pressure groups, labor czars, and socialists; these persons manipulated the

THE PUPPET!

puppet strings. Thomas was shown dancing on a globe; his feet were touching the United States.

Thomas was portrayed as a typical politician. The face, aside from its bald head, resembled President Roosevelt's. The man in the cartoon wore glasses, his eyelids were pulled together, he was laughing and his teeth were conspicuous. The figure wore a checkered, single-breasted, one-button suit and bow tie; wavy, loosely-gloved fingers held a soft hat. Thomas' alleged masters were drawn with even more typically caricatured countenances. "Pink pressure groups" was depicted with a crew cut, an unshaven face, and thick glasses. "Labor czars" was represented with a derby hat, a short, stubby cigar, and a large diamond stickpin. "Socialists" was shown with a long, arch-crowned nose, long hair, and thick, horn-rimmed glasses. The mouth was open and revealed large buckteeth. "ILO" was given the most respectable appearance of the lot. The head was bald, with a deep crease in the middle. This figure was shown smoking a cigarette and wearing glasses. All the faces were given smug, self-satisfied grins.

The seven cartoons on the third page introduced various aspects of the theme; the stories were carried throughout the paper. Number one showed a hatted, brim-turned-down, unshaven, sneering "American Commie" holding up a copy of Thomas' book, *The Four Fears*, in his right hand and saying, "This sure is meat for us." The caption over the cartoon read: "In 1945 Senator Thomas wrote a book entitled 'The Four Fears.' It was so pro-radical that the 'New Masses,' Communist monthly magazine, offered Thomas' book on a subscription with the magazine." In truth, the book had been published in 1944 during the peak of Allied attempts to bring the Soviet Union into World War II as a full partner. It had been advertised widely in Utah weeklies and had been almost completely ignored by the Utah voters before the 1950 elections.[1] Indeed, from a careful sampling of more than one hundred articulate participants in the 1950 senatorial campaign, no one admitted having read the book prior to 1950, and only five persons admitted having read it at that time. They accepted quite uncritically the garbled accounts and slanted interpretations in Quigley's paper.

The next cartoon in the *United States Senate News* was omitted. The material intended for this space was so inaccurate and in such bad taste that even the thick-skinned Republican campaign leaders refused to publish it. It dealt with Thomas' alleged attendance at a pro-Communist function—which Thomas had never attended. This material had been sent previously to Quigley by Republican propagandists; he had no way of determining its authenticity. Indeed, the main difference between the Utah edition of the *United States Senate News* and Quigley's usual product was the fact that its contents were based almost entirely on materials sent to him and not on his own research on his victim's voting record.

Cartoon number two represented a Congressional hearing room which showed Thomas objecting with the words, "No! No! We don't!" to the declara-

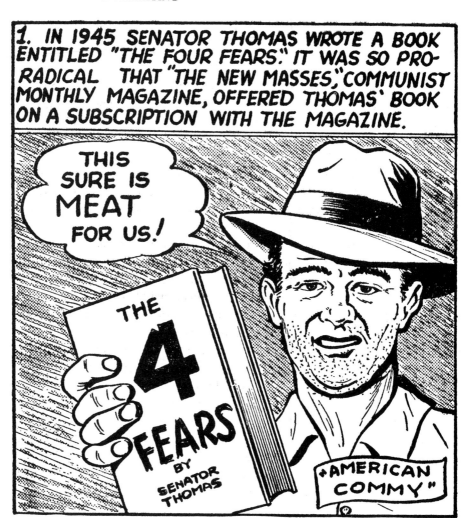

tion by a witness that "We want strong military forces for protection." The caption read: "In 1949 Thomas worked and voted to cut the Air Force to only 48 groups. In previous years he opposed making our Army, Navy and aviation strong. Read that record in this paper."

Number three depicted an unshaven, rather repulsive " 'Red' Laborer" saying, "I've got to sign an anti-Communist affidavit and I don't want to," and Thomas answering, "Let's repeal that kind of law." The caption read: "The Taft-Hartley labor law made union officials sign an oath that they were not Communists. It also gave union members the secret vote and the right to an accounting of their money. Thomas fought this law and even in 1950 he is trying to repeal it."

Quigley was at his best when he could find that a congressman or senator had voted for pay raises or pensions for members of Congress, especially during a war period or a depression. His next cartoon exploited this theme. It showed Thomas' head, a happy expression on his face, resting on a bird's body, covered with feathers. The bird was shown sitting in a luxurious nest of leaves. The title, "Well feathered nest," referred to Thomas' vote for "the law to raise his salary fifty percent, or from ten thousand dollars to fifteen thousand dollars," according to the caption. This cartoon was supported by a front-page, six-inch-long story which was headed, "Thomas Votes Self Raise; Says No To One for GI's." It was, however, the most irrelevant item in the paper. Such action by a member of Congress is generally unpopular. In 1955 Republican Senators A. V. Watkins and Wallace F. Bennett voted for a pay raise and received considerable criticism, but in 1956, when Bennett stood for reelection, the same objection

5. HE VOTED FOR THE LAW TO RAISE HIS SALARY FIFTY PERCENT, OR FROM TEN THOUSAND DOLLARS TO FIFTEEN THOUSAND DOLLARS AND HE DOES NOT PAY INCOME TAX ON $2500 OF THAT. HE CAN DRAW A PENSION OF MORE THAN $600 A MONTH FOR LIFE WHEN YOU VOTERS DEFEAT HIM.

WELL FEATHERED NEST

was not raised concerning his vote the previous year, as was made in 1960 to Thomas' vote of nine years earlier. However, there was a further propaganda element in the Quigley story. Senator Thomas was charged with having voted against a pay raise of $7.50 for army privates in August 1941. This reference was intended to bring the soldier into the picture and arouse his resentment against Thomas. There was no explanation of the reason for the senator's vote, nor any acknowledgment of all the GI pay raises for which he had voted. By implication, the cartoon and story were intended to question Senator Thomas' patriotism. Actually the story disclosed that what Thomas had voted for was a pension program rather than a pay raise. Quigley admitted sadly that he had been caught in an error; he prided himself on his factual accuracy.[2]

Cartoon number five portrayed General Douglas MacArthur with his head high in the air and his face turned up stating, "We must be strong in Asia" and President Truman pronouncing that "Secretary of State Acheson and I agree. Let's abandon Korea and Formosa! This, early in 1950." The caption read: "High Democratic officials were warned many times that war in Korea was coming. However, the Communists in Washington prevailed and America is now in a real shooting war."

The sixth cartoon showed four figures: a dentist, a nurse, and a doctor all clothed in white, and a long-haired radical with clenched fist and angry mien, perspiration drops flying into the air. He says, "We'll tell you what to do from now on!" while the dentist says to the nurse, "We should have studied law." The caption read that "Thomas introduced bills to socialize medicine, even though the Utah State Senate opposed it. This would cost billions and destroy the greatest medical system in the world." A full column-and-a-half story headed, "Thomas Sponsored Bills To Socialize Medicine," amplified Thomas' connection with so-called socialized medicine. This was intended to associate Thomas further with communism. Soviet Russia has socialized medicine, Thomas favors socialized medicine, therefore Thomas is a Communist, was the completely fallacious reasoning by arbitrary association. This part of the paper greatly reinforced the mammoth campaign being waged against Thomas by the influential American Medical Association; or perhaps, the saturation bombing of the doctors' campaign had prepared the voters for this clincher.

Cartoon number seven offered a contrast to the figures in the other cartoons, and the solution to the alleged errors made by Senator Thomas and to the mess he and the Communists were supposed to have created in the American government. Two handsome persons, a young lady and a young man, holding up a ballot marked with an "X" in the squares after the Republican national and state offices, assert that "We are voting Republican this year right down the line. No more bunglers and wasters for us!"

The fourth page of the paper contained reprints and replicas of the *New Masses*, the *Daily Worker*, and dinner programs; these showed Thomas as an author of articles published in Communist publications, or as a sponsor, or as the recipient of praise from pro-Communist promotional events. The charge that he had served as cochairman of a *New Masses* fund-raising dinner was repeated, and the fateful cover of the *New Masses* of June 22, 1943, which listed Senator Elbert D. Thomas as a contributor, was reproduced.

The front page contained long stories which amplified the themes of the cartoons. Most persons would never read beyond the cartoons and headlines. But for the few who would read some of the stories, the task was made easier by the use of a larger type than is usually found in daily newspapers. Quotations from Thomas' book or points the writers wanted to emphasize were in capital letters generally or in capitalized boldface.

The page was made up so as to emphasize the headlines and to call attention to the words, "Communism" "*Daily Worker*," "Paul Robeson," "Vito Marcantonio," and other items and persons. Actual quotations were in small print which was barely legible, or they were partly covered over by dark guidelines or by overlapping portions of other replicas, which obscured, sometimes completely, what Thomas actually had written or published. Heavy guidelines in one connected series of three items were drawn around the printed words, "The Worker," and the typed-in words, "Communist Daily Worker and Senator Elbert D. Thomas." His name was encircled with heavy, black ink in four other places. The formula ran: The *Daily Worker* was Communist, Senator Thomas' name and picture appeared in the *Daily Worker*, therefore Senator Thomas was a Communist. This formula, designed to create guilt by association, was repeated over and over again throughout the paper.

In one of two leading articles, the two-column headline read "Thomas To Stand On Record." The subheadline stated that he voted against defense, against the GI's, farmers, and workers, and that he was praised by Communist publications. It was interesting to note how the story was prepared to protect itself from attack; it warned the readers that it would be attacked, stating that "The present administration will, immediately on publication of this paper turn loose a barrage of propaganda to discredit it. They will scream that the people from outside the state are attempting to interfere in Utah politics." Quigley characteristically anticipated an attack on the paper's assertions; he reassured the reader beforehand that "Every item in this paper is documented either by photostatic evidence or by specific reference to an official government document." Quigley usually wrote a similar warning in each one of his papers. Not only did he want to establish the accuracy of the paper's content, but he also wanted to do everything possible to prevent a boomerang, always a haunting fear of those propagandists who employ the negative approach in political campaigning.

Quigley used name-calling generously. Thomas' supporters were "labor czars," and his two running mates, Representatives Granger and Bosone, were "political cronies." "The political propagandists on the federal payroll will spend untold amounts and stop at nothing to insure the election of the Senior Senator from Utah," was the warning of the Republicans. This was precisely what the Republicans were doing, "spending untold amounts" and "stopping at nothing" to insure Senator Thomas' defeat. The object of this type of propaganda is to attack first and hard; it is to call the enemy by the very names and to accuse him of the very things you know that he will call you and accuse you of doing.

This lead story concluded by repeating the items of the cartoon agenda; "Thomas to Stand on Record," Thomas voted against the Mundt-Nixon bill, cochaired the Awards Dinner with Paul Robeson, wrote *The Four Fears*, contributed to the *New Masses*, and was praised by the *Daily Worker*. As something new, Thomas was accused, with no further elaboration, of purchasing a school "with others . . . at Washington, Connecticut, to educate American youth along Russian educational ideas." If Thomas participated with others in purchasing a school, the members of his family did not know about it. He did become a member of the Board of Trustees of the Romford School in Washington, Connecticut. This small boys' boarding school, housed on an estate donated by a wealthy family, was founded in 1930 and then discontinued during the war. In 1946 J. W. Frazer, president of the Kaiser-Frazer Corporation, Will B. Ziff, whose firm published *The Four Fears*, and Geoffrey van Bibber Slagle were responsible for reviving the school with an enrollment of thirty-two boys. Frazer was chairman of the Board.[3]

Suddenly, on February 3, 1947, after a "lengthy discussion" on the problems confronting the school between the board and the headmaster and owner of the school, Joseph K. Stetson, six board members resigned, including Frazer, Ziff, Slagle, Joseph B. MacMullin, Herbert W. Rogge, and Senator Thomas. Thomas had never purchased a piece of the school. In retrospect, it is impossible to see what his alleged purchase of this school had to do with communism or his campaign in Utah for reelection.

The other lead story carried the banner headline, "Thomas Philosophy Wins Red Approval," and then in subheadlines stated that "Commies Use Book to Raise Dollars" and quoted Thomas as telling America that it was absurd to fear Red propaganda. Then followed a number of quotations from Thomas' book, *The Four Fears*, which were truncated and garbled. No coherent passages from Thomas himself, by which the reader could judge his philosophy, were reproduced. Passages were represented as an expression of Communist sympathies, with editorial comments which attempted to link Thomas with the Communists. So effective was the propaganda that Thomas was not able to dissociate himself from this book for the remainder of the campaign, although it had been written six years earlier under conditions which were totally different from those which existed in 1950. When the book was written, the United States was in the midst of a war, and the Soviet Union was one of her Allies. It was designed to assist in creating friendly relations with that nation. The book discussed four fears. One of the propaganda techniques of the Allies during World War II was embodied in the expression "the four freedoms." One of these was freedom from fear. When fear dominates, the ability to succeed is greatly impaired. Could there be anything wrong in advising people not to fear something? Thomas' opponents quoted relentlessly from a chapter entitled, "Fear of Russia," lifting passages out of context, sometimes deleting words or entire sentences, and thereby distorting the meaning.

The very first quotation illustrates this device. It began:

> What Russia needs in the way of geographical security she will insist on and get. She will have to ask favors of no one. But the hangover of ill will against her is still so powerful that what seems reasonable for other nations to do will be called Bolshevik plotting if the Russians do it, and I have no doubt that anti-liberal forces everywhere [from this point the words are in capital letters] are at this very minute working overtime to find ways of creating distrust of her. We shall hear that she means to Bolshevize Europe, that she means to grasp all the helpless little countries next to her. . . .

The quotation in its original context did not begin in this manner. Thomas actually had said: "We may take for granted—*and Mr. Churchill's speech of February 22, 1944, confirms it*—that what Russia needs. . . ."[4] To have left Churchill's name in the newspaper or to have reproduced the whole context would have been embarrassing to the Thomas attackers.

Other quotations from the book emphasized Thomas' alleged Communist leanings. Such material as the following was easily misused:

> Now that Russia has shown herself the strongest country in Europe . . . how does she stand with us? It is not easy to say, but I feel very certain that anti-Russian forces throughout the world are still strong, and they will make every attempt to discredit Russia, to throw doubt on her motives and intentions, and to make Americans, especially, believe that Russia is the most to be feared of all powers. They will work on our continued ignorance of her, and our dislike for Communism. They will make us believe that the Russians have deep-laid plans to rule the world, to change all governments by force, to absorb all Europe.
>
> . . . But are they likely to send an armed force over here to take our democracy or our property from us? Do they refuse to work with us because our economic ideas differ? To be sure, they sent agents everywhere to discredit the private property system, but propaganda is not soldiers, and even the propaganda has stopped.[5]

This statement was certain to appear pro-Communist to a reader in 1950. It would have been equally easy to quote passages from the same chapter showing Thomas to be a profound Democrat and a great American. A typical example follows: "If we are so terrified of communism, it must be because we have lost confidence in ourselves. It must be that we have a very uneasy feeling about the reality of our own democracy. I have no uneasy feeling about the reality of our democracy."[6] This quotation suggests the tone of the whole book. Thomas did not fear Russia. Neither did he believe other Americans should do so if they believed in the destiny of America. He asserted that the American spirit represented the faith of the people in themselves and the hope of all mankind, and that this faith and this hope could hardly flourish in an atmosphere of fear and hatred.

The book was well received when it made its appearance. For example, an editorial in the St. Louis *Post-Dispatch* stated:

> Senator Elbert D. Thomas has embarked on an interesting effort to help insure American participation in the peace. As he sees it, the chief danger ahead in this country is neither bad bargains by the White House or State Department, not intransigence from isolationist senators and congressmen. What he apprehends is that fears will sweep the people, as in the fall of 1919, and kindle a new isolationism, because of which peace will again be blocked in the Congress by a minority.
>
> Four fears have seemed to him so dangerous that he has published a book to show the menace of these hobgoblins, and to get the true light on them before the people, that they might be overcome. . . . Surely this is the time and thought and talent well spent. If more of this spadework had been done in 1919, it is possible that the tragedy of the rejection of the Versailles Treaty would have been avoided. For the irreconcilables could not have had their way without the backing of those liberals who didn't like Shantung, or the mandates in the Pacific, of Fiume, or the Saar. The perfectionists sustained the isolationists in the refusal to enter the League. Such folly should not be repeated this time, and education of the Thomas type may help forfeit it.[7]

Another critic, writing in the *New York Times*, did not agree with Senator Thomas' idealistic premises as he set them forth in *The Four Fears*, but he had this to say about the man himself: "Any disagreement with Senator Thomas must rest on a different view of human nature. If all politicians were of his stature, and if all citizens measured up to his belief in the common man, we should be ready to call a constituent assembly for a world state."[8]

Quigley's implication that someone had influenced Thomas to write *The Four Fears* and that someone had ghostwritten at least parts of it was true. Perhaps Thomas himself had the original idea for the book. More likely, however, William B. Ziff of Ziff-Davis Publishing Company suggested the preparation of the manuscript. Ziff acquired the services of Mrs. Howard Mumford

Jones as writer and copy editor. Her husband, a professor of English at Harvard, was listed as a sponsor with Senator Thomas of the National Council of American-Soviet Friendship, Inc. In the preface to the book, Senator Thomas acknowledged his greatest debt to Mrs. Jones for editorial and research assistance. Actually, she wrote the chapter on Russia which received so much emphasis by Quigley and which was so effective in ruining Senator Thomas' chances for reelection. Thomas made very little change in Mrs. Jones' "original." Earl Wixey, his administrative assistant at the time, protested the contents. Thomas answered: "I don't know much about that chapter. Mrs. Jones knows the field better than I, so I left it pretty much as she wrote it."[9]

Twelve years after the book appeared, Mrs. Jones admitted that the analysis of possible causes of postwar friction did seem a little naïve. She stated that no student who failed to see in Senator Thomas's career, pronouncements, or positions a fundamental integrity and deep concern for the welfare of the country should evaluate his services to the nation. She said that he certainly was no radical, and anybody who tried to make him appear so in 1950 was simply a premature McCarthy. "He loved the country, he loved peace, he wanted people everywhere to share in the benefits America could confer." Shrewdly she added: "I have no doubt that he was on occasion outsmarted by the more clever and more aggressive political operators."[10]

In fact, Thomas was completely unaware of the propaganda brew that would be concocted, with the book in the middle of the pot, by public relations and advertising men, political dynamiters and researchers, opposition campaign managers and candidates' staff members on the governmental payroll, which would finally blow the lid off of his hopes for reelection to the United States Senate. But it was Quigley's newspaper which did the most damage.

Quigley filled up the rest of the paper with irrelevant and unrelated items as far as Senator Thomas' record and candidacy were concerned; but once having established the fact that Thomas had spoken to a Communist-front group or had had an article published in the *New Masses*, he had only to make a statement and then connect Thomas and Soviet Russia to that statement. For example, he wrote, "Thomas' Tariff Cut Hurt All Utah." He then placed the alleged effects of the administration's free trade policy on Thomas' shoulders. After this he concluded that as a result of the "Trade Agreements program which Senator Thomas has initiated and supported since its inception in 1934, . . . the country has been flooded with hundreds of millions of dollars worth of Russian furs." In retrospect, this conclusion seemed absolutely ludicrous. This trade policy existed during the entire Eisenhower Republican administration, and some of the quota acts of 1934 which replaced tariff acts were still "on the books" in 1962. Indeed, their repeal or modification was opposed by Utah Republican conservatives, including United States Senator Wallace F. Bennett.

Much was made of Thomas' having voted for a fifty-eight- instead of a seventy-group air force. Thomas followed administration policy at the time. This, along with another negative vote on national defense, was supposed to reflect Thomas' patriotism and personal judgment. Again the reasoning produced guilt by association; Communists were opposed to a large American air force and national guard; Thomas voted for "little air power" and to "kill the Reserve Officers' Training Corps law"; therefore Thomas was Communist.

In another front-page article, entitled "Birds of a Feather" and "Thomas Woos Red Serpents in Garden," words were put into Thomas' mouth. At a Madison Square Garden rally in 1946, held in honor of three Soviet journalists, Thomas had said that "we're gathered here tonight to honor not only the three most outstanding good-will ambassadors of people who helped to make victory over tyranny and barbarism possible, but all the peoples of the Soviet Union."[11] This was paraphrased into the statement that "These good-will ambassadors whom Senator Thomas said he loved like brothers are the serpents who today are responsible for the vile Communist propaganda which has maligned and undermined the good will of the American people. . . ." But Thomas had praised A. A. Gromyko and Ilya Ehrenburg, Politburo member, and had said that "the Russians can be firm friends, as we have found."

Some articles did not carry Thomas' name. He was connected with Communists and Communist action by the association of persons and subject matter. For example, one headline read, "Hoover, FBI Chief, Warns of Red Threat to America." Another stated, "Yalta Agreement Led to Korean War." Was Hoover warning the American people against Senator Thomas who had associated with people whom he had warned against in general? Was Thomas responsible for Yalta and therefore the Korean War? Then followed the typical reasoning in all the stories in this newspaper. The only way to *clean out the Commies* was to elect a Republican senator from Utah. Halfway measures simply would not work. Korea was the result of Yalta. The administration was responsible for Yalta. Alger Hiss, a Communist sympathizer, was President Roosevelt's chief adviser at Yalta. Truman verified the Yalta Agreement at Potsdam. The story concluded with the allegation that the Communists worked a clever game over the years in getting Roosevelt and Truman to be friendly with the left-wingers, and that left-wingers are in control in Washington; therefore, clean out the mess by ousting Thomas, for this is the only way to get rid of the Commies.

The stories on the third page just below the seven cartoons seemed to be fill-ins. In one the headline read: "Granger and Bosone Should Be Defeated." Having tainted Senator Thomas, perhaps the Republicans thought some of the stuff should be rubbed off on his stablemates.

A rather lengthy story attacked Thomas' labor record. It was a good summary of the arguments against the Taft-Hartley bill. This story, too, would have been irrelevant had it not been tied in with communism. The appeal in the last two paragraphs was to the American fighting forces. Soldiers and sailors should remember when they go to the polls on November seventh that the striking union bosses, who allegedly had Thomas in their grip, were making money out of the soldiers' sacrifices on the battlefield.

Two stories now appear ludicrous. "Thomas Voted 'No' on School Lunch" was one. The school lunch was only an issue because it was provided by the federal government. Republicans opposed its cost but some saw it as a method to reduce farm surpluses, and teachers and school districts were divided in their support of the program. The other article was entitled "Vote vs. 'Voice' Shocked Utah." Senator Joseph McCarthy and the Republican administration, which succeeded Thomas in office, all but wrecked the Voice of America. Utah was not shocked.

The *United States Senate News* graphically reiterated, amplified, and summarized the charges which had been levied against Senator Thomas by the Republican party and all its allied interest groups. Here is a partial list of the charges that had been made against him during the campaign:

1. Senator Thomas was communistically inclined.
2. Senator Thomas was a Communist sympathizer and a fellow traveler.
3. Senator Thomas wrote a book praising the Communists, communism and its program; and the book was so enthusiastically received by the American Communist party that it was used as a subscription incentive for their official magazine, the *New Masses.* (It was offered as a subscription bonus on March 13, 1945.)
4. Senator Thomas sponsored rallies to honor the Communist party and the Soviet Union.
5. Senator Thomas advocated socialism, described as creeping socialism, which was completing the socialization of America. For example, he sponsored the National Health Insurance bill then pending in Congress.
6. Senator Thomas contributed articles to the Communist press.

These charges portrayed Thomas as a Communist sympathizer and as so much putty in Communist hands. They pictured him as naïve in interpreting the realities of international relations generally and soft on the Soviets particularly. In giving the impression that he was a Communist, they sought to crystallize the doubts they created in the minds of the voters into action at the polls.

Was Thomas actually a Communist? On balanced judgment, the answer to that question must be in the negative. When he wrote his book, he was very much interested in the thesis that the American people were thinking only of the war, and not of the future problems of peace. He felt strongly that preparation for peace should be begun during the war, since peace could come about only by agreement between the United States and the Soviet Union. To make that agreement possible, an atmosphere of faith must be created, not of fear.

> It must be noted that in his speeches advocating friendship with the Soviet Union and expressing admiration or praise for the Russian fighting forces that repelled the German army, *Thomas made no comments which could be construed as demonstrating esteem for the Russian government. Neither are there any allusions to Russian "democracy."* His policy seemed to speak well of the Soviets when he could, and to build the foundation of friendship with the materials at hand, leaving to the Russians themselves their own internal affairs. Believing firmly that an enduring peace was dependent upon Russian-American friendship, Thomas thought that a "Red Scare" reaction was more dangerous than Russia herself. Commenting on this point, Thomas said, "I always like to recall that the doctrines of our own American Revolution were condemned by the same kind of little minds as seek today to utilize the spectre of Red Russia.[12]

His was an idealism which transcended national boundaries. But his own country came first. Certainly his utterances in the Senate reinforce the judicious appraisal which makes his devotion to his country seem indisputable. On March 25, 1949, Thomas said:

> I realize that Russia today, in what she is doing and in the way in which she operates, under the theory of her government, is just the opposite of what America has stood for in the hundred and seventy years of her history. We cannot accept the single will in government and survive. Therefore, we hate what she is doing.[13]

In 1945, he stated:

> The American Government is still the only Government on earth where the spokesman for that Government and the leaders in it carry on not for the benefit of the Government, but for the people for whom the Government functions.[14]

In 1950, the year it was alleged that he was a Communist, he said:

> He who would like to bring destruction to the Government of the United States today is not only a traitor to his country, he is a traitor to all civilization and to the people of the whole earth, because it happens that the last bit of hope that is lodged in the minds of the people of the world everywhere is the hope born of faith that the Constitution of the United States will survive, and that the people of the United States, with their ideals of carrying on government for the benefit of the people, will endure.[15]

To anyone who knew Senator Elbert D. Thomas, how he lived and worked and thought, these were no idle statements to camouflage any hidden political goals. They were the essence of what he believed and representative of what he really thought. Thomas' basic motives were to serve his God, his country, and his fellow-man. He was pragmatic at times, an idealist at other times. In politics, he was a Democrat in the tradition of Thomas Jefferson and Woodrow Wilson; in political thought he was democratic in the tradition of those who placed a concern for others around them above an effort to ingratiate themselves with others for the sole purpose of self-advancement.

Even Quigley said later that he did not think Senator Thomas was a Communist. He did think, however, that "these clever Commies used him as a front." He said: "Certainly his book indicates a genuine sympathy for the Commies, but it is my judgment that he let himself be shoved around by them unwittingly."[16] He said he did not know who influenced Senator Thomas to write *The Four Fears.* Thomas, he thought, was carried away with the idea of trying to cement a friendship with Russia.

The *United States Senate News* touched off widespread repercussions. There arose from the pro-Thomas Democrats the shrieks and shouts of moral and righteous indignation; there was talk of seeking out the culprits and holding them to account at law. Many persons anticipated that the sheet would boomerang; Republicans feared it would do so. In Provo, Utah, T. W. Adams published an ad in the Provo (daily) *Herald* on October twenty-fourth, which stated that he had made a one dollar contribution to the Republican party for printing the next smear sheet in Utah instead of in Minneapolis or Philadelphia; he invited others to do likewise. He then said of the Quigley sheet, "it boomeranged into the best Democratic campaign stuff of the year." But the truth was that the paper did *not* boomerang. Many persons thought that where there was smoke there might be fire. Others actually believed that Thomas was a Communist. At the moment when a popular reaction might have been anticipated because of the outrage to fair play and the lack of any solid basis for the innuendoes, the Korean situation began to worsen and began to scare the electorate into escapism.

Had the election been two or three weeks later, Bosone and Granger, the Democratic congressional nominees, might also have gone down in defeat. Events in Korea synchronized perfectly with Republican local propaganda releases. The Republicans undoubtedly could have won the senatorial race without Quigley's smear sheet had they known in advance that events in another part of the world, played heavily on the front pages of the newspapers, would have so much influence on the election.

But there were other reasons for the failure of the Quigley sheet to boomerang. The Republicans had laid the groundwork for its reception before and during the active campaigning period. Their greatest effort, although hardly of their own planning, was the all-out doctors' campaign to discredit Thomas for his alleged role in the Senate in behalf of "socialized medicine." The ground had also been prepared by the Farm Bureau Federation and other political groups in livestock and agriculture, who had dropped their traditional policy of opposing or supporting only legislative measures and who now openly opposed the Democratic and supported the Republican nominees. The ground had been fertilized by numerous political fringe movements which had started up during the campaign—the Democrats for Bennett; the attack, led by Senator Watkins on Senator Thomas' appointee, Willis Ritter, to the Federal District Court Bench; the attitudes and activities of the leaders of the Mormon church; the annual state convention resolutions of various groups, for example, the American Legion and the League of Business and Professional Women; endorsements by many more groups of Thomas' opponents and by a hard core of local political dynamiters, state Senator Rue L. Clegg, United States Senator Arthur V. Watkins, former L.D.S. Mission President Selvoy Boyer, Governor J. Bracken Lee, former Congressman William Dawson, local Mormon leader Leonard Love, to name only a few.

The campaign had become an all-out affair, a "knock-down, drag out" brawl; it was to become even dirtier. The Democrats published a full-page newspaper advertisement soon after the appearance of the *Senate News.* Its headline was taken from the Ninth Commandment, "Thou Shalt Not Bear False Witness." Immediately under this headline was another which read, "We Deplore Dishonesty in Politics." "Republicans," the Democrats observed, "are attempting to mislead the voters of Utah. They mis-state, they misquote, they misrepresent. Nothing they charge Senator Thomas with saying is as strong as the following." Then followed quotations from leading Republicans who had said the same things Senator Thomas had said during the war.

Reportedly, General Douglas MacArthur had said, "The world situation at the present time indicates that the hopes of civilization rest on the worthy shoulders of the courageous Russians," and the "free peoples of the world . . . salute . . . that great army and great nation which so nobly strives with us [the United States] for victory, liberty, and freedom." Senator Robert A. Taft was quoted as having stated that we are "eternally grateful" for the Russian aid which did more to bring about a "German defeat than any other army [this includes the United States army] in the world." Wendell Willkie was quoted as having asserted: "There are many things in Russia that we can admire." Representative Clare Booth Luce allegedly admitted that "some of [her] best friends" were "Communists." The *New York Times* said that "continued cooperation between the United States and Russia is so essential to future world peace that no remaining differences can be permitted to interfere with it."

General Dwight D. Eisenhower was quoted as having said he saw "nothing in the future that would prevent Russia and the United States from being closest possible friends." Senator Arthur Vandenberg was quoted as having asserted: "There is little doubt that true peace does finally depend upon a 'live and let live' accommodation between their Eastern Communism and our West Democracies." Cordell Hull was reported to have praised the "courage and self sacrifice . . . of the whole people of the Soviet Union," adding that all "liberty-loving peoples of the world . . . admired the armed forces and the entire population [which includes the leaders] of the Soviet Union." Captain Eddie Rickenbacker was said to have predicted that "Russia is likely to come out of the war the greatest democracy in the world," and the darling of the extreme isolationists, Colonel Robert McCormick, must have made an extra effort when he was recorded as having said: "In Russia's fight to survive as a nation lies the great hope of the world for early peace."

At the conclusion of this list, the Democrats pointed out that "these men, *and Senator Thomas*, did not speak today, or yesterday. The quotations came from public statements during the dark days of World War II. Hitler's hordes were storming the gates of Stalingrad, and every loyal and patriotic American citizen was urging cooperation with our Russian ally." In conclusion, the Democrats called upon the Republicans to "be truthful, or have the grace to be quiet!" They asked the voters to "vote for honesty and decency, and for Elbert D. Thomas."

Although this defense by the Democrats was designed to bring Senator Thomas into a select company of men who were Republicans, great public servants, and distinguished citizens, whose statements should have been acceptable to the Utah Republicans particularly, it did not change the subject under discussion nor the object of attack. The object was still Senator Thomas and the subject was his past actions and utterances. The Republicans showed greater propaganda sense when they retaliated on October twenty-seventh with a full-page advertisement in which they changed the object to the record of Senator Arthur V. Watkins, who was not running for office, a fact which only pointed up the misfiring of Democratic propaganda.

The Republicans also began with a scriptural quotation. After reminding the public that the Democrats had said, "Thou shalt not bear false witness," they asked the readers to consider the following piece of scripture, "Thou hypocrite, first cast the beam out of thine own eye; and then . . . ," reproducing the Democrats' words, " 'We deplore dishonesty in politics,' say the Mis-Dealers—but DO they? Read their smears. . . . Then read the Truth!" To be noted was the name-calling which was absent in the corresponding Democratic advertisement. Thomas was alleged to have stated on September twentieth that

Senator Watkins "opposed the Marshall Plan" and on October thirtieth that "Joe Stalin" got comfort out of "the kind of hesitation, fear and vacillation shown by Senators Watkins and Taft, and Representative Vito Marcantonio." The Republican ad listed some items in legislation related to foreign aid or national defense which Senator Watkins had either voted for, supported, or demanded. The first item stated, "He supported ECA [the Marshall Plan] every time it was before the Senate." The other items stated categorically that he had voted for all defense appropriations and for all curbs on Communists.

The Democrats, according to the Republican ad, had charged that in practically every instance, Senator Watkins had voted against legislation designed to curb the aggressive attitude of Russia, that he "has given more aid to the Kremlin than any other Senator in Washington," and "He's just 'agin' everything—any piece of legislation that has been made a law in the past eighteen years, Senator Watkins automatically is against."

After a brief reference to the "totalitarian technique . . . of the Big Lie and the Big Smear!" the Republican ad listed on the right side of the propaganda ledger a formidable array of things Senator Watkins had voted for, supported, defeated, and kept in behalf of the nation and the Republican party. Reportedly he voted for such liberal measures as housing, federal aid to education, and civil rights, defended the Constitution, and kept Republican platform pledges of 1946 and 1948. The ad further claimed he had secured seven items of national legislation in behalf of Utah dealing with water development, highways, mining, the acquisition of federal land by the University of Utah, and the transfer of Bushnell Hospital to the Indian administration, thereby saving it for a Navajo school.

The ad concluded with the statement that Thomas, Granger, and Bosone had never repudiated any charges, and with the plea to the voter to elect Bennett to the Senate. The gimmick in this kind of propaganda was that if one does not deny what others charge him with, he is automatically guilty, even if the person had not even had an opportunity to read the charges and answer them.

Another large Republican newspaper advertisement was headed, "That Lame Excuse for Elbert Thomas Just Won't Do." The thesis of this ad was stated in a few single-sentence, lead paragraphs: "The Democratic Party bosses must have a pretty low opinion of the intelligence of Utah voters. They seem to think that Utahns are too dumb to see the difference between: 1. Recognizing the fighting qualities of the soldiers in a wartime Russian army which was battling on our side, and 2. Praising the political leadership and the aims and practices of the Communists." The ad completely distorted what Thomas had said and written on this subject.

In another advertisement which was typical of the Republicans' blows during the waning moments of the campaign, the same persons who signed "The Lame Excuse" ad asked in a boldface, three-column headline, "What Makes This Man Thomas 'Sling Mud' and 'Smear'?" The very first paragraph turned on Thomas almost precisely what he said of the Republicans and what he could have said of Bennett, "What spur drives Elbert D. Thomas into the frenzy of mud-slinging which he has made the burden and brand of his vituperative campaign against Wallace F. Bennett for election to the U. S. Senate?" This was the theme, Thomas smears Bennett, which was repeated in paragraph after paragraph of unrelated and garbled statements and taken out of printed context from random sources by the Republicans. One wondered if the signers of the ad (one of whom was a completely disgruntled former Democratic state legislator, whose frustrations had made practically a recluse out of him) were giving vent to their own feelings of hatred and anger which had developed from their personal experiences in local politics unrelated to the 1950 campaign.

In an open letter to Elbert D. Thomas, the writers presented their conceptions of the ingredients of the "American Way of Life." For example, the "American Way of Life" was both Standard Oil and United States Steel, big business and apple pie, porkchops, hot cakes, soda pop, the World Series, the Chicago Stockyards, and the Mormon Tabernacle. The conclusion to this potpourri was the dichotomy of free enterprise and socialism. As usual, Thomas was identified with the socialized state.

The doctors published their clincher as a newspaper ad with the words, "A Vote for Wallace F. Bennett is a Vote Against Socialized Medicine." In another ad they asked the reader to listen to a radio address by Selvoy J. Boyer, Jeffersonian Democrat and prominent Mormon church dignitary, on the subject, "Do *You* Want Socialism or Freedom?"

One small incident illustrates the Republican propaganda style. State Senator Rue L. Clegg had discovered that Thomas had appointed young men to the United States Naval Academy who were not residents of the state. In one case, the Naval Academy records gave an address for a boy which had never been his residence or that of his father. In another case Clegg could not find any record of a boy's father having resided or voted in Utah since 1918. The records showed that the boy had been born and educated in another state. Clegg, in a quarter-page ad, then asked Senator Thomas: "Is this an example of your devotion to the youth of Utah? Our boys are good enough to be selected to go to Korea; why then did you have to go outside of Utah to select someone to go to Annapolis?" Multiplied by dozens of similar contributions from independent and unexpected sources, the incident revealed how the negative campaign against Thomas became overwhelming to the Democrats.

But in all the Republican propaganda, what hurt Thomas the most were a very simple statement and a very innocent question. The first was a quotation from *The Four Fears.* "All close students of development in Russia agree that she has given up her early hopes of world-wide revolution," and the second, the question, which was asked in print hundreds of times, "Did you not say this, Senator Thomas?" The statement read in 1950, in the face of Soviet Russian imperialistic movements in various parts of the world, made Thomas appear less than a "statesman" and a "wise and able leader," as the Republicans averred; in truth, it made him appear not only unrealistic but naïve. Thomas could not answer the question. He could not explain in the heat of a political campaign why he had said it six years earlier, nor could he very well admit that not he but a ghost writer had actually written it.

As the campaign progressed, Democratic party officials made some effort to meet the ads and the Quigley newspaper with a counteroffensive. In particular they did some thorough research on the preparation and production of the smear sheet. The promise of the Democratic state chairman, Grant MacFarland, to tie the "scurrilous attack on Senator Thomas" to Republican leaders of the state fell somewhat flat. In a legal notice, the Utah State Republican Central Committee and the County Central Committees of Utah, over the name of State Republican Chairman Pratt Kesler, took full responsibility for the preparation and circulation and financing of the publication. But the attempt to seek some outside state connections bore fruit; the Democrats did not find any previously unknown "out-of-state political groups," but they did find a professional public relations man, Walter E. Quigley of Minneapolis, whose specialty was political publicity, or, as he described it, political dynamiting.

From a batch of photostats they received from Minneapolis, they discovered that Quigley, the researcher, had a record of having been disbarred from the practice of law and dismissed from positions a number of times. His record was altogether unsavory.

Democratic campaign managers had not been without propaganda sense when they responded to the Quigley sheet by ferreting out its source. They followed this effort with some expensive and effective political dynamiting on Quigley himself, but the information they had on him was neither edited nor issued in a mass-appeal form. It was sent to Drew Pearson, who used it in his broadcast the Sunday before election day and who attempted to discredit Quigley. But this was a one-shot effort and reached a comparatively limited audience. Drew Pearson would be read or listened to by the voters who would have voted for Thomas in any event. Pearson was not very popular in Utah generally. He was disliked for his methods of securing and disseminating information by the very conservative and religious groups who would tacitly approve of Quigley's methods or at least close their eyes to them because Quigley helped to uproot Senator Thomas. Defeating Senator Thomas had become, in some quarters, almost a religious crusade. Nor did the attack on Quigley in any way discredit any other Republican propaganda. Quigley had no connection with any parallel campaign which was waged by a pressure group, party organization, public relations counsel, or individual candidate. For example, when he was asked for some information about the AMA campaign in Utah, he replied with characteristic frankness: "The American Medical Association campaign is handled by a man and his wife who did a similar job in California. . . . I tried to get into the act, but they had it sewed up tight."[17]

Quigley related later that when he was in Salt Lake City he "read a speech by either Cal Rawlings [Calvin Rawlings, national Democratic committeeman] or Black [Parnell Black, Salt Lake County Democratic chairman] calling me a 'character assassin' or some other names. However, the repercussions were mild. Drew Pearson blasted me in a Sunday afternoon broadcast which I happened to hear. It brought me national attention and more clients, and I would like to have him open up on me again."[18] Earlier, Quigley recalled that he had met "Cal Rawlings in the Trainmens Legal Aid office here [Minneapolis] some years ago. He and Parnell Black gave me hell after the paper hit, but I expected that. You can't toss as many bricks as I have done for 40 years and not catch a few."[19]

Statements made by newspapers and organizations decrying the smear campaign were impotent. The *Salt Lake Tribune* protested mildly the "display of bitterness," the almost libelous charges, and the "personal elements in the American democratic form of government."[20] The *Deseret News* remained silent. The *Telegram* reported the exception to the campaign tactics taken by the Utah Chapter of the American Association of Social Workers. Although they addressed letters of protest to the state chairmen of both parties, they said for publication that "We do not feel that Senator Elbert D. Thomas' writings, actions, and statements were out of order at the time they were made or indicate in any way that he is not and has not always been a loyal and responsible American."[21]

Only once had Thomas himself struck back in violent protest. He had directed one great blast against the Anti-Communist League broadside displaying his picture side by side with Paul Robeson's, which he called "the most false, defamatory, insidious, dishonest, and hateful attack upon a man's good name and character that I have ever seen," adding that it was "such a low effort of mudraking servility as to be unbelievable," and "how low can men sink." He threatened to bring the responsible persons to task and clean up the dirty business. But after that he remained silent on the smears in the campaign. After the campaign, he did not support the feeble efforts made in his behalf to have the campaign investigated by the Senate's Sub-Committee on Elections. He was tired and completely disillusioned about the "common man" and particularly about the Utah people. All his pet illusions about his fellow American citizens and his conception of American politics had been completely shattered.

Quigley claimed that his paper was the decisive factor in the election. This is a claim difficult to dispute or to sustain. There were several other hard-hitting campaigns, masterminded by out-of-state public relations men but implemented by local hatchet wielders, which made it difficult to evaluate the effectiveness of any one factor. In every case, all the separate propaganda, most of which were aimed at individual blocs of voters, had the same objective, to pin the Socialist or Communist tag on Senator Thomas. The doctors' campaign was enormous and all-embracing in its execution. Using the newspapers and radio and working through all the allied medical groups and many business groups, it probably reached as many individuals eventually as the Quigley sheet did with one fell swoop.

But Quigley insisted that his paper was decisive. He reasoned, "if properly cartooned, etc., [they] are picked up usually by all adult members of the family, even those on the opposite side. I have found them decisive over the years—far more than TV or radio and *much* cheaper. Campaign papers cannot be turned off. In 30 years of issuing them, I find they 'tip over' states within a week of their issuance."[22]

Quigley would not reveal the cost of the paper to the Republican National Headquarters, by whom he said he was paid, nor the amount of his fee. Usually, he explained, private persons paid him but that was not the case in Utah. Pratt Kesler, state Republican chairman, admitted that the state Republican organization had paid Quigley a substantial sum in addition to what he had received from other sources.

Thomas' managers, in a last-minute, desperate stand during the final campaign week, also spent huge sums, especially for full-page newspaper advertisements, but this expenditure did not touch the large sum spent to prepare, produce, and distribute the single missile, the *United States Senate News.* Generally, however, neither side lacked money in this election year. The Republicans complained loud, long, and often about the huge sums labor organizations raised locally or brought into the state and spent for the Democratic candidates. However, the Republicans raised locally and brought into the state equally large sums, or perhaps even larger.

The chief significance of the type of campaign waged by the Republicans in 1950 for the political process in the United States was in the part played by the public relations man, particularly by the political dynamiter who is in a separate or special class of public relations men. Stanley Kelley observed that the "Public relations men and their close relatives, advertising men, have moved into politics in a big way."[23] It is evident, however, that the nature and extent of this movement differed from case to case. Kelley gave examples of their contributions. In the campaigns he studied they served as producers of propaganda, as press secretaries, as fund raisers, and as strategy consultants. His findings on the campaign of the AMA would apply to Utah, with variations owing probably to the preponderant Mormon population of the state and the fact that Mormon doctrine and public policy would seem to support automatically, but certainly superficially, the AMA position, and that Mormon-trained speakers were available to make the labors of Whitaker and Baxter, who managed the medical campaign, significantly easier.

In summary, Quigley came to Utah for only a day or two. He was hired to do a hatchet job on Senator Thomas. His skill as a one-shot artist was purchased early. His specialty was a four-page newspaper called the *United States Senate News*, which required months of research. Such material cannot be dug out, processed, and delivered once a campaign is underway. It must be on hand in useable form when needed. He set one charge and released it, but it took in the whole state, the entire electorate; it was mass appeal which used cartoons and the printed page in the style of yellow journalism and in the form of a newspaper. It depended upon efficient mass distribution for its effectiveness, which consisted in hitting hard all at once all over the state.

It is doubtful if the paper would have been quite so effective as it seemed to be, and as Quigley himself claimed, if it had not been for the great number of individual and interest group campaigns being waged simultaneously and continuously over a long period of time. These campaigns had already won blocs of votes for the Republicans and had broken into ranks of support from labor, education, and agriculture which had been promised to Thomas by leaders of these groups and his own managers. They had broken down the moral resistance of the electorate and numbed its critical judgment. The explosion of Quigley's bomb at the moment in the campaign when there was still some hope for Thomas to pull through, wrecked completely the resistance of the Democrats; their morale was shattered completely and irretrievably. The Republicans, without relenting in the propaganda efforts which had characterized their entire campaign, had only to wait for the collapse of their opponents.

The campaign has been interpreted from the standpoint of Thomas' defeat. The Republicans were responsible for this interpretation. Their campaign was more one of attack on Thomas than one of support for Bennett. The doubtful voter considered whether he should vote for or against Thomas, not whether he should vote for Bennett.

After the campaign, Drew Pearson gave the following account of what took place in a meeting of senatorial assistants:

> The "prime targets" in 1950, he said [the speaker was Ab Herman, assistant to Guy Gabrielson, National Republican Committee chairman in 1950], were Scott Lucas in Illinois, Francis Myers in Pennsylvania, Elbert Thomas of Utah, and Millard Tydings of Maryland. Turning to Frank Smith, assistant to Senator John M. Butler, who defeated Tydings, Herman continued: "We did a beautiful job in Maryland and Utah, Frank. I don't see why the Democrats yelled so much about the composite picture in your campaign, when, by comparison with the anti-Thomas newspaper in Utah, your publicity was like a country gentleman's."[24]

Four years after former Republican state senator Rue L. Clegg had caused eyebrows to lift and murmurs to roll over an audience by holding up a photostatic copy of the *New Masses* magazine on which Senator Thomas was pictured as a contributor of an article entitled "World Citizen,"[25] he wrote in a letter to the editor of the *Salt Lake Tribune*:

> I notice Senator Bennett is introducing a new resolution calling for censuring McCarthy for accusing his fellow solon, Senator Watkins, of acting as a "handmaiden to the Communists."
>
> That reminds me of an election four years ago when I was competing with Mr. Bennett for the Republican senatorial nomination. I was running the interference at every intersection and crossroads in the state, accusing Senator Thomas of being "putty in the hands of the pinks" . . . but at the same time not questioning his good intentions or loyalty.
>
> Mr. Bennett was bringing up the rear with his sermons on faith, hope, and charity, but at the same time silently acquiescing in all that was being said about Senator Thomas. And what is more, he remained silent during the balance of the campaign while much more vicious and unfair statements were being circulated about his opponent. Is there so much difference in silent acquiescence and the outspoken accusations of Senator McCarthy?
>
> As I look back on that campaign, I regret very much the part I played in it—not so much for what I said but because of the misconceptions that developed in the public mind.[26]

The "misconceptions" added up to the murder of a reputation—they killed United States Senator Elbert D. Thomas politically.

NOTES

1. For example, in Ephraim, Utah, a typical Mormon village in an agrarian area, Ross Cox, the publisher of the local paper, said in a 1944 editorial: "After three weeks of advertising in daily and weekly newspapers, over the radio, and on the front page of the local paper," the merchant who had stocked the book had "not sold a single copy . . . not only that, he had not had so much as an inquiry about the book from a single New Dealer or other person."

Cox then concluded: "It could get people to thinking that it doesn't require much time to be a yes man in Washington, but leaves ample time to write a book. We hope a thorough reading of *The Four Fears* will dispel this fifth fear which has been haunting us lately." *Ephraim Enterprise*, October 13, 1944.

2. He added that the writer was the only person, as far as he knew, who had read the story closely enough to detect the mistake. Most persons, especially during a campaign, do not look for discrepancies between the headlines and the story in an account they know at the outset to be a propaganda effort and to have as its sole purpose the discrediting of a candidate for public office.

3. The policy of the school was stated by Slagle in the proceedings of the first meeting of the board on August 6, 1946, in New York City. It read:

> We have one policy, gentlemen, and this has been definitely set and will never change. This is that this school stands absolutely square-shouldered and two-footed on the American way of life, on the American way of government, on the American way of living, on free enterprise. None of this flimflam stuff Mr. Ulhope and I were speaking about just the other day. Frankly, this school has been put together by sheer American guts. What we want to do is to produce men who are of the same category and the same stripe. On that policy we will stand from now to the day that this place is under the ground.

Report of the Board of Trustees, Romford School, August 6, 1946.

4. Elbert D. Thomas, *The Four Fears* (New York: Ziff-Davis Publishing Co., 1944), p. 60.

5. *Ibid.*, p. 63.

6. *Ibid.*

7. February 25, 1945.

8. *New York Times*, September 10, 1944.

9. Letter from Earl Wixey to author, October 26, 1955.

10. Letter from Mrs. Howard Mumford Jones to author, August 31, 1956.

11. U.S., *Congressional Record*, 79th Cong., 2nd Sess., 92 (June 10, 1946), 3317.

12. Mont Judd Harmon, "The Political Ideas of Senator Elbert D. Thomas" (M.A. thesis, University of Wisconsin, 1950), pp. 160-61. Harmon's research covered forty-six magazine articles, eighty-eight addresses, seventy-five radio talks, and three books by Thomas. Italics supplied.

13. U.S., *Congressional Record*, 81st Cong., 1st Sess., 95 (March 25, 1949), 3172-75.

14. *Ibid.*, 79th Cong., 1st Sess., 91 (June 5, 1945), A2817.

15. *Ibid.*, 81st Cong., 2nd Sess., 96 (April 24, 1950), 5598.

16. Letter from Walter E. Quigley to author, March 5, 1952.

17. Letter from Walter E. Quigley to author, March 7, 1955.

18. Letter from Walter E. Quigley to author, November 13, 1955.

19. Letter from Quigley to author, March 7, 1955.

20. November 1, 1950.

21. *Salt Lake Telegram*, October 24, 1950.

22. Letter from Quigley to author, November 13, 1955.

23. Quoted from William Lee Miller, "Can Government be Merchandised?" *The Reporter* (October 27, 1936), p. 11, in the introduction to Stanley Kelley's final thesis chapter entitled "The Political Role of the Public Relations Man." This excellent thesis has now been published under the title, *Professional Public Relations and Political Power* (Baltimore: Johns Hopkins Press, 1956).

24. July 16,1951. Later, Richard Cardall verified personally the authenticity of the event and the accuracy of Pearson's account.

25. *Deseret News*, August 8, 1950, and *Ephraim Enterprise*, August 18, 1950.

26. November 20, 1954.

SPINNING
THE RED WEB
IN MONTANA

A DRAMATIC contest for James E. Murray's Senate seat took place in
1954 in Montana between the Democratic senator and his Republican
challenger, Congressman Wesley A. D'Ewart. A veteran of twenty years in the
Senate, Murray was a person of high standing not only in Montana but in the
country as a whole. His opponent, D'Ewart, had an impressive career in politics
as a member of the House of Representatives for nearly ten years from the
Second District. The 1954 battle was noteworthy, not only because of the
closeness of the margin by which Senator Murray ultimately won, but also because of the use of political dynamiting in the campaign.

The Montana Senate race was significant to the Democratic and the Republican parties both in the state and in the United States as a whole. One vital
consideration was control of the United States Senate.[1] Republicans, recently
victorious in the executive branch, were anxious to gain firm control of the
Senate in order to advance the program of President Eisenhower. On the other
hand, the Democrats wished to establish control as a prelude to victory in the
1956 presidential election.

Quite apart from its vital relationship to national affairs, given the pre-
carious partisan balance in the Senate, there remained the perennial issue of
party ascendancy in Montana affairs. Would the Murray organization, firmly
entrenched, continue in power? Or would Republican Congressman D'Ewart
extend his successful organization, which controlled the eastern district, to the
entire state? The stakes were high in 1954 from the standpoint of the state, the
nation, the political parties, and the fortunes of the individual candidates and
their supporters.

Despite a growing urban population, Montana in 1954 was essentially rural.
There were six cities of more than ten thousand population, but no city exceeded fifty thousand. More than half of the people in the sparsely populated
state lived either in small farming communities or on farms. In this environment a tradition of personal politics has been nurtured. Since its frontier years
Montana has witnessed a procession of colorful personalities who have pro-

jected sharply etched images upon the political canvas. Political party organization has not developed to a point where it can be described as "disciplined." A tradition of "voting for the man," rather than for party or issue, has survived.

In national affairs, Montana in 1954 had a record, unbroken since 1900, of voting always for the successful presidential candidate. Oddly enough, Montana had elected but one Republican to the Senate prior to the 1954 campaign.[2]

In 1954 the Republicans controlled the governorship of the state, which they had captured two years earlier with colorful Hugo Aronson, who was hailed as the "galloping Swede." The Republicans had carried Montana in the 1952 presidential election and captured both houses of the legislative assembly. Democrat Lee Metcalf held the Western Congressional District seat, won in 1952 by a slim margin. Republican Wesley A. D'Ewart had been reelected to a fifth term in Congress from the Eastern District by a resounding thirty-five thousand votes, exceeding even President Eisenhower's plurality there. The barometers pointed to rising Republican prospects in Montana and it appeared to Republican leaders that 1954 would be a year of further gains.

The dominant interests in the Democratic coalition included farm groups, notably the Farmers' union, and labor. The Republicans relied upon cattlemen and business interests, as well as farmers in the irrigated valleys of western Montana. The Anaconda Company (known in 1954 as the Anaconda Copper Mining Company, or A.C.M.) was the single most powerful economic force in the state. For years the Anaconda Company and the Montana Power Company had maintained a united front in politics, which by 1954 was beginning to disintegrate. These two corporate giants were referred to either as "the Company" or "the Twins," and their political strength was a factor with which to reckon.

From a business standpoint, 1953 had been a good year in Montana, but farmers were already beginning to experience a decline in agricultural income. This decline continued in 1954, when the wheat harvest was 34 percent under the record 1953 crop.[3] A major strike of workers in the copper industry, which idled more than ten thousand Anaconda Company employees during September and part of October 1954, was finally settled in mid-October. A lumber strike in the Missoula area in late summer was also a factor in the economic setting. By autumn the economic indicators were pointing downward in many areas. Unemployment was up substantially over the preceding two years.

Political dynamiting was by no means unknown in Montana. Dynamiting tactics had been used on occasion by both parties before 1954. The practice grew naturally out of an early tradition of personal politics in which each candidate blasted his opponent and no quarter was asked or given. The early titanic struggles of the copper barons left a lasting imprint which has not yet been eradicated from the Montana political scene.

In the 1920's Joseph M. Dixon, who was governor from 1921 to 1925 and had been a leader in the Progressive movement, was frequently the target of vituperative attacks by political adversaries and the press. Leif Erickson, a liberal Democrat who defeated Senator Burton K. Wheeler in the 1946 Democratic senatorial primary, benefited from a propaganda paper entitled the *Montana News*. This publication was prepared by the expert dynamiter, Walter Quigley of Minneapolis, who was employed by A. F. Whitney, president of the Brotherhood of Railroad Trainmen, for the express purpose of blasting Wheeler.[4] In the election, the tables were turned as Erickson's Republican opponents alluded to "The Red Streak over Montana," pointing to Erickson's ultraliberal associates. In the 1952 Senate campaign between Mike Mansfield, the Democratic nominee who was ultimately successful, and Senator Zales Ecton, the Republican incumbent, one Harvey Matusow was brought into the state by supporters of Senator Ecton and made sweeping accusations regarding Mansfield's alleged connections with the Communist party.[5]

Before examining the 1954 Senate contest, it is appropriate to consider the backgrounds of the opposing candidates.[6] A scrutiny of their differing temperaments, careers, and political philosophies will help place the events of the campaign in proper perspective.

James E. Murray, who was destined before his retirement to serve in the Senate longer than any other Montanan, was born in Ontario, Canada, May 3, 1876. After completing his education in Canadian schools and at the New York University Law School, Murray moved to Butte. There he was admitted to the bar in 1901, beginning an association with Montana and Butte which was to endure until his death in 1961. He originally was attracted to Butte in part by the fact that it was the home of a wealthy uncle, whose attorney Murray became. He managed his uncle's sizable mining properties and later inherited a substantial portion of his uncle's estate. There is little agreement in Montana as to the exact extent of Murray's wealth, but it was assumed that he was a millionaire. At the time of his death, Murray's estate had shrunk to lesser proportions, which may have reflected a transfer of part of his holdings to other members of his family prior to his death.

Murray was of Irish-Catholic origins and retained throughout his life a strong allegiance both to the Irish nationality and to his Catholic faith. Both were useful attributes in Butte where Irish-Catholics were powerful. The significance of Butte in Montana politics throughout Murray's career was measured by the decisive pluralities it gave him, thereby launching him on the road to political victory.

He plunged into politics soon after his arrival in Butte and was elected to one term as attorney of Silver Bow County in 1906. His continuing interest in politics was evidenced by his service as a delegate to the Democratic national convention in 1920 and 1932. An early and active supporter of Franklin D. Roosevelt for the presidency, Murray served in 1933 and 1934 as chairman of the Montana Advisory Board of the Public Works Administration. In this capacity, he proposed the building of Hungry Horse Dam.

Murray's opportunity for advancement in politics occurred as a result of the resignation of Senator Thomas Walsh, who vacated his Senate seat in 1933 to accept appointment as attorney general in Roosevelt's Cabinet.[7] The vacancy was filled temporarily by Governor John Erickson, who was appointed after resigning as governor. In 1934, Murray narrowly defeated Erickson in the Democratic primary and won the Democratic nomination for the seat. Elected in November 1934 to the two remaining years of the unexpired term, Murray was subsequently reelected to the Senate for full six-year terms in 1936, 1942, and 1948.

After his arrival in Washington, Murray quickly distinguished himself as a "hundred percent New Dealer." Throughout his senatorial career he consistently supported the New Deal and Fair Deal measures of Roosevelt and Truman. He became a warm friend of conservation, public power, the small businessman, and labor. His service on the Senate Labor Committee led to national eminence among liberals. In 1954, he was ranking minority member of the Senate Interior and Insular Affairs Committee.

Senator Murray was the author of the Small Business Administration Act, and he brought about the creation of a Senate small business committee, which he served as chairman. Of all legislation for which he was responsible, he regarded the Employment Act of 1946 as being of greatest significance. He promoted the cause of compulsory health insurance by sponsoring the controversial Murray-Wagner-Dingell bill. He advocated a Missouri Valley Authority to do for the Great Plains what the Tennessee Valley Authority had done in the Tennessee Valley, thereby incurring the disfavor of the Montana Power Company.

The senator's liberalism was something of a paradox. Although he was an Irish-Catholic of substantial wealth, associated with legal and banking interests throughout most of his life, he emerged nevertheless as one of the outstanding liberals of his era. How was such incongruous behavior possible? The best explanation is that he spent his adult years in Butte. An individual associated with the unique Butte environment invariably acquires a liberal outlook as an inevitable consequence of such association.

The liberalism of Murray stands in stark contrast with the conservatism of Wesley A. D'Ewart who represented a different background, albeit one familiar to many Americans. D'Ewart was born in Worcester, Massachusetts, on October 1, 1889. The family, of French Huguenot origin, had migrated first to Scotland and later to the New England area. Wesley D'Ewart retains in his speech and mannerisms some of the flavor of the New Englander. Educated in the public schools of Worcester, he moved West and became a forestry student at Washington State College. After graduation, he served in the Wilsall, Montana, area as a ranger in the Forest Service for six years.

From forestry, D'Ewart moved into ranching by acquiring a ranch near Wilsall which eventually grew to five thousand acres. Through the years his interests broadened to include reclamation and conservation. He organized the Montana Reclamation Association and was its first president. He also organized and served as first president of the Park County Rural Electric System. As D'Ewart prospered, he also became a director of a bank in Park County. The growing esteem in which he was held by friends and neighbors led to his election to the Montana House of Representatives in 1936. He was reelected in 1938, and two years later was elected to the Montana Senate where he served through three sessions.

In 1945 Democratic Congressman John O'Connor, a fixture in the Second District, died unexpectedly. Both parties held conventions to nominate candidates for the special election to be held in June of that year. At the Republican convention it was assumed that no Republican could win since O'Connor had won the seat by some fifteen thousand votes in the previous general election.[8] D'Ewart was nominated after the convention deadlocked on other possible candidates. He defeated his Democratic opponent in the special election, launching a career of nearly ten years of service in the national House of Representatives.

During his years in the House, D'Ewart served on the Interior and Insular Affairs Committee. He introduced and supported legislation dealing with reclamation, resources management, and recreation. He was a dependable friend of the National Park Service and the United States Forest Service. Known as a fiscal conservative, he tended generally toward a conservative position within Republican ranks. The most controversial legislation which he sponsored, a bill affecting leases on public grazing lands, would have been most favorable to livestock interests but was blocked by recreation interests.[9]

D'Ewart's conservative outlook mirrored his Yankee upbringing and the impact upon his life of the Puritan-Protestant ethic. His years as a rancher, identified with the livestock interest, reinforced his conservative point of view. Through the years, however, his conservatism was tempered by a practical recognition of the value of certain measures which strictly speaking did not fall within the gambit of conventional conservative ideology. For example, he supported rural electrification cooperatives, reclamation, conservation, and some welfare measures. A frugal man by temperament, he has always been cautious and prudent in his management of affairs. During his years in Congress, he earned the respect of friend and foe alike by the diligence and dispatch with which he handled the duties of his office.

These two men were to occupy the center of the Montana political stage in 1954. In strikingly different ways each had risen to prominence in politics. Each was a seasoned veteran of many campaigns. Each represented a venerable political tradition which belonged to a passing generation. If one can speak with any precision regarding liberalism and conservatism, it must be said that in 1954 Montana voters were to have a clear choice between these contrasting ideologies, a choice offered in the persons of D'Ewart and Murray.

Flushed by their one-sided victories in the July 20, 1954, primaries of their parties, both incumbent Senator Murray and his adversary, Congressman D'Ewart, could count political pluses and minuses on their respective sides. Although the mathematics of politics permits no precise measuring of strength and weakness, the candidates and their supporters were well aware that certain factors, however intangible, might be assessed in calculating the probable outcome. In retrospect, after more than a decade, it is impossible to determine precisely how the various factors affected the relative strength of each candidate. Nevertheless, these factors must be identified, evaluated, and weighed to whatever extent possible.

Senator Murray possessed substantial pluses, not the least of which was the fact that he was the incumbent and had already served twenty years in the Senate. His name was well known to Montana voters and there was no problem of establishing a political image for 1954. Another plus for Murray, repeatedly stressed throughout the campaign, was his seniority. He was the ranking minority member of the important Interior and Insular Affairs Committee of the Senate. Should the Democrats gain control of the Senate in the 1954 elections, Murray would become chairman of this committee which was of vital importance to Montanans.

Murray's Irish-Catholic background was an advantage, given the complexion of Montana's ethnic and religious forces. Moreover, he was a partisan Democrat closely identified with the Democratic organization in a state in which only one Republican had ever won a Senate race.

On the minus side, Murray's age (he was seventy-eight) was used as an argument against him. At the end of the term for which he was a candidate he would be eighty-four. Democrats privately commented about Senator Murray's growing senility. As early as 1954, and during the years that followed, this factor came increasingly to weigh against him.

Another minus factor in 1954 was Senator Murray's family, several of whom had benefited from their father's status. One son had been appointed to a federal district judgeship in Montana, and another served as the senator's administrative assistant. The impression was growing that the latter, Charles A. Murray, was the senator in all but name. Some of the activities of other members of the family, who allegedly had used the senator's connections in furthering private business ventures, were to be alluded to in the campaign.

Senator Murray labored under the disadvantage of all incumbents in that he was an "in" and had acquired the liabilities of a long period of office holding. Murray's liberalism, a point of strength in the 1930's and 1940's, had, during the conservative renaissance of the 1950's, become something of a liability. His proposals for MVA, for health insurance, and for other reforms were on the shelf, and he was fighting for his political life against a conservative tide which had crested two years earlier in the overwhelming triumph of Dwight D. Eisenhower.

Congressman D'Ewart also brought substantial plus factors to his campaign. He had won five victories in succession in the Eastern District against strong Democratic opposition. His most recent victory, that of 1952, had been by an impressive thirty-five thousand votes over his Democratic opponent, a margin greater than Eisenhower's in that district. D'Ewart had a solid record of hard work and achievement in Washington. He maintained cordial relationships with his constituents; his news letter was one of the better ones produced in Washington.

D'Ewart had developed an excellent organization consisting of loyal supporters scattered throughout the Eastern District. Presumably their support would be available in 1954. He had also the endorsement and support of President Eisenhower, who, along with other Republicans, regarded the Senate race in Montana as one of the nation's most critical 1954 contests. D'Ewart's many Republican friends in Washington could be expected to respond to any call for help and come to Montana to campaign in his behalf.

Along with these pluses Congressman D'Ewart, too, possessed some minus qualities. Republican leaders privately conceded that he lacked color and political glamour. His speaking manner, while sincere, was not especially dramatic or effective. Lacking these attributes, it was necessary for him to compensate by harder work in other areas. He faced also the necessity, which did not confront Murray, of quickly extending his organization to the western portion of the state, a section where he had not previously ventured in politics. D'Ewart was confronted, too, by the farm revolt, which was evident throughout the country and was destined to cost Republican candidates dearly in farm states.

The day after Labor Day found the Murray organization in its headquarters in Great Falls. Murray's campaign manager, his son Charles, had extensive experience in working in the Murray organization and was regarded in Montana

Democratic circles as a man of considerable skill and a "power operator" in politics. Other key persons in the Murray organization included attorneys Joseph J. McCaffery, Butte, and Leif Erickson, Helena. Charles Murray and McCaffery made most of the campaign decisions. Erickson, whose connections with the "liberal" wing of the party were close, canvassed the state for Murray.

Relations with national and state Democratic organization leaders were excellent. There were no important defections from Democratic ranks except that of former Senator Wheeler which was expected and discounted. The national committeeman, Leo Graybill, Sr., of Great Falls, who had been chosen in 1951, was generally regarded as belonging to the liberal wing of the party. His relations with both Murray and Murray's organization were friendly. The state chairman, Jack Toole, had been elected in 1954, but he brought drive and imagination to the position and worked closely with the Murray organization.

Raising money was a minor problem for the Murray organization in 1954. Contributions flowed in ample quantity unsolicited to the senator's office and were earmarked for the campaign in advance. Financial records of the campaign show that $37,714.04 was received by the Murray for Senator Club in contributions.[10] This sum is considerably less than the extravagant amounts claimed in Republican charges just as Democrats charged Republicans with spending far more than actually was spent.

Senator Murray's campaign organization was well established and had been repeatedly tested. It was necessary merely to revive it for the 1954 campaign. Murray's advantage over D'Ewart in having had years of service in the Senate made it possible for him to use his federal patronage powers to reward loyal friends and supporters with appointment to federal political posts in Montana; they, in turn, rallied to the Murray banner.

Wesley D'Ewart, on the other hand, began his campaign in 1954 with the necessity of establishing a statewide organization for the first time. In D'Ewart's previous congressional races, William Jameson, a Billings attorney, and Ralph Bricker, a Great Falls real estate man, jointly had managed his highly successful campaigns. As president of the American Bar Association, Jameson was unable to work actively in the 1954 campaign and Bricker chose to play a somewhat limited role.

Some of D'Ewart's advisors felt that a different approach was needed in 1954 and that a fresh face in the campaign manager's seat would be desirable. Albert A. Schlaht, a Billings publisher and businessman, was invited to manage the D'Ewart campaign. Schlaht, who had served previously in the Wyoming legislature, had managed his Billings business interests with acumen. He brought both energy and new sources of financial support to the campaign. Some Republican leaders thought that Schlaht lacked the political "touch" of

Bricker and Jameson. Critics pointed out that Schlaht distributed campaign literature on the basis of requests from county chairmen. His predecessors, by contrast, had known in advance how much literature each county chairman or organization worker could use and had provided the proper amount without waiting for a request. As a result of the Schlaht approach, literature was not distributed properly or in ample quantity. But no one could criticize Schlaht's direction of the campaign so far as zeal and imagination were concerned.

Matt Himsl, a Kalispell businessman and chairman of the Flathead County Republican Central Committee, served as chairman of the D'Ewart for Senator Club. Ralph Bricker continued to serve as chairman for the Eastern District although his participation was less active than in previous campaigns. Henry Sawtell handled finances for the D'Ewart organization. The principal headquarters was located in Helena.

Relations of the D'Ewart organization with the regular Republican organization were generally satisfactory but left something to be desired in spots. The state chairman, William Mackay, had just been chosen for that position in August of 1954 and was able but inexperienced. The national committeeman, Wellington D. Rankin, an influential Helena attorney with enormous land holdings in Montana, was at odds with D'Ewart and did virtually nothing to support him. This friction undoubtedly harmed D'Ewart, especially in Butte, a center of Rankin influence.

Finances were available to the D'Ewart organization in ample quantity. Official records show that the D'Ewart for Senator Club spent a total of $51,816.53.[11] Approximately three thousand dollars in available funds was unexpended and was distributed in 1956 to Montana Republican state and national candidates.[12] The Republicans, of course, were charged with spending larger amounts. It is difficult to estimate total campaign costs inasmuch as in both parties sums were spent by the state organization as well as by the candidate's club. There were local candidate clubs scattered around the state which raised and spent funds. One probably would not be far from the mark if he estimated the total cost of the campaign on each side at one hundred thousand dollars.

One of the mystery men in the Republican organization was Frank Kluckhohn, who came to Montana on loan from the Republican National Committee to assist the D'Ewart organization in public relations. Kluckhohn is a well-known journalist and author. His public relations firm has been employed frequently by the Republican National Committee on a consulting basis. He was in Montana for a number of weeks during the closing phases of the 1954 campaign to handle press relations for the D'Ewart organization. There was great respect for his ability but the consensus among D'Ewart people seems to have been that Kluckhohn was, in D'Ewart's words, "a little rougher than I like to be."[13]

The 1954 senatorial race between Murray and D'Ewart was contested during the eight weeks between Labor Day, September sixth, and Election Day, November second. Prior to the opening of the campaign in Montana, both Congress and President Eisenhower had helped lay its foundation. On September first, the president signed legislation granting increased benefits and extending coverage under social security. In mid-August he had signed a major piece of Republican-sponsored legislation, granting tax reductions totaling nearly 7.5 billion dollars. Overriding objections of the Eisenhower administration, Congress had outlawed the Communist party. This was to be a weapon Democrats could use to counter Republican charges that the Democrats had been soft on communism. Legislation granting substantial salary increases to federal employees was also adopted.

The McCarthy-Army hearings occurred during the summer of 1954. The McCarthy Era was nearing its close although the impending demise of the Wisconsin Republican was not yet visible. During the campaign a special Senate committee headed by Senator Arthur V. Watkins of Utah issued its report recommending Senate censure of McCarthy on a number of counts. However, the Senate would not reconvene to vote on its committee's recommendation until after the November election.

Other events provided part of the backdrop for the 1954 campaign all over the United States. It was the year in which the Illinois branch of the American Legion adopted a resolution asking withdrawal of support for the Girl Scouts because of "un-American influences in the Girl Scout handbook and its publications."[14] The controversial Dixon-Yates plan with its implications for TVA was hotly debated. Finally, in 1954, Charles E. Wilson, secretary of defense, pronounced his famous parable about bird dogs and kennel dogs; unemployed workers were equated with the kennel dog who is unwilling to go out and search for a meal when hungry.

Murray and D'Ewart stated their platforms during their primary campaigns. Senator Murray summarized his position in the following statement:

> One hundred percent parity price supports for all agricultural products; expansion of public power and rural electric programs; development of Montana resources; tax relief by raising the personal exemption from the present six hundred dollars to one thousand dollars for individuals and removal of unnecessary excise taxes to stimulate business; abolition of discriminatory tax rates; expanded social security, more liberal old age assistance, improved health facilities; a sound foreign policy based upon international cooperation; avoidance of American involvement in foreign wars and a strong national defense program; international control of Atomic and Hydrogen weapons and gradual disarmament to achieve lasting peace and security.[15]

More than a month before the Republican primary, Congressman D'Ewart presented his platform as follows:

> Develop and widely use natural resources; promote progress for agriculture which gives producers a fair share of national income; encourage prosperity and welfare of labor and industry; foster mutually beneficial relations with Indians; stop unnecessary expenditures; continue equitable tax deductions for all taxpayers; eliminate subversives from government; maintain an invincible defense force; pursue international policies which preserve liberty and peace for the United States.[16]

At the Democratic convention in Billings in late August, Murray outlined the issues at stake in the campaign as "farm parity, the balanced budget, foreign affairs, the off-shore oil 'give-away,' communism, conservation, and public power."[17] Looking backward in 1963, D'Ewart recalled the principal issue of the campaign in these words: "I was a conservative; he was a liberal. That was the fundamental issue. The question was: 'Did the state want a liberal or a conservative in the United States Senate?' "[18] Before the Republican convention in August 1954, D'Ewart saw the basic issue as "constitutional Republican representative government versus a Socialist centralized Bureaucracy."[19]

As the campaign opened it was evident that the farm problem would be a liability for the Republican candidate. Montana farmers had grown increasingly restive because of the substantial reduction in wheat acreages. Senator Murray recognized the critical significance of the farm issue in a statement at Glendive: "I regard the action of the Republican Congress in respect to America's farmers as a direct and complete violation of the pledges made by Eisenhower in 1952. . . . I am convinced the people will return the Democrats to control and we will return full parity prices."[20] Murray continued to discuss the farm question throughout the campaign. At Malta, near the Canadian border, Murray asserted that the people of northeastern Montana were "indignant at Republican attempts to hamstring Democratic programs for land utilization, soil conservation, and rural electrification."[21] At Glasgow, Murray expressed the wish that "Secretary of Agriculture Benson would tour Montana's vast wheat acres to learn the facts of agricultural life. . . . Our wheat farmers are in a bad way. They tell us they can't take another year of Benson's flexible parity plus rigid control."[22]

In a major speech on farm policy delivered at Bozeman in mid-October, Murray vigorously attacked the farm policies of the Republican administration. He stated: "We should guarantee our farmers full equality with city folk so long as they do produce, which is what parity means. We should put an end to Benson's vacillating shilly-shallying, on again, off again idea of controls which makes it impossible for good farmers to plan production with intelligence and certainty."[23]

Congressman D'Ewart valiantly defended the Eisenhower program. Ironically, he had not voted for the Benson flexible price support program which had been so disastrous for Montana wheat farmers. He assailed the activities of Charles Brannan, who was speaking frequently at Democratic gatherings in Montana, and raised the question: "Montana members of the Farmers Union would like to know whether they are paying the expenses of their $36,500 a year chief counsel to speak for Democratic candidates or if it is charged as it should be to the Democratic campaign fund."[24] In mid-October D'Ewart asserted: "Farmers are recovering from the price drops of the last two years of the Democratic administration and they are doing it without the artificial stimulus of war." In the same vein he added: "Wheat farmers in Montana this year are getting about $2.15 per bushel compared with $1.78-$1.92 during the 1951-1952 period. The Eisenhower administration is proving that we can have prosperity in peace—we do not need war to make good prices."[25]

Democrats nationally were making much of the Eisenhower administration "give-away" program by charging that the Republicans were allowing private interests to acquire control of valuable natural resources belonging to the national government. D'Ewart replied by asserting that "left-wing Democrats" are "being careless with the truth" in making such charges. He stated further:

This charge is humorous when we consider that it comes from the Democrats who, in the course of 11 years, gave away to foreign nations 131 billion in American dollars and resources.

No less than one hundred sixty-six foreign nations and nine national organizations passed through the give-away shop, Mr. Murray and his fellow New and Fair Dealers set up.

At a time when Senator Murray's friend, President Truman, said he could not build the Tiber Dam in Montana and was forbidding new projects for flood control and irrigation, they gave 135 million dollars to foreign nations for the same work.[26]

The peace issue was introduced by D'Ewart, who noted that during the Republican administration no war had occurred and added: "We have had war in every Democratic administration this century . . . not a single American boy has died in this century under a Republican administration. . . . They spent 133 million [sic] dollars of our taxpayers money without buying a real friend."[27]

Near the close of the campaign, attempting to link himself with the Eisenhower administration, D'Ewart said: "The real issues in this campaign are the accomplishments of the Eisenhower administration as against the destructive policies of Trumanism."[28] Murray had commented earlier upon this theme of identifying the D'Ewart fortunes with President Eisenhower by stating: "Apparently in this campaign, Wesley D'Ewart . . . isn't aware that the programs he's attacking are those now sponsored by Republican President Eisenhower.

... Either D'Ewart's playing both sides against the middle and consciously trying to mislead our people, or as seems more likely, his mind has grown confused and wandering and he's just too old at 65 for the job he seeks."[29]

One of Murray's strongest claims was that his seniority and standing in the Senate would enable him to do more for Montana. He noted that if reelected, assuming a Democratic-controlled Senate, he would become the first Montanan to be chairman of the Senate Committee on Interior and Insular Affairs. He stated:

> The Senate's Interior Committee controls all legislation affecting mines and mining, oil resources, Indian affairs, public lands, reclamation, and power development.
> It is of tremendous importance in our state. The chairman of that committee is in a position to get things done for Montana. . . .
> But it takes 15 to 20 years in the Senate before a man can possibly become Chairman. . . . I will automatically become chairman with the election of a Democratic Congress this year.[30]

Speaking in Miles City a week later Murray again reminded Montana voters that he would become chairman of the Interior and Insular Affairs Committee if the Democrats gained control of the Senate and added:

> I shall use all the influence my seniority in the Senate confers on me, not only to bring about full development and stability of our oil industry, but also to half excessive imports of foreign oil. Not only do they retard the development of our own resources, but I feel strongly that any dependence on foreign oil might leave the nation extremely vulnerable in war.[31]

Murray's emphasis upon his seniority inevitably attracted attention to his advanced age. D'Ewart did not allude directly to Murray's age although other Republicans sometimes did. D'Ewart did point out in Butte that all of the Republican candidates for the Senate in 1954 nationally were under sixty-five years of age. Senator Murray evoked both interest and amusement in his reply: "I am so decrepit I would welcome D'Ewart to come on this platform and we'd see who is the old man. I am willing to run a foot race any day of the week and I will give $2,000 to any charity you have if he wants to put on the gloves with me."[32] D'Ewart declined to accept the challenge: "I would not want to endanger the life of a 78-year-old man. I am sorry Senator Murray obviously is sensitive because I said publically in Butte that all Republican candidates for the Senate this year are 65 years of age or under. I regret that the Senator has seen fit to enter into personalities."[33]

Prosperity and the tax cut were issues. D'Ewart noted that the country and people were "generally prosperous." Senator Murray responded:

> My opponent in this campaign insists on going around saying things are "generally prosperous." He must be thinking of General Motors. Certainly our farmers and stockmen are not feeling too prosperous. Certainly America's five million unemployed and

their families and the many more millions who've lost all over-time pay and are working a short week are not feeling too prosperous, and most certainly the small businessmen of America are not happy with their situation.[34]

Speaking in Missoula, D'Ewart remarked: "The Senator is still talking about the depression of the '30's and the tide of misery on which he first ran for office."[35] Murray charged that "only a few select families in the low and middle income groups will realize any savings from the Republican tax bill."[36] D'Ewart countered:

> Murray is weeping crocodile tears for the taxpayer he hurt and would hurt more. I don't think Montanans will be fooled by this phony act.
> The fact is that every earning American paying taxes had his taxes cut at least 11 percent for this year and even Senator Murray should be able to understand this simple fact.[37]

The veteran was injected into the campaign by Murray who charged that D'Ewart voted against veterans interests on three specific bills. D'Ewart accused Murray of "distorting and misrepresenting my record on veterans' legislation."[38] In an advertisement in the *Great Falls Tribune*, D'Ewart attempted to explain his voting on veterans bills by stating that the issue against which he voted involved a ten-million-dollar appropriation item which the Veterans Administration said it could not use.[39] Murray continued to emphasize the "no votes" by D'Ewart, doubtlessly assuming that some veterans would conclude that a congressman who voted "no" on any veterans legislation opposed their interests.

The impending vote in the Senate on the censure of Senator McCarthy evoked lively debate. Republican State Chairman MacKay asked whether "the people of Montana don't have as much right as the people of Ohio to know how their Senator is going to vote on the McCarthy censure."[40] Murray responded that he would "vote my conscience" on the issue.[41] In mid-October the issue was still alive. Speaking in Butte, D'Ewart said:

> All Montanans have the right to know how my election opponent, Sen. Murray, intends to cast his ballot on the committee recommendation that the Senate censure Sen. McCarthy.
> I personally have never criticized Sen. McCarthy. I would have no vote, of course, on the censure proposal, but I am wondering what Sen. Murray plans to do—how he plans to vote.[42]

Murray answered D'Ewart's query by inviting D'Ewart to "tell us how he would vote if he were a Senator" on the censure question.[43] Murray concluded:

> As for myself, I think it is completely un-American and subversive of American ideas

of justice and decency for anyone to judge a fellow until he has heard the accused confronted by those who would indict him and until the accused has had an opportunity to present his defense.

 . . . I shall listen to the presentation of the charges against the Senator from Wisconsin and I shall listen to his defense, then I shall vote my conscience. . . .[44]

The speeches of Murray and D'Ewart were reported in the press. Only a part of a political campaign, however, can be viewed from the perspective of the candidate's formal speechmaking. Other factors inevitably intrude, some of which are beyond the control of either candidate. It is the interplay of an endless, and almost incalculable, array of factors which frustrates all efforts to reduce the art of political campaigning to an exact science. The tangled web of a political campaign is woven from the interaction of candidates and other personalities, party organizations, powerful interest groups, the press, religion, economic conditions, and cultural and historical factors. To place the activities of the candidates in perspective, some of these factors are explored below.

The role of religion in the campaign, obscured by the passage of time, was probably minimal. Murray was a Catholic and D'Ewart was a Protestant. Montana's population is so well balanced between religious and ethnic groups, however, that neither religion nor race has been a powerful factor in any campaign. Both Democrats and Republicans who were interviewed with regard to the role of the Catholic church were emphatic in their assertions that it remained strictly neutral throughout the campaign. The D'Ewart organization included a number of Catholics in positions of responsibility, while some top officials in the Democratic organization were Protestant. It is possible, although there is no evidence to prove it, that Catholics in both parties who had planned to vote for D'Ewart switched to Murray at the last moment because of the charges associating Murray with communism that were leveled at him in the closing weeks of the campaign.

Religion contributed indirectly to D'Ewart's defeat in that Democrats circulated among Catholics copies of the so-called "Ole Fallan letter." The letter had been employed originally by some of D'Ewart's Masonic friends in Wilsall, including a close associate, Ole Fallan, in an earlier D'Ewart campaign for Congress against a Catholic Democratic opponent, John J. Holmes. In part the letter stated: "John Holmes is a product of Southern Ireland and has never had any experience in public affairs, a yes man. . . . And DON'T let the Catholics have another voice in Washington."[45] Among Catholics in 1954, the letter was regarded as having had D'Ewart's knowledge and approval when first used. A separate sheet distributed with the letter explained that Fallan and D'Ewart were neighbors and political associates. The Republican national committeeman, Wellington D. Rankin, asserts that "the thing that beat him was this and the 'Red Web.' At least 20,000 copies of this letter were sent out by Democrats."[46]

The press played a minor, albeit indeterminate, role in the campaign. Murray enjoyed the editorial support of six newspapers, of which two, the *Great Falls Tribune* and the *Dillon Tribune*, were dailies. D'Ewart fared better with press editorial support, as his candidacy was endorsed by eleven papers, of which three, the *Daily Inter Lake* (Kalispell), the *Miles City Star*, and the *Havre Daily News*, were dailies.[47] The "Company Press," a group of leading daily newspapers in Montana having approximately one-half of the daily circulation in the state and controlled through a subsidiary by the Anaconda Company, remained editorially silent. Apparently the Anaconda-controlled papers gave equal coverage to both candidates, although the D'Ewart organization, in the early phases of the campaign, complained about the unfair treatment they were getting in the news columns.[48]

Montana's two corporate giants, the Anaconda Company and the Montana Power Company, are deeply and perennially involved in Montana politics. With a well-earned reputation for concerted action in earlier years, the so-called "Twins" of Montana politics were, by 1954, drifting into separate courses. Neither corporation publicizes its political choices for obvious reasons. Both have long served as convenient "whipping boys" of Montana politics. Anaconda was generally regarded as being sympathetic to the reelection of Murray, despite his liberal views. Top leaders in the firm were personally close to Murray. Although most Montanans were probably unaware of it, the chief Washington lobbyist for A.C.M. was frequently Senator Murray's chauffeur in Washington. Although Anaconda representatives had offered some encouragement to D'Ewart prior to the beginning of the campaign, neither he nor his organization expected or received more than perfunctory support from Anaconda. A different story can be told with respect to the Montana Power Company, which sided with D'Ewart. Gilbert LeKander, D'Ewart's administrative assistant, described the utility's position in these words: "Montana Power employees probably were in our corner. They should have been. Murray tried to put them out of work."[49]

A record number of out-of-state political speakers toured Montana in 1954. Both candidates drew heavily on out-of-state support, wherever available. An imposing array of Republican talent, topped by President Eisenhower who spoke at Missoula September twenty-second in connection with the dedication of a Forest Service installation, came to Montana in behalf of Wesley D'Ewart. Others included: Vice-President Nixon, Secretary of Agriculture Benson, Senators Barrett, Bennett, Carlson, Dirksen, and Payne, and Congressmen Martin (the Speaker) and Phillips. Senator Joe McCarthy sent a letter endorsing D'Ewart, stating: "His strong opposition to Communism and his high type of Americanism would act as a great strengthening force in the . . . Senate. . . . It would be a great victory for real Americans and for anti-Communists if Wes D'Ewart is elected."[50] Principal out-of-state speakers for Senator Murray included former Secretary of Agriculture Brannan; former Commissioner of Reclamation Michael Strauss; Senators Gore, Johnson, and Morse; and Congressmen Cooley and Kirwan. Murray received communications from Senators Clements, Humphrey, and Sparkman in support of his candidacy.

Far more indefatigable in their efforts in behalf of the two candidates were Montana's own political leaders. Governor Hugo Aronson and his fellow Republican and the former governor, Sam Ford, worked extensively for D'Ewart. He also received the endorsement, in a statewide radio address, of former Democratic United States Senator Burton K. Wheeler. A bitter foe of Murray's, Wheeler's intense personal animosity toward Murray detracted from the effectiveness of his endorsement of D'Ewart. Attorney General Olsen campaigned for Murray. The most significant support Murray received, however, came from his junior colleague in the Senate, Mike Mansfield, who literally covered the state from one end to the other in behalf of Murray. Mansfield, who in 1954 was nearing the pinnacle of bipartisan support he now enjoys, worked mightily to transfer his enormous popularity as a moderate to a more liberal colleague. One leading Montana Democrat feels that Mansfield's energetic support was the decisive factor accounting for Murray's victory.

As the campaign neared the final weeks it had become evident that Congressman D'Ewart would have an uphill fight to unseat Senator Murray. Writing from Billings, William S. White reported in mid-October that "persons high in this campaign concede in private that only on the so-called 'Red issue' which has not thus far been visibly important in this state could Senator Murray possibly be beaten by the Republican aspirant. . . ."[51]

The Communists-in-government issue had been simmering for some time in the 1954 national campaign. Senator McCarthy was largely silenced as a result of the investigation of charges against him by the special Senate committee, but others in the Republican party were still raising the Communist issue. Vice-President Nixon had repeatedly stated that the administration was "kicking the Communists and the fellow travelers and the security risks out of the government not by the hundreds but by the thousands."[52] As the campaign was nearing its close, Senator Lyndon Johnson voiced concern that Republicans in Washington, Montana, and Wyoming were planning "one of the worst smear campaigns in history."[53]

During the last two weeks of the campaign, the Republican high command decided to introduce "dynamiting" tactics in a final effort to prevent Murray's reelection. The publication of a sensational booklet entitled *Senator Murray and the Red Web over Congress* injected into the campaign the charge that Murray, if not an actual Communist himself, was tainted with the Communist conspiracy in the United States. The booklet was of sufficient importance to require detailed analysis.

Montanans, accustomed as they were to unorthodox campaign methods, nevertheless were jolted by the appearance of this publication on October 15, 1954. It was modeled after a similar booklet which had been used by Senator Smathers in his campaign against Senator Pepper in Florida in 1950.[54] *Senator Murray and the Red Web over Congress* was produced by a photo-offset process. It consisted of 24 pages, 10 3/4 inches long by 8 1/4 inches wide. The inside pages were entirely in black and white, but the front and back covers used red abundantly to emphasize the significance of the Communist issue. On the front cover, below the title, was a picture of the capitol of the United States, over which was spread in net-like fashion a red web; crawling over it was a large, red spider, with a hammer and sickle emblem on its back. At the bottom of the page was printed in black on red "THE STORY OF COMMUNIST IN-FILTRATION OF YOUR U.S. CONGRESS FROM OFFICIAL RECORDS AND COMMUNIST DOCUMENTS."

Inside the front cover appeared the statement: "This record is based on carefully verified records and documents, available for inspection in the Senate Internal Security Subcommittee, the House Committee on Un-American Activities, the Congressional Record, and the Library of Congress." A price of fifty cents was shown and it was stated that the booklet was compiled and published by a Montana for D'Ewart Committee. Two names were listed, those of Ralph Studer of Billings, as chairman, and H. T. Porter of Bozeman, as secretary-treasurer.

Pages three through ten attempted to exploit the fact that a number of Senator Murray's committee employees had been associated with Communists or Communist-front organizations. It was asserted that this information had been gleaned from the hearings of the Senate Internal Security Subcommittee on interlocking subversion in government departments. The pamphlet stated:

> Nine persons formerly employed on Congressional committee staffs have been questioned concerning affiliations with the Communist party and rather than reply have claimed their privilege against self-incrimination under the Fifth Amendment of the Constitution.
>
> Six of the nine were employed on committees of which Senator James E. Murray was chairman or ranking Democrat member. Several were members of organizations with which Senator Murray has been identified and which have been designated as Communist or Communist front organizations by the Attorney General and Congressional or legislative committees.[55]

On pages four and five the booklet dealt with the relationship between Senator Murray and Henry H. Collins, Jr. Portions of three documents, reproduced by photo-offset, established that the material was taken from the report of the Senate Subcommittee to investigate the administration of the Internal Security Act. A letter, dated April 2, 1941, from Senator Murray to Colonel Philip B. Fleming, an administrator in the Department of Labor, expressed Murray's interest in obtaining the loan of Henry Collins for use on the special committee to study problems of American small business.

> According to Whittaker Chambers, Collins was a member of the Communist General Staff, in government and treasurer of the "Ware Group" a Communist cell within the government. . . . Collins has declined to answer, claiming his privilege of self-incrimination under the Fifth Amendment of the Constitution.
> This is the man whom Senator Murray as chairman selected to direct the study of American Small Business.[56]

A similar treatment was accorded, on pages six and seven of the publication, to the relationships between Senator Murray and Harry Magdoff, who was also a member of Murray's staff on the select committee on small business. Photo-offset reproductions of portions of correspondence from Henry Wallace, the secretary of commerce, to Senator Murray in April 1945 indicated that at Murray's request Magdoff was being made available as a consultant to the Murray committee. Testimony which disclosed that Magdoff had declined, under the Fifth Amendment, to state whether or not he was a member of the Communist party, was reproduced. Alfred J. Van Tassell, who became a member of the Murray Small Business Committee on loan from the War Production Board, like Magdoff, refused to answer questions regarding his relations with communism.

On page eight a full-page photograph of Charles Kramer, a former employee of Senator Murray's committee who later was named by Elizabeth Bentley as a member of a spy ring, was reproduced. As a member of the Senate Committee on Labor and Public Welfare, of which Senator Murray was at one time the ranking Democrat, Kramer was responsible for developing

> federal health programs modeled on the "cradle to grave" program of the British Socialist Party. . . . Senator Murray's compulsory health insurance, the "socialized medicine bill" was one of these.
> Charles Kramer has consistently refused to answer questions concerning Communist affiliation. . . .[57]

Reference was also made to two other "Fifth Amendment witnesses" who served on the Committee on Labor and Public Welfare. They were Mrs. Margaret Bennett Porter and Charles S. Flato, both of whom refused to answer questions regarding their Communist connections. At the top of page eleven was the caption, "Murray and Pepper," beneath which was the comment that Senator Murray and Senator Claude Pepper had "a long and close association."

Reproductions of statements made by J. Edgar Hoover, director of the Federal Bureau of Investigation, with respect to the "menace of communism" appeared on page twelve. The caption at the top of the page read, "Identifying

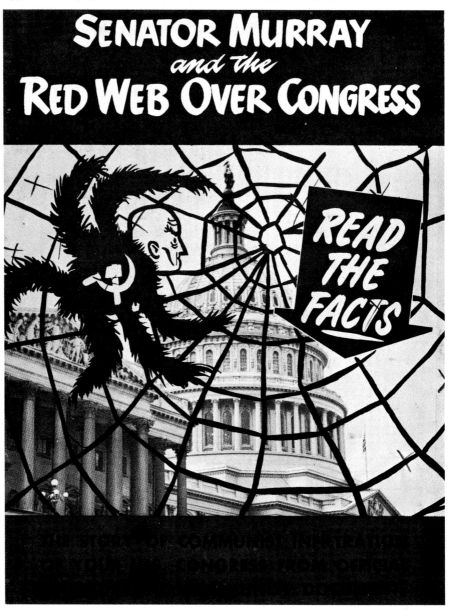

The employment of Collins, Kramer, Magdoff, Porter, Van Tassel and Flato, six of the nine "Fifth Amendment witnesses" discovered on Congressional Committees, tells only part of the story.

The official files, records and publications of the Committee on Un-American Activities of the House of Representatives in Washington, D. C., show that Senator James E. Murray has been identified by membership, sponsorship or association with thirteen (13) Communist front organizations, all of which have been designated or cited as Communist or Communist front organizations by the Attorney General of the United States, Congressional or legislative committees, or both. They are:

1. American Slav Congress.
2. National Council of American-Soviet Friendship.
3. Russian War Relief, Inc.
4. Washington Tom Mooney Committee.
5. Greater New York Conference on Inalienable Rights.
6. Abraham Lincoln School of Chicago.
7. National Lawyers Guild.
8. International Workers Order.
9. American Youth Congress.
10. Conference on Constitutional Liberties in America.
11. National Federation for Constitutional Liberties.
12. Washington Committee for Democratic Action.
13. American Committee for Yugoslav Relief.

Fellow-Travelers." Hoover's article listed some of the criteria by which a Communist-front organization might be identified. The remainder of the booklet, beginning with page thirteen, was devoted to "Senator Murray's Red Record." Thirteen organizations, to which Senator Murray had been related either as member, sponsor, or speaker, and which later were cited as Communist or Communist front, were named. The organizations listed were: American Slav Congress, National Council of American-Soviet Friendship, Russian War

Relief, Inc., Washington Tom Mooney Committee, Greater New York Conference on Inalienable Rights, Abraham Lincoln School of Chicago, National Lawyers Guild, International Workers Order, American Youth Congress, Conference on Constitutional Liberties in America, National Federation for Constitutional Liberties, Washington Committee for Democratic Action, and American Committee for Yugoslav Relief.

Materials showing how Senator Murray was related to each of the Communist-connected organizations were introduced (pp. 14-19). One item, for example, bore the caption, "Murray Addresses Red Rally." The *Chicago Daily Tribune* for December 2, 1943, carried a report of Murray's appearance before the Abraham Lincoln School in Chicago. To the right was photographed a 1953 congressional committee report entitled "Guide to Subversive Organizations and Publications" which contained the information that the Abraham Lincoln School had been cited as an adjunct of the Communist party by the attorney general in 1947, by the Committee on Un-American Activities in 1944, and by the California Committee on Un-American Acitivities in 1948. On page nineteen it was stated that "Senator Murray was an early backer of Marshall Tito, as shown in this *New York Times* report of February, 1945, before Tito broke with the Soviets." To the left of this statement were photographs of clippings from the *New York Times* noting Senator Murray's remarks praising Tito as a " 'great leader.' " On page twenty of this booklet, Senator Murray's relationship with the Committee of Catholics for Human Rights (honorary national chairman) was discussed. Material indicated that the Committee had been exposed as a Communist-front organization. On page twenty-one appeared a photograph of the Russian publication, the *Soviet News*, with the caption, "The Only Senator Who Regularly Receives a Communist Newspaper from Overseas." There was also a photograph of a mailing label showing Murray's name as the recipient of the *Soviet News*. Material concerning the publication, *Soviet Russia Today* (pp. 22-23), pointed out that Senator Murray had contributed two articles. Photo reproductions of parts of the two articles, one entitled "A Quarter Century of Progress" and the other "Tribute to Lenin," appeared side by side. The latter was also produced as a separate publication and circulated in Montana during the campaign.

A red-colored reproduction of the masthead of the *Daily Worker* for January 2, 1947, with a banner headline, "Murray Calls for Labor, Progressives to Unite," graced the back cover. Part of a column, reproduced from that issue, contained the statement, "The heroes of the 80th Congress are few. They include a dozen senators led by Pepper of Florida, Taylor of Idaho and Murray of Montana." The remainder of the back page carried this final comment:

In this manner and for these reasons, the Communist Party from coast to coast has looked with favor on Senator James E. Murray. . . .

You have read the record. You have seen the evidence. Apply the tests outlined by J. Edgar Hoover on page 12. Determine for yourself whether Senator James E. Murray has truly and faithfully represented the patriotic citizens of Montana. Determine for yourself whether Senator James E. Murray has represented YOU in these matters.

How the booklet, *Senator Murray and the Red Web over Congress*, came to be produced, how it was distributed, and what effect it had on the campaign are questions deserving careful consideration. Gilbert LeKander, D'Ewart's administrative assistant, commented that "very little additional research was needed to adapt the anti-Pepper booklet used by Smathers in Florida to the Murray campaign.[58] During the summer and early fall of 1953, members of D'Ewart's staff had gathered material for use in the campaign. Much of the material related to Murray's alleged connections with communism. The booklet took shape gradually in mimeographed form and was available for production before the beginning of the campaign.

At a meeting of an inner circle of political friends and supporters of D'Ewart, which was held in Helena shortly after the primary, the possibility of using the booklet in the ensuing campaign was discussed. Apparently no one spoke then in opposition to the proposal. However, one important D'Ewart supporter, Ralph Bricker of Great Falls, opposed the use of the booklet and later refused to have anything to do with its circulation.[59] One other person who was present at the Helena meeting where the booklet was discussed later privately expressed his regret for not having had the courage to speak out against it at the meeting.

The technical production of the booklet presented some problems. The cover received considerable thought. The artist employed to design the cover created in the original drawing a likeness of Senator Murray enmeshed in the red web over the capitol building. Murray's picture was later deleted at the insistence of Albert Schlaht, the campaign manager, and William McKay, chairman of the Republican State Central Committee. Even toned down, the cover was the most flamboyant and controversial aspect of the booklet. Virtually every Republican closely associated with the campaign subsequently expressed a dislike for the cover.

Forty thousand copies of *Senator Murray and the Red Web over Congress* were printed in Montana. The publication cost approximately eight thousand dollars.[60] Production costs were financed outside of regular Republican organization funds. Where the money came from to pay the cost of publication remains a mystery. No reliable information is available. Frequent Democratic charges that the booklet was financed by Texas oil millionaires or other outside forces have received wide currency, but lack documentation. H. T. Porter of Bozeman, the secretary-treasurer of the committee which produced the publication, is no longer living. The man closest to the campaign, Albert Schlaht, probably reflected the sentiment of other Republicans when he remarked that there were a lot of things that "I didn't want to know about."[61]

Republicans who were interviewed in connection with the publication frequently pointed out that it was documented. D'Ewart and Schlaht detailed the care with which the documentation was checked by separate researchers. The material was thoroughly checked for libel by several able attorneys.[62] The fact that no libel action has been brought may be a source of comfort to its Republican sponsors. At any rate, Republicans repeatedly emphasized that nothing was included in the publication which was not a part of the official public record.

Who wrote *Senator Murray and the Red Web over Congress*? The publication contains only the statement that it was "Compiled and Published by Montana for D'Ewart Committee." Ralph Studer of Billings, who was listed as chairman of the committee, had been known for years as a self-advertised foe of communism. For years he had placed display ads opposing communism in the *Billings Gazette*. Studer was quite willing to allow the use of his name as head of the organization sponsoring the booklet.[63]

The distribution of the *Red Web* was delayed as long as possible. Republican strategy was to use it only as a last resort. It was released about October fifteenth, in time for use during the final two weeks of the campaign. It was made available to regular Republican organizations as an optional item. Some county organizations expressly opposed its distribution and some Republican workers reported strong adverse reactions to its use among fellow Republicans. Its biggest distribution was concentrated in three urban counties in western Montana—Flathead, Silver Bow, and Missoula. The booklet was distributed in the working-class areas of Great Falls, but its distribution elsewhere outside of urban areas was limited. Matt Himsl, the chairman of the Flathead County Republican Central Committee, recalls its door-to-door distribution in Kalispell.[64]

The publication of *Senator Murray and the Red Web over Congress* produced an immediate and devastating impact. No campaign material used in Montana since the end of World War II has created a greater sensation. Its precise effect on political attitudes and behavior is difficult to assess, but apparently was two-way in character. Some working-class Democrats were attracted to D'Ewart as a result of the publication. On the other hand, many moderate Republicans and independents were offended. Democrats who had been tiring of Murray because of his growing senility were alienated.[65] Some Republican workers refused to have anything to do with the publication. The "Company Press" ignored it in its news and editorial columns. Only four weekly newspapers commented on the booklet.[66]

Democrats responded vehemently to the publication of *Senator Murray and the Red Web over Congress*, expressing not only their outrage but also the feeling that a violation of campaign fair play of serious proportions had occurred. The response came from Democratic leaders other than Murray, who said little regarding the pamphlet. Near the end of the campaign, Murray made one public reference to it saying: "False and vicious propaganda has been imported into the state to brand some candidates for high office as Reds, left-wingers, Communists, sympathizers, and fellow travelers."[67]

The attack the Murray organization and other Democrats aimed at the *Red Web* took four main forms. One tactic which greatly irritated Republicans was the use of a large advertisement, placed in leading newspapers, containing personally autographed pictures for Senator Murray of three presidents of the United States—Franklin D. Roosevelt, Harry S. Truman, and Dwight Eisenhower. President Eisenhower had written on his picture: "For Senator James E. Murray with best wishes to a distinguished American, Dwight Eisenhower." The advertisement stated that "Big Jim" Murray cosponsored the bill (now law) to outlaw the Communist party in America and deserved the confidence and support of the voters in his bid for reelection.[68] Republicans charged that the president had not intended his picture as an endorsement. President Eisenhower seized the occasion to write expressing his unqualified support for D'Ewart's candidacy. Nevertheless, the advertisement undoubtedly had an effect upon some Montana voters, who must have wondered how a man whom President Eisenhower called a distinguished American could be tainted with communism.

The comments of Democratic leaders in Montana with respect to the publication were scorching. The chairman of the Democratic State Central Committee, Jack Toole, said: "Republicans are now issuing smear pamphlets and booklets that reach a new low in American political campaigns."[69] Speaking in behalf of Murray's candidacy, his junior colleague, Senator Mike Mansfield, said that it was "a shocking fact that politics has sunk to a new low in the campaign, not only in Montana but in other states."[70] Arnold Olsen, the attorney general of Montana, asserted that "Montanans are disgusted with this campaign of sneak and smear that is being waged by the Republicans."[71] Leo Graybill, the Democratic national committeeman of Montana, speaking to Cascade County Democrats in Great Falls, stated that the new Republican tactic was a "diabolic approach to Americanism and a reflection on the American way of life. . . . They know they cannot beat Murray on the issues and they know Murray has no Red tinge."[72]

Murray's Democratic colleagues in Congress reacted with equal promptness. Senator Hubert Humphrey of Minnesota wired D'Ewart:

> Shocked to learn from press that your agents are trying to depict Montana's great and patriotic Sen. Jim Murray as pro-Communist. . . . I want to tell you and the people of Montana that Senator Murray co-sponsored my bill to outlaw the Communist Party as part of an international conspiracy. While others talked about it, Jim Murray did something about the Communist menace.[73]

Writing to Democratic State Central Committee Chairman Jack Toole, Senators Clements of Kentucky and Sparkman of Alabama praised the "sturdy patriotism and fine Americanism of Jim Murray" and denounced "his detractors for such gutter tactics. . . . "[74] The Democratic Senate minority leader, Lyndon Johnson, telegraphed Toole regarding Murray: "I am confident that the people of Montana will resent and reject the incredible campaign now underway to portray Murray as a left-winger. I have served with Murray for many years and I know him to be a patriotic American. . . ."[75] And a Democratic House minority leader, John McCormack, was reported as stating that Murray "has been years ahead in the fight on Communism, not only in America but throughout the world. He said that he was amazed at the 'contemptible attempts to smear Murray.' "[76]

A final facet of the response of the Murray organization to the Republican charges was explained by Joseph J. McCaffery, Murray's manager. This strategy was to make use of local centers of influence throughout Montana. In this sparsely populated state, its centers of influence in the persons of attorneys and business community leaders in both parties can be reached quickly. Through such a network of influence, the Murray forces were able quickly to counteract the *Red Web* and appeal to the fair play instinct of opinion leaders throughout Montana.[77]

In evaluating *Senator Murray and the Red Web over Congress*, the question may be asked: how effective was the publication? About as many Republicans who were interviewed felt that the publication was harmful as felt it was helpful to the candidacy of D'Ewart. Those who were closest to the D'Ewart campaign in 1954 and participated in the decision to use the pamphlet generally felt that the publication had been helpful. On the other hand, prominent D'Ewart supporters who were not especially close to the campaign's management tended to view the publication as harmful to their candidate. By marked contrast, Democrats who were close to Murray's campaign felt that the publication was harmful, whereas those who were less closely involved felt that it actually helped Murray's candidacy.

Was the publication within the bounds of accepted political morality? D'Ewart, his administrative assistant LeKander, his campaign manager Schlaht, and members of the D'Ewart staff answered "yes." Feelings among other Republicans were mixed. Democrats uniformly took the position that the publication was beyond the bounds of accepted political morality and that Democrats never resorted to such tactics. Wesley D'Ewart summed up the attitude of the Republicans who supported the publication of the *Red Web* on ethical grounds when he said, "When a man's record is so bad that a truthful discussion is labeled a smear, the time has come to remove him from office."[78]

The effect of the pamphlet upon the career of Wesley D'Ewart did not end with the campaign. When D'Ewart was nominated by President Eisenhower to be an assistant secretary of the Department of the Interior, hearings were held before the Committee on Interior and Insular Affairs of the Senate. Senator Murray was chairman of the committee. At these hearings held on July 11 and 13, 1956, D'Ewart was asked about his connection with the "smear campaign" against Senator Murray in 1954. Some sections of the testimony are pertinent.

Senator Anderson. You do recognize that the campaign in its close was based almost entirely on the claims that Senator Murray was a Communist sympathizer?

Mr. D'Ewart. Not on my part.

Senator Anderson. That was not my question. I asked you if you recognized that the campaign toward its close was based entirely on claims that Senator Murray was a Communist sympathizer.

Mr. D'Ewart. That kind of material was used in the campaign, but I personally did not use it.

Senator Anderson. What did you do about it when it came to your attention?

Mr. D'Ewart. I did not do anything about it. It was not my organization. I did not contribute to those radio broadcasts or television shows. We did not take part in them. They were not sponsored by me or by my organization. . . .

Senator Anderson. When did you see this "Senator Murray and the Red Web over Congress"? In October, September, or earlier?

Mr. D'Ewart. I think it was in October. It was late in the year.

Senator Anderson. What did you do when you saw that?

Mr. D'Ewart. I did nothing, sir.

Senator Anderson. Did you read it through?

Mr. D'Ewart. Yes. It was called to my attention. I saw it. . . .

Senator O'Mahoney. Did you, yourself, believe in any of these things that were said about Senator Murray, that they were true?

Mr. D'Ewart. I have not examined them as to the truth, sir. . . .

Senator O'Mahoney. The implication was that Senator Murray was associated with the Communists. Do you wish the committee to understand that you now think he might have been.

Mr. D'Ewart. Absolutely not.

Senator O'Mahoney. Do you repudiate this sort of attack?

Mr. D'Ewart. I had no part to do with it, sir, and would not use it in any campaign. If you mean by that would I personally use it, I would say "No, I would not."

Senator O'Mahoney. Well, would you accept the benefit of it?

Mr. D'Ewart. Well, I would rather not. Let's put it that way.

Senator O'Mahoney. You would rather not. But if it should happen to come your way, you would take it?

Mr. D'Ewart. Well, it is pretty hard to control all the things that happen in a campaign. . . .

Mr. D'Ewart. And I also disavow any connection with this publication.

Senator O'Mahoney. But you took the benefits of it, sir. You did not disavow it while it was being circulated, and you knew it was being circulated.

Mr. D'Ewart. You are correct.[79]

That *Senator Murray and the Red Web over Congress* was "documented" is beyond question. Nevertheless, the booklet is open to serious criticism on three specific counts: the camouflaged responsibility surrounding its publication; the contents; and the misleading cover. Those who produced the pamphlet evaded responsibility for its publication by using a "front organization." It is, therefore, difficult to assign responsibility, but the publication would not have been used without some understanding on the part of the D'Ewart organization. In interviewing various persons associated with the 1954 Republican campaign, it was impossible to find agreement on how the publication actually was put together. Each person had a different version of what had happened, highlighting the difficulty of assigning responsibility. The refusal of key participants in the campaign to answer questions concerning the cost of publication, the place of publication, the name of the printer, and how the booklet was financed implies at least that there was something to conceal. Answers may be forthcoming later, but obviously we are much too close to the event to have access to the whole story.

The publication may be criticized with respect to content. While it purports to be a documented exposé of Red infiltration into Congress, implicating Senator Murray, the case rests heavily upon highly circumstantial evidence. The persons who later were unwilling to testify on charges that they were Communists were not being labeled as Communists at the time that Murray was associated with them. Alleged Communist connections came to light a number of years after the men in question had been associated with Murray. Moreover, Murray's associations with the Soviet Union and with so-called "Communist-front" organizations occurred before those organizations were so labeled and while the United States and the Soviet Union were allies in World War II. It seems unwarranted to infer from such activities and associations, however zealously pursued and ill advised, that Murray was a Communist or an abettor of the Communist conspiracy.

Finally, the cover on *Senator Murray and the Red Web over Congress* was entirely unwarranted. Nothing within the publication could justify the extreme statements made on the cover, including the innuendo that Murray was himself a Communist or Communist sympathizer. This must have been the conclusion that the sponsors of the publication expected readers to draw. The contents simply were incorrectly labeled, but the great bulk of those who saw the publication probably never examined the contents closely.

Another spectacular instance of political dynamiting which occurred in the 1954 campaign involved the activities of one Martin Littleton who came to Montana and made a number of telecasts and broadcasts from Billings. A New York attorney by background, Littleton had lived in Wyoming and was an attorney for ranching interests there. About three weeks before the election he was induced by some ultraconservative Republicans in the Billings and Bozeman areas to come to Montana and make three or four television addresses which were broadcast statewide from Billings. Littleton depicted himself as a Wyoming rancher. He insisted that James E. Murray was, if not an out-and-out Communist, certainly a fellow traveler. Much Republican pressure was brought to get the Littleton programs canceled in Billings but without success. Littleton's broadcasts boomeranged and, at the very least, cost D'Ewart some labor votes in the Billings area.[80]

A piece of campaign literature which was distributed throughout Montana was a mimeographed publication entitled "Red Record and Communist-Front Associations of James E. Murray." This also was published verbatim as a full-page advertisement in a weekly newspaper, the *Poplar Standard* of Roosevelt County, over the signature of the Roosevelt County Republican Central Committee.[81] Murray's "Tribute to Lenin" was printed as a separate leaflet and used extensively.

In retrospect, the Montana Senate election campaign of 1954 retains a fascinating hold upon the observer. The outcome of this close, hard-fought struggle remained in doubt for some time after the returns began to come in on election night. Finally, as the returns came in numbers sufficient for analysis, it became evident that a classic pattern in Montana politics had reasserted itself. Murray had won by the narrow margin of 1,728 votes, receiving a total of 114,591 votes to 112,863 which were cast for D'Ewart. The forecasts had predicted a Murray victory, but no one had expected the vote to be quite so close.

In winning the Senate seat he had held for twenty years, Murray carried most of the wheat counties along the Canadian border, adding the mining counties, and the lumber counties. D'Ewart carried the livestock counties south of the Missouri River as well as the irrigated farming counties of western Montana.

Murray carried twenty-three counties to thirty-three carried by D'Ewart. An urban-rural cleavage was not apparent. D'Ewart carried 59.2 percent of the counties with more than 40 percent of the population *rural-farm*. He carried 58.8 percent of the counties with more than 40 percent of the population *urban*. He carried 56.2 percent of the counties with more than 40 percent of the population *rural-nonfarm*. Hence D'Ewart's appeal was equally strong to all segments of the population spectrum. Where Murray had the decided advantage was in Silver Bow and Deer Lodge counties, both of which he carried by two-to-one margins, thus obtaining here an eight-thousand-vote lead which was enough to withstand the strength D'Ewart generated in other areas of the state.

No single factor may be isolated as the definitive cause of Murray's victory. His organization, carefully nurtured with patronage through the years, his incumbency, his seniority, his partisan affiliation in a state that has elected but one Republican to the Senate, plus the sensitivity of Montana to the 1954 national trend toward Democrats—all of these were of some significance. In explaining D'Ewart's defeat other factors may be added: some divisiveness in Republican ranks, notably the coolness of Rankin, the strong swing of the winter wheat farmers away from D'Ewart, and D'Ewart's lack of political "color."

As long as the 1954 election is remembered, however, the most vivid recollections will center around the publication, distribution, and impact of *Senator Murray and the Red Web over Congress*. The place of this missile in political history is assured. It is unforgettable as an example of political dynamiting. However, given the sparse population of Montana and its political tradition of personalism in politics, such a tactic could not be employed effectively along the lines developed in eastern, urban areas. The *Red Web* was poorly timed in appearance. It was too overwhelming an indictment of Senator Murray to be plausible. It evoked distaste among both Republicans and Democrats. A powerful but poorly conceived and poorly designed instrument, it backfired. Had the *Red Web* never appeared, Wesley D'Ewart might well have won the Senate election of 1954.

NOTES

1. As 1954 dawned, Senate seats were distributed as follows: forty-eight Democrats, forty-seven Republicans, and one Independent.

2. Between 1916 and 1954, Democrats had defeated Republicans in thirteen Senate con-

tests. This record of success has been preserved since 1954 in spite of substantial Republican challenges.

3. *Great Falls Tribune*, September 11, 1954, p. 5.

4. Frank H. Jonas, "The Art of Political Dynamiting," *Western Political Quarterly*, 10 (June 1957), 379.

5. Matusow swore in an affidavit filed in January 1955 that he had lied before Congressional committees and courts regarding Communist charges he made earlier.

6. Murray and D'Ewart were nominated in their respective primaries on July 20, 1954, winning over token opposition. Murray's plurality over his closest opponent was 60,935, and D'Ewart won over his nearest rival by a margin of 39,258.

7. Walsh, however, died en route to Washington before his Cabinet service could begin.

8. Interview with Wesley A. D'Ewart, September 18, 1963.

9. H.R. 4023, 83rd Congress, 1st Session.

10. Records from the office of the secretary of state, Helena, Montana.

11. *Ibid.*

12. Interview with D'Ewart, September 18, 1963.

13. *Ibid.*

14. *People's Voice*, August 20, 1954.

15. *Great Falls Tribune*, May 6, 1954, p. 5.

16. *Ibid.*, June 9, 1954, p. 6.

17. *People's Voice*, September 3, 1954.

18. Interview with D'Ewart, September 18, 1963.

19. *Great Falls Tribune*, August 23, 1954, p. 1.

20. *Ibid.*, September 18, 1954, p. 12.

21. *Ibid.*, October 7, 1954, p. 5.

22. *Ibid.*, October 8, 1954, p. 5.

23. *Ibid.*, October 19, 1954, p. 5.

24. *Ibid.*, October 7, 1954, p. 5.

25. *Ibid.*, October 19, 1954, p. 9.

26. *Ibid.*, October 13, 1954, p. 4.

27. *Ibid.*, October 12, 1954, p. 5.

28. *Ibid.*, November 1, 1954, p. 5.

29. *Ibid.*, October 15, 1954, p. 16.

30. *Ibid.*, October 4, 1954, p. 1.

31. *Ibid.*, October 12, 1954, p. 6.

32. *Ibid.*, October 14, 1954, p. 1.

33. *Ibid.*, October 14, 1954, p. 1.

34. *Ibid.*, October 26, 1954, p. 5.

35. *Ibid.*, October 29, 1954, p. 5.

36. *Ibid.*, October 24, 1954, p. 5.

37. *Ibid.*, October 25, 1954, p. 4.

38. *Ibid.*, October 17, 1954, p. 4.

39. *Ibid.*, October 20, 1954, p. 2.

40. *Ibid.*, October 19, 1954, p. 5.

41. *Ibid.*, September 28, 1954, p. 1.

42. *Ibid.*, October 14, 1954, p. 4.

43. *Ibid.*, October 17, 1954, p. 4.

44. *Ibid.*

45. Letter circulated by Ole Fallan and others, Wilsall, Montana, (n.d.).

46. Interview with Wellington D. Rankin, October 31, 1963.

47. George Bousliman, "The 1954 Campaign of Senator James E. Murray" (M.A. thesis, Montana State University, Missoula, Montana), pp. 63-68.

48. Interview with D'Ewart, September 18, 1963.

49. Letter from Gilbert LeKander, October 30, 1963.

50. Quoted in *Great Falls Tribune*, October 27, 1954, p. 4.

51. *New York Times*, October 17, 1954.

52. *Great Falls Tribune*, October 3, 1954, p. 1.

53. *Ibid.*, October 18, 1954, p. 1.

54. Letter from LeKander, October 30, 1963.

55. *Senator Murray and the Red Web over Congress*, p. 3.

56. *Ibid.*, p. 5.

57. *Ibid.*, p. 9.

58. Letter from LeKander, October 30, 1963.

59. Interview with Ralph Bricker, October 15, 1963.

60. Interview with Albert A. Schlaht, September 18, 1963.

61. *Ibid.*

62. Interview with D'Ewart, September 18, 1963.

63. Interview with Schlaht, September 18, 1963.

64. Interview with Matt Himsl, October 25, 1963.

65. Interview with Mel Engles, chairman of the Republican State Central Committee, September 17, 1963.

66. Bousliman, "The 1954 Campaign of Senator James E. Murray," pp. 32-34.

67. *Great Falls Tribune*, October 29, 1954, p. 5.

68. Political advertisement in the *Missoulian* (Missoula, Montana), October 30, 1954.

69. *Great Falls Tribune*, October 26, 1954, p. 16.

70. *Ibid.*, October 27, 1954, p. 5.

71. *Ibid.*, October 26, 1954, p. 5.

72. *Ibid.*, October 20, 1954, p. 2.

73. *Ibid.*, October 21, 1954, p. 1.

74. *Ibid.*, October 26, 1954, p. 1.

75. *Ibid.*, October 29, 1954, p. 12.

76. *Ibid.*, October 27, 1954, p. 5.

77. Interview with Joseph J. McCaffery, September 18, 1963.

78. *Great Falls Tribune*, October 27, 1954, p. 4.

79. U. S. Congress, Senate, *Nomination of Wesley A. D'Ewart to be Assistant Secretary of the Interior*, hearings before the Committee on Interior and Insular Affairs, United States Senate, 84th Congress, 2nd Session, July 11 and 13, 1956 (Washington: Government Printing Office, 1956), pp. 6-9.

80. Interview with Al Himsl, February 5, 1964.

81. *Poplar Standard* (Poplar, Montana), October 8, 1954.

THE NEWSPAPER
AS A GIANT PUBLIC
RELATIONS FIRM
IN POLITICS

TWO personalities and two events appeared to dominate in interest in the senatorial campaign in the 1958 Arizona elections. The personalities were United States Senator Barry Goldwater and Stephen C. Shadegg, his campaign manager: the events, the Al Green exposé and the Stalin leaflet affair. Yet these were by no means the only events and the sole personalities which played significant roles in a political struggle characterized at best "by bitterness, deceit and personal attack."[1]

Over and above all the personalities and events in a political battle labeled the "bitterest" and by some observers the "dirtiest" in Arizona's history was the position of the Phoenix newspapers—sometimes called the Pulliam Press—the *Arizona Republic* and the *Phoenix Gazette*. Indeed, the brand of journalism sometimes displayed by these newspapers, especially in political campaigns, has been called "Pulliamism," in tribute to their owner and operator, Eugene Pulliam, a newspaper publisher from Indianapolis who took great pride in calling a spade a spade.

Shadegg claimed that he masterminded the whole campaign and that whatever came into it from Goldwater's camp had come out of "his own little head." Republicans and Democrats alike attributed to him able and astute management. He himself described his blueprint for the campaign:

> We had a single theme for the entire campaign from the beginning to end and we felt it was important to understand Barry as a forthright individual committed to opportunity rather than subsidy. There was a great deal of *loose talk* about one of the state labor boss' attempt to control Arizona politics, *but this was mainly authored by officials of the Republican Party in Arizona.* We knew in advance there would be some attempt by outsiders to influence the election, but I felt it would be harmful to cry "wolf" until we could name the wolf, describe him and *print his picture.* From the beginning I was fortunate to have available to me day to day reports from a *friend* who was close to the top labor organization in Arizona. Through this individual we were able to identify the "wolf," *secure his photograph*, discover that he had been in Arizona most of the time since March, and name him as Regional Director for C.O.P.E. [Committee on Political Education]. When we printed his picture we showed him coming out of a restaurant after a luncheon conference with the state Democratic chairman.[2]

The "friend" in the enemy's ranks was George F. Fowler. The "wolf" Shadegg fingered was Al Green.

The *Arizona Republic* played the major part and almost an exclusive role in making public the identity of Al Green and in exposing his past record and current activities to its readers, who, incidentally, were also voters in large numbers. The investigation that was done on Al Green falls accurately into the category of political research, or political dynamiting as Walter Quigley would define it.

While this investigation was being planned, the primary elections took the spotlight. The newspapers directed that spotlight from the very beginning, taking an active part in the several bitter Democratic primaries. The *Republic* encouraged Stephen W. Langmade, national Democratic committeeman, against Governor Ernest McFarland, contestants for the senatorial nomination, and Dick Searles against Robert Morrison, gubernatorial aspirants. In one issue this newspaper ran the following three-column head at the top of its front page: "Town Bully Cries Wolf, GOP Chief Accuses Walton of Covering Up for COPE." Below, a two-column head read: "Demo Chieftain [Langmade] Regrets Muscle-in by COPE." This was accompanied by: "Paul Fannin Charges Demos Use State-Paid Staffs in Campaigns."[3] This type of reporting by the *Republic* was typical of its treatment of candidates throughout the campaign.

The "bully" in this case was Joe Walton, state Democratic chairman, who had made a mild attack on Gene Pulliam, the publisher of the *Arizona Republic*, accusing him of destroying the two-party system in Arizona. Actually Walton was a mild-mannered man who suddenly in print became the "town bully." Walton was accused of "flippantly dismissing his close association with an out-of-state COPE hatchetman" and of imposing "his will upon the members of his party." Moreover, he was accused of purging "life-long Democrats who have refused to accept COPE dictation," and of compelling state legislators to sign loyalty oaths promising "to jump like puppets on a string at his command." As for Langmade, Democratic national committeeman, he played Goldwater's game, reinforcing the Republican anti-COPE theme with telling blows.

Langmade hit McFarland hard as his opponent in the primary, charging that McFarland worked very closely with labor and had made several "secret deals" with organized labor. Voters are attracted by the word "secret," and will react negatively to its use.

Insinuations from other than official Republican sources were quite prevalent at this stage of the primary campaign that McFarland had entered the Senate as a poor man but after twelve years had returned to Arizona very wealthy.

McFarland's opponents did not openly document the charge that the governor had used any public office for personal gain.

After his defeat, Langmade sent a telegram to McFarland stating that he would speak for both the party and McFarland in the coming election. No evidence was found to indicate that Langmade worked very hard either for McFarland or against Goldwater. He did say that "Goldwater's defeat should be the principal aim of Arizona Democrats."[4] Langmade undoubtedly hurt McFarland by openly criticizing his COPE support. In a front page article entitled "Demo Chieftain Regrets Muscle-in by COPE," the *Republic* quoted him as expressing regret that COPE had sent outside representatives of labor into Arizona "whose interests are not entirely those of Arizona."[5] Langmade was referred to repeatedly in the press as one of the Democratic "leaders" who resented COPE's "invasion" of Arizona. He certainly considered it unwise to send into Arizona "outside" regional or national labor union political organizers. Democratic and labor leaders appeared to be insensitive to the long anti-labor invasion buildup which had been cultivated by the Phoenix press in Arizona and by Goldwater himself as a member of the Senate committee investigating labor practices. Many local Democratic leaders have expressed the same opinions about labor union organizers from outside the state as Langmade did, but usually they have not expressed themselves publicly during the heat of a campaign, to the detriment of their party nominee. Tough primary races almost without exception greatly damage the winner and the party.

Langmade may be taken as the prototype of the Democrat in Arizona who aided and abetted Goldwater's bid for reelection.[6] Many of those found their way into, and allowed their names to be used by, the Democrats for Goldwater organizations sponsored by the Republicans.[7]

The Democratic nomination for governor was one of the most bitterly contested in the state's history. In the Republican primary, there was only one gubernatorial candidate—Paul Fannin. The principal candidate in the Democratic primary was Attorney General Robert Morrison of Tucson, a so-called "liberal." He had engaged in a long-standing feud with the Phoenix newspapers, which therefore supported his primary opponent, Richard Searles, a Democratic conservative who had served for a time as an undersecretary in the Interior Department under President Truman. Some of the animosity toward Morrison was personal. A staff member of the *Arizona Republic*, who did most of the research for the campaign against Morrison, did not like the man. He was dispatched to Morrison's California hometown to unearth a series of derogatory stories on his background.

Morrison probably made a tactical mistake in going almost completely on the defensive. Not only did he shout "Pulliamism"—a name given to the tendency of Pulliam's Phoenix newspapers to editorialize politically outside their editorial columns—but he also described the details of his past in public in an attempt to evoke sympathy. This approach apparently had helped Richard M. Nixon in 1952 and Justice Hugo Black in 1933. When the Al Green exposé was published by the *Arizona Republic*, Morrison's explanation was lost in the overall impression that the whole Democratic campaign somehow was characterized by the criminality of its candidates or of their supporters.

One incident illustrates the lengths to which a paper will go in order to support a candidate. The *Arizona Republic* featured on its front page an interview-type story in which a Scottsdale resident told why he was going to vote for Searles rather than for Morrison. The man had written a letter to the editor. The chief editorial writer called it to the attention of the managing editor with the suggestion that something might be developed from it. Apparently the city editor then called the letter writer to request permission to use the letter as a news story and then wrote it up as an interview. One former staff member of this newspaper considered the story nearly libel and the action itself a misuse of the press.

The question may then quite justifiably be raised, if the Pulliam press was so powerful in this area, why did Searles, whom it supported, lose, and his opponent, whom it went out of its way to attack, win in the primary? Searles took a firm stand on public versus private power, and personally incurred "the hostility of a number of groups, most important of which was Salt River Valley Water Users Association." Himself a former president of this group, Searles proposed in the closing stages of the campaign that the "water users make a payment in lieu of taxes on its earnings, which accrue in considerable part from an electric power system."[8] This stand doomed him. Despite the fact that he was the newspapers' choice as candidate, Searles did not even carry Maricopa County.[9]

The *Arizona Republic* found some solace in the fact that Morrison had only a plurality. Even a monopolistic newspaper cannot completely sway the "public's mind" when that "mind" is made up of powerful opinion leaders in their own area. The Phoenix newspapers appealed to ten conservative anti-governmental groups, but some of these were not so conservative when it came to a question of government aid for the development of water resources in arid Arizona. The beneficiaries of the Salt River Valley Project were not irresponsible liberals nor even sober New Deal Democrats; they were solid Arizona citizens who had not experienced the dangers and threats of a governmentally aided or lien operated enterprise. Much the same situation obtained in the "conservative" South, especially in the region covered by the Tennessee Valley Authority, where politicians and editors, Democrats and Republicans, almost to the man would rise to the defense of that public power facility.

This incident is interesting in that it reveals an issue which was debated, albeit in a primary election. Issues were rare–in fact practically nonexistent in the 1958 Arizona campaign. This campaign seems to indicate that if a party will campaign on an issue, a *real* issue, it can win even with an extremely vulnerable candidate and against the opposition of a monopolistic and completely one-sided press. Public versus private power is one of the few genuine issues which now and then, here and there, has been found in the elections of western states in recent years.

The defeat of Searles may be viewed as evidence that the Phoenix newspapers did not have the political influence in the 1958 campaign attributed to them, especially by its victims at the polls. But it is not strong evidence. It may be postulated that these journals were not unhappy that Morrison won in the primary. His remaining in the campaign gave the Republicans a thoroughly discredited target to shoot at, and Searles might have been a more difficult candidate to defeat in the final run. Although the newspapers had supported Searles in the primary, they suddenly diverted their all-out support to Fannin. To have remained neutral in regard to the gubernatorial candidates would have deprived the Goldwater campaign of much of its strength, for the support given to Fannin simultaneously worked favorably for Goldwater and rallied local interest groups to his campaign.

With the primaries out of the way, the Pulliam press got down to real business–the support of the Republican cause and the destruction of its opponents. The tool which was used, primarily by the *Arizona Republic*, was an attack on labor, aimed at COPE's area representative, Al Green. The attack was launched in the paper's October nineteenth issue, with a typical *Republic* streamer in boldface type almost an inch and a quarter high across the top of the entire page: "COPE AGENT 'MUSCLES IN.' " A smaller type, half-banner headline read, "Arizona Democrats Resent Invasion." This was an appeal to the Democratic vote, a technique which was blueprinted in Shadegg's initial plan for his management of Goldwater's campaign. Then came a one-column, three-line head reading: "Goldwater Removal Prime Aim."

Most viciously devastating were the two mug shots of Green, a front and a profile view, with the inscription on one, "Refer to CII-423,866, Bureau of Criminal Identification and Investigation, P.O. Box 1859, Sacramento, California," and on the other front view, "Stanislaus Co., 9030, Dec. 21, 1940." The caption read: "Record of Violence–Charles Alva Green, California labor figure was 'mugged' in California after his arrest for malicious destruction of property. This is the man sent to Arizona by Reuther and Hoffa to beat Goldwater, elect Morrison and get control of Arizona State Legislature."

Unfortunately, although the public record does not show that he said or did anything which warranted the description in the *Republic* of his method of entry into the state and into the campaign, Green was vulnerable. An official from COPE national headquarters later stated frankly that COPE offices knew this and that they acted foolishly in sending Green into Arizona. Indeed, this COPE official added that Green got what could be expected on the sole basis of his appearance in Arizona, if not precisely what he deserved on the sole basis of his conduct in that state. Also, he (the COPE official) admitted that had he been on the "other side," he would have done exactly the same as Shadegg, Goldwater, Eugene Pulliam, and the Republicans.

The *Republic* was not long in repeating its familiar technique of associating very closely Reuther and Hoffa, an association which had no basis in fact, except that each man was the head of a separate labor union.

The lead in the Al Green story referred to the subject as "One of Walter Reuther's political muscle men, who has a record of criminal violence. . . ." In reality, nothing more needed to be said to achieve the object of the attack. The story went on, however, to rehash the familiar theme and techniques of Goldwater's campaign to date. According to this story, many Democrats were voicing resentment at Green's "arrogant manner." Green was not only allegedly financing their campaign, but he was also accused of "giving orders." The story stated that with "unlimited funds" at his disposal, Green was well on his way "toward control of the Democratic party" which could be the "political control of the whole state." Reference was made to the reports—usually made previously by Goldwater and the *Republic*—of $450,000 which COPE had earmarked and allocated to defeat Republican candidates in the 1958 election campaign.

Then the story reviewed Green's record in California. In 1941 he had been arrested in Modesto for hiring two men to throw hot creosote on new homes allegedly built by nonunion labor. He served six months in a county road camp. In 1943 Green was arrested again in Modesto on charges of displaying firearms in a threatening manner.

The *Arizona Republic* stated that it "had assembled evidence" (it did not note how it got this evidence) indicating that Green had spent nearly seventy-five percent of his time in Arizona since July first. Then came the transition from Green to the Democratic party. This technique removed the account from the realm of a straight news story to the province of propaganda. The story, reportedly written by Bill King of the *Republic* staff, reported that

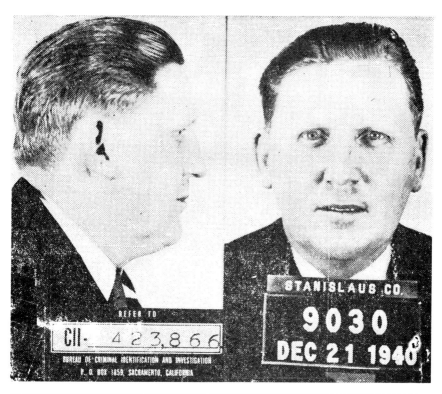

Green's observed contacts in Arizona included Democratic Chairman Joseph F. Walton as well as many local chiefs. Just beneath the two mug shots in a large photo, Green was shown chatting with two men. The caption read: "Sidewalk Chat—This picture shows Al Green, left, in a sidewalk conversation with Joseph F. Walton, center without hat, Democratic state chairman. They had just finished lunch together inside the restaurant."

The caption omitted the name of the third man, James Browne, a Democratic party worker in the employ of the National Senatorial Democratic Campaign Committee. Actually Browne had set up the luncheon. His wife, identifiable but also not named in the caption, was seen standing behind Green. Browne said he wanted to introduce his wife to two of his favorite "characters," Green and Walton. The luncheon had been purely social. The fifth person in the photograph was not identified. Part of his head was blocked by a traffic signal pole. His left hand shielded his face from the front, suggesting that perhaps he had seen the photographer. He would not have known at the moment that his face would not be seen in the picture in any event.

Later the man was identified as a feature political writer for the *Phoenix Gazette* who wrote pro-Goldwater stories.[10] One or two days later this writer called union headquarters and determined that the eating place was a "scab" restaurant. He made some mileage with this discovery. Browne later heard that the Chambord restaurant was "scab," but both he and Green claimed they were not aware of the fact—or of the rumor—at that time.[11]

Browne explained that his expenses were paid by Walton, whom he had learned to appreciate very much during earlier trips to Arizona. He stated: "Joe was one of the rare birds in that state who showed either gumption or ability in party affairs. Both Mrs. Browne and I have enjoyed the Waltons' company on several occasions. It would be more appropriate to think of my job at the time as sort of aide to Walton, outside of National Committee venue." Browne added, "My superiors had earlier asked me where I wanted to spend pre-election days. There was great reason to suspect a tremendous debacle in Arizona; I was on excellent terms with Walton; so I chose Arizona."[12]

Browne's presence in Arizona contradicted the impression created by Goldwater's propaganda aides that *only* COPE had sent personnel to Arizona and that *only* Reuther and Hoffa had supplied the principal funds to finance the Democratic campaign, particularly McFarland's.

Browne commented:

> Both organized labor and organized Democrats have been in a great state of disorganization and disunity for a long time. It is best to think of both groups in at least three terms, Phoenix, Tucson, and the remainder. I understood on several occasions that at least one or two of the labor hierarchy were in the Goldwater fold. Without equivocation I can say that both labor and the party shared equally in effectiveness and in coherence.[13]

Labor's unity was greatest in Tucson. Browne added:

> Phoenix was, and is, a great problem. If Pulliam would only print a story of how weak
> Arizona labor really is I'm certain it would attract great readership. But I fear that the
> ordinary citizen has no idea of the nuances of labor politics and antagonisms. The same
> might apply to our party, too.[14]

Here, then, would be a clue to Goldwater's great triumph in 1958. Saddled with
inept and vulnerable nominees, torn with intraparty conflicts and damaged
more than helped by a potentially powerful, politically minded interest
group—labor—the Democratic party was at its lowest ebb in several decades.
The sparkle of Goldwater's victory and Shadegg's craftsmanship would be
dimmed by the measure of their foe's weaknesses. This, however, in no way
disparages the highly efficient campaign waged for Goldwater by Shadegg and
the Pulliam newspapers in Phoenix. Theirs was a magnificent performance.
They located the enemy's weaknesses and hit his sore spots with a relentless
bombardment of propaganda missiles.

The *Arizona Republic* story which exposed Al Green and associated him
with the Democrats slopped over onto another whole page. No one yet has
estimated the cost of these two full pages of propaganda in behalf of Senator
Goldwater and other Republicans. It would far exceed the cost of two full
pages of straight commercial advertising. Not only are political advertisement
rates higher, but one would also have to include in the accounting the salaries
paid to researchers and especially to writers. One would have to include the fees
paid to the public relations firm or to the "research division" which had assembled and compiled the data on Green. The operation covered several weeks or
even months and sent the original researchers, whoever they were, to several
cities in California—Sacramento, Modesto, Stockton, and Los Angeles. Above
all, apart from the actual cost, the value of this newspaper effort to Goldwater's
campaign was inestimable.

The second page was devoted mainly to pictures. These were four columns
wide. The top picture was captioned "Political Mission." It showed Green,
"*California* agent of AFL-CIO, Committee on Political Education currently
concentrating on Arizona," clutching his coat and boarding a "limousine for
trip from Adams Hotel to Sky Harbor." The caption under the second picture
was headed "Beck's Boy Here." It read further that Teamster Einar O. Mohn,
once administrative assistant to Dave Beck, is shown with teamster brass from
Colorado and *California*. The "brass" were two unidentified men. However, in
the third picture, two men, rather hard-looking characters, were identified.
Both seemed to be looking contemptuously and disapprovingly at the photographer. That they appeared to be making no move toward him could have been
due to the fact that the picture was taken with a telescopic lens. The caption

read: "Out-of-state Teamsters—Shown at airport here after Phoenix conference with other unionists are Edward Woodard, left, Mountain States teamster
representative from Colorado, and Carl Windschanz, officer of a Los Angeles
teamster local."

Published, precise data on the movements in Phoenix of these Teamster
officials indicated that they had been shadowed by private detectives. The data
on Green was equally precise. Green, the reporter wrote, "was registered at the
Adams [Hotel, Phoenix] or Santa Rita [Hotel, Tucson] for 26 days." The report on Green's movements ran on and on in considerable detail. It cited by
name the people he called on the phone, the number of long distance calls he
made, where he called to, and the occupation of the person he had called.
Shadegg and the members of his research division kept all the information
about Green and his activities a secret until the day they wanted to release it
with explosive impact. In this campaign, secrecy was the hallmark of Republican maneuvers.

Also in the *Arizona Republic* of October nineteenth there was an example
of how a newspaper can strengthen its own propaganda output by printing on
the same page press dispatches from other parts of the nation on the same sub-

ject and with the same slant. Running down the entire length of the second page of the dynamiting story on Green was a single column headed, "AFL-CIO Influence Hold Peril." The lead in this UPI dispatch from Hot Springs, Virginia, printed in larger type than the remainder of the story, read, "Ralph J. Cordiner, board chairman of General Electric Co., yesterday described the AFL-CIO as 'the most aggressive and successful force in politics' and as powerful as 'all other groups and individuals combined.' "

Regardless of the content, the dispatch can be considered campaign propaganda because of its timing and because it appeared to be placed in this newspaper space to strengthen the impressions which the other stories on the page had been designed to create—that of the presence in Arizona of this "successful force in politics," a force more powerful than "all other groups and individuals combined." If it is good journalism to place a story of this kind in this position, then good journalism itself can be used as a technique of propaganda.

The *Republic* editorial page in the same issue contained much of Goldwater's campaign strategy and tactics. Columbus Giragi, a local columnist, wrote a piece designed to attract the "Democratic Pintos" (conservative Democrats) to the Republican cause. He defined a Pinto Democrat as "one who refuses to vote for or support the ambitions of any person who is inferior to his or her political opponent, Republican or Democrat; one who refuses to vote for 'a yellow dog' simply because he is on the Democratic ticket." Giragi then explained that Pintos

> resent and oppose those political parasites who use the Democratic Party for their own personal profit and aggrandizement. They become Pintos to retain self-respect and to set themselves apart from those political *wolves* of whom they are ashamed.
>
> These predacious politicos are rough on Pintos, and do not spare their fangs in punitive purges and abuse. They usually toss their grenades from ambush, and their favored associates are the political ingrates—the drones of the party hive.

On this same editorial page Holmes Alexander, a conservative syndicated columnist, stated that Senator Barry Goldwater was fighting both the Underworld and the Other World for his reelection. "In the Underworld, there are the criminal elements of the labor movement, the goons and racketeers who dread the return of Goldwater with added seniority to the McClellan committee. In the Other World, there is Goldwater's Democratic opponent [McFarland]. . . ." In the Underworld were the "top labor leaders" who "are opposing him on the principle that conservatives and states righters are not good for big labor. But the bitterest opposition comes from shady characters with skeletons in the closet who fear and hate him." Holmes ended his column on a patriotic if not precisely a heroic note: "McFarland, seeking federal aid for everything, calls himself 'the man who puts Arizona first.' Goldwater likes the challenge, saying: 'I put the United States first.' "

In reality Al Green did not appear to everyone to be the shadowy or sinister figure in Arizona as he was pictured in the exposé. He had been in and out of Arizona on political errands for COPE since the 1954 campaign, in which he participated to help defeat Republican Governor Howard Pyle who was trying for reelection. In 1958 his daily life appeared to be conspicuously in the open.[15] One charge against him was that he lived lavishly in the Santa Rita Hotel in Tucson and in the Adams Hotel in Phoenix; but no description was given either of his extravagant life or how he hid himself or covered his tracks.

National or regional union leaders or COPE personnel might take up lodging and establish personal headquarters in a modest motel removed from the heart of the city or located on its outskirts in order to avoid and even to evade publicity. Citizens generally resent carpetbaggers or out-of-state organizers telling them what to do in a union or political campaign. Even local union leaders might oppose the intrusion of national political organizers on the grounds that these are not sufficiently acquainted with the local mores, and their advice could do more harm than good. In Al Green's case, he was accused simultaneously of both ostentatious and surreptitious living.[16] By innuendo the impression was developed by the Republicans that he was like a rodent who had to be ferreted out of his hole by espionage and counterespionage methods.

After the election Paul Sexson, who was in charge of Goldwater's Phoenix office, stated that Goldwater and his staff knew nothing about the forthcoming Al Green story until they all read it in the *Republic*. Sexson was insulted and incensed when his statement was questioned. He turned the interrogator's letter over to Bert Fireman, Goldwater's press release man, who answered indignantly and angrily—he had reason to do so for he had been erroneously credited with having written the Al Green story. He volunteered the information that the story had been written by Bill King, the *Republic* feature writer, in a period of several days, from materials assembled from available files in the newspaper's library.[17]

References in the story itself indicated, however, that the data had been gathered over a period of time from various places. When George F. Fowler was interviewed, he let it be known casually that he had discovered and uncovered Al Green and that he had taken the pictures. Indeed, he had been in Al Green's company and in his Santa Rita Hotel room. He had gone to lunch with K. S. Brown, state COPE director, and Al Green. Green later rationalized his own position by saying that he used Fowler to convey information to Shadegg that he wanted him to receive. Brown apologetically admitted that he had given

Fowler his visiting card with a scribbled endorsement of the man, but he stated he did so only for a limited purpose, for Fowler to use in a town outside Phoenix in carrying out an errand. When Earl Anderson, a labor union agent who was to figure prominently late in the campaign, heard about Fowler he located and investigated him. He described him as a "political leech" who had served both sides simultaneously, commuting between Shadegg's office and the state labor headquarters.

Fowler undoubtedly tended to overdramatize his part in Goldwater's campaign, but he could have been the first person to inform Shadegg about Green's presence in Arizona; he also could have kept Shadegg informed as to Green's whereabouts and activities throughout the campaign.

Fowler did not claim that he had acquired the mug shots of Green from the files of the California Bureau of Investigation and Identification. It is very likely that they were obtained either from private or from police files by others for use elsewhere, presumably in Texas. In any event, a careful reading and a correct interpretation of the California statute would suggest that the way these mug shots were acquired could be questioned and that their use in a political campaign in the manner Shadegg or the *Arizona Republic* used them might be considered illegal.[18] This had always been a troublesome point to the researcher of Goldwater's campaign: how did Shadegg get possession of the mug shots and how did the *Arizona Republic* dare to use them?

Apparently the original request for information concerning Green came from a California source who submitted his name as Alva C. Green. Reportedly, Clarence Oliver, an investigator in the Dallas district attorney's office, on September 23, 1958, asked Detective Sergeant R. E. McHugh of the Stockton police force to secure the criminal record and mug shot of one "Charles Al Green" from the CII at Sacramento. McHugh was on vacation at the time, but secured the information from the San Joaquin County sheriff's office and from a captain of the Sacramento police department. McHugh sent the photos and record of Alva C. Green to Oliver. Apparently there was some confusion about Green's correct name. Later, on September twenty-seventh, Sergeant McHugh personally requested and obtained the photo and record of Al Green from the CII in order to verify that Al Green and Alva C. Green were the same person. Green's name was reported in the *Arizona Republic* on October 19, 1958, as "Charles Alva Green or Al Green."

When questioned and shown the information obtained from the Dallas district attorney's office investigator, W. F. Alexander, the assistant district attorney, took full responsibility for procuring the mug shot of Green from California. He said that he had the investigator get the mug shot in connection with a felony pending in Dallas County, Texas. The office also communicated with

Oklahoma and Louisiana officials as well as with private corporations which he said were involved. The mug shots and other materials he procured, he said, were in the Dallas office files before and after the 1958 Arizona election. He did say that copies of the same materials were on file in the offices of other interested agencies. At no time did Alexander offer any further detail. He did not expand on Green's implied connection with the felony in Dallas County, or on the specific interests in the case of the officials in Oklahoma and Louisiana, or on the investigators hired by private corporations. He did not specify the other "interested agencies" which had the mug shot and materials in their files. Alexander then concluded by discrediting the information offered by the investigator in his office. This investigator had had some mental problems and subsequently some other troubles (1962) with law enforcement agencies.

The mug shots could have been obtained only on the grounds that Al Green was "violating the law" or that he was a fugitive from justice. He was not charged in Arizona during the campaign with violating any law or with campaigning in any unusual or illegitimate manner. Indeed, his main technique—a widespread telephone network and filing-card system to reach principally the members of labor unions and to induce them to register and vote—was used in scope and in size, and then matched, if not exceeded in expense, by Goldwater's Republican organization to reach prospective Goldwater voters.

It may be surmised that someone on Goldwater's staff, or on his behalf, had available or had hired outside help to obtain the mug shots and to do the "research" on Al Green and other labor leaders, mostly officials of the Teamsters union. In fact, all these "services" could have been donated to Goldwater's campaign. The Democrats claimed that considerable money came into his campaign coffers from Texas. No one publicly denied this allegation.

Later, in a report by a public relations counsel in Washington, D.C., to the national COPE office, it was stated that a public relations firm in Dallas had done the research on Green. This report read:

[This public relations firm] reportedly used a dozen investigators in Arizona. They employed bugs, wire taps, long-range cameras, etc., in their work. They took, for example, the telescopic pictures of Al Green and Joe Walton, the State Democratic Chairman, which were employed on the front page of the *Arizona Republic*. They had men posted in front of the state AFL-CIO to copy the license plate numbers and photograph everybody going in and out. They checked all airline passenger arrivals in and out of Phoenix and Tucson and were responsible for the pictures of Einar O. Mohn and other teamster officials at the airport between planes, which were employed to convey the fiction that teamster leaders were participating in the campaign to unseat Goldwater. The head of this firm was an ex-FBI agent and used his law enforcement contacts to get the picture of Al Green from the California enforcement bureau in California.[19]

Another part of the blueprint for Goldwater's campaign was the decision to keep all Republican speakers and outside help out of Arizona. Only Fred Scaton and Ezra Taft Benson, two Cabinet members, came to the state. The intention was to establish a contrast between a stream of outside COPE and labor union officials busily going in and out of Arizona in behalf of Democratic candidates, and Goldwater, the native son, who was going it all alone.

It is ironic that an out-of-state public relations firm was retained in the face of the Goldwater staff's avowal not to have any out-of-state people active in Arizona in behalf of their nominee. If these public relations or private detective firms were hired to assemble explosive ammunition for Shadegg's and the *Arizona Republic* blast at Al Green, and if their hired operatives did secure the data which the Republicans used on Green and other labor leaders and organizers, then what Green did and how he did it would not have been any different from what this firm did. The rationalization would be that the Arizona Republicans were fighting some tough foes, labor union gangsters, and that fire had to be fought with fire. An unbiased observer might conclude that in this campaign, as perhaps in political campaigns generally, the participants on both sides were tarred with the same feathers and wore the same leopard spots; that in given similar political situations the antagonists use comparable techniques at least in terms of intensity if not always in skill of application. As a corollary, would it not be valid to assume that in analyzing a political campaign one should look closely at the actions of men and not accept at face value the protestations from both sides about the immorality of the opposition's techniques and the righteousness of one's own cause?

In any event, according to Shadegg, by the middle of the summer Goldwater's campaign staff had compiled a dossier on Al Green. Shadegg described him as a veteran political organizer for labor unions with a record of violence in California. Someone had provided Shadegg with official arrest photographs which showed the identification number across Green's chest, and that was all Shadegg needed to crush his client's opponent.

Apparently the *Arizona Republic* began an independent investigation of Green's activities. Shadegg then counseled with an alert reporter and his editor. The principal point to settle was the timing of the release of the material. During the conversation the editor predicted that this thing could swing the election. He also observed that it could push the gubernatorial candidate along with the senator, as well as two or three other Republicans.[20] In retrospect, it can validly be asserted that he was correct.

The fact that Governor McFarland might win called for a hard-hitting blueprint, an extreme position in naming and pinpointing a theme, and some devastating bombardments released early. Goldwater's campaign could "run down"; it was difficult to pace an initially aggressive campaign, and a strong Democratic tide was rising which could engulf Arizona, as it did other western states. That Goldwater's organization picked up momentum as it approached election day was to the credit of the Republican leaders who managed the campaign. Indeed, Goldwater's lead before the Green exposé indicated that he scarcely needed this technique in order to win. When the Al Green material was released, however, it provided the shocker that actually turned back the tide. What followed seemed an anticlimax.

Goldwater, Shadegg, and the Republicans, however, had no intention of alienating all organized labor. They tried by various means to make this clear to union members and the electorate at large. Goldwater was presented as a candidate who was championing the freedom of the individual worker and who was challenging the dictatorial orders of out-of-state union bosses.

Goldwater's opponents had many more obstacles to overcome. The Republicans had in Senator Goldwater a more salable commodity than the Democrats had in Governor McFarland. But a greater difference was apparent. In the demoralization, and in a political sense, the utter destruction of McFarland's forces by propaganda and political techniques, the Goldwater forces simply were superior to their Democratic counterparts. Goldwater threw haymakers, but he also was a great infighter.

Much was written both during and after the campaign comparing the Goldwater and McFarland personalities. Dubbing their race a "personality affair," *Time* described a day of whirlwind campaigning by "first-rate Army Air Forces pilot" Barry Goldwater, and compared it with the plodding tactics of "Homespun Ernie" McFarland who, "elected Arizona's governor in 1954, nursed his grudge against Goldwater, never missed a ribbon-cutting, a chance to wave at the gathering of constituents or shake an Arizona hand."[21] Another critic stated that McFarland's entire political life had been a "vague, sweet, bumbling confusion."[22]

In Barry Goldwater the public relations men had a "star." Goldwater had "youth" and "appeal" on his side and working for him. He was a responsive candidate and an energetic campaigner. His approach appeared "modern," especially when he used his jet plane; he was advertised as the only licensed jet pilot in Arizona.

Goldwater was an able and articulate speaker. His views, expressed in terms either of glittering generalities or name-calling, were often extreme, but instead of raising his voice as his emotional temperature rose when speaking about his *bête noire*, COPE, he would talk forcefully but quietly, with excellent control, as if he were master of the situation. Indeed, he seldom lost his poise. He exuded confidence and authority.

Goldwater possessed the principal asset of charismatic leadership. His listeners gained the impression that he was sincere and honest. They also gained the impression that he was a man of conviction and courage and that he was a fighter for just causes. This does not imply that he was none of these things nor that he did not have any of these qualities; it means that what counted in the election was the fact that the voters, at least enough of them to work fanatically for him and to vote for him, believed these things and saw in him these qualities which they liked in a political candidate.[23]

Goldwater on occasion could be an actor. He could be dignified and become righteously indignant, and then in the next moment or on another occasion, when he was on stage, he could give a performance bordering on the melodramatic. His television appearances were purposely few in number, but these were organized extremely well.[24] One of Goldwater's telecasts, presented on October 29, 1958, entitled, "Breakthrough" (to labor), was given the advantage, without additional cost, of generous front-page treatment by the *Arizona Republic.* The next day the paper ran a posed photo which showed in the background, hanging on a stage curtain, a blown-up facsimile of the front page of a newspaper with the masthead, "LABOR," Arizona edition. Goldwater, immaculately groomed, was seen slightly bent forward in an action pose, just after he had broken through the large facsimile. Though parts of the paper's headline were blocked by Goldwater's figure, the masthead and the picture of McFarland were left untouched and in full view. The caption on the picture read: "Everybody Calls Him Mac."

One sentence from Goldwater's television speech was quoted in the photo's caption. It read: "For six years newspapers such as this one have been telling you that Barry Goldwater hates the union men, and for six years I have been trying to get through this union curtain of thought control." This sentence drew an analogy with Communist thought control behind the iron curtain. Goldwater, speaking "quietly" but with "grim seriousness" elaborated that he was in favor of union members but against the excesses of the "union bosses." This was an aspect of Goldwater's campaign theme, BIG LABOR and LABOR BOSSES, not in Arizona but in Detroit and elsewhere, where Reuther, Beck, and Hoffa were conspiring to defeat him, then to enter Arizona and finally to become "dictators."

Two years later, during the 1960 presidential campaign, Robert F. Kennedy visited Arizona to campaign for his brother. He contended that Phoenix Newspapers, Inc., published by Eugene C. Pulliam, are "probably the most unfair in the United States." Kennedy further stated that Vice-President Richard Nixon was being backed by James Hoffa, Harry Bridges, Senator Goldwater, and Mr. Pulliam. Governor Fannin, a perennial favorite and beneficiary of the Phoenix press, came to Pulliam's defense. In so doing, however, he made

an honest appraisal of the technique used by himself, the Republicans, Goldwater, Shadegg, and the Pulliam press against the Democrats in the 1958 campaign. Fannin said, "To link Barry Goldwater and Gene Pulliam with Harry
Bridges is practicing guilt by association." He then claimed that it was this type
of thinking which prompted "two union members in 1958 to anonymously

publish a cartoon linking Senator Goldwater with Joe Stalin." And then, apparently with tongue in cheek, he said, "Mr. Pulliam's editorial policy favors the Republicans, and I appreciate this. I am proud to have Mr. Pulliam's support. But I would remind you that in his news columns Mr. Pulliam leans over backwards to give the Democrats and their candidates *more than an even break*."[25]

In commenting on this, Shadegg reverted to an analogy in applied logic. He said: "There would be as much logic in claiming that the Bishop of Arizona and Lucky Luciano are blood brothers because they both like peanut butter as there is in linking Pulliam and Bridges because both are opposed to John Kennedy as president." One astute observer of the Arizona political scene then asked for the purpose of analysis, a pertinent question. How much logic was there in Shadegg's campaign tactics when he linked Reuther and Hoffa and then both of these to McFarland? In truth, many observers, Democrats, and labor leaders interpreted McFarland's statements on his so-called labor support as a repudiation of that support and then gave that as a major reason for the Democrats' defeat in that campaign.

The rationalization for linking the names of Hoffa and Reuther stemmed from two separate events. Allegedly the Teamsters had given $5,000 to McFarland's campaign—how, when, and where was not revealed by Goldwater's managers—and $450,000 had been pledged by Reuther at a labor convention in Miami, Florida, to defeat Goldwater and other Republican antilabor nominees. It was never made clear if this sum was to be spent in Arizona alone or throughout the nation in an attempt to defeat several nominees. There was no evidence of any kind that any such sum was received or spent by McFarland. Goldwater, however, did not want to alienate completely all the individual labor union membership vote. His most complete effort to placate individual union members was the brochure entitled, "Barry Goldwater, 'Where I Stand' " and subtitled, "I have absolutely no quarrel with rank and file labor." For three pages this brochure tried to demonstrate that the "wage earners" need "Barry" to "get rid of the union dictators, racketeers, and crooks."[26]

Another technique along this line was the "Report of the Arizona Labor Committee for Barry Goldwater." This was a brochure which contained Goldwater's "favorable" voting record on labor legislation and on bills which labor favored or in which labor had an economic or social interest. His "favorable" votes on legislation which would provide or retain jobs for the working man were graphically portrayed. The "record" ended with the statement, "Every Arizonian has benefited in some way from the inspired services of this young, courageous, dedicated United States Senator."

The *Arizona Republic* issue of October nineteenth had contained a large advertisement apparently paid for by Aubrey Barker. Barker, with Theodore

Cogswell and three other persons, was a member of the Arizona Labor Committee for Barry Goldwater. Barker's name, with those of Cogswell and the three representatives of labor, also appeared on a brochure entitled, "The Voting Record of Barry Goldwater on Labor and Jobs." While Goldwater was blasting away at Al Green, Reuther, and Hoffa, he was simultaneously courting local labor groups and individuals.

Theodore Cogswell stated that the members of the committee actually never met as a committee. Cogswell did no research or work in preparing the materials for the brochure, or in writing it, and contributed no money towards its publication. All the work and expense were borne by the Republican State Committee.[27]

Goldwater, "urbane and engaging," with very few variations of his campaign theme, avoided the danger of sounding like a rundown record on a worn-out phonograph by his stunts and poses in his television appearances. He created and cultivated the impression of the young, vigorous "action" candidate, the dynamic "sales manager" for the "Republican Old Guard—with a New Look," as one weekly periodical put it.

In contrast, according to the Republican propaganda, "folksy" McFarland—"Mac" to his friends—with his "plodding tactics" had been a "no-boat rocker" in Congress and a "do-nothing" governor in the state, who for six years had waited—just sat—for the chance to satisfy a grudge by regaining his senatorial seat.

One knowledgeable analyst earmarked the "breakthrough to labor" telecast as the turning point of the campaign. He said:

> On October 23, Senator Goldwater used all four television channels to present his key telecast of the campaign. The program was aimed at picturing labor union bossism as the central issue confronting the nation and Arizona. He struck hard at Walter Reuther and James Hoffa, and featured film clips of hearings before the McClellan Senate Committee on Union Corruption. All at once Goldwater seemed to have snatched the offensive from McFarland.[28]

Suspicion of "union hoodlums" by this time had stemmed from the Goldwater fight against "corrupt union factions." Goldwater, Shadegg, and Company had generated a great deal of "heat" over alleged financial contributions by COPE to McFarland's campaign in a completely distorted form with grossly exaggerated figures.

While Goldwater was accusing McFarland's supporters of smearing him,[29] the Democrats pointed to a few Goldwater "smears." In this category they placed Goldwater's entire treatment of COPE money in the campaign. He stated that COPE had allocated $450,000—which would be spent from Detroit to Phoenix—to defeat him.[30] One columnist sympathetic to Goldwater raised the figure to five hundred thousand dollars. In the meantime, Goldwater repeatedly cited a sum of five thousand dollars which reportedly the Teamsters union had donated to McFarland's gubernatorial campaign in 1954.

McFarland, in a memorable television appearance, made a spectacular retreat; he denied any knowledge of having received any COPE money, thereby practically disavowing his entire labor support. Labor leaders were furious, and to this day they attribute their setback and the Democratic defeat in this election to McFarland's "giving up" at this point. To support their contention they pointed to the successful Democratic attorney general, a former state labor official, Wade Church, who not only did not avoid the stigma of labor but who was quoted repeatedly as having said in public, "I am proud to wear the badge of labor."[31] McFarland seemed to have been hammered into submission by the constant pressure from Goldwater's camp. Such pressure forces mistakes by the opponents which are exploited instantly by alert opposition propagandists. McFarland's "breakdown" in public was another highlight of the campaign.

Shadegg and Goldwater never allowed any labor money, either from within or from outside the state, to be spent in behalf of labor itself as an interest group; it was always spent, they alleged, for Democratic candidates. On the other hand, if the American Medical Association through AMPAC (American Medical Political Action Committee) spent thousands of dollars in behalf of a Republican candidate, dollars which came from outside the state of Arizona, these dollars would always be spent, according to Republican propaganda, in behalf of the democratic way and to fight creeping socialism, never in behalf of a particular candidate.

In any event, Goldwater, in his more politically sober statements, chopped the COPE financial figure from $450,000 to $14,000. Fulton Lewis, who always had a kind word for Goldwater and his counterparts in other states, cited the figure as thirteen thousand dollars. "At least $13,000," he reported.[32]

Unfortunately for McFarland, the timetable for filing financial reports was against him. Goldwater discovered a record of fourteen thousand dollars which had been sent by COPE into Arizona, with one thousand dollars specifically earmarked for McFarland. Actually, in view of the cost of senatorial elections—Goldwater filed contributions of over $150,000 from wealthy men across the country and from other sources, practically all *outside* money—$1,000, or even $14,000, is a paltry sum. First by suggestion, then by impression, created and made possible by continuous repetition in or out of a valid context, the electorate had had pressed into its consciousness a figure of $450,000. Subsequently, having been lodged in the subconscious, it was this figure of $450,000, and not a more realistic or exact figure, which immediately came to mind whenever mere mention was made of COPE or BIG LABOR financing of political campaigns.

In reality, one thousand dollars reportedly was a contribution to McFarland's campaign by the Garment Workers union in New York. What has made it bad per se for labor union members and garment workers to contribute to a candidate's campaign and what has *not* made it equally bad for the factory owners, their bosses, to do so defies all reason. Yet this is precisely the condition in American politics, and candidates can base and then win a campaign on the assumption that Republican sources for campaign funds are legitimate while Democratic sources are made to appear somewhat tainted. Yet in this campaign no Republican allegation was ever made that a Democratic or labor union financial transaction was dishonest or illegal. Much financial aid for Democrats did come from local unions and from local labor sources. After all, labor is nationally organized. Other national business and professional organizations or their political fronts have made financial contributions to local candidates.

The COPE donation to McFarland did not pass through his hands. In this sense, he had no knowledge of it. The damage occurred when he denied his "campaign" had received it or that it had been given to his finance committee. The record showed otherwise. His disavowal made him appear something less than honest. Shadegg was quoted as saying, for example, that he had reports coming to him that COPE was spending $37,500 a day for hiring workers to repeat the pattern of a Michigan campaign. Shadegg remarked carefully that the amount involved was secondary to the fact that *here again* was an example of Mac's refusal to tell the truth.[33] This facile transition from the amount and above all the source of the money revealed Shadegg's genius as a propaganda specialist.

Goldwater lost no time in emphasizing and repeating his observations on this discrepancy between the record and McFarland's disclaimer. In fact, Goldwater previously prepared the groundwork for this *coup de grâce*. In October he was reported as having said: "We will probably never know 'whether outside money is pouring into Arizona to help Governor McFarland' because he forgot to report a [previous] $4,000 contribution from the teamster's union."[34] Sometimes no mention would be made of the fact that that particular incident was supposed to have taken place in 1954 and not in 1958. The *Arizona Republic* again issued a headline which dramatized the discrepancy for the entire Arizona electorate.[35] Preceded by a half-banner line in comparatively smaller type, stating "Governor Disclaims Knowledge," the boldface banner line directly beneath read: "COPE GIFT TO MAC ON FILE." The story which followed then rehashed the whole threat of labor money brought into the state from the outside for the Democrats.[36] Aspects of the dynamiting job this newspaper had done on Al Green and Robert Morrison then were reviewed. This was a pattern of reporting followed by the Phoenix newspapers right down to election evening; Al Green's name was the "clincher" in each story.

McFarland said he welcomed the disclosure for it enabled him to "give the lie to the fantastic tales of out-of-state money coming to [his] aid." Noting the Pulliam press' claim that his "campaign had received $450,000 of outside contributions, he then quoted a Chicago newspaper as saying Goldwater's campaign was receiving financial help from the same Texas oil people who contributed to the late Joe McCarthy." The reference to "Texas oil people" and to "Joe McCarthy" was a belated attempt by McFarland to match this sort of technique with Goldwater's. The *Republic* was quick to call this alleged smear of Goldwater and of the memory of the late lamented (in Arizona) Joseph McCarthy to the attention of its readers.[37]

Goldwater had also accused McFarland of having signed a "sweetheart" contract.[38] When McFarland himself (who operated a television station) and United States Representative Stewart Udall stated categorically that this was not true, the Republicans insisted that it was.

The Phoenix press continued its favorable news and feature treatment in behalf of Goldwater and the other Republican nominees to the very last day of the campaign. One staff member of the *Arizona Republic* documented his paper's coverage of the McFarland-Goldwater contest. His article, published in the *New Republic*,[39] was completely descriptive: "There Weren't Two Sides to the Story in Phoenix." As an afterthought, this reporter agreed that these two papers acted as a "giant public relations firm" for Goldwater. "Liaison," he said, "between Shadegg and the *Arizona Republic* and *Phoenix Gazette* was supplied by Bert Fireman, a columnist for the *Gazette.*" Republicans insisted that Fannin paid for the publicity he received in the Phoenix press.

Certainly an important category for the analysis of this subject is the amount and the location of the space that was given to one side and the propaganda devices which were used to fill this space. The *Arizona Republic* published a series of stories and photographs which could be classified as the "plain folks" device or perhaps the "lilacs and lace" technique. These were generally sentimental in nature, featuring Democratic housewives with their children, who were greatly concerned about what would happen if the Democratic candidate for governor, Robert Morrison, were elected. Therefore, they intended to vote for the Republican candidate for this office, Paul Fannin.

The photographs, generally five by four inches (two columns wide) were attractive and in good taste. The series, with captions, that ran from October twenty-ninth to November third in the *Arizona Republic* was typical. Seated at a desk, with pen in hand and about to write in a looseleaf notebook, was Mrs. Ruth Dunlap, a businesswoman and a "registered Democrat," who, after "careful consideration," endorsed and supported Fannin because of his "business record" and his "cautiousness in making promises." Her three children, all of voting age, were Democrats. She held out against them, not to be contrary, but to exercise her belief that voting was a "personal matter."[40] Another "registered Democrat," Mrs. Don E. Johnson, a medical secretary who filed records, explained that she would vote for Fannin because she thought he could do more for Arizona than his opponent.[41] She said that Morrison's "past had set me against him." Previously the newspaper, in revealing and publicizing this "past," had done a complete dynamiting job on Morrison.

Next a mother was shown with her five children, holding the youngest on her lap. A "Demomother," she was "thinking of the children's future and what is going to happen to our country if it gets into the hands of people who are pursuing their own selfish interests, and not thinking of the welfare of the state."[42] Blaming inflation on the "misuse of labor's power," she could trust Fannin, who was for the labor man and not against him "like the labor bosses." This was followed in the next issue by a picture of a "Democratic housewife who thought Fannin was best." She was pictured with her three children. In this case, however, she was also going to vote for Goldwater, who had "the intelligence necessary for the job."[43] Another picture showed "another Democratic housewife" for Fannin.[44] She also was impressed by the Republican candidate's business ability.

The only somewhat comparable story in behalf of McFarland appeared on a back page of the *Republic* November first issue. Pictured were a Buckeye pharmacist, who praised "Mac" for his record, and his wife, who was scanning some newspapers. In no case, however, did the newspaper picture a Republican housewife, surrounded by her children, who was quoted in support of a Democratic candidate.

On November third the *Arizona Republic* published a full-page advertisement headlined, "Who is Supporting Barry Goldwater's Campaign?" This included a photograph of Goldwater and six long columns of names of "voluntary contributors to Goldwater-for-Senator Committee."

The Phoenix papers also conducted their own campaign to "get out the vote." This effort was calculated to help Goldwater. Although the registration was heavily Democratic, the assumption underlying this effort was that many registered Democrats were either conservative or disgruntled; in either case, once in the ballot booth, they would vote for some Republican candidates, particularly for senator and governor. Banner headlines were placed above the masthead and banner captions at the bottom of the front page. Typical head-line streamers were: "If You're Proud of Arizona and Want to Insure Your Future, Vote Tuesday."[45] "No One Knows How You Vote Except Yourself," and "Plan to Vote! If You Fail, Don't Sob and Wail."[46] Another read: "Read Columbus Giragi Text, Section 2, Page 6." The "text" on page six was banner headlined (all but one column), "Here's Text of Address by Columbus Giragi."[47]

In a radio broadcast Giragi had given the case of the Arizona Pinto, the Democrat who voted for Goldwater. He told his hearers to think for them-selves, the typical appeal for support to the "other side." Goldwater became the "thinking man's" candidate. The remainder of the text dealt with the famil-iar theme and phrases, "the Hoffas, Reuthers, and the Becks," the "real ene-mies of labor," who are interested only in "dictatorial powers," in "special privilege and personal profit," in "concentration of power," and in the "under-regulated, under-criticized, under-investigated, tax-exempt labor organizations and in their belligerent, aggressive, and too often lawless and corrupt man-agers." Why do those persons work for the defeat of a man (Goldwater) who is a "better friend of labor than Walter Reuther, James Hoffa, and Dave Beck."

Giragi referred to the "*invaders* specially trained at political brain wash-ing," an obvious reference to Al Green. In reality Al Green personally made no radio broadcasts or television appearances, gave no speeches, and did not en-gage in such propaganda activities. There was no evidence that he did anything, nor did any labor official do anything, comparable to this radio address which subsequently was given the benefit of full newspaper coverage heralded by a top front-page headline. This address was hardly news; it was a rehash of the campaign theme, the mean, bad labor bosses versus the real friend of labor, Barry Goldwater. The entire treatment appeared to be free space and free pro-paganda donated by the *Republic* to Goldwater's account.

The Phoenix press also provided propaganda for a favored candidate by reprinting nationally syndicated columns—by Raymond Moley,[48] Holmes Alexander, and Victor Reisel—all of which endorsed Goldwater. Moley's col-umn from *Newsweek* was reprinted in the *Arizona Republic.*[49] Moley spent two or three days in Phoenix around October first to gather his material. He then observed that "many COPE workers were abroad, contacting workers, publishing and distributing propaganda, and inspiring word of mouth sto-ries."[50] This statement helped to create an exaggerated impression of COPE activities. By COPE workers he could have meant only Arizona union members and their wives. COPE supplied some cash, far short of the amount claimed by Goldwater, and a few professional organizers in residence.

Holmes Alexander had Goldwater fighting the criminal elements of the underworld, the goons and racketeers of the labor movement, and the shady characters with skeletons in the closet who feared and hated him. Alexander compared Goldwater, a handsome jet pilot who had energy and color and a stainless record in the Senate, with McFarland, "known jocularly," he said, "as the Gray Ghost because of his elusive and unsubstantial campaign tactics."[51] Victor Riesel's column also appeared in the *Arizona Republic*.[52]

The newspapers also always gave Goldwater and Republican candidates the benefit of any possible advantageous news play. On its front pages, invariably the *Arizona Republic* would publish an anti-McFarland story above the fold and a disclaimer by the governor below the fold. In the October sixteenth issue, above the fold was a three-column headline: "Goldwater Would Return Big Stick Foreign Policy." Below the fold was a two-column headline: "McFarland Accuses Foe of Neglect on Water." A similar news play appeared in the issue of October thirtieth. Above the fold was a three-column headline: "Goldwater Fears COPE Tactics May be Copied." Below was the two-column headline: "Mac Says Opponent Press Spread HATE." Invariably also, regardless of the "spill-over" onto back pages, the Goldwater story would receive the greater length on the front page. In this instance, Goldwater received twenty-one column inches, McFarland thirteen.

In the October twenty-second issue, which contained three stories damaging to the Democrats, not a single item appeared either favorable to the Democrats or damaging to the Republicans. The second page contained the following headlined stories: "Rhodes Alone On Platform," "Fannin Trades Verbal Blows With Morrison," "GOP Farm Plan Lauded," and "4 Candidates Tell Farm Bureau They Oppose Production Control." Among these four candidates were three Republicans. In fact, every one of the top stories, covering almost the entire page, with the exception of some small advertisements, either favored the Republicans or impugned the Democratic cause. Though the newspaper had supported conservative Joe Haldiman as the possible contestant for John J. Rhodes' congressional seat, the newspaper gave preferred news coverage to the court-contested case of the election result—ostensibly to provide additional embarrassment to the Democrats and to fan the fire of factionalism which had raged in the bitter Democratic primaries.

On this page was also a recurrence of another theme pursued by the newspaper in order to embarrass Democratic candidates. Time and time again the reporter would point out that invited Democrats did not show up for panel discussions or debates with their Republican counterparts. On this occasion Rhodes spoke alone because Joe Haldiman did not appear, though someone on his staff reportedly had made a firm commitment that he would do so. At a Farm Bureau luncheon, Governor McFarland and Haldiman failed to put in an appearance. In this period of American politics, if a nominee did not appear at a debate, even though he had not accepted an invitation to do so in the first place, he was accused of being afraid to debate his opponent.

This technique was used particularly against McFarland. In his case, the opposition would either stack the panels when he was expected to be present or it would not publish the invitation and probably not extend it to him clearly or in good time, when the place and date of the panel debates were announced. Then when McFarland did present a paper, the newspaper would ridicule his speaking style or the content of his speech while praising his opponent's presentation. On occasion they would note that McFarland had forgotten parts of his speech or had to be called back to finish reading a manuscript.[53] Incidents of this kind took place toward the close of the campaign.

Goldwater had cultivated the image that he was forthright and had nothing to hide, that he was fearless and courageous and that he welcomed headlong verbal clashes. He was an abler speaker than McFarland. He was young and had a good memory. Although McFarland had been in the Senate previously, Goldwater, the incumbent, had a ready knowledge of current policies. Challengers to incumbents have overcome this advantage; but if an incumbent is alert and manages to assume the offensive and maintain it, he does have a firmer grasp of public policy. McFarland was neither an alert Hubert Humphrey who could overcome his incumbent opponent, Joseph Ball, in the 1948 Minnesota senatorial campaign, nor a youthful Frank E. Moss, who, in the 1958 Utah senatorial contest, could outshine his elderly opponent Arthur V. Watkins. Moss also had help from a formidable array of congressional visitors. McFarland had none of these assets. Naturally he would hesitate to appear with Goldwater in public; Goldwater had all the tactical advantages, both personal and political.

In the issue of the *Arizona Republic* reporting McFarland's failure to appear at a Phoenix Urban League Forum, Richard Kleindienst, state Republican chairman, complained that "large orders for the use of television and radio stations during the remainder [of the campaign] have been placed by the Democratic Central Committee."[54] This observation was to be used later in the campaign to account for the huge expenditure of COPE funds in support of the Democrats. It is difficult to account for Kleindienst's additional statement that "We do not have the money to buy time on such a scale." He implied that the Republicans did not have comparable time on the air and perhaps could not purchase what they needed to answer the Democrats, who had bought up most of the remaining time available.

The Republicans had already purchased time on a large scale and had plenty of money to pay for it. They were not placed in a disadvantaged position by this last-minute Democratic action.[55] The Republican campaign was very well financed—indeed, at the end of the campaign, the Republicans had a surplus. The Democratic opposition claimed that it was Goldwater who had $450,000 to spend, the exact amount he accused COPE of supplying to his opponent and the other Democratic nominees in the nation.

On November second the *Republic* announced that Goldwater "will address a Maryvale district rally tonight and will wind up his campaign with a 30-minute TV show at 9 P.M. tomorrow." No mention was made in this announcement that McFarland had been invited to appear at this rally. Actually McFarland had scheduled and announced that he would make an individual telecast. In fact, he did so—and at the same hour—a technique which he thought would be more beneficial to him than meeting Goldwater personally. His aides said that he had never agreed to meet Goldwater. Either he was not invited to do so, or an invitation might have been extended deliberately with the knowledge that his prior commitment made it certain that he would not show up at the rally so that the observation could again be made that he did not put in an appearance.

The next day the *Republic* front-paged and headlined its story of the rally with these words: "Afraid of Questions? Goldwater Asks, Mac Misses Final Rally." After acknowledging the lead to justify the headline, the *Republic* then gave an account of McFarland's address, selecting paragraphs which it answered by excerpts from Goldwater's panel remarks on his telecast which followed that evening. Apparently to accomplish this purpose it ran two stories in different editions of the same issue. A later story that same day was headlined: "Goldwater Tells Voters: Influence Real Poll Issue." The lead was Goldwater's question the evening before in answer to McFarland's "accusation" that Goldwater had painted his political opponent as something grotesque; the question was "whether the opportunities inherited by the coming crop of citizens will be limited by remote labor bosses and monopolistic business." The inclusion of monopolistic business was unusual for Goldwater. Perhaps at the last moment he sought to create the impression of balance in his views, decrying bossism and monopoly in both big labor and in big business.

In other instances the Phoenix paper stacked the cards in favor of Goldwater in editorials and in so-called news stories. At all times it maintained the fiction of "good" journalism by reporting events and statements of important persons. Sometimes the fiction became quite transparent; at other times it seemed to vanish entirely. *Republic* news stories on Democratic meetings and candidate speeches would frequently point out what the speaker did *not* say. For example, one *Republic* story reminded its readers that "he [Morrison,

Democratic gubernatorial candidate] did not mention any issues related to the conduct of state government, such as school taxes, development of new industries, and water problems."[56]

Democrats also pointed out that the "Letters to the Editor" were "loaded" with pro-Republican and anti-COPE letters. On one day there appeared one twenty-one-inch-column letter against McFarland, another four inches against Democratic candidates, and seven and one-half inches which was headed "Union Intimidation of Voters Defied" and signed "A Concerned Mother."[57] This writer appealed to all Arizona mothers not to sit by and let organized crime come in and take over the state. "How sad it would be for them in a short time if union bosses take over our state government and federal government," she concluded. The irony in this observation was that crime in Arizona had little or no connection with organized labor. No proof was offered in 1958 that any such connection or relationship existed in that area at that time. On another day "The People Speak" contained the following titles: "Union Man Warns Against COPE," nine inches; "Reuther Is Menace," seven inches; and "Housewife Defines Political Standards," fourteen inches.[58]

The *Republic* gave special play to Goldwater's appearances. To open his campaign, Goldwater returned to his "home town," Prescott, Arizona. Speaking from "between the four huge pillars atop the Yavapi County Courthouse steps," he "dramatically warned" Arizona against "New Deal and Fair Deal political conditions." Goldwater, in this address which was heard by five hundred persons and thousands more listeners on the largest network—twenty stations—ever operated in Arizona, "lashed McFarland's record."[59]

In another feature Goldwater was pictured receiving a plaque for outstanding services as soldier, citizen, and public official from Malcolm Bayley in behalf of the Sons of the American Revolution.[60] The SAR did Goldwater a service by presenting the plaque during the heat of a political campaign.

It would be difficult to single out and separate the role played by the newspapers in their successful efforts. Before the elections were under way, Goldwater was reported as saying that the only "issue" the Republicans had was precisely the one he used—BIG LABOR BOSSES. Former Senator Robert A. Taft's 1950 Ohio campaign was pointed to as the prototype of the hard-hitting campaign with labor—the CIO in that day—as the "wolf" or the "devil." Taft won over great odds. If he did so, others can do it, was the reasoning. The fact that Goldwater won and other Republicans who did adopt Taft's theme and tactics lost, added tinsel and glitter to Goldwater's victory. He became as a result the standard-bearer of his party's hopes.

Republican leaders generally seemed to be advocates of the Taft thesis, that BIG LABOR could be beaten at its own game, in spite of its great political advantage of adequate finances and large union memberships. Part of this thesis is that the labor "bloc" can be split and its ranks divided along union and individual member lines. It can only be concluded that Pulliam and his associates gave the order to the newspaper staffs to pull out all the journalistic—actually in this instance, propaganda—stops in order to defeat the Democrats, especially individual Democratic candidates, and to support Goldwater and Fannin. No other Republican candidate received as much attention in the paper's pages. While these newspapers supported some Democrats in the primary, the principal result, it would seem, was dissension, confusion, the routing of Democratic forces in such measure that they could not be reassembled easily and quickly, if at all, in a concerted effort for the final run. If Pulliam did not plan this result, he got it anyway; he contributed a great deal toward it.

Another factor in Goldwater's favor was the complete unity of the Republican elements and factions behind him. He had helped organize the party beforehand and made it for all practical purposes his party. Any ill feeling which turned up in his organization was directed at others and not at the senator, who apparently remained aloof from the dynamiting techniques employed by his staff and the Phoenix newspapers in his behalf, even to the extent that he could deny foreknowledge of their tactics, incomprehensible as that may appear. One cannot rule out entirely the possibility that Shadegg and the Phoenix press did not make Goldwater and his senatorial office staff privy to their every move in his behalf. Conceivably Goldwater, Sexson, and others could have been telling the truth, at least as they understood it, when they denied that the Al Green exposé had been planned considerably in advance of its detonation, and maintained that it was a spontaneous journalistic outrage based on materials normally gathered on any prominent individual and filed in the expectation that the news media might have use for them in the future.

In a political election, the payoff for nominees and managers is at the polls. In 1958, incumbent Senator Barry Goldwater kept his seat, defeating Governor Ernest McFarland by 164,593 to 129,030 votes. His winning share of the total vote cast, "an off-year vote (300,004) larger than that cast in the record presidential year of 1956 (297,552)," was 56 percent.[61] Republican Paul Fannin replaced the Democratic governor, and United States Representative John J. Rhodes easily retained his seat for a fourth term. Democrats won the remaining major national and state offices.

Senator Goldwater's victory stood out like a sore thumb, particularly in the West where the Democrats won nine of the ten senatorial seats up for election. This brought him into the national spotlight. Editorials speculated that if he, a conservative Republican, could win by such a decisive margin running against the sweeping Democratic tide, why could not other Republican candidates, especially incumbents such as Arthur V. Watkins of Utah, George Malone of Nevada, Frank A. Barrett of Wyoming, and perhaps even William Knowland of California?[62]

As usual, conservative journals editorialized that Senator Goldwater had stood courageously and unrelentingly on his principles. Having voiced his firm conviction in defense of the existing political, economic, and social order and against the enemies of this order, dramatically personalized in the figure of Walter Reuther, with Jimmy Hoffa lurking ominously in the shadows, Goldwater had stood not only firm but he had ridden out on his charger, undaunted by the odds and obstacles against him, with lance in hand, to meet the enemy on his own ground and at his own game.

Typical of such writings was the *Saturday Evening Post* editorial:

> Conspicuous among politicians who didn't let the supposed "trend" prevent them from standing on their principles is Senator Barry Goldwater of Arizona, who took all the rocks the political propagandists of the AFL-CIO had to throw at him and won the election. . . . Just why Goldwater survived obstacles which were too much for other conservatives is a matter for political analysts to explore.[63]

Close analysis of Senator Goldwater's campaign would seem to permit the deduction that he did not win precisely because he stood on his principles. Watkins, Malone, Knowland, and Barrett also stood on their principles and lost. The contention here, however, is that Goldwater won because he threw as many rocks at his opponents as they threw at him. Indeed, if he did not throw more rocks, he threw them harder and timed them better. He hit his target more frequently and more accurately. Furthermore, he had the entire strength of a monopolistic press behind him.

Not only did Goldwater's public relations counselors match COPE technique for technique, but they simply overwhelmed Goldwater's avowed enemy by transfer devices and insinuations by association, discrediting his opponent, Governor McFarland, and with him the whole labor movement and Democratic party in Arizona. Perhaps more accurately it would be the other way around; Shadegg and Goldwater thoroughly discredited out-of-state labor organizers and leaders and thereby Governor McFarland and the Democrats. The *Arizona Republic* summarized the whole routine of the Goldwater campaign on November second, just two days before election day. It stated:

> Political observers in Arizona attributed the Goldwater smear to those supporting McFarland. The AFL-CIO Committee on Political Education (COPE) has centered its attack on the junior senator, using money sent in from the Reuther-Hoffa Committee. These funds are being administered by Al Green, a Californian with a record of criminal violation.

It seemed to matter little to the *Republic*, Goldwater, and Shadegg when only one day later the paper reported that "Hoffa Looses Bitter Attack on Reuther."

Apart from Goldwater's political personality, Shadegg's managerial skill, and the continuous bombardment of the Phoenix newspapers, the Al Green exposé—with its satellite exposé of Robert Morrison—stands out as the great dynamiting event of the campaign and therefore, from a technical standpoint, its highlight. Goldwater's "breakthrough" and McFarland's "breakdown" came conceivably as a result of this blockbuster. This was Shadegg's brainchild, the result of his technical ingenuity: he was the principal architect. The *Arizona Republic* was the construction firm which supplied the physical materials, the construction personnel, and even some advice which conceivably it forced on the architect during the final stages. Shadegg's office supplied most if not all the propaganda materials. His job was the basic research, the locating, the gathering, and the assembling of the ammunition.

One section of the Fair Campaign Practices Committee's code commits a signee to refrain from "scurrilous personal attacks," but neither Morrison nor Fannin signed the code. Neither did Congressman Rhodes, the Republican candidate for reelection in the First District. All other major candidates did so, including Senator Goldwater, who early suggested that the Committee investigate COPE.

One Democratic strategist in this campaign observed:

> When you have two daily newspapers such as Eugene Pulliam's *Arizona Republic* and *Phoenix Gazette* (whose combined circulation is greater than all the other dailies in the state) emphasizing a given theme and carefully censoring out efforts to combat that theme, the situation is critical. I think it would be summed up by stating that Arizona neither voted against McFarland nor for Goldwater but rather against what was believed to be a monster labelled LABOR. This monster, incidentally, still remains somewhat vague and undefined in the minds of most people. That in itself must be regarded as a tribute to the effectiveness of the Pulliam press.[64]

McFarland himself states that "with everything else Goldwater could not have defeated me without the help of the Phoenix papers."[65]

However, other Democratic party officials were not so sure that these newspapers deserved all the credit for Goldwater's victory. Charles L. Hardy, chairman of the Democratic Central Committee of Maricopa County concluded that "it is a mistake to blame too much on the newspapers." He observed that in the southern part of the state (Tucson), Goldwater beat McFarland even though the *Arizona Daily Star* (one of the two newspapers in Tucson) endorsed McFarland, adding that "there was something more than the paper."[66]

The Phoenix press made all of Goldwater's campaign techniques effective. Its bombardment of the opposition was continuous and unrelenting. But the services and contributions of the Phoenix press must be seen in a different light as a campaign technique from that of Goldwater's energy and presence, Shadegg's ingenuity, and McFarland's succumbing to pressure. These were human aspects and actions. None of these, however, would seem to have had the effect on the election results that they did without the publicity carried by the mass media, particularly the printed page, which went into the homes to be picked up and read by all members of the family.

The nature of this particular printed page would seem unique. It consisted of two daily newspapers, one morning and one evening, with no competition in Phoenix and virtually none in the environs, giving almost all-out support to one candidate or to one party slate and apparently never overlooking a single opportunity to do so. In order to do this they employed many known propaganda devices and techniques. The result appeared to observers to be a perversion of the canons of good journalism and the ethics of a national honorary journalistic fraternity which the publisher, Eugene Pulliam, helped to found in his younger days. The managing editor of the *Arizona Republic* was the president of the organization at the time. Not very often have two newspapers, with a virtually daily press monopoly in a key population area, used their facilities in behalf of one or two candidates or a political party. One might conceivably conclude that they converted their establishment into a giant public relations firm during a political campaign.

NOTES

1. *Arizona Republic*, November 2, 1958. For a good account of this election, see Ross R. Rice, "The 1958 Election in Arizona," *Western Political Quarterly*, 12, Part 2 (March 1959), 266-75.

2. Letter from Stephen C. Shadegg to Frank H. Jonas, December 18, 1958. Shadegg's reply was in response to a request from the writer for some help in securing data on the "elections in the eleven Western states" for a biennial report which was to appear in the *Western Political Quarterly*. This journal had published such reports since its inception in 1948. Shadegg generously responded. The understanding was implicit that the data he supplied would be used in recording, analyzing, and interpreting the events and personalities in the 1958 Arizona elections campaign. He answered subsequent questions on the same event. Acknowledgment is hereby gratefully made for Mr. Shadegg's supply of data and commentary. Italics throughout are the writer's.

3. October 22, 1958. Fannin was not then aware that Goldwater was using his federal government paid staff in his campaign.

4. *Arizona Daily Star*, September 1, 1958.

5. October 22, 1958.

6. In this context, James C. McDevitt, national director of COPE, observed, "We not only had the unfortunate actions on the part of several representatives of the IA and M [Interna-

tional Association of Machinists], but more particularly the Democratic party itself in Arizona really dealt us a death-blow. It should be recalled that Mr. Langmade, the National Committeeman, did his best to kill the Democrats' chances in the Primary. I am told that he made his sound truck and other equipment as well as manpower available to the Republican candidate for campaign purposes." Letter from McDevitt to George F. Fowler, July 1, 1959.

7. Langmade remarked in the primary that he would like "to return the junior senator from Phoenix [Barry Goldwater] to his dry goods counter where he and his brother Bob can draw straws to see which is the Republican and which is the Democrat." Reported by R. John Eyre, letter, May 28, 1959.

8. Rice, "The 1958 Election in Arizona," p. 269.

9. Apparently the *Republic* did not expect political opposition to its stand on this question from the water users' group. It seemed surprised when it editorialized:

> The Salt River Power Distict's entry into the gubernatorial campaign was unprecedented in state politics. Never before has an organization with tax-free municipal status thrown its entire weight behind a candidate in such blatant fashion. Sooner or later the false and spurious claims of the project will be rejected by the taxpayers, who will insist that the project come under the rate-fixing, profit-limiting authority of the corporation commission, just as other power companies do. The use of tax-free, semi-public power revenue to favor one candidate over another is unheard of in American politics, and should not be tolerated.

Arizona Republic, September 11, 1958.

10. Browne personally believed that Virgil Hill of the *Phoenix Gazette* was not the "gentleman pictured, as it had been alleged, although the gentleman could well be a 'tip off.' " Letter, August 16, 1959.

11. *Ibid.*

12. *Ibid.*

13. *Ibid.*

14. *Ibid.*

15. "As to Mr. Green, whom I had known in other states, his activities were often surprisingly 'open.' "*Ibid.*

16. Shadegg, in his book *How to Win an Election* (New York: Taplinger, 1964), gives the impression that he and his research division knew exactly where Green was during his stay in Arizona in 1958. In the research done after the campaign in Arizona, the writers neither heard any allusions to Green's alleged clandestine movements nor found any evidence otherwise to support such allegations. On the other hand, they found that the effort to "get the goods" on Green and to keep these "secret" afterwards were far more "cloak and dagger" in nature than any action which possibly could be attributed to Green. Likewise, interviews with Green and observers of the Arizona election cast doubt on the authenticity of the charges that Green was living elegantly during this period.

17. Cates, an *Arizona Republic* staff writer, said that Art Heenan, the city editor, had written the story: Heenan denied authorship. The confirmation that King wrote the story came from a *Phoenix Gazette* staff writer who also worked part-time in Shadegg's office.

18. "The Attorney General shall furnish, *upon application*, all information pertaining to the identification of any person, a plate, photograph, outline picture, description, measurement, or any data of which person where is a record in the bureau [CII, or Bureau of Criminal Identification and Investigation]. *The information shall be furnished to a peace officer* *of the state,* to United States officers, or officers of *other states* or territories, or possessions of the United States, or peace officers of other countries duly authorized to receive the same, upon *application in writing by a certificate signed by the officer, stating that the information applied for is necessary in the interest of the due administration of the laws, and not for the purpose of assisting a private citizen in carrying on his personal interests or in maliciously or uselessly harassing, degrading or humiliating any person."* West's *Annotated California Code,* Penal Code, sec. 11,105. Italics added.

19. Letter, November 18, 1959. The letterhead of this firm read, "Business Consultants —Former FBI Agents." The report also revealed that officers of this firm were very close to the Murchison-Richardson-Hunt interests in Texas and the firm does investigative work for them as well as for the Texas legislature. Reportedly they had hired this firm for an investigation of COPE.

20. Shadegg, *How to Win an Election,* p. 75. Actually, the *Arizona Republic* seemed as anxious to have Fannin elected as Goldwater. It did as much or more for Fannin with positive publicity, and with the dynamiting job it did on his opponent Morrison, as it did for Goldwater with its dynamiting of Green or discrediting of any Democratic candidate.

21. September 29, 1958. This *Time* article was shot full of minor errors. No one, for example, ever called McFarland "Ernie." McFarland was "Mac" to Arizonians, some of whom—if campaign buttons could be believed—wanted to "Send Mac Back" to the Senate. Others said they wanted to send him back to his cotton farm.

22. Robert Creighton, *Arizona Legislative Review,* November 4, 1958.

23. It was these qualities which were to attract national politicians and public relations counsels to him as a possible presidential candidate in 1960 and 1964. They thought they saw in Goldwater a highly competitive spirit. However, in 1964, he more than met his match. It was his opponent, President Lyndon Johnson, who was the whirling dervish, always moving, unrelenting in his showering of propaganda missiles on Goldwater and the Republicans. According to F. Clifton White, who was in charge of securing the Republican nomination for Goldwater, he "quit" in 1964. He began to "explain." He lacked "fire." He did not want to be president. This was White's estimate of the man and his campaign. Interview, March 19, 1965.

24. "While Governor McFarland utilized hundreds of hours of canned television film on various innocuous subject matters, Mr. Goldwater used three 30-minute statewide telecasts as a means by which, to state in person, what he stood for." Letter from Richard G. Kleindienst, Arizona Republican State Committee chairman, March 4, 1959.

25. *Arizona Republic,* October 19, 1960.

26. Anderson and Goldberg pointed out that this brochure carried no signature nor any identification mark of publication: as a result, they contended that Goldwater was also equally guilty of distributing unsigned and unidentified scurrilous campaign literature. Letter from Earl N. Anderson, November 10, 1959.

27. Interview, reported April 27, 1959. The brochure, however, stated explicitly that it was "prepared by" Aubrey Barker, chairman, Communication Workers of America Local 8532, AFL-CIO; Theodore Cogswell, Phoenix Local 352, Typographical Union, AFL-CIO; Don Sherrill, International Alliance of Theatrical and Stage Employees, Radio and TV Department, Phoenix, AFL-CIO; Henry Lorona, American Railway Supervisors Association No. 351, Railroad Brotherhoods; Earl S. Gymon, Communication Workers of America, Local 8532, AFL-CIO. This brochure also graphically portrayed "how employment and wages increased in Arizona 1951-1957, during Barry Goldwater's service as United States Senator," and reviewed "Goldwater's *personal* labor record" in the Goldwater firm, concluding that this personal record was "excellent."

28. Rice, "The 1958 Election in Arizona," pp. 270-71. Rice attributes the highlight to a more positive action by Goldwater than the Al Green exposé, which was without a doubt a "smear." After the campaign, Eugene Pulliam frankly admitted that the target, and therefore the opponent, in this campaign was Walter Reuther.

29. For the "smears" against Goldwater, see Shadegg, *How to Win an Election*, p. 86, and Stepnen Shadegg, *Barry Goldwater: Freedom Is His Flight Plan* (New York: Fleet Publishing Corp., 1962), Chapter XV, "Smear, Slander, Sabotage and Victory," pp. 217-32.

30. "Speaking to the Tucson Rotary Club at noon Goldwater said that COPE, the AFL-CIO Committee on Political Education, has a $450,000 campaign fund, the *large share* of which will be devoted to attempts to unseat Goldwater and Sen. Charles Potter (R, Mich.)." *Phoenix Gazette*, October 15, 1958.

31. Church had been a business agent for the Construction, Production, and Maintenance Union and later served as president and secretary-treasurer of the Arizona State Federation of Labor, 1943-1947. He admitted that COPE gave him money and verified the fact that he had said "labor is one of the brightest badges I wear."

32. *Arizona Republic*, November 1, 1958.

33. *Ibid.*, November 28, 1958.

34. *Phoenix Gazette*, October 15, 1958.

35. October 28, 1958.

36. After the campaign, the following figures were found on file in the state capitol. Goldwater's reported expenditures for the general election were $134,010.72; contributions received in his behalf, $175,748.33. McFarland reported expenditures of $137,606.94 and contributions of $107,911.25.

One statement showed contributions collected by Stephen C. Shadegg, who was designated as "Financial Agent for Goldwater," in the amount of $25,100.22, and expenditures in the amount of $18,934.28. Other payments made especially to Shadegg amounted to $4,332.61. Another payment was made to the S-K Research Laboratory, a building owned by Shadegg. The total paid to or retained by Shadegg and to the S-K Research Laboratory, according to this sketchy report, amounted to $13,047.10. This figure might well represent an approximate amount received by Shadegg for his services as campaign manager plus rent for Goldwater's Phoenix headquarters, which were housed in the S-K Laboratory Building. Reportedly Shadegg received $7,500.

37. As late as October thirtieth, McFarland challenged Goldwater "to tell the people of the state where his campaign money is coming from." McFarland also

> pointed out that one political commentator has reported most of Goldwater's money coming from the same Texas oil men who supported the late Senator McCarthy (R., Wisc.).
>
> William Barnes, Young Democratic chairman, told the group that Goldwater reported receiving $22,000 from Texas oil interests in 1952.
>
> McFarland said he would not accuse him of allowing that contribution to influence his vote, but he voted against an amendment to the tidelands oil bill, which the Arizona legislature memorialized him to support and which would have provided $55 million for Arizona schools.

Arizona Republic, October 30, 1958. The next day (October thirty-first) the front-page story headlined, "Mac Drags McCarthy into Campaign."

"Twenty phone calls came into the *Republic* in one hour and the callers said they were members of the 'Hover Over the Dead Society.' They said numerous groups were resentful at 'vicious' attacks by McFarland and COPE on the memory of the late Senator Joseph McCarthy of Wisconsin, who died 17 months ago. 'Joe cannot answer but we will answer back at the polls,' one caller said. 'McFarland talks about smears but he's the only one to attack a man who is dead.' " *Arizona Republic*, November 4, 1958.

38. The "sweetheart" contract is an agreement between a union and a company. It is not considered legitimate since it is not the result of employee bargaining. The implication is that there has been collusion and that the union membership is being "milked."

39. December 1, 1958, pp. 6-7. This staff member wrote under a pseudonym. His real name has been withheld upon request.

40. *Arizona Republic*, October 29, 1958.

41. *Ibid.*, October 30, 1958.

42. *Ibid.*, October 31, 1958.

43. *Ibid.*, November 1, 1958.

44. *Ibid.*, November 3, 1958.

45. *Phoenix Gazette*, November 1, 1958.

46. *Arizona Republic*, October 29, 1958. On the last three days of October, the *Phoenix Gazette* published three streamers on the front page. These read: "It Is Simple to Vote a Split Ticket, Either by Machine or Paper Ballot," October twenty-ninth. This was obviously an "instruction" to the Democrats to vote Republican. "Don't Surrender Arizona to Reuther, Be Sure to Vote," October thirtieth, and "The Eyes of the Nation Will Be Upon Arizona Today. Do Not Fail to Vote," October thirtieth.

47. *Arizona Republic*, November 2, 1958. Giragi, a native Arizona Democrat, was a columnist who viciously attacked the foes of the Republicans, both real and imaginary.

48. One Moley pro-Goldwater column appeared in the *Phoenix Gazette*, October 3, 1958.

49. The October 13, 1958, issue of *Newsweek* appeared on the newsstands on October eighth, and Moley's column was reproduced on October tenth.

50. Later, Moley admitted that since he was a writer of opinion and not by any means "a purely objective reporter," he favored Goldwater and Fannin. He also admitted that timing was important not only in political strategy but in news commentary and that he had what it took for both, since he had been active in both politics and journalism for twenty-five years. He said: "It's part of both trades to watch timing." Letter from Raymond Moley to Frank H. Jonas, May 29, 1959.

51. *Arizona Republic*, October 19, 1958.

52. October 10, 1958. At the time, however, Riesel appeared to be a regular columnist for the *Republic*. The question here is whether the paper reprinted an earlier Riesel column for Goldwater's benefit in the campaign. The *Republic* regularly carried conservative columnists almost exclusively, so that the publication of these columns during the campaign was not a change of newspaper policy.

53. *Arizona Republic*, October 31, 1958.

54. *Phoenix Gazette*, October 31, 1958.

55. "Fortunately, from our standpoint, we did have an opportunity to answer, since I had purchased three TV telecasts covering the state for the last *ten days prior to the general* *election*, and we had 30 minutes on election eve for a statewide television hookup." Letter from Stephen C. Shadegg to Frank H. Jonas, February 25, 1959.

56. November 1, 1958.

57. *Arizona Republic*, October 29, 1958.

58. *Ibid.*, October 31, 1958.

59. *Ibid.*, September 11, 1958.

60. *Ibid.*, October 27, 1958.

61. Rice, "The 1958 Election in Arizona," p. 271.

62. All were U.S. senators: Knowland was running for the governorship; Watkins, Malone and Barrett, for reelection.

63. January 10, 1959, p. 10.

64. Letter from Larry B. Marton to Frank H. Jonas, December 4, 1958.

65. Interview with Ernest McFarland, June 16, 1959.

66. *Ibid.*

THE UNINTENTIONAL
SMEAR

ONE day late in the turbulent Arizona election in 1958 a modest touring car from California, laden with ten neatly wrapped packages in the trunk, rolled into Yuma and came to a stop in front of the Desert Sands Motel. At approximately ten o'clock in the evening of that day, Wednesday, October twenty-ninth, a two-door yellow sedan from Arizona pulled up alongside the California vehicle. With hardly more than a greeting,[1] the drivers transferred the packages from one car to the other and then retired for the night, the man from Phoenix at another motel. Both men knew the nature of the "cargo" but neither knew that it was "hot."

Although he knew he had transported some printed matter across state lines, T. E. McShane had served merely as a convenient courier for a lodge brother, Earl N. Anderson.[2] McShane and Anderson were Grand Lodge representatives of the International Association of Machinists in Los Angeles.

These somewhat surreptitious actions were the result of the meeting previously arranged by telephone between Anderson and the driver from Phoenix, Frank Goldberg, a minor official of the same union in the Arizona capital.[3] Anderson and Goldberg knew that the packages contained fifty thousand political leaflets intended for distribution in the election campaign.

The next day, Thursday, October thirtieth, Goldberg began placing the leaflets singly in, or under windshield wipers of, parked cars. By five o'clock he had disposed of approximately three thousand in this manner. He then divided the remaining two thousand from the one package he had opened and left them in two labor union halls.[4]

Tired and hungry, he ate dinner. About seven o'clock he turned his car toward Phoenix. En route he dropped off some leaflets in Buckeye.[5] He was completely unaware that his distribution of the handbills subsequently would result in a series of political explosions which would cover the state, absorb the attention of the politicians and voters in both parties for the remaining six days until election day, result in some unusual political behavior by the candidates and their campaign managers, reverberate sporadically for more than a year afterwards, and finally end in a court trial of himself and his friend, Earl N. Anderson. The affair was to become known as the incident of the "Stalin leaflet." The entire senatorial election campaign would be described as the bitterest[6] and the dirtiest[7] in the state's history.

Simple in design, the leaflet was a sheet of cheap paper approximately seven by eleven inches, on which was printed a cartoon likeness of Joseph Stalin. The reverse side was blank. The former Soviet dictator was caricatured as winking, smiling, and holding a smoking pipe between the teeth on one side of his mouth. The lower lip of the other side curled downward. The ends of the mouth were flanked by the drooping ends of his heavy mustache. With cropped hair, and a long, thick nose curled halfway over the mustache, the likeness suggested the sly but benign grandfatherly type.

Three captions were meant to convey a message that could be understood only if one had followed the senatorial contest between incumbent United States Senator Barry Goldwater, Republican, and incumbent Arizona Governor Ernest McFarland, Democrat, who was trying desperately to recapture the coveted seat he had lost to his younger and more flamboyant rival in 1952, the year of the Eisenhower landslide.[8]

Over the cartoon a two-line head read, "Union Lauds Goldwater, 'Honest, Sincere,' Miners Say." The words had been taken directly from the banner front-page headline of the *Arizona Republic* for October nineteenth. Under the cartoon were the words, "Goldwater fully endorsed by Pulliamism and lauded by Mine-Mill Smelter Union which was expelled from organized labor for Communist domination. Politics makes strange bedfellows!!" Within the lined square frame around the cartoon in the upper left-hand corner were five simple words, "Why Not Vote for Goldwater?"

In Phoenix, Friday morning, October thirty-first, Goldberg continued the distribution by placing single handbills in or on cars in the Park Central parking lot. This was a newly constructed shopping center with several large retail outlets, including Goldwater's Inc.[9]

By noon the leaflet had come into the hands of the politicians of both parties, but Goldberg continued his hand distribution during the afternoon in various shopping centers, business parking areas, and in the evening at the Dog Race Track. Goldberg left no stacks at any place except in two locations in the lobby of the Adams Hotel, where he dropped two or three hundred leaflets.[10]

The next morning, Saturday, November first, Goldberg had planned to drive to Tucson, work all day there in the same manner as he had in Yuma and Phoenix, and then be back in the capital to distribute what he had left at the

Union Lauds Goldwater "Honest, Sincere," Miners Say

GOLDWATER fully endorsed by Pulliamism and lauded by Mine-Mill-Smelter Union which was expelled from organized labor for Communist domination. Politics makes strange bedfellows!

state fair.[11] But he noticed that the Pulliam paper, the *Arizona Republic*, had a front-page article about the leaflet, and various radio stations carried the story. These news releases referred to a Senate investigation and to the questionable legality of the leaflet due to the fact that its source was not identified. Leland Glazier, a paid investigator for the Democratic party, reported that Goldberg "had told him he had started to Tucson but on the way he heard radio reports of an investigation of the cartoons."[12] In any event, Goldberg drove to Chandler, Arizona, and then turned back to Phoenix, where he called his associate in California, Earl N. Anderson, who said that he would be in Phoenix the next day, and that in the meantime Goldberg should destroy the remaining leaflets.

Saturday night Goldberg drove on West Van Buren to a location between Tolleson and Avondale, about fifteen miles from downtown Phoenix. There, just off the highway, where they could be seen, he dumped the remaining seven packages containing thirty-five thousand leaflets—a peculiar way to "destroy" them.

Anderson arrived in Phoenix Sunday afternoon.[13] Goldberg called his home at about six o'clock and the two men arranged to meet at Seventh Avenue and Camelback. About midnight both men drove in Anderson's car to "an area on the south side of West Van Buren near Avondale" which "appeared to be a sandy-like river bed."[14] As the car lights were put on the packages, Goldberg said that the packages were not as he had left them and *some appeared to be missing.* The two men then quickly decided that someone had discovered the packages and they departed at once.[15] They returned to Phoenix and secluded themselves for the remainder of the campaign, not even going to their union headquarters until the day after the election. They were not identified as the actors in this political drama, which so far was only a prelude to what was to follow, until February 10, 1959, when, after what appeared to be a long, intensive search to ferret them out, their identities were revealed publicly by officials of the Democratic party.

Goldberg did not handle his piece of political dynamite as explosive material, and hardly anyone considered it to be so at first glance, a point yet to be belabored. Had Goldberg had any experience in the art of political dynamiting or had he consulted any available expert on the subject, he would have learned that in this kind of political campaign propaganda, the statutes required that someone had to be designated, with a name and address printed on the leaflet, as the person responsible for the issue. He therefore would have asked a legal resident of Arizona to lend his name for this purpose. Then, had he been more skillful, he would have arranged to have the leaflets hit the electorate all at once by a mass distribution through the mail, by a shower from the skies, or by a well-organized and simultaneous door-to-door handout or car-to-car deposit in various cities, towns, and rural places. All he did in two days was hit a few areas crowded with automobiles in Yuma and Phoenix and dribble between towns and between parking lots in these cities, disposing of only one-third of his fifty thousand leaflets. Goldberg said that he had intended to cover the state. Had this really been his intention, he would not only have chosen a method of mass distribution, but he would have had printed at least three hundred thousand leaflets, not a paltry fifty thousand. The state was covered for him by the *Arizona Republic* when, in its November first issue, it published a replica of the leaflet on its front page, with a slanted commentary on its meaning.

It is doubtful that anything which happened after Goldberg began his distribution in Yuma had been outlined by him or by anyone else, but it is possible that he did some things deliberately after he had heard that his leaflet was "hot." He did not seem too concerned about his leaflet becoming widely distributed and read: he wanted certain persons and groups to see it. This may account for his having chosen labor halls in Yuma to dispose of part of one package. It may also account for his beginning his Phoenix distribution in the Park Central parking lot near the Goldwater store. Goldberg said he chose this spot because it was the largest parking area in that part of Phoenix. However, Stephen C. Shadegg, Goldwater's campaign manager, observed that

> the pamphlets were distributed in a better section of town, and I believe it was intended that we would come into possession of them. If someone really wanted to distribute a scurrilous pamphlet about Goldwater, I should think they would choose for their area of distribution those sections of town which would most likely be against Goldwater to start with. Actually, the major distribution was made in the parking area surrounding Goldwater's store in the northern section of the city.[16]

Goldberg has stated unequivocally that his leaflet was not intended to smear Goldwater. In fact, the insinuation that Goldwater was sympathetic to communism in any manner or form—an attribution so absolutely contrary to the facts and particularly to the impressions universally and conclusively held by the voters—would be considered such a stupid propaganda device that one would be constrained to accept Goldberg's view on this point. However, Goldberg did want his leaflet to fall into Goldwater's and Shadegg's hands, apparently at the earliest possible moment.[17]

Next, Goldberg has admitted that he left "small stacks of the leaflets in some places [in Phoenix]," but he added that he could not recall the exact locations.[18] Later, however, he said he left only two "small stacks" in the lobby of the Adams Hotel.[19] He denied having left any stacks at bus stops,[20] where the very first reports stated the leaflets had been picked up along with those in the Park Central area. He further denied any knowledge of how so many leaflets got into Republican headquarters[21] and in several other places where they were found in numbers and where some were picked up by the police.[22] He denied all knowledge of how Shadegg and the Republicans obtained so many copies; he even refuted the statement by a Goldwater aide[23] that a girl from Goldwater's store, Mary Jane Haskins, following in his footsteps collected anywhere from one hundred and fifty to five hundred copies and took them to Shadegg's office.[24]

Bundles of leaflets were picked up by the police at Thirty-fifth Avenue and Van Buren, at Thirty-second Avenue and Indian Road, and just outside the Republican headquarters. The first two places played a role in a little postelection drama, and at this point there walks on the stage a shadowy figure, called a friend by a Republican campaign strategist and a spy by others.

After the campaign Shadegg revealed: "From the very beginning I was fortunate enough to have available to me day to day reports from a friend who was close to the top labor organization in Arizona."[25] This man was located and identified as George F. Fowler.[26]

According to Fowler, the day following the distribution of the cartoons in the Goldwater store area, Shadegg received an early morning telephone call that someone had dropped a lot of Stalin cartoons in a box in the northeast section of Phoenix. Shadegg then called two employees who worked in his drug plant and told them to "go out where the cartoons are and stand guard over them until Goldwater's campaign truck could come out and pick them up."

Shadegg's secretary, Joan Faris, told a different story. She stated that the foreman or head chemist in Shadegg's pharmaceutical establishment received a call very early on Monday, the day before election. According to Miss Faris, when he received the report of the phone call, Shadegg dispatched two youthful employees to stand guard over the bundles. He then called the police, she said, who, when they arrived on the scene, involved the employees, who had to be extricated by Shadegg. Shadegg subsequently denied the details in these reports, discrediting both Fowler and Miss Faris as reliable persons, but he did not supply adequate details of his own.

The only public mention of a pickup truck appeared the day following the election. The *Phoenix Gazette* reported that the "Phoenix city police today had information linking a green pickup truck, believed to be a 1953 or 1954 Chevrolet, to the smear sheet. They were told that a truck of that description was driven away from 20th and Van Buren yesterday moments before about 500 copies of the cartoon were found on a bus stop bench there."[27]

What, then, really had happened? Goldberg and Anderson asserted and reasserted that Goldberg personally distributed the leaflets, that he left no completely intact bundles anywhere, except the seven he disposed of on Saturday night near Avondale, and that he left no stacks or piles anywhere except in the lobby of the Adams Hotel and in a few other hotel lobbies and two union halls in Yuma. By stacks or piles Goldberg meant fifty to one hundred leaflets, or at most two or three hundred. Where, then, did all the bundles which had been found at various places and all the leaflets which were still being distributed the day before election come from?

The allegation was made that persons associated with Goldwater's campaign or with the *Arizona Republic*, which had become identified actively and almost exclusively with the Goldwater campaign, might have had reprints made. Indeed, the Maricopa County Republican chairman, Charles H. Garland, who was doing professional public relations work for the Republican party at the time, stated that this was the case, that "reproductions" had been made.[28] But he did not say who had had them made.

Goldberg indicated that there was a strong possibility that reprints of the original leaflets were made which may have been distributed without his knowledge.[29] The most plausible explanation for the appearance of thousands of leaflets in bundles and stacks is that these were the ones abandoned by Goldberg and Anderson near Avondale at midnight between Sunday and Monday. From the number brought to Shadegg's office by individuals, he would have had enough in any event for his mailing list to news media and some labor organizations.

Only months later, after his statement to the FBI, did Anderson recall that when he and Goldberg drove to Avondale in his car that the packages were "still intact."[30]

Goldberg could hardly deny that leaflets other than the fifteen thousand he himself distributed made their appearance. Even Shadegg understood that "the FBI [had] picked up 150,000 which were left in bundles at bus stops on the day or so before the election." He also said that "forty thousand or so were dumped on election day, with no attempt made at distribution."[31] The *Phoenix Gazette* reported that leaflets were still being distributed on election day.

By denying that he knew anything about these other leaflets, Goldberg might have been trying to implicate others in the distribution or simply trying to provide some protection for himself in the forthcoming court trial. His only chances at this trial were either to implicate others in an anonymous distribution or to create a circus out of the proceedings and thereby embarrass prominent politicians and public officials, Republicans and Democrats alike. Reasons for his actions both before and after the election were not difficult to find; they could have been found in Goldberg's own personality, for apparently Goldberg did not like "anyone." He appeared to have no use for the Phoenix press, the Mine, Mill and Smelter union, and COPE. Apparently he did not like Al Green, K. S. Brown, and Governor McFarland. He specifically stated that he did not like Senator Goldwater.

The impact of the Stalin leaflet was probably not what Goldberg had envisioned. The explosion it detonated was to come after he had played his part and left the stage. It was Stephen C. Shadegg, Senator Goldwater's manager, who set it off, for he lost no time in using the leaflet as a dynamiting technique to blast Governor McFarland clear out of public office. In this effort he was aided and abetted by the bungling of the Democrats.

Indeed, the record indicates that the Democrats were the first to hear about the leaflets after they had been delivered to Goldberg in Yuma on October twenty-ninth. That evening, Governor McFarland and United States Senator Carl Hayden attended a Democratic rally in Yuma. McFarland asserted repeatedly that shortly before he boarded a plane to return to Phoenix that night someone told him about the leaflet. His informant described it as a smear, indicating that he had seen it or had heard about it from someone who had seen it. Yet Goldberg stated that he had not distributed a single leaflet that evening.

At about the same time, the Republicans were distributing an alleged smear publication against United States Representative Stewart Udall, Democrat, who was running for reelection. In fact, on Friday, the *Yuma Sun* bemoaned both smears, the Republican piece against Udall and the leaflet, already attributed to the Democrats. Rumors of smear were flying thick and fast at the time in this area. Perhaps it was the piece intended to discredit Representative Udall which Governor McFarland had learned about in Yuma.

Since Senator Hayden remained in Yuma for the night and learned about the leaflet on Thursday morning, it is probable that he actually saw a copy. A member of Congress since Arizona became a state in 1912, Senator Hayden had been through many political battles. He did not appear to take the leaflet very seriously. When he returned to Phoenix he mentioned the leaflet casually to both Democrats and Republicans, including Senator Goldwater's manager, Shadegg.

On Thursday Governor McFarland—irked by the charges Goldwater had leveled at "organized McFarland supporters" who, he said, had spread "scurrilous rumors" which "smeared" Goldwater's private life—retaliated by telephoning Senator Theodore Green (D—R.I.), the chairman of the Senate Subcommittee on Privileges and Elections. The call, placed on Thursday, did not reach Green until the next day, when McFarland told him that the leaflet was a Republican smear and suggested that an investigator be sent at once to Phoenix.

When this communication was made public, Shadegg said: "To allege that we had anything to do with them was the act of a desperate man." Then Shadegg said: "These [leaflets] were circulated two days ago in Yuma. Senator Hayden told me this."[32] Shadegg stated that he had not heard of the leaflets until during a noon luncheon on Friday, October thirty-first. Senator Hayden said:

> I returned to Phoenix via commercial airline on the afternoon of October 30. I have no recollection of having advised Governor McFarland of the leaflet, nor did I tell Senator Goldwater's campaign manager about it. If my memory serves me correctly, each of them knew about the existence of this leaflet by the time I arrived back in Phoenix. I am sure that I discussed the leaflet with Governor McFarland, but I cannot pinpoint the exact time, just as I cannot say definitely when I discussed it with Mr. Shadegg, though I know that I did so in the days that followed the Yuma visit.[33]

When asked what had prompted him to take this emergency action, Governor McFarland replied that a strong rumor had been circulated persistently to the effect that Goldwater's office would release a bombshell in the waning moments of the campaign. The appearance of the leaflet seemed to confirm this rumor.[34]

To release a final piece of propaganda, even a roorback, as a clincher or as insurance during the last few days of a campaign would not have been unusual. The Goldwater campaign, between the primaries and October thirtieth, had been exceptionally well executed, with excellent pacing and superb timing. The heat Senator Goldwater had already generated by personal dramatizations on his theme—Reuther, Hoffa, Big Labor Bosses, and COPE agents who were trying to become dictators in Arizona—and by his effective efforts to expose Al Green, the COPE area representative, and thereby to discredit Democratic candidates, had been such that the electorate could have expected anything as a campaign technique not only from that source but also from the Democrats in retaliation. But before it had become known publicly that the Democrats had reacted to the leaflet by assuming that the Republicans themselves were responsible for it and before James H. Duffy, the Senate investigator, landed in Phoenix on Saturday morning about ten o'clock, Shadegg had begun to turn the leaflet into a boomerang. Shadegg probably knew that the Democratic party had not launched it. Later he said that they could not have been that stupid. However, when he first saw the leaflet in his office shortly after two o'clock Friday afternoon, he appeared very surprised—and disgusted—and said, "How could they be that stupid?" He never explained who he meant by "they." Undoubtedly he was already thinking of hanging the responsibility on COPE and thereby indirectly on the Democrats and Governor McFarland.

In any event, Shadegg saw immediately the possibilities in using the leaflet as a weapon to discredit Governor McFarland. Moreover, his own attack on Al Green, a COPE political organizer, and on COPE itself, had been very vicious. He would be able to justify his own hard-hitting techniques by making it appear that his candidate had been hit hard. If Goldwater were attacked with an alleged defamatory missile, then Goldwater certainly could more easily account for his own attack on COPE. One would have been hard put to find any attacks by the Democratic party or by COPE as dramatic as the Republican attacks on COPE and the Democratic candidates. The few Democratic propaganda techniques, which the Republicans called smears, were limited in scope and duration compared to those employed by the Goldwater forces which could be defined in the same way. In addition, if one established a precise timetable, one might be able to say that most of the Democratic countermeasures were retaliatory or defensive in nature.

A public relations man could not wish for a better roorback to assail his client than the kind represented by the Stalin leaflet. Indeed he might welcome a defamatory attack that was so patently and ridiculously contrary to fact that no one would believe it. No one would have had a chance to make a poisonous verbal dart stick which associated Senator Goldwater in the least way with communism. Indeed, the Stalin leaflet was so potentially limited as a possible propaganda explosive that had neither party taken any action, it probably would have been ignored generally by the electorate. It certainly would have had little or no effect on the outcome at the polls. It had none of the qualities of a successful roorback in behalf of the Democrats, for its message, though apparently very simple and obviously very brief, was too obscure; it could not be grasped immediately nor even with some study unless one had followed very closely the entire campaign and all the factors involved in it.

Shadegg acted characteristically, skillfully, swiftly, and above all, offensively, but perhaps on this occasion a little too precipitously. Many of the leaflets had been collected in the Park Central area and brought to his office. He immediately sent a copy to everyone on Senator Goldwater's mailing list, along with a note saying, "This is being widely circulated in the Phoenix area."[35]

But he mailed the leaflets anonymously. This was his mistake. The message was typed by his secretary on a regular letter-size sheet of paper and mailed, with the leaflet, in a plain envelope with no return address. Later he realized his mistake, for he made a second mailing explaining the first to the persons and organizations on the same list, but this time he did so on Senator Goldwater's campaign letterheads.

That evening the staff of the *Arizona Republic* busily prepared the shocker that was to confront its morning readers. It was the distribution of the newspaper itself which provided the real propaganda bomb. Actually it was a *second* bomb, very much larger, and much more effective than Goldberg's puny effort. Its distribution and effect were in the Quigley formula; it hit the whole populace and the whole state with devastating and shattering effect.

On Saturday morning, November first, the cartoon was reproduced on the front page of the *Arizona Republic*, on the right side above the fold, but *with-out* the captions on the original leaflet, except those words which were a part of the cartoon itself, "Why Not Vote for Goldwater?" The omission of the top caption, "Union Lauds Goldwater, 'Honest, Sincere, Miners Say,' " was doubly significant, for it carried the message Goldwater intended, a fact which the *Republic* publishers and editors certainly understood when others were still puzzling over its meaning. The entire front-page display and story by the *Republic* can be examined closely for a brief analysis of the political position of the *Republic* and especially for its treatment of candidates.

Al Green was one of the major reasons for producing the Stalin leaflet. Goldberg wanted to point out the sheer hypocrisy of the *Arizona Republic* in blasting a labor leader who had done nothing more than ordinary election-eering, while at the same time speaking favorably of a labor union which had been ejected from the AFL-CIO for having been tainted with communism. The *Republic* staff undoubtedly understood the message on the leaflet at once, for this paper lost no time in producing a replica and replacing Goldberg's intended

FURTHER evidence of the type of political campaign conducted by COPE appeared here yesterday in thousands of pamphlets attacking Sen. B a r r y Goldwater.

The "smear type" brochure is a favorite weapon of COPE used in political contests in Michigan, Wisconsin, Washington, and Oregon.

JOE STALIN, pipe in mouth, is pictured in the pamphlets as saying, "WHY NOT VOTE FOR GOLDWATER?"

The pamphlets, distrib u t e d over the state by opponents of the incumbent senator, implied that both Goldwater and the independent International Union of Mine, Mill, and Smelter Workers were Communist dominated.

THE HANDBILLS drew a grim and coldly angry reply from Goldwater.

The senator stated:

"From the inception of this campaign, there have been scurrilous rumors circulated by organized McFarland supporters.

"My family life, my business, my mother, my brother, and my

SMEAR ON GOLDWATER — This slanderous cartoon is being distributed over the state by forces opposed to Senator Goldwater (R-Ariz). It does not bear a union label as required by anything printed in a union shop. Text accompanying the smear sheet seeks to imply that Goldwater is friendly with a Communist-dominated union.

message with one of its own. The newspaper interpretation was that it was nothing more than a smear of Goldwater, and this interpretation diverted attention from itself.

The three-column head to the news story read, "Mac In Tears About Smears; What Does He Say Of This?" There was little or nothing in the news story to warrant this headline. Certainly the "lead" did not justify it. The first four-fifths of the story dealt with Senator Goldwater's "indignation"; only one-fifth with McFarland's "disavowal." By using the word "tears," the headline writer referred dramatically to the protests Governor McFarland had made against the alleged "smears" his opponents had used against him.

The news story barely missed stating categorically that COPE had issued the leaflet. Specifically the report stated that "the 'smear-type' brochure is a favorite weapon of COPE used in political contests in Michigan, Wisconsin, Washington, and Oregon."

One voter who wrote to the *Republic* editor asked if the paper had some knowledge that COPE had issued the Stalin leaflet. Shadegg and Goldwater both pointed their fingers at COPE as the guilty party. Some suspicion was cast on Goldberg and on the Machinists union, but these suspicions were confined to small groups or a few individuals. Certainly they were not widely prevalent during the last three or four days of the campaign. Goldberg asserted later that no one, no one at all, could have known that he was the originator of the leaflet.

Perhaps the *Republic* felt itself justified in taking its offensive position—besides the reason that this is the calculated position of any expert and efficient propagandist—since many persons thought that the *Republic* and Shadegg were implicated somehow in the production and distribution of the leaflet. This hypothesis, though disproved finally, was neither unprofessional nor far fetched *at the moment.*

In the substitute caption at the bottom of the cartoon—none appeared at the top—the *Republic* said: "Text accompanying the smear sheet seeks to imply that Goldwater is friendly with a Communist-dominated union." But the text was *not* reproduced in the story. One must recall that only a very limited number of voters had seen the original cartoon. Goldberg had distributed only fifteen thousand copies in Yuma and Phoenix. Some distributions in Phoenix were reported by the press but these were reported *after* the *Republic* had published its replica and its slanted story. Even so, this later distribution must have been limited to far less than the total of thirty-five thousand leaflets deposited by Goldberg near Avondale. The police had already begun to pick up bundles and piles of leaflets, with five thousand in a bundle and several hundred in each pile. The impact on the electorate was made by the *Republic* reproduction, not by Goldberg's distribution.

That the *Republic* effort was a political technique has been suggested by the report from a staff member that the editors wanted to publish the reproduction and the biased story on Sunday instead of on Saturday, in order to get the close to fifty thousand more circulation of the Sunday edition. This placed the publication in the realm of propaganda technique rather than in that of journalism.

In any event, the original caption beneath the cartoon was quite factual. Broken sequentially into its component parts it read: "Goldwater fully endorsed by Pulliamism. . . ." Except for the connotation of the word "Pulliamism," this statement was true. Eugene Pulliam, publisher of the *Republic* and the evening *Gazette*, had endorsed Goldwater unequivocally and uncompromisingly. If the type of journalism Pulliam practiced in the Goldwater campaign could properly be labeled Pulliamism, the label was hardly a misnomer. Indeed, the news play given by the Phoenix Pulliam papers to the appearance of the Stalin leaflet perhaps alone merited the appellation.

And then the caption went on, "[Goldwater] lauded by Mine-Mill-Smelter Union. . . ." Actually, when this union action endorsing McFarland and not Goldwater was reported, the statement of the union's Arizona counsel, Carl Krass, was reported as having read that, though "Sen. Barry Goldwater did not receive endorsement of the Arizona Mine-Mill Council . . . the delegates were convinced of his 'basic honesty and sincerity.' "[36]

Goldberg had copied his top caption word for word from the *Republic* headline. This headline had read: "Union Lauds Goldwater." If Goldberg had made an intentional error, then the *Republic* had made it in the first place. The statement, though not the real lead in the newspaper story, was substantially correct since the union's council chairman had said that the delegates were convinced of Goldwater's "honesty and sincerity." How the chairman had ascertained this conviction of the delegates was not explained, for their officially recorded vote had rejected Goldwater.

The third part of Goldberg's original caption read, "Mine-Mill-Smelter Union which was expelled from organized labor for Communist domination." This would seem, even from newspaper stories, to have been a true statement. Goldwater had said that this union was the most democratic in Arizona. He had repeated this on the day he reacted to the leaflet,[37] and indeed, he said it again after the election. Goldwater had spent at least two hours with the members of this union when he appeared at the meeting where the delegates screened the candidates for possible endorsement. Also, after a visit at the national headquarters in Washington, D.C., of the International Association of Machinists, he called this union the most efficient labor organization. Afterwards, he published his views and sent copies to the local in Arizona. He seemed desperately to seek the good will of those unions which were either independent (Machinists) or not affiliated (Mine, Mill, and Smelter) with COPE, an action which would indicate he was interested chiefly in using COPE as a propaganda target in his reelection effort.

Goldberg's caption ended, "Politics makes strange bedfellows!" This was merely an axiom in politics generally accepted as true. Lacking in Goldberg's literary effort, which revealed his ineptness, was the treatment by Goldwater and the *Republic* of Al Green, the COPE area director, who was blasted right out of Arizona politics by a "smear job" which hardly had a parallel in any campaign in the West in 1958.

Actually, Goldwater's words about the Mine, Mill, and Smelter union were friendly, as were the words of the Union Council chairman. Certainly these were "friends" talking about each other, not enemies, not even political opponents. No one would have associated Goldwater with communism, but this apparently deliberate seeking of union favor by Goldwater, especially the favor of the Mine, Mill, and Smelter union, did appear somewhat anomolous. Indeed, they seemed to be "strange bedfellows."

In its front-page reproduction of the Stalin leaflet on November first, the *Republic* omitted the statements which could be established or construed as true, even those statements which had been copied from the pages of its own previous issues, and left standing the one single allusion associating Goldwater with communism, "Why Not Vote for Goldwater?" The accompanying story was also a recapitulation of the theme of the campaign and its treatment of the candidates. The *Republic* charged that the "thousands of pamphlets" which had appeared in Phoenix on the previous day were further evidence of the political campaign conducted by COPE. Actually COPE had nothing to do with the leaflet, and Goldberg had absolutely no use for Green, COPE's representative in Arizona.

In its follow-up story on November second, the *Arizona Republic* implied that McFarland, COPE, and Al Green were connected somehow or other with the leaflet. This connection was established by placing three separate sentences in sequence *without a direct reference* in any single sentence to an item in a previous one. The first sentence was "Political observers [who were these observers?] in Arizona attributed the Goldwater smear to those supporting McFarland." The next sentence, although it did not state that COPE was one of these supporters, read, "The AFL-CIO Committee on Political Education (COPE) has centered its attack on the junior senator using money sent in from the Reuther-Hoffa controlled committee." It followed that anyone who attacked Senator Goldwater must be a supporter of Governor McFarland. One could infer that Reuther and Hoffa, names which were much more familiar to the readers of the paper than the name of COPE, had sent the money. A further inference could be developed that Hoffa and Reuther were close associates and that both together or each separately controlled the committee. The last sentence in this paragraph read, "These funds are being administered by Al Green, a Californian with a record of criminal violence." In propaganda analysis, the principal device used—as it was in this instance and throughout nearly all the stories published about the Stalin leaflet—is called transfer. Previous stories make this transfer possible in the reader's mind. In this technique, sentences which contain separate references to materials already familiar to the reader are placed in sequence or close to each other in the same paragraph.

Senator Goldwater himself indicated that he was aware of this technique when he was reported as stating: "I am shocked that a man with the reputation of McFarland should accuse my supporters of this act."[38] It was true that McFarland had stated: "My opponents have deliberately circulated a phony attack on the Mine, Mill and Smelter Workers Union, which is supporting me." Later it was revealed that Goldberg, who prepared the leaflet, was more an opponent than a supporter of McFarland's.

Goldwater then stated that "I have not charged my opponent as being *directly* responsible for smears against my family and my business. I have not said that the governor was *personally* responsible for these tactics." Then in a startling statement intended to absolve the McFarland opponents from their attacks, Goldwater was quoted as having said, "But when McFarland failed to denounce the aid of COPE he should expect these tactics."[39] In other words, if one does not deny an accusation, he is guilty. Goldwater, on the other hand, never denied that his campaign had received money from outside the state, nor had he denounced at any time any source of financial aid. Indeed, it would appear from an analysis of the Pulliam papers that the *Arizona Republic* and the *Phoenix Gazette* were the largest contributors indirectly to any *individual* campaign in the 1958 Arizona elections.

The weight on the publicity balance at that time was heavily in favor of Goldwater and the Republicans. The Democrats were trying desperately to get back on the offensive. If the Stalin leaflet affair had been launched by them and intended as a roorback, it had boomeranged. However, the boomerang had not returned by itself. Shadegg had picked it up and had thrown it back. Goldwater supported his campaign manager at every step and with effective statements on the subject of the man's character.

Also, the fact that the boomerang was being returned accounted for the apparently slanted reporting by the Phoenix newspapers. One should not blame the Pulliam papers for their reporting in this affair, for they had already established themselves as a giant public relations firm with Senator Goldwater as their "client." It was to be expected that they would do all within their means to serve him. The one-sided political positions of the Phoenix newspapers and their publisher, Eugene Pulliam, were at all times consistent and honest.[40]

The *Republic* repeated its approach in the second paragraph of its November first story. The leaflets, the paper declared, implied that both Goldwater and the independent International Union of Mine, Mill and Smelter Workers were Communist dominated. In any event, the paper reported that "The handbills drew a grim and coldly angry reply from Goldwater." His words at this point were significant: "From the inception of this campaign, there have been scurrilous rumors circulated by organized McFarland supporters." The transition from COPE to McFarland as the responsible party was made by the newspaper in the statement that "the pamphlets [had been] distributed over the state by *opponents* of the *incumbent senator*. . . ." This phrase bridged the gap between COPE and McFarland; both had been named alternately and interchangeably as Goldwater's opponents. Neither the *Republic* nor Goldwater at the time these statements were made had any evidence that COPE or McFarland had produced the leaflet, yet they were able to make such allegations and insinuations without being held responsible for them. Goldwater continued:

> My family life, my business, my mother, my brother, and my personal actions have been smeared. Until this moment I have said very little.
>
> I will not keep silent and accept this latest smear accusing me of being supported by Communists and *attacking the largest and most democratic union in Arizona*.
>
> To charge [this union] . . . with still being Communist dominated is a vile and despicable act.

Then Goldwater made a strange statement: "Barry Goldwater is not supported by Communists, and the men of the Mine, Mill, and Smelter unions in Arizona deserve better than this."[41] Was Goldwater trying to leave the impression that he had been endorsed by this union?

By this time the pot was boiling, although the lid had not yet been blown off. This was to come on Monday, the day before the election, when Duffy made his spectacular statement that the only persons he could see or find who were distributing the leaflets were Republicans. Over the weekend charges were hurled back and forth, thick and fast.

McFarland and the Democrats had not been idle. In Yuma the Democratic county offices had learned about the leaflet around noon on Thursday.[42] Several persons who had seen a man passing them out brought copies to the party headquarters, saying that the man was on Orange Avenue going from car to car.

The county secretary took a copy to Bert Helm, Yuma county attorney and county chairman. Soon thereafter Ben F. Howard, a conductor on the Southern Pacific Railroad, came into headquarters and told the same story, saying that the man was driving a yellow station wagon with Goldwater and Fannin stickers.[43] Only later, when the Democrats in the county headquarters realized what was going on, did they call Howard back to their office, and obtained his affidavit which read: "On Thursday, October 30, I was coming from the Southern Pacific yard office when I noticed a man distributing handbills. The man got into a station wagon which bore Goldwater and Fannin stickers. When I returned to my own car, parked nearby, I found a handbill which showed a picture of Stalin, and the words, 'Why Not Vote for Goldwater?' "

Although this affidavit was dated November 3, 1958 (Monday), the Yuma County Democrats read the statement on a television program on Thursday night, October thirtieth.[44] The evening before the election, Howard's affidavit was used by McFarland on television and radio about every fifteen minutes. Although based on circumstantial evidence, the statement associated the Republicans with the distribution of the leaflet.

The *Arizona Republic* made the developments in the Stalin leaflet incident its leading story in the Sunday edition, November second, prior to election day. These included, in addition to comments from Shadegg, Goldwater, McFarland, and Duffy, a disavowal of responsibility and an abhorrence of the "hate handbill" by K. S. Brown, Arizona COPE chairman, but it placed Brown's statement at the very end of its long story—where many persons would not bother to read it. The one-column subhead to the story read: "Fund Used By COPE Is Cited." The paper apparently was not going to let COPE off the hook if it could prevent it, particularly after Senator Goldwater was attributing the leaflet to COPE and to labor sources outside the state. At this moment, Arizona state COPE officials were as much in the dark as anyone else about the source of the leaflet.

The newspaper account was typical of its treatment of the candidacies throughout the campaign. One paragraph read: "Duffy moved into the investigation immediately and warned, 'if we're not able to run down anything we'll probably call in the Department of Justice.' " The following paragraph read: "Political observers in Arizona attributed the Goldwater smear to those supporting McFarland. The AFL-CIO Committee On Political Education (COPE) has centered its attack on the junior senator, using money sent in from the Reuther-Hoffa-controlled committee. These funds are being administered by Al Green, a Californian with a record of criminal violence." The next paragraph began: "*Those responsible* for the cartoon are guilty of violating a federal law. . . ."[45]

The explosion in this incident came on Monday morning when James H. Duffy released his statement to the press. It read:

> I have conferred with representatives of both sides and found no concrete evidence to the effect that Governor McFarland or his supporters had anything to do with the leaflets. I have no direct evidence that Senator Goldwater printed the leaflets but Mr. Stephen Shadegg, campaign manager for Mr. Goldwater, has admitted that he received four or five hundred copies of the leaflets which were sent to everyone on the Senator's mailing list. This is the only evidence of a large-scale distribution of the leaflets that I have discovered.

This release was reported immediately to Shadegg. When he read it, all hell seemed to break loose. Senator Goldwater, usually quite placid in his office, according to his staff, "hit the ceiling." The statement appeared to them a whitewash of McFarland and a confirmation of the suspicions that somehow, in some way, Shadegg was involved in the leaflet.

Labeling Duffy's statement a "gross distortion of the truth," Shadegg attempted to set the record straight. Assuming that the "scurrilous cartoon" implied that Senator Goldwater enjoyed Communist support, he stated that the cartoon was brought to his attention for the first time at two o'clock Friday afternoon. Omitting any reference to the fact that a Goldwater employee, Mary Jane Haskins, had been instructed to pick up leaflets in the Park Central area, he said that "friends" of Senator Goldwater had brought them to the senator's headquarters.

Shadegg then admitted that he had mailed copies, with a statement that the cartoon was being distributed in the Phoenix area, to the daily newspapers. He did not say that he had made two mailings, the first an anonymous one.

He stated categorically: "I did not mail four or five hundred copies to any general mailing list, and I told Mr. Duffy exactly the facts as stated in his statement. This same information was given to Mr. Duffy by Mr. Bert Fireman who has been handling the Senator's press releases."[46] Duffy related that he had received his information from Shadegg's statement, which he quoted directly. Shadegg had said: "Friends started bringing them in and by four o'clock we had 400 or 500 of them in the office. Then we sent one copy to everyone on our mailing list. . . ."

After the campaign, when Shadegg's attention was called to an apparent inconsistency or contradiction in his own or in newspaper statements, he exclaimed: "Don't you know you can't believe everything you read in the newspapers!" There is no public record that he had at any time previously attempted to correct a statement made by the Phoenix press which had supported his client completely and consistently. Moreover, Fireman, Goldwater's part-time press-release man, was a full-time staff member of the evening *Phoenix Gazette*. He was the liaison between Goldwater's headquarters and the newspaper offices. The Phoenix press would be generally disinclined to publish anything that would damage either Shadegg or his client, Barry Goldwater; it would be inclined to correct any error.

Duffy explained to Fireman that he had obtained his information from Shadegg during his conversations with him on Sunday afternoon and evening. Duffy's opinion was that the distribution of four or five hundred copies of the leaflet to Senator Goldwater's mailing list constituted a re-publication of defamatory material and a very improper action on the part of Mr. Shadegg. This Shadegg undoubtedly knew, and perhaps he was already apprehensive; but Duffy's saying it apparently disturbed him, for he and the Phoenix press began a campaign to discredit Duffy and thereby his testimony.

Shadegg related that "on Friday morning, October 31, *before* the pamphlets had appeared in Phoenix, I was reliably informed that COPE had put up some $10,500 to buy additional radio and television spots for Saturday, Sunday and Monday."[47] This time, he said, was used to repeat Duffy's statement that he could not find anyone except Shadegg who had made a wide-scale distribution. In this statement, as in others, Shadegg appeared to want to show that just about everyone in Phoenix had foreknowledge of the leaflet's issue except himself and the personnel in Goldwater's entourage. Shadegg had not forgotten, however, that Duffy had not made his statement until nearly noon on Monday.[48]

In another statement Shadegg said that McFarland or his aides had requested Theodore Green to send an investigator to Arizona to identify the author of the pamphlet fully twenty-four—perhaps forty-eight—hours prior to the distribution in Phoenix.[49] If one were to accept the forty-eight-hour time period, then McFarland, or someone in his office, would have had to make the call early Wednesday morning. No one had heard about the leaflet or had seen it in Yuma until Thursday morning.

McFarland has related that he himself made the calls; that he tried to call Senator Green on Thursday before he saw the leaflet, but he did not complete the call until Friday. In this conversation he told Senator Green that he *suspected* a smear and wanted him to send an investigator to Phoenix. McFarland saw a copy of the Stalin leaflet for the first time at noon on Friday, when Robert Morrison handed him one at a luncheon in Scottsdale. When he returned to his office that afternoon he called Washington again and gave a precise description of the leaflet. He said neither he nor anyone in his office had contacted the newspapers. When he first heard about it in Yuma on Wednesday, he thought it was a "harmless thing." He insisted that he had heard about the leaflet on Wednesday. Even Senator Goldwater made reference repeatedly to Wednesday night as the date the leaflets first appeared in Yuma.[50] If Goldberg was truthfully stating that he did not distribute a single leaflet until Thursday, their statements could not be correct.

Shadegg was constructing a timetable which would have placed Duffy in the position of having received precise prior knowledge of the leaflet in Washington, D.C., from his associates there *before* he boarded the plane for Phoenix. Shadegg asserted he either purchased his plane tickets or made arrangements to do so on Thursday.[51] McFarland's call, however, which was based only on a vague suspicion of a smear, was not completed until Friday morning. Governor McFarland's secretary, Larry Marton, stated that a telegram was sent to Senator Green on Saturday morning, November first, requesting an immediate investigation of the leaflet. According to Marton, the newspapers made up the fact that Duffy had left Washington before he had received the telegram; they shouted collusion, he said.

Shadegg was ably assisted by the Phoenix papers in the effort to discredit Duffy. According to Marton, "the Goldwater camp, including the Phoenix daily newspapers, accused Duffy of lying, of being McFarland's tool, of being a hatchetman for the Democrats, and of everything else under the sun."[52] They claimed that "Gov. Mac" paid Duffy's bills while he was in Arizona and did everything but tuck him into bed at night. "In short, on November 3 and 4, they tore us to pieces and we had no chance to reply."[53]

Marton's statement would indicate that the leaflet incident resulted in a roorback against the Democrats. This was somewhat of a new twist in political campaigning, the turning of a propaganda piece which Goldwater claimed was launched to discredit him into a roorback which thoroughly rent his opposition into shreds.

In a telecast on Monday evening, Goldwater reviewed briefly the leaflet incident. When he came to Shadegg's distribution, he said:

> The investigator for the Senate committee on privileges and elections, who came here at the behest of Governor McFarland, this morning [Monday] issued a statement in which he stated that my campaign manager had admitted distributing 400 or 500 of these leaflets.[54] When indignant friends of ours brought the pamphlet which had been left in their cars, we sent a pamphlet and a statement—as I have said before—condemning the pamphlet to the news media in Arizona. The question you must decide is whether to believe this man who came here on a partisan errand, who never contacted me—and that's difficult to understand—though he was in consultation with Governor McFarland's assistants; or whether you are going to believe that what I have to say is the truth.[55]

Goldwater resorted to a technique used by the charismatic leader, an

appeal to his personal honesty and authority. The senator then went into his
COPE routine and impugned Duffy's honesty and courage. He ended his part of
the campaign on this negative note, much as he had begun it after the primary
two months before. For him everything had gone according to plan.

Goldwater had also gotten Senator Carl Curtis of Nebraska, who was sitting
at home, to denounce Duffy's report.[56] The denunciation, from such long
range and on such short notice, came automatically as a favor to Goldwater, on
information supplied by him. In any event, Curtis sent an investigator, Vernon
Johnson, as a representative of the Republican minority, to Phoenix. When
Johnson arrived, he conferred with Duffy and then remained absolutely silent.
Johnson made a report to the committee after he returned to Washington.

The *Arizona Republic* headed its election day story on Senator Curtis with
these words: "Senator Says Duffy Act 'Cheap Trick.' " Curtis called Duffy's
action in Phoenix an "attempted character assassination," and "was shocked to
find that a staff member would *stoop* to the acts committed by this man."[57] He
also charged that Duffy had failed to contact Goldwater and that Goldwater
tried without success to contact him. Actually Duffy said he did try to contact
Goldwater and that Goldwater did contact him.

After his press release on November third, Duffy moved from the Sahara
Hotel in Phoenix to the Valley Ho Hotel in Scottsdale, in order to be able to
work according to his own schedule without being continually harrassed by
radio and newspaper representatives and others who had no additional information to offer, and who in many instances were very abusive. Within five minutes after he left the hotel to have dinner, Goldwater and several assistants arrived and asked for him. Duffy was not aware of this call until he had returned
to the hotel at about eleven o'clock that night. He said he had used his time to
make calls on outside phones and from various locations. Goldwater's manager
said he had been closeted with McFarland. At 2:30 A.M. he answered a knock
at the door and Dean Burch, Goldwater's administrative assistant, and Shadegg
forced their way into his room. For an hour and a half Duffy was forced to
listen to abusive language to the effect that he had lied, slandered Senator Goldwater and his assistants, twisted the facts concerning the leaflets, refused to
meet with Senator Goldwater, and had issued a false statement.

Burch and Shadegg demanded that Duffy get dressed to meet with Goldwater and further demanded that he change his statement. Burch wanted Duffy
to sign a three-page, handwritten statement for release to the press. Duffy refused claiming it contained misrepresentations and untruths which purported
to discredit the work he had done in Arizona and the statement he had released
on November third. About 4:30 A.M., November fourth, Burch and Shadegg
left Duffy's room.

During a conversation Duffy had with Herb Surrett of the United Press International during the early morning of November fourth, Surrett stated that his office had received an envelope with no identifying marks or names on it which contained a copy of the Stalin leaflet and a piece of plain paper with one sentence saying in substance, "These are being widely distributed in the Phoenix, Arizona area." Soon afterwards another envelope arrived from Senator Goldwater's headquarters containing the senator's denial of responsibility for the printing and distribution of the pamphlet. Both envelopes were believed to have been sent from the same source.

On Tuesday the voters went to the polls with the politicians' roars still ringing in their ears and their minds cluttered with the confusion of charges and denials and countercharges. If a single issue remained in this campaign, it had to be picked out of the garbage can during the days to come when attempts were made to restore some sanity to politics in the Grand Canyon State and to find some clear answers to the mystery of the Stalin leaflet incident.

What then was the effect of the Stalin leaflet on the election results? Opinions vary, ranging between the two extremes of little or none at all to considerable or decisive. In those which attach great significance to it, there is usually the reservation that what made it important was the wide distribution and one-sided slant given it by the Phoenix dailies, especially the *Arizona Republic.* Important in this connection is not the leaflet itself or the limited use made of it by its creators and initial distributors, Goldberg and Anderson, but the attempts made by the Democrats to pin the responsibility for it on the Republicans, and above all, its exploitation by the latter to discredit the Democrats.

When Walter Quigley examined a copy he commented: "The Arizona stuff [Stalin leaflet] is crude. I can't see where it would affect a vote."[58] Indeed, had neither the Democrats nor the Republicans taken more than passing notice of it, Quigley's evaluation probably would have been correct.

The distribution by Goldberg alone would have been too limited for either a "dynamiting job" or a roorback. In the first instance, there was little or no "revelation" based on "research" in the few sentences of the leaflet, which were poorly stated and presented; the meaning was not immediately clear even to those who were engaged actively in both parties. Felknor has summed up this aspect of the leaflet in terms of Goldberg's "editorial ineptitude." Goldberg simply failed to make his point, which was that the *Arizona Republic* in its support of Goldwater was damning the "innocent," or at least anti-Communist, unions and using a Communist-tainted union to advance the cause of the paper's choice, Senator Goldwater.[59]

In the contest between the Republicans and Democrats to discredit each other by exploiting the leaflets through various techniques, the Republicans had the edge. The cartoon caption did relate the leaflet to Goldwater in such a way that he could assume it was a "smear" against him. By deleting all other captions which might have clarified the purpose of the propaganda piece, the *Arizona Republic* attributed exclusively and solely this intent to it. The Republicans took advantage of an initial revulsion of the electorate to a "smear." Goldwater successfully essayed the role of the underdog, thereby evoking sympathy for himself and his side. Also, assuming the Republican thesis, that the "smear" came from COPE, an organization which had endorsed McFarland, the Republicans were able in the last days of the campaign to pin a major "smear" attempt on the Democrats, a label that McFarland and other candidates had avoided scrupulously and quite successfully, at least on the record if not in the electorate's mind.

Though Senator Goldwater gained the most from the use his manager made of it, he evaluated it as being very low in effect. It had been suggested to him that the leaflet had helped him. He answered: "Relative to the Stalin photograph, I disagree with you that this was an asset. Frankly, I don't think it helped or hurt, and that would apply to my opponent as well as to me."[60] He further stated: "I can tell you that it didn't affect my election one way or another."[61] Here he implies that had he ignored the leaflet, he would have won in any case. Indeed, he admitted: "Frankly, it never gave me much concern. I knew we had the election won at that point and nothing could change that, particularly a cheap attempt like the Stalin cartoon."[62] In retrospect, this evaluation appears to be correct; but an interesting point is why he rated the effect of the leaflets so low. At the time he acted as if it were the most important technique in the campaign. He made spur-of-the-moment statements, motivated by the leaflet, which appeared to be somewhat irrational if not incorrect. On the day before election he added to the list of threats against himself and the members of his family, which he had issued at the press conference the previous Friday, that "they had threatened to kill me." On television that night he had drawn himself up to his full stature as a senator and an honest man, one who had authority and would not—could not—lie, and categorically stated that Shadegg had not made the large anonymous distribution with which he had been credited by the Phoenix press.

Shadegg himself later dismissed the Stalin leaflet as a "phantasy of unbalanced thinking, a ridiculous bit of phantasy." Six months after the election he still thought that the "leaflets were a concrete example of what labor was doing with Union funds," although he must have known, as others did, that the leaflets were very inexpensive to produce and that subsequently Goldberg and Anderson individually had taken full credit for their production and had paid the printing cost. The entire expense of distribution was borne by Goldberg himself. When asked how he knew the leaflets had been produced outside the state and with union funds, Shadegg replied: "You'll have to ask Senator Goldwater." He estimated that they might have contributed a small, net, overall gain for Goldwater.[63]

Bert Fireman, *Phoenix Gazette* feature writer and Goldwater's press release man, stated that the "Stalin leaflets did not significantly affect the election."[64] He admitted, however, that they helped Goldwater a little but could have hurt him considerably if the affair had not been followed closely." If Duffy, who investigated the affair for the Senate Committee on Privileges and Elections, had been able to clear McFarland and COPE, the responsibility for having printed the leaflets would have been placed at Goldwater's feet.

Although he did not evaluate its effect at the polls, Richard G. Kleindienst, state Republican chairman and an ardent Goldwater supporter, did attribute great prominence to it, an estimate which was in contrast to Senator Goldwater's postelection attempts to downgrade the part it played.[65]

Not all the Democratic leaders were agreed on its impact. McFarland's secretary, Larry B. Marton, felt that the leaflet was the straw that broke the camel's back. This view was affirmed by Leland Glazier, Maricopa County Democratic party assistant executive officer. "Straw" is hardly the best word to use in this context. Marton actually felt that the leaflet was the most significant factor in McFarland's defeat.[66] On the other hand, Michael Morris admitted that the leaflet contributed a small part in the overall plan. "In itself," he said, "it was not too significant, just one of the small things."[67] According to Charles Hardy, Maricopa County Democratic chairman, "the leaflet might have had a cumulative effect."[68] Stephen Langmade, Democratic national committeeman, did not think the leaflets were particularly important. "They only confused the people," he concluded.[69] Harry Mitten, executive secretary of the Republican State Central Committee, conceded that the leaflet had a great deal to do with the campaign. He reasoned as follows: "The American public is interested in fair play and the leaflets hit below the belt. It is an example of an unfair technique." One may suggest, however, that this is generally true only when personally one is not emotionally involved in or actively concerned with the fate of a candidate. One tends to discount or even overlook the charges made by one's favorite candidate and to place great emphasis on those made against him. Not too much attention is given by the voter to a precise definition of a "smear." If he is vitally interested in the fortunes of a particular candidate, he will tend to accept that candidate's definition and interpretation.

Probably the best and most balanced view of both the highlight part played by the leaflet and its effectiveness was expressed by Orien Fifer, managing editor of the *Arizona Republic.* Pointing to a copy of the Al Green article he said:

"It was this article and the Stalin leaflet that elected Goldwater. Every public opinion poll taken in the valley favored McFarland up until ten days before the election. *Those two articles elected Goldwater.*"[70] This judgment also implicitly suggests the role played by the *Arizona Republic* in the campaign because it was this paper which gave great circulation to both stories, which were written by its own staff members. The *Arizona Republic*, and its sister paper, the *Phoenix Gazette*, can take substantially the credit for reelecting Senator Goldwater and for electing Paul Fannin governor. The *Arizona Republic* was prepared with both skilled personnel and a giant organizational and mechanical apparatus to act on a moment's notice.[71] It would have taken the usual commercial public relations firm, or even a candidate's immediate staff, hours or even days to prepare their attack or counterattack for publication. Then the cost of distribution to cover an entire state would be immense if not prohibitive. The Democrats had no such assets. Rarely in American political campaign history has any party had such advantages, which, in Goldwater's case, were enhanced by the fact that all the newspapers in Phoenix were owned and operated by one man who apparently was also one of the principal strategists for the senator's reelection campaign. Such a situation may certainly be described as extraordinary.

Probably the best evaluation which can be assigned to the part the *use* of the leaflet played in the campaign is that it served Senator Goldwater as a "clincher." The Goldwater forces *used* the Stalin leaflet to justify their own hard-hitting campaign, especially the Al Green "smear." Although the Goldwater interpretation of Green's personality and his actions in the campaign had already been accepted by the electorate, including many Democrats and labor union members, the Stalin leaflet, attributed to COPE and outside-the-state personnel and money, justified the vilification of Green, if any doubt remained in anybody's mind. Shadegg, by attributing the leaflets to Goldwater's opponent, succeeded in pinning on the Democrats the only major public or documented smear of Goldwater used by them during the campaign, while he was using a series of techniques which upon close examination could themselves be construed as smears or very close to this designation. Ironically the Democrats he aimed at had nothing to do with the leaflet. The possibility that the leaflet could be turned against McFarland was a result of the editorial ineptitude of its authors; they had not intended it as a "smear" of the governor. For this reason Bruce Felknor would have been justified in labeling it an "unintentional smear."

The leaflet provides the student of campaign propaganda not only with an example of the "unintentional smear," but it demonstrates how a very simple and comparatively minor printed "missile" can be turned into a major episode and almost a decisive technique in a political campaign by an astute and alert campaign manager. In fact, the whole affair became so prominent that interest in it continued long after the campaign, and in the ensuing years it will be re-called perhaps more readily and more often than any other propaganda in Arizona politics.

So the 1958 election campaign came to a close. But it remained for the FBI to provide the epilogue by ferreting out the source of the leaflet and placing the responsibility squarely on Anderson and Goldberg. At first Senator Goldwater appeared to have been eager to pursue the trail, but as time passed, he seemed to be content to drop the whole matter. Surprisingly the Phoenix press, which had carefully and at considerable cost researched Al Green's and Robert Morrison's records, particularly in California, showed very little interest in the case. Staff members protested that they made every effort to determine the identity of the responsible persons, but the public record does not bear out their allegations.

Stories were prevalent in Arizona that the FBI, with as many as ten or twelve agents in the field, was trying frantically to find the perpetrators. Finally they closed in on Goldberg and Anderson in California by putting pres-sure on the leaflet's printer in Santa Monica. Bothered for several days by visits from federal agents, the printer appealed to Machinists union officials in Los Angeles to "get these people off my back."

Goldberg was suspected early, soon after the election. When one national Democratic public relations man saw the leaflet in Arizona on Friday, October thirty-first, he said spontaneously, "that looks like the work of the Machin-ists." He had seen the cartoon earlier in California. In fact, some suggestion had been made that it might be used in other campaigns, including those in Utah and Nevada.

Having the clue that the cartoon had come from Machinists headquarters in Los Angeles, every interested person began to look around that union for some-one who might have produced the leaflet. The searchlights soon fell on Frank G. Goldberg. He had been an outspoken critic of McFarland and Morrison, of COPE, of other unions, and of everyone and anyone who did not share his views against the right-to-work measure in effect in Arizona. He charged that the cooperation of labor leaders with the McClellan Committee would only lead to a setback for labor. He and Anderson had derided Arizona state labor leaders whom they accused later of tacit collaboration with Senator Gold-water, if not by their precise actions, then by their silence on vital labor inter-ests. In a way Goldberg had been the "bad boy" in Arizona labor politics—"the kind of person" who would or could bring out the leaflet. He and Anderson later even boasted at their trial that they would blow the lid off Arizona politics, involving the Democrats, Republicans, the state AFL-CIO organization, and especially Senator Barry Goldwater and Stephen Shadegg.

In Arizona Leland Glazier was carrying on his intensive search. Working on the hypothesis that Shadegg somehow, in some way, had been involved with Goldberg in the leaflet episode, he apparently was beginning to get close to a powder keg. Suddenly Goldberg and Anderson met the FBI agents in Blythe, California, and made their statements, assuming full and exclusive responsibility. They then retained an attorney, a Democrat, in Phoenix, thinking they would need his services. But the FBI did not announce its findings. Soon after, Goldberg received a telegram from Glazier requesting an immediate meeting. He complied and "confessed" to Glazier, who immediately called a press conference and gave the information to the press.

Hardy, the Maricopa County Democratic chairman, thought it would look better if "the Democratic party were to break the story, particularly since Goldberg was one of our Precinct Committeemen." Later, Hardy learned that the two men had already told their story to the FBI which withheld any public announcement until it presented its information to the grand jury.

With straight journalism, the *Phoenix Gazette* played the revelations on the front page of its February 11, 1959, issue. The Democratic release was in the form of a telegram by Hardy to Senator Goldwater giving some details and emphasizing that "the Democratic party organization had nothing to do with the printing and distribution of the cartoon, and deplores such tactics."[72] Goldwater had admitted this point one month earlier but could not resist the conclusion that "it points up the fact that out-of-state forces were at work in the Arizona election." In reality Frank Goldberg could not have been considered an "out-of-state" person.

When asked why they "confessed" to Glazier, after already having told their story to the FBI, Anderson and Goldberg said that they did not want Glazier to get hurt, that he was getting too close to Shadegg. They also said Glazier and the Democratic officials who hired him wanted them to make statements that would implicate Shadegg, and that this was a dishonest intention. They wired this charge to Senator Green and also to FBI Director J. Edgar Hoover. The *Arizona Republic* headlined this development, with a large picture of Goldberg above the fold, "Democrats' Investigator Accused, Tried to Frame Shadegg!"[73]

Apparently the two men were angry, but had they wanted to protect the Democrats as well as the Republicans, they could have put Glazier's alleged suggestions aside without any fanfare. Later they were somewhat sorry they had acted hastily, not in rejecting Glazier's suggestion but in appearing to de-fend Shadegg. At a trial, their only chance at justice—which is what they said they sought—would be to link both Shadegg and the *Arizona Republic* with the leaflet, Shadegg for his anonymous distribution and the *Republic* for its dis-torted use of the leaflet in behalf of Senator Goldwater. In fact, another lawyer they retained later separated himself from the case by stating that he could not make an all-out effort to defend the two men unless he tried both Shadegg and the *Republic*. This he could not do, he wrote, because in doing so he would embarrass his law partners who were good friends of Shadegg's.

Anderson and Goldberg asserted that Glazier did not "solve the case," that it had already been solved by the FBI; indeed, that nobody had solved it, since they voluntarily agreed to meet with FBI agents and make their statements. They claimed that Glazier had learned what he knew from the FBI statements which they had entrusted to their lawyer, who, they claimed, failed them in his professional capacity by divulging the information to Glazier.

The grand jury indicted only Anderson and Goldberg.[74] Subsequently these men could not get a lawyer in Arizona to defend them. Obviously no one wanted to oppose in any way the dominant political interests in the state. The trial record contained little in addition to what has been recorded in these pages. A reading of the trial transcript might suggest that the California lawyer who was brought in as defense attorney made a few feeble attempts to create one or two political scenes. The judge kept the trial proceedings to the single charge that was actually involved, that of having failed to have their leaflet signed by a responsible person. The defendants were found guilty, given sus-pended jail sentences, and fined one thousand dollars each—the maximum pen-alty. The Phoenix press gave the trial only perfunctory notice. Anderson and Goldberg slipped away into anonymity. Arizona labor organizations deserted them, as did everyone else, even their own Machinists union. In politics, appar-ently, neither the Democratic nor Republican party, and hardly anyone else, likes to have the applecart upset. To do so only spoils the game for the ambi-tious, as well as for the incumbent, rulers of the land.

The men who masterminded the 1958 campaign will long be remembered. Stephen C. Shadegg emerges as a new type of dynamiter, one who insisted that he was not a professional in the public relations field,[75] even if others so re-garded him. A press report described him as "the coming campaign genius of the Republican party" and reported that *Roll Call*, a weekly newspaper circu-lated on Capitol Hill in Washington, predicted Shadegg "will be the new Murray Chotiner of the Republican Party." Stephen C. Langmade, Arizona Demo-cratic national committeeman, said of him: "Shadegg has a good basic philosophy. He is considered not as a member of either political party, but as a professional public relations man."[76]

Asked if public relations was his hobby, Shadegg replied that it was more than a hobby, that it was his "over-consuming interest." He said that "battle for survival" exists between competing ideologies, that the next four, six, or ten years would determine whether or not all the freedoms we have enjoyed will disappear. His "consuming interest" is to help preserve these freedoms. "Politically," he has said, "I am a passionate conservative, in the tradition of Burke, John Adams, Randolph, etc." Then he summarized his personal philosophy by quoting from Edmund Burke, "Private property is inseparably connected with freedom." He then elaborated further with this analogy: "Government ought to make sure that everyone starts at the line, but not limit the distance each one may travel." As a conservative, he emphasized that he is "opposed to any form of egalitarianism."[77]

His career evidences his widely varied interests, from the days in 1927 when he joined the Pasadena Playhouse School of Drama just out of high school, had several professional theatrical engagements, spent about ten years as a professional writer for radio, motion pictures, and national magazines, until he became interested in, and eventually owner of, a small manufacturing business in Phoenix, the S & K laboratories, a wholesale drug research and distributing company. Although this solved the economic problem for him, writing remained his favorite career. He recalls: "In 1937 I left radio and started freelance writing. First sale was in February, 1938. Since that time I have written and sold more than 500 detective stories" (all under pen names).[78] He became interested in politics early and joined the Democratic party. "I became of age in California," he said, "where a corrupt Republican administration was in power. In a moment of rebellion against this type of administration, I became a Democrat." Although he stated that "I have always been an anti-Roosevelt, anti-Truman, anti-New Deal,"[79] he remained a registered Democrat until 1956 or 1957 when he joined the Republicans.

In the 1950 campaign he did some writing for Democratic Senator Carl Hayden. Somewhere along the line the story started and spread that he had managed Hayden's campaign. Inside the dust jacket of his book, *How to Win an Election*, the biographical note reads, "Involved in the political arena for more than 14 years, he ran his first statewide campaign for Democrat Carl Hayden in 1950." However, Senator Hayden himself has said that "Stephen Shadegg was not my manager in 1950. All he did was to assist in the preparation of radio scripts in a very satisfactory manner."[80]

The story is prevalent in Arizona political circles that Shadegg approached

Governor McFarland, offering to manage his campaign for ten thousand dollars, but that his offer was rejected. On this point McFarland reported:

> Mr. Shadegg did not come to me personally and offer his services for $10,000. A friend of mine who knew him well conveyed the information to me that he was willing to work for $10,000, and indicated that if I did not accept immediately he was going to work for Goldwater. He is an able writer and has a wicked pen. That is why I say that it might have been a good thing had I accepted the offer.

Shadegg admitted that he had been approached by "friends of McFarland" and asked if he would manage McFarland's 1952 campaign, but insisted that he had used his right to exercise a preference and decided to help Goldwater. Without any suggestion from the interviewer, Shadegg quickly stated that his choice had not been determined by the prospects of commercial gain.[81]

He managed Goldwater's campaign from his office. In addition, Goldwater rented adjoining space in Shadegg's building for his representative in Arizona, Paul Sexson. It is difficult to ascertain just how much research and writing Shadegg himself did in Goldwater's campaign. Apparently, with ample if not inexhaustible financial resources, he hired investigators and purchased research data. Shadegg never complained publicly or privately of being short of funds.

Bert Fireman, the able feature writer for the *Phoenix Gazette*, was hired for part-time work during the campaign as the press release writer, and in this capacity he acted as a liaison with both Phoenix newspapers. At times Shadegg worked directly with the editors, and Goldwater was in touch with Eugene Pulliam, the publisher. Shadegg also hired George F. Fowler, who did investigative work for him, especially in labor circles.

Much ammunition for Goldwater's campaign was gathered by a research division and then assembled with that gathered by others in Shadegg's office. Shadegg said that he did not hire the Dallas public relations firm, nor did he know who did; he said he did not know that they were operating in Arizona until well into the campaign. In any event, the explosive charges were planned and prepared in his office under his direction.[82]

When the McFarland Democrats attempted to fix the responsibility for the Stalin leaflet on Shadegg late in the campaign, they were ineffective, both because Goldwater stood behind him, and because Shadegg was protected by a shield of civic virtue. Since 1945, although he had devoted a great deal of his efforts to his private business and his writing, he had found time for the following community activities: president of the Phoenix Little Theatre for three years, during which time a new $185,000 theatre was constructed; president of the Phoenix Community Council for two years, during which period all of the United Fund agencies were evaluated; General Fund chairman of the American

Red Cross; chairman for three years of the American Cancer Crusade; an active Episcopalian and chairman of the Eighth Province for the National Committee of Laymen's Work.

In 1952 Shadegg was named Phoenix "Man of the Year." He said that he mentioned this only because it is his conviction that the Democrat's charges might have been more effective had he been less well-known in the state, or had he not enjoyed the warmth of many friendships throughout Arizona as a result of his various community and civic activities.

In spite of his protestations that he is not a public relations man, of his affirmations of a personal conservative philosophy, and of his many community and church activities, the feeling has persisted among both Republicans and Democrats in Arizona that he is opportunistic and that he is interested in personal prestige and power. The fact that he has worked both sides of the political fence, Democratic and Republican, lends credence to this feeling.

Shadegg was to extend his activities to other states in 1960 when he was asked to help some Republican senatorial candidates in the Middle West. In 1964 he participated in the Republican national campaign with emphasis on Western states. He was not on Goldwater's staff in this election year. In 1966 he managed the successful campaign of Jack Williams for the governorship. In Arizona he will be remembered for his engineering of Goldwater's return to the Senate in 1958 in a Democratic state and with a Democratic tide running against Goldwater. He will be remembered best for his dynamiting of Al Green, which routed the Democrats, and his manipulation of the Stalin leaflet from an apparent smear of his client into a final blast which helped defeat the Democratic opposition.

NOTES

1. According to Anderson, the man in California who had sent the packages, the two men "were not acquainted." Letter from Earl N. Anderson to Frank H. Jonas, August 5, 1959. Unless otherwise noted, all letters cited hereafter were received by Frank H. Jonas.

2. After delivering the packages, McShane disappeared from the stage where a bizarre political drama was about to unfold. On January 16, 1959, he signed the following statement for two FBI Special Agents:

> On October 27, 1958, I was in the IAM [International Association of Machinists] office in Los Angeles, California. I mentioned to Mr. Earl Anderson that I was going to Arizona two days later. Mr. Anderson asked me if I would deliver some packages to Phoenix, Arizona. I told him I was only going to Yuma, so he stated he would have someone pick up the packages there. On October 29, 1958, I went to a printing company in Santa Monica, Calif., the name of which may be the Weaver Printing Co., where I loaded about eight or ten sealed packages in the trunk of my car. None of the packages

I delivered had been opened. I am of the opinion the printing and delivering of these cartoons was *not an official project of the Machinist Union*. The request of Mr. Anderson for me to deliver these cartoons was *not made as a result of official union business* but was a *personal request* on his part.

3. At the time Goldberg was employed by the Goodyear Aircraft Corporation in Phoenix. He had been a shop steward in this plant for the Machinists union in Phoenix. He had also been local and district chairman of the Machinists nonpartisan Political League.

4. Letter from Anderson, August 5, 1959. Neither Anderson nor Goldberg was acquainted with the union halls in Yuma. Goldberg guessed that the two where he left the leaflets were the Central Labor Council and the Carpenters Hall. They were actually the Laborers Local, 903 Third St., and the Carpenters local No. 1153, 448 West Thirteenth Street. The secretary of the laborers union was present when Goldberg "just opened the door and threw them in," about one thousand tied in a bundle with no wrapping. Letter from Thelma Murphy, September 24, 1959. Miss Murphy said the leaflets were placed in a safe. Another correspondent reported that they were thrown in a trash can after an official of the union picked up a copy and saw what it was. Letter, August 25, 1959, name of writer withheld by request. The county attorney and Democratic county chairman, Bill Helm, stated that "very few leaflets were distributed in Yuma and the bundles that were left at the two union halls were quickly confiscated and not distributed." Union officials, he added, "paid little attention to them, except to throw them in the trash barrel." Letter from Bill Helm, July 8, 1959.

5. Goldberg claims that no bundles containing large numbers of leaflets were left in Yuma or Buckeye. Interview with Frank Goldberg, May 10, 1959.

6. "One of the bitterest campaigns in Arizona's political history will come to a close today and tomorrow. Starting immediately after the primary, the campaign has been marked almost daily by bitterness, deceit and personal attack." *Arizona Republic*, November 2, 1958.

7. "Most observers concluded it was Arizona's dirtiest campaign." Virgil Hill, *Phoenix Gazette*, November 5, 1958. Hill, a feature writer on politics for this newspaper, observed, "the campaign charges and countercharges often have a way of disappearing quickly after an election but this year's election seems likely to leave scars for years to come." *Ibid.*

8. For an account of the entire election, see Ross R. Rice, "The 1958 Election in Arizona," *Western Political Quarterly*, 12, Part 2 (March 1959), 266-75. See also Frank H. Jonas, "Western Politics and the 1958 Election," *ibid.*, pp. 242-44. Senator Barry Goldwater commented on the Rice article as follows: "I want to tell you that the article by Ross Rice is, on the whole, very factual and I find no fault with it whatsoever, and I want you to know that I thoroughly enjoyed reviewing it." Letter from Barry Goldwater, May 18, 1959.

9. "[Goldwater's, Inc., is] a cross between an elegant department store and a high-fashion women's specialty store. It includes four stores in Phoenix, one in suburban Scottsdale, and one in Prescott. The combined annual gross is approximately $6,500,000." Paul F. Healy, "The Glittering Mr. Goldwater," *Saturday Evening Post*, June 7, 1958 (reprint).

10. Letter from Earl N. Anderson, November 2, 1959.

11. Frank H. Goldberg, signed statement to the FBI, Blythe, California, January 14, 1959. Most of the account of Goldberg's activities to this point was taken from this statement. Hereafter it will be cited as Goldberg's FBI Statement.

12. *Phoenix Gazette*, February 10, 1959.

13. This part of the account of Anderson's and Goldberg's activities was taken from the

signed statement of Earl N. Anderson to the FBI agents, Blythe, California, January 14, 1959. Hereafter it will be cited as Anderson's FBI Statement.

14. *Ibid.*

15. *Ibid.* Goldberg gave much the same account. "I noticed that the pile had been distributed and some appeared to be missing. Some cars came along and I thought they had been discovered, so we departed." Goldberg's FBI Statement.

16. Letter from Stephen C. Shadegg, February 25, 1959.

17. One might ask if Goldberg had wanted Shadegg to have a copy as soon as possible, why did he not take it to him personally or at least send it by mail? Either course might have been personally incriminating. One public relations man who worked for the Republicans did make the following statement in denouncing the role that a Senatorial Committee investigator, James H. Duffy, played in the Stalin leaflet incident: "He [Duffy] tried to hang the distribution of these pamphlets on Shadegg simply because *Shadegg had been sent one through the mail and had copies and reproductions* thereof sent to certain labor and political leaders pointing out the type of campaign smear tactics being used by enemies of Goldwater." Letter from Charles H. Garland, July 20, 1959.

18. Interview with Frank Goldberg, May 28, 1959.

19. Letter from Anderson, November 2, 1959. He used the Adams Hotel lobby to dispose of a remaining package because Al Green, the COPE area representative, stayed there; he wanted this man to see them, a man who had been the target of a vicious campaign against outside labor leaders by the Arizona Republicans, the *Arizona Republic*, and Senator Goldwater. In a way, the leaflet could have been construed as coming to Green's defense, but Goldberg had had unpleasant dealings with the man and had no use for him.

20. "The FBI has picked up 150,000 which were left in bundles at bus stops on the day or so before the election." Letter from Stephen C. Shadegg, December 18, 1958. "Fireman [Bert Fireman, a member of Goldwater's staff] and Glazier [investigator for the Democratic party] both said that bundles of leaflets were placed at various bus stops the day of election." Letter from R. John Eyre, May 23, 1959. Eyre had interviewed both Fireman and Glazier on this point.

"About 500 copies of the cartoon were found on a bus stop bench there [Twentieth Street and Van Buren]." *Phoenix Gazette*, November 5, 1959.

21. Anderson stated that they—he and Goldberg—were unofficially advised by the FBI that five thousand or ten thousand showed up at Republican headquarters on election day. Letter from Anderson, August 5, 1959. Anderson affirmed, however, that "Goldberg has no knowledge of leaflets at Republican headquarters." Letter from Anderson, November 2, 1959.

22. When asked for a report, which was considered a public record, on the police pickups of leaflets at Thirty-second Street and Indian Road and at Thirty-fifth Avenue and Van Buren, the Phoenix police chief construed the request as "political" and refused the report. He referred the writer to the newspaper account. Letter from Charles B. Thomas, chief of police, city of Phoenix, September 21, 1959. The newspaper record revealed that in addition to the above two places, the police picked up a large number of leaflets "just outside Republican headquarters." *Phoenix Gazette*, November 5, 1959.

23. Statement by Bert Fireman, *Phoenix Gazette* columnist, who handled press releases for Goldwater. Fireman added that copies of the leaflets were sent to the newspapers and about

"200 were turned over to the FBI." When interviewed on this point, Goldberg stated that he did not accept Fireman's statement though he refused to indicate how Shadegg could have obtained so many copies. Letter from Eyre, May 23, 1959.

24. Miss Haskins was regularly employed at the Goldwater store in Scottsdale. For two months previously she had worked with Dr. Dwight Hudson and Robert Herberger on a volunteer basis in behalf of Senator Goldwater. This office was at 3500 North Central Avenue in Phoenix. After she had received a phone call from Shadegg, she and another person, a man she refused to identify, went to the Park Central area and picked up about three hundred and fifty leaflets from within cars. She saw no bundles of leaflets lying around. Interview with Miss Haskins, June fifth and sixth, reported by R. John Eyre, letter, June 10, 1959.

25. Letter from Shadegg, December 18, 1958. Fireman said that "a volunteer—a spy—from within labor had kept an eye on Green." Interview, May 12, 1959; letter from Eyre, May 23, 1959.

26. Several years after the campaign Shadegg denied that Fowler was the man he referred to as a friend, but he would not say who this friend was. However, Fowler frequently visited Goldwater's headquarters. At one point Shadegg found Fowler examining the contents of his own office wastebasket. For whom was Fowler spying? Who was the real friend or spy for the Republicans?

27. November 5, 1958.

28. Letter from Garland, July 20, 1959.

29. Interview with Frank Goldberg, reported by R. John Eyre, May 17, 1959. Lack of even acceptable circumstantial evidence would seem to discount completely this hypothesis but not remove it entirely from the realm of possibility. However, Fowler did present the writer with one of the leaflets which appears to have been printed on a different kind of paper than that used in the original leaflets. No chemical tests were applied to verify this.

30. Anderson was asked: "Is it possible that someone found these packages and took some either to Republican headquarters or to Mr. Shadegg's office?" Letter from Frank H. Jonas to Earl N. Anderson, October 20, 1959. Anderson answered: "It is possible that some of these were taken to Republican headquarters—but doubtful. . . . Read our statements and you will note that we were at this location on Sunday night, November 2, 1958, and it appeared that they were *still intact*." Letter from Anderson, November 2, 1959. Both Anderson's and Goldberg's statements to the FBI averred in almost identical language, that "the packages were not as [Goldberg] left them and some appeared to be missing."

31. Letter from Shadegg, December 18, 1959.

32. *Arizona Republic*, November 2, 1958. Shadegg's statement for the press was made on Saturday, November first. Two days previously would have been on Thursday, October thirtieth.

33. Letter from U.S. Senator Carl Hayden, July 8, 1959.

34. Larry Marton, the governor's secretary, wrote that "Gov. Mac" had feared some "last minute shenanigans" and had therefore requested the investigator to "check any last minute developments." After the campaign, Paul Butler, chairman of the Democratic National Committee, talked with McFarland about the factors which had a bearing on the outcome of the election. Marton then wrote Butler a two-page letter naming and summarizing seven factors. Letter from Larry Marton to Paul Butler, November 27, 1958.
    Marton also wrote:

Significantly, it was Governor McFarland who initiated the investigation—not Senator Goldwater. Furthermore, the leaflet itself is rather a weak and ineffectual attack on Senator Goldwater. Those of us associated with Governor McFarland are convinced it was a calculated plan designed to reflect adversely on the Governor. The Phoenix newspapers were quick to publish the leaflet on the front page and attribute its authorship to Governor Mac.

Letter from Larry Marton, December 4, 1958.

35. *Arizona Republic*, November 2, 1958. In the newspaper account Shadegg is reported as having said that "the leaflets were found on the street and in cars in the Park Central shopping area Friday afternoon." Goldberg has stated that he did not leave any leaflets in the streets or otherwise lying around either singly or in piles. On the other hand, an Arizona newspaperman said the copy he received and which was reproduced in his newspaper on Saturday morning, November 1, 1958, was dirty and marked as if a tire had run over it.

36. *Arizona Republic*, October 20, 1958.

37. His exact words on this occasion were: "The largest and most *democratic* union in Arizona." He would defend these workers who "deserve better than this." He would not remain "silent." *Arizona Republic*, November 1, 1958.

38. *Arizona Republic*, November 2, 1958. Goldwater did not state what kind of reputation McFarland had in the community. The implication was that the Governor had a *good* reputation, with integrity and honesty. However, during the campaign, Shadegg had done his best to discredit McFarland and to create the impression that McFarland was less than an honest man. On the other hand, McFarland made room for a direct hit by Shadegg when he denied a one thousand dollar contribution from a labor union source, which had been made an item of record. At the moment, however, it was advantageous to imply that McFarland was a man of *good* reputation. This generally *good* reputation of an opponent then throws into sharp relief an accusation that in a particular instance he was not so honest or at least so honorable. Also, it is always a good technique to be *shocked* at an opponent's tactics. At least one can always "view with alarm" the low state of morality in the enemy's camp. This helps divert attention from one's own low state of morality, if such a low state exists.

39. *Ibid.*

40. About a month after the election, a staff member of the *Arizona Republic* wrote an article entitled, "There Weren't Two Sides to the Story in Phoenix." *New Republic*, December 1, 1958. This staff member was thought of highly by his editors. In subsequent statements, this reporter said:

> Senator Goldwater has a number of advisors. He is his own boss. E. C. Pulliam ditto. Pulliam supports Goldwater because Goldwater espouses a political philosophy that Pulliam likes. Shadegg is strictly a hireling . . . Mr. Fifer [Orien W. Fifer, Jr., managing editor, *Arizona Republic*] is merely a poorly paid editor who does what the boss wants. Mr. Pulliam is boss. . . . Goldwater's office, I believe, could not and cannot dictate policy to Mr. Fifer. But they could, can, and will go to Fifer through Mr. Pulliam.

Letter, February 24, 1960, name of writer withheld by request.

41. *Arizona Republic*, November 2, 1958.

42. "If Senator Hayden and Governor McFarland knew about the leaflet the night of our rally [Wednesday], they did not tell us [Yuma County Democratic party organization officers]." Letter, August 25, 1959, name of writer withheld by request.

43. Goldberg drove a two-door, yellow sedan. He said he had no stickers of any kind on his car. This information was supplied by Earl Anderson after his and Goldberg's confessions.

Could it have been possible that Goldberg had placed Fannin and Goldwater stickers on his car to avoid close attention from others while he was distributing the leaflets?

44. One Yuma County Democratic officer thought Goldberg had been "scared off" by this TV program. Letter, August 25, 1959, name of writer withheld by request.

45. November 2, 1958.

46. Initially Fireman answered the telephone when Duffy called Senator Goldwater's headquarters, but Duffy did not state that Fireman had told him how many copies of the leaflet Shadegg had mailed. In fact, Shadegg, in his prepared press release, carefully avoided giving the exact number. Later Fireman revealed in an interview that three hundred and fifty leaflets had been received and that two hundred of these had been picked up by the FBI.

47. Letter from Shadegg, February 25, 1959.

48. *Ibid.*

49. *Ibid.*

50. "Last Wednesday in Yuma . . . a particularly vicious leaflet was distributed in parked cars." Barry Goldwater, quoted in *Arizona Republic*, November 4, 1958.

51. "While Duffy was buying his airline ticket to Phoenix, he was apparently shadowed by an operative who reported the purchase. . . . Two other operators discovered Duffy's whereabouts in the early hours of election day morning." Holmes Alexander, "Arizona Election Scored with Stupid Propaganda," *Standard-Examiner* (Ogden, Utah), November 19, 1958.

52. Letter from Larry Marton to Paul Butler, December 4, 1958.

53. *Ibid.*

54. Actually, Duffy reported that Shadegg had "admitted that he had received 400 or 500 copies which were sent to everyone on the Senator's mailing list." The number Shadegg would have admitted mailing would have depended on the size of the mailing list. Shadegg had not revealed previously how many names were on the list. Later he did limit it to newspapers.

55. *Arizona Republic*, November 4, 1958.

56. Senator Carl Curtis (R., Neb.), relying solely on information relayed to him by Goldwater or by Goldwater's office, asserted: "Duffy checked out of his Phoenix hotel after releasing his statement to the press and later checked into a 'swanky resort' in Scottsdale reserved for him by McFarland and was driven there by Mr. Bibolet, McFarland's personal assistant." *Arizona Republic*, November 4, 1958.

57. *Ibid.*
When James H. Duffy, the investigator for the Senate Subcommittee on Privileges and Elections, came to Phoenix to investigate the distribution of the Stalin leaflet, he revealed that the committee chairman, Senator Theodore Green, had instructed him to investigate a letter sent out by an organization called "Democrats for Arizona."
Arizona Republic, November 2, 1958.

58. Letter from Walter E. Quigley, March 28, 1959.

59. Fair Campaign Practices Committee, Inc., Bruce L. Felknor, director. Report on California trip, March 3-16, 1959, dated March 31, 1959.

60. Letter from Barry Goldwater, August 7, 1959.

61. Letter from Barry Goldwater, August 18, 1959.

62. Letter from Goldwater, August 7, 1959.

63. Interview with Goldberg, May 10, 1959.

64. Letter from Bert Fireman, May 12, 1959.

65. Letter from Richard G. Kleindienst, March 4, 1959.

66. Marton admitted, however, that it was the newspaper's use of the leaflet that made it effective. "Without the papers," he said, "the leaflets would not have been important." Interview with Larry Marton, reported by R. John Eyre, letter, June 16, 1959.

67. Interview with Michael Morris, reported by R. John Eyre, letter, June 16, 1959.

68. *Ibid.*

69. *Ibid.*

70. Interview with Orien Fifer by R. John Eyre, May 23, 1959.

71. For example, Fifer stated: "As soon as I saw a copy of the Stalin leaflet it was on its way to the engraver's to be used on Page One."

72. *Phoenix Gazette*, February 11,1959.

73. *Arizona Republic*, February 11, 1959.

74. Reports circulated in Phoenix that Republican party and campaign leaders made every possible effort to avoid being called by the grand jury. Senator Goldwater at first said that he would come to Phoenix to appear at the trial—which he did not do.

75. Letter from Stephen C. Shadegg, June 2, 1959.

76. Interview with Stephen C. Langmade by R. John Eyre, June 19, 1959.

77. Interview with Stephen Shadegg by R. John Eyre, May 5, 1959.

78. Letter sent by Shadegg to the *Arizona Republic* office and on file in the *Republic* library under "Shadegg." The letter was not dated but the article about him containing this information appeared in the *Republic* on February 10, 1952.

79. *Ibid.*

80. Letter from Shadegg, June 2, 1959.

81. Interview with Shadegg, May 5, 1959.

82. Interview with Goldberg, reported by R. John Eyre, letter, June 10, 1959.

POLITICAL
CACOPHONY
IN CALIFORNIA

C ALIFORNIA was the focus of national attention during the 1962 congressional and gubernatorial elections. Shortly after the campaign, the state became the most populous in the union, thereby qualifying it in future years for the prerequisites of primal representation in party conventions, the electoral college, and Congress. Dramatizing this newly acquired eminence was the return of Richard M. Nixon, native son and former vice-president of the United States, to enter the gubernatorial campaign, intended presumably as an initial step toward winning a second Republican presidential nomination.

The fate of Nixon as a gubernatorial candidate in 1962 presents a provocative analogy with the experience of the former majority leader of the United States Senate, William F. Knowland, who trod the path toward the state's electoral votes with similar motivations, against the same opponent, and with strikingly comparable results! In each instance a nationally established leader of the Republican party, long absent from the councils of state politics, returned to attempt to capture the governorship as a springboard to the White House. Both encountered deep schisms and bitter personal animosities within the state Republican party, marked by public recriminations more devastating than those mustered by the opposition during the general election. Each held the common opponent in light regard, completely miscalculating the determination and electoral appeal of the unpretentious, but voter-oriented, incumbent governor, Democrat Edmund G. "Pat" Brown. Both went down to crashing defeat, Knowland leading the conservative wing and Nixon the moderate wing of their party. In spite of the loud protestations of innocence by Democrats and Republicans alike, both campaigns were violent and unprincipled and rank among the most unedifying in the recent history of the state. Finally, each of the two GOP candidates chose to ignore the Warren-Knight formula for past gubernatorial successes: a policy position in the center of the ideological spectrum and an avoidance of undue partisanship.[1]

Since the turn of the century, the political environment which hosts partisan campaigning in California has been conditioned by two singular circumstances: a weak party system and Republican manipulation of a predominantly Democratic electorate. Bossism and machine control of state politics in the 1880's and 1890's generated a counteracting reform movement culminating circa 1915 with the adoption of a series of regulations which destroyed the traditional basis of party power. Gradually patronage appointments disappeared within a network of civil service laws; party discipline vanished before the practice of "cross-filing" wherein candidates were privileged to file on the primary tickets of opposing parties; the electorate was given a standing invitation to participate in legislation by the adoption of initiative, referendum, and recall measures; and, ultimately, party loyalty was affected at the grass roots when local offices were declared to be "nonpartisan."

Over the years the Republican party adapted to the novel conditions with greater finesse than the Democrats. By 1934, when faced with minority status within the electorate, the party leadership perfected a seemingly unbeatable formula for defeating the opposition. The key was the creation of a preprimary endorsing auxiliary, the California Republican Assembly, used by influential Republicans to sort out the aspirants for elective office beforehand, thus mobilizing party support in the campaign behind a single designated candidate. Another valuable tactic was the exploitation of cross-filing in a manner which neutralized the party identity of both issues and candidates. Containment of dissident factions within party boundaries, commandeering professional campaign management, marshaling party auxiliaries for precinct work, prodigal financing, and virtually unanimous press support purposefully employed to support candidates acceptable to the hierarchy, were contributory factors to Republican successes.

The Republican triumphs were aided and abetted by a political malaise which plagued the Democratic party for the four decades preceding the smashing success of 1958. The leadership was weak, proving incapable of reconciling the deep ideological fissures within the party membership. During the depression of the 1930's the party was cannibalized by left-wing factions such as the "EPIC" movement led by Socialist-turned-Democrat Upton Sinclair. The challenge to conservative control over the state economy caused the creation of a conservative coalition which straddled party lines. Led by an aggressively managed press, the conservative influence created an extremely hostile environment for "liberal" Democratic politicians. Leaders of the party often defected to support Republican candidates, or at least refrained from endorsing their own. A macabre legacy of the period was the perennial allegation by Republican supporters that the Democratic party harbored traitors to the nation.

The Democratic formula for winning national elections, which established an effective liaison between politically malleable racial, religious, and national minority groups, disciplined labor unions, and viable big city political machines, could not be employed on the state level. No adequate preprimary endorsing mechanism existed; potential nominees engaged in civil war. The run of candidates was generally inferior to those of the opposition, and Democrats frequently suffered the supreme ignominy of losing their own primary nominations to Republicans. A by-product of the Republican control of the state legislature was a series of district gerrymanders which created incumbent empires within each party. The Republican organization graciously awarded a few sinecure legislative seats to cooperative Democrats. Since incumbency practically guaranteed reelection usually in the primary, Democratic legislators frequently assumed nonpartisan positions on campaign issues and often refused to be identified with their party. For five successive national elections from 1932 to 1948, while Democratic presidents were being elected by the state, the party was unable to establish control over the state legislature and placed only one partisan governor, Culbert Olson, in the state capitol for a single term.

Lacking the conventional pattern of two-party rivalry in state politics, Republicans and Democrats alike elected Republican Governor Earl Warren three times and Goodwin Knight once, between 1942 and 1958. Both men stood as nonpartisans and preempted the broad middle of the ideological spectrum, thus winning the tacit support of the electorate and creating the presumption that Democratic candidates were "left of center" in their political orientation. By assiduously creating and tending the myth that the Democratic party and its leadership was infiltrated by, or oriented toward, or associated with, left-wing elements, Republican candidates and their supporters exploited with amazing virtuosity the most rewarding single campaign issue in the past three decades.[2]

The 1958 election shattered the traditional pattern of Republican ascendancy in state politics with a smashing Democratic victory. For the first time since 1889 the Democrats effectively bid and made the grand slam of state politics, winning six out of seven statewide elective offices including the governorship, control over the state senate and assembly, a majority of the congressional delegation, a United States senatorship, and even the entire five-man State Board of Equalization as a bonus.

As in most sudden reversals of established political trends, the dramatic results tend to obscure the underlying causes. The accepted hypothesis ascribes roughly equal weight to the rejuvenation of the Democratic party and the collapse of Republican leadership into internecine warfare. The 1952 presidential candidacy of Adlai Stevenson brought forth volunteer political clubs across the state which, the following year, were formed into a viable state party auxiliary organization, the California Democratic Council (CDC). At long last the Democratic party had a preprimary endorsement and campaign apparatus which rapidly grew to five hundred clubs with fifty thousand members, a formidable rival to the California Republican Assembly. A change in the election law in 1952 permitted the identification of the party affiliation of candidates on the primary ballot beginning in the 1954 election, thereby paving the way for a return of partisanship to state politics. For the first time in modern history the Democrats, guided by able leadership, selected and backed candidates with some degree of coordination and discrimination, and competed for each state and national elective office. The trend toward mobilizing the latent Democratic majority within the electorate had been established.

The dominant conservative wing of the Republican party had never been genuinely content with the Warren-Knight brand of moderate Republicanism and regarded the "nonpartisan approach" as an expediential device to maintain nominal party control over state politics. In 1952 former Congressman Thomas Werdel of Bakersfield attempted to rally the conservative wing of the party in an unsuccessful "dump Warren" campaign. Conservative discontent found full fruition in the 1958 campaign with a representative candidate in former United States Senator William F. Knowland.

Such an eventuality might not have occurred, however, if Governor Warren had chosen to remain in his gubernatorial post in preference to accepting appointment as chief justice of the Eisenhower court in 1953. Although Lieutenant Governor Goodwin J. Knight maintained the nonpartisan tradition as governor throughout the remainder of Warren's term and his own subsequent incumbency to 1958, he considerably broadened his support base with labor unions and conservative elements within the Democratic party. Frustrated and goaded by the brand of Republicanism represented by Eisenhower at the national level and Knight within the state, the conservative faction was preparing to recapture control of the party. It is a supreme irony of party history that the very gambit of "personality politics" created by this group to contain the opposition, became impaled upon the ambitions of three strong Republican personalities.

It would be unwise to oversimplify the complex series of events culminating in the Republican defeat in 1958, but certainly a prime consideration was the classic feud of political alienation between Warren, former Vice-President Nixon, Knowland, and Knight. Bitterness between Nixon and Knowland developed in the days before the 1952 Republican national convention when both were pledged to an Earl Warren favorite-son delegation from California. Both Warren and Knowland were seriously disconcerted when Nixon indicated an early interest in the Eisenhower candidacy and was subsequently nominated for the vice-presidency. In 1954 Knowland sided with Knight to defeat a Nixon bid to elect a state party vice-chairman who would be elevated to the state chairmanship in time for the 1956 election. By 1956, however, Knight began a "dump Nixon" campaign shortly before the San Francisco convention and Knowland sided with Nixon in a plan to discipline Knight. Subsequently the California Republican delegation was divided into three groups, with only one-third assigned to Knight—from whom was exacted the promise of a unanimous vote for the Eisenhower-Nixon ticket as the price for the chairmanship. In this manner, playing the "balance-of-power" game, Knowland had at least temporarily checked the ambitions of his two most formidable rivals in state politics.

Knowland announced on January 7, 1957, that he would retire from the Senate in order to see more of his family; within ten months he had become an active gubernatorial candidate. The maneuver anticipated defeating incumbent Governor Knight in the primary and leading the California Republican delegation to the 1960 national convention in search of the presidential nomination, thwarting in transit any similar ambitions Nixon might cherish. The Senator encountered the implacable opposition of Knight, who stated frequently and with considerable exuberance that his only immediate ambition was to continue to serve the people of California as governor.

In this instance Nixon sided with Knowland, and amidst anguished cries charging that a "deal" had been made, Knight was forced from the gubernatorial into the United States senatorial race against Democratic Congressman Clair Engle, for the cause of "party unity." The coercive instruments used upon unhappy Governor Knight were noted for simplicity and effectiveness: denial of funds and press support. Democratic leaders enjoyed a politicians' field day characterizing the Knowland-Nixon-Knight arrangement as a "cynical deal," a "big switch," "musical chairs," and the "big fix." The grim picture of partisan political mayhem being committed upon a popular, nonpartisan, electable governor was undoubtedly a major factor in Knowland's defeat.

Intrigued by the suicidal strife within Republican ranks, the California Democratic Council endorsed state Attorney General Edmund G. "Pat" Brown as the party's gubernatorial candidate. Brown was also an advocate of the middle of the road in political philosophy in the best Hiram Johnson and Earl Warren tradition. As a former Republican-turned-Democrat he was the only elected member of his party holding statewide elective office and had supported Franklin Roosevelt, Harry Truman, and Adlai Stevenson in past years.

Since Brown had only token opposition, and Knowland none, the primary election of June 3, 1958, served as a popularity contest between the two gubernatorial candidates in the last election before the abolition of cross-filing. The primary campaign was literally "no contest" with Brown rolling up a 662,050 margin and the opinion polls indicating that he was at no time in jeopardy of defeat. Knowland ran on one implied and two overtly stated issues. Campaigning only fourteen days in the state, he attempted to convey the impression that he was "tending the store" in Washington as the minority leader of the Senate, which was still in session. He embraced the affirmative side of the ballot Proposition 18, dubbed the "right-to-work issue," seeking to turn California into an open-shop state. There is reason to believe that this position on such an explosive issue was not his personal choice, but was made the quid pro quo for active support from the conservative wing of his party. Finally, Knowland developed the thesis that he would correct alleged failings in the state administration. Impartial observers noted a tendency toward overconfidence in the Republican camp and, indeed, the precipitous resignation of Knowland's campaign manager, former National Committeeman Edward S. Shattuck, immediately following the primary lent credence to this view.

Brown followed a "lone wolf" pattern of campaigning which had become his political trademark. He disassociated himself from the Democratic party ticket and from individual Democratic candidates. His speeches and other public activities were pitched in a low emotional key. He dealt with "bread and butter" issues: the need for more schools, the water problem, unemployment, small business support, and the negative position on the "right-to-work" measure. He accepted financial support from both parties and carefully avoided blatant partisanship out of thoughtful consideration for the independent voter and the uncommitted Democratic and Republican conservatives. The strategy quickly earned the sobriquet of "the nice guy campaign." This view was not shared by the other candidates in his party who lacked the attorney general's secure political moorings.

Charles P. Taft, chairman of the Fair Campaign Practices Committee, has stated that his file on campaign smear tactics contained more material from California than all of the other states combined. Leaders and candidates in both parties agreed that this was one of the "dirtiest" campaigns in their experience.

Against the background of the Eisenhower-Nixon "radicalism" charges, several "hate themes" were developed, as well as many techniques for misrepresentation of alleged political support on both sides. The presence of the "right-to-work" Proposition 18 on the ballot was the source of employer-employee, class-warfare propaganda. Proposition 16, advocating the return of parochial school property to the public tax rolls, instigated a veritable flood of religious and racial prejudice campaign tracts. The now historic Nixon-Chotiner formula for linkage-with-communism has practically become standard operating procedure for Republican campaigning in California.

The "right-to-work" measure was not a partisan issue per se. The overwhelming majority of Republican candidates tried, almost desperately, to disassociate themselves from Knowland's position. Nevertheless the senator persisted in developing the thesis that Brown was the "willing tool" of "corrupt labor bosses." The distribution by Mrs. Helen Knowland of several hundred copies of the Joseph Kamp pamphlet, *Meet the Man Who Plans to Rule America*, irretrievably identified her husband and his party as bitterly anti-labor in sentiment.[3]

The subject of the pamphlet is in the character assassination category, with Walter P. Reuther, vice-president of the AFL-CIO, the target. Reuther is characterized as a Marxist and both a former Socialist and pro-Communist. He is further stigmatized as a "pseudo-intellectual nitwit," "a smart, smug, arrogant labor boss," "a bold, shrewd, foul-mouthed agitator," "a ruthless, lawless labor goon," "a cunning conspirator," and a "slick, sordid, conniving politician."[4]

Democratic party leaders and many Republicans repeatedly called for public repudiation of the charges and immediate withdrawal of the pamphlet from circulation. Knowland was quoted in the press as saying: "I don't think that I am called upon to answer for every piece of mail that comes into my office."[5] Mrs. Knowland admitted that she had temporarily discontinued circulation of the pamphlet at her husband's request because of the absence of a union printer's label. She stated that she had ordered several thousand more copies and complained because the exposure had made her the victim of "intimidation and sabotage."

Another interesting attempt at "linkage" was launched by Knowland in mid-October when he attacked Paul Ziffren, Democratic national committeeman, as an "associate" of individuals who were "affiliated" with the old Chicago Capone gang, and then charged that Ziffren was the "chief architect" of the Brown campaign. This gambit purported to prove that Brown was associated with, if not actually responsible for, an alleged "crime wave" developing in the state.[6]

There were at least three phases of the religious issue interjected into the campaign. Brown was attacked as a member of the Catholic church and because of rulings he had made as attorney general relating to the use of the Bible in public schools. The religious belief of some Jewish candidates was made an adjunct to anti-Semitic propaganda. Representatives of all major religious groups in the state became involved on one side or the other of Proposition 16.

Typical of the attack on Brown was a leaflet published by Heritage Manor, Inc., entitled *It Happened in Spain, It Could Happen Here*, posing the rhetorical question, "Could Roman Catholic . . . Brown, if elected Governor, be loyal to the state of California and the Vatican at the same time? . . . The Roman Catholic Church says No!"[7]

In a twenty-two page booklet entitled *Brown Bans the Bible*, the California Christian Citizens Association took exception to the ruling the attorney general made relating to use of the Bible in public schools. The authors stated: "We suggest as a slogan for 1958—'Return the Bible to the Schools and Mr. Brown to Private Life.' "[8]

A blatant anti-Semitic attack was made on behalf of Craig Hosmer of Long Beach, the incumbent Republican congressman standing for reelection in the Eighteenth District. The flyleaf purported to contrast the public records of Hosmer and his opponent, Democrat Harry S. May, by presenting the incumbent as a native-born gentile and his opponent as a foreign-born Jew. Under the various categories listed in the parallel columns, May's former occupation was given as rabbi, Zionist director, and scrap metal dealer; his birthplace, Berlin; his educational background, the Jewish Theological Seminary of Breslau, Germany; and his children's names as Sharon Avivah, Judith Arlene, and Tamar. His organizational affiliation, Americans for Democratic Action (characterized as "a left-wing faction with a program of 'laundered Communism' "), was placed opposite Hosmer's American Legion affiliation. His military service was listed as "none," while Hosmer allegedly served "in all war theaters." *Who's Who in America* was cited as the source of Hosmer's record and *Who's Who in World Jewry* for May's background.

An organization known as Californians for Public Schools placed the highly controversial initiative, Proposition 16, on the ballot. Proponents of the measure to repeal the tax exemption of private school, undercollegiate property emphasized the principle of separation of church and state, alleged that religious doctrine as taught in parochial schools militated against this principle, and quoted freely from a textbook used in Catholic high schools entitled *Living Our Faith* to support these contentions.[9] Campaign literature for this group carried such slogans as: "Californians Should Not Pay Taxes for a Foreign Religious Dictator."

The leaders of the Catholic and principal Protestant and Jewish denominations joined in an intensive campaign in opposition, basing their main contention upon the tax savings to the state effected by private education of children of precollegiate age. As the chief target of the proposed amendment, the Catholic clergy made extraordinary efforts in urging their adherents to "Vote 'NO' on 16." Worshipers were exhorted by parish priests many weeks before the election to register and vote, children were enjoined to alert their parents, and registration clerks were strategically placed near Catholic church lobbies throughout the state for the convenience of communicants.

Protestant and Catholic leaders alike sent vigorously worded telegrams to President Eisenhower, the Federal Communications Commission, and the FBI when spot radio announcements appeared one week before election, allegedly implying that the Vatican had directed Roman Catholics to vote against the proposition. The insinuations of the advocates of the affirmative, claiming that Nixon and the president endorsed their views, brought a denial in the first instance, and a statement from a spokesman for the president that he had never taken a stand on the issue.

The effect of the religious controversy on the outcome of the election is difficult to gauge since the sentiment on Proposition 16 crossed both party and denominational lines. The measure was defeated by more than a 2 to 1 ratio, 67.2 percent voting against and 32.8 percent in favor. California poll results indicated that 78 percent of the Catholic vote was against the proposition, 14 percent in favor, and 8 percent undecided. The same source revealed that 64 percent of the Catholic vote favored Brown, with only 19 percent for Knowland and 17 percent undecided.

Protestants were rather evenly divided: 43 percent opposed the measure, 38 percent were in favor, and 19 percent were undecided, while 44 percent favored Brown, 39 percent, Knowland, and 17 percent were undecided. It would seem that the generalization that the majority of Catholics were registered Democrats, and voted against Proposition 16 and for Brown, was probably correct. It does not follow, however, that Catholics voted for Brown because he is a Catholic. Congressman Patrick J. Hillings, candidate for attorney general, is also a Catholic, but the same poll results found 51 percent of the Catholics preferring his rival Stanley K. Mosk, a Jew, while only 20 percent supported Hillings.[10]

The linkage-to-communism technique was emphasized in several areas. As a practicing Catholic, Brown proved to be relatively invulnerable to direct attack as a Communist or leftist. Nevertheless a committee identifying itself as the Citizens for the Right to Know, published full-page advertisements in the California press linking Brown with crime, narcotics, and smut, and "either ignorance and/or indifference to the Communist conspiracy."[11]

The inspiration for the latter allegation was a publication issued from the attorney general's office entitled *Guide to Community Relations for Peace Officers*. Cited in this pamphlet, as bibliographical sources on race problems, were publications by Carey McWilliams, Franz Boaz, and others, alleged to have been affiliated with the Communist party or its fronts.

Another attempt at linkage with communism was a reprint from *Human Events* authored by Oliver Carlson and entitled "Your Pink Slip is Showing, Mr. Brown: The Truth About Knowland's Opponent."[12] Some of the allegations were that Brown belonged to the National Lawyers Guild before World War II; in February 1945 he supported a move to grant United States citizenship to Harry Bridges; as a candidate for attorney general in 1946, he was endorsed by five "Communist-infiltrated or dominated at that time" organizations, including the CIO Council of California; and that, according to the *People's World* for June 17, 1946, he spoke at a rally in Los Angeles which was "under the auspices of a commie front, the 'Mobilization for Democracy.' " The article closes with the comment: "Of course he's no communist; he's just an opportunist whose pink slip is showing."

Senator Knowland's campaign manager, Stewart Hinckley, reported to the Fair Campaign Practices Committee a pamphlet issued by the Communist party in California on the grounds that Knowland was characterized as a "cold, scheming ruthless politician" and "Political Enemy No. 1 of the People of California." The senator was also accused of accepting aid from a "pro-Fascist lunatic fringe that flourished when Hitler came to power in Germany." Hinckley also charged Brown with having "voiced on television substantially this same charge."[13]

Probably the most reprehensible single advertisement in the campaign supporting Knowland was the picture of a teen-age schoolgirl under a posed hypodermic needle, accompanied by the caption, "Brown's Black Record on Narcotics," and insinuating that Brown was responsible for an alleged increase in the use of narcotics by juveniles.[14]

The campaign to defeat Proposition 18 by attacking Walter Reuther undoubtedly had an oblique effect on the Brown-Knowland race. An expensive, full-page advertisement discrediting Reuther appeared in the Pacific Coast edition of the *Wall Street Journal* bearing such headlines as "Will You Let Reuther Get Away With It?" "What Is Reuther Up To?" and "How to Stop Reuther."[15]

Both major parties followed the time-honored practice of claiming substantial support for their candidates from the opposition group. Knight's Republican proponents, however, produced a well-organized, expensive, and extensive campaign of misrepresentation of Democratic support. Under a letterhead entitled "Los Angeles County Democrats," with an address of 808 South Vermont (Knight's headquarters), and signed by two individuals without designation of status, a deliberate attempt was made to lead the voter to believe that the Los Angeles County Democratic Central Committee (located at 311 South Vermont), was supporting Knight rather than Democrat Clair Engle. Both signers were Democrats, neither had seen the letter, one had not authorized his name to be used and the other had given permission for use of his name only by a Democratic Committee for Knight. Similar letters were reported by Democratic leaders in six other northern and central California counties.[16]

In somewhat the same vein, but without any attempt at anonymity, Senator Kefauver was charged with "trickery" by Knight backers because of a letter circulated in the state, purportedly on official stationery of the United States Senate Committee on Judiciary, endorsing Engle and carrying the names of

Brown's
Black Record
on
NARCOTICS

Attorney General Brown, the man who wants to be governor, has been in charge of the State Bureau of Narcotics for eight years (1950-58). It was his duty to provide leadership in the fight against the growing narcotics menace. He has failed. Here is his record:

237 % INCREASE in statewide narcotics adiction (1953-1957)

877 % INCREASE in the number of youngsters under 18 committed for treatment (1950-1958)

19 % INCREASE in drug addicts, first six months of 1958 over first six months of 1957. (During the same period, New York state had a decrease of 12%. Illinois a decrease of 43%.)

"NARCOTICS is a million-dollar-a-day business."
(Assemblyman Jack Beaver, R)

CALIFORNIA is "a cesspool of narcotics."
(State Senator Edwin Reagan, D)

This is Brown's black record on narcotics. It is a shame. The shame of California.

Hard-working and dedicated city and county police have admitted the state-wide narcotics menace is beyond them. They need help.

What has Brown done?

He has made speeches. But as of February 1958 he did not even have a basic policy manual for the guidance of his agents.

He has only deplored the situation. Despite the growing narcotics menace, his 1958-59 budget made no request for additional narcotics officers as urged by legislators.

Brown has failed the people. He has failed the parents. He has failed our children.

This is Brown's black record on narcotics.

And yet he asks that we promote him. That we make him governor.

You owe it to yourself and to your children to study Brown's black record on narcotics. Is this what you want for governor?

Citizens for the Right to Know is an independent, non-partisan comittee. Its purpose is to reveal Brown — the man behind the myth. To help, send your contributions to Citizens for the Right to Know, Room 1010, 609 South Grand Avenue, Los Angeles 17, Calif.

CITIZENS FOR THE RIGHT TO KNOW *James G. Law, William V. Thompson; Co-Chairmen*
609 So. Grand Ave., Los Angeles 17, California

eight Republican members of the committee on the letterhead. Knight supporters claimed that "by implication" the eight Republicans had endorsed Engle and that "presumably" the letters had been mailed at government expense.

Knight supporters became embroiled in another questionable project when their candidate was vying with Mayor Christopher for the endorsement of the California Republican Assembly. A pamphlet entitled *The Political Odyssey of George Christopher*, alleging that the mayor was registered as a Republican in 1930, a Progressive in 1932, a Democrat in 1936, and a Republican in 1948, was distributed at the convention. The title and other matter in the publication was interpreted by Christopher as reflecting upon his Greek ancestry and caused him to state: "Yes, I am of Greek descent and when the ancestors of the gentleman who disparages me were but savages in a cave, mine were preaching doctrines of culture in the shadows of the Parthenon."[17]

In the major races the Republicans employed "Compare the Record" fly sheets, placing their candidates in a favorable light in contrast with the opposition. The "selective evidence" technique employed extensive listing of detail on the one hand and a bare outline of the Democrat's record on the other; concentration on Republican war records and particularly patriotic group membership; contrast of religious affiliation; conservative versus liberal organizational affiliation; extensive quotations favorable to the Republican and extremely rude and derogatory remarks about the opponent; citations to the *People's World* (Communist party paper), referring only to the activities of the Democrat; a positive statement of the constructive stand on public issues by the Republican, contrasted with sly innuendo, patent misrepresentation, or quotations taken out of context to represent the Democrat.[18]

Several circumstances conspired to intensify the pressures which beset the 1962 campaign. Although the California electorate favors the Democrats three to two in registration, the voter is not so imbued with partisanship that he is unwilling to split his ticket, as the substantial victory of Republican Senator Thomas H. Kuchel proved. No Republican candidate for statewide office, however, can afford to ignore the "political percentage game" of winning from 85 to 90 percent of his party's vote, while capturing from 20 to 25 percent of the opposition strength.

The compromises which Nixon felt forced to make in attempting to heal the break in his own party in order to obtain maximum support, and yet to appeal to the conservative elements in the Democratic party, were virtually beyond reach. Assemblyman Joseph C. Shell, heading the Republican conservative wing, fought a hard-driving and pointedly personal campaign in the primary. He aimed his ammunition at Nixon rather than at Brown and drove a wedge deeply between the conservative and liberal wings of the party. Nixon's compromise was to ignore Shell and concentrate on Brown. He was unable to heal the breach in the general election. Moreover, his stand on the John Birch Society was equivocal to the extent that ultraconservatives in both parties appeared to be alienated, and the rank-and-file Democrats were given a prime issue. Nixon won comfortably over Shell 1,285,151 to 656,542, but the significance of the vote was that the Shell conservative partisans captured one-third of the Republican total.

Brown changed his tactics, ran as a "slate" candidate, and polled 454,641 more votes than Nixon. Once again the citizenry reinforced the stereotype of unconventional behavior: over 250,000 voting Democrats did not cast a ballot for governor; 294,313 voted for minor Democratic candidates; 66,712 wrote in Joseph Shell and another 35,833 wrote in Richard Nixon's name!

Herbert Phillips, the political sage of the *Sacramento Bee*, called it the "year of the smear"! In this free-wheeling political milieu, the campaign for the gubernatorial contest became so dramatic that it soon dominated the entire election scene. On the positive side, each candidate produced a program on the major issues of public policy: agriculture, water, education, conservation, tax and budget reform, full employment, the economic climate for business, government efficiency, law enforcement, recreation, and future planning. In order to capitalize upon his experience on the national and international scene, Nixon also introduced various issues of foreign policy, usually in the form of admonitions to President Kennedy.

On the negative side, each candidate attempted to impeach the other's motives and suitability as a chief executive. Brown charged Nixon with inexperience in state affairs and with using Sacramento as a stepping stone to the White House. Nixon claimed that Brown was unfit to govern and that he played partisan politics, indulged in nepotism, and appointed incompetents to public office.

As the campaign progressed, the tempo accelerated and the dialogue became exceedingly acrimonious. Supporters on each side called the opposing candidate "a liar," while the candidates themselves claimed to be the victims of vicious smears. Three issues predominated throughout: the imputation by the Democrats of ethical turpitude on Nixon's part because of a family loan made several years before by a prominent defense contractor; the Republican revival of that hoary but durable litany on Democratic loyalty, "soft on communism"; and the entirely fortuitous Cuban drama, which both sides strove valiantly to reconstruct in partisan terms.

Bludgeoned in the past by repeated Republican attacks on the linkage-with-communism issue, the Democratic leadership viewed the 1962 campaign as an ideal opportunity to settle a real or fancied score with Richard Nixon, made in his 1946 race for Congress and 1950 bid for the Senate. By common consensus, if not by design, the "new Nixon," statesmanlike, vice-presidential image was brushed aside. In its place was invoked the "old Nixon," a ruthless, unprincipled seeker after power for its own sake.

The Democratic indictment contained three major charges supplemented by a host of lesser allegations tailored to reach specific areas of sensitivity relating to the interests of such special groups as old-age pensioners, labor unions, Negroes, and the Mexican-American and Jewish communities.

Nixon's personal and family financial problems have been the subject of Democratic party interest and exploitation since the revelation of his eighteen-thousand-dollar "sponsor's fund" during the 1952 campaign. In 1962 the Democrats revived an issue of the 1956 campaign by demanding an explanation of a very complicated financial transaction between Nixon's mother, a businessman brother, Donald, and an individual connected with the Hughes Tool Company, among other business interests. Apparently a loan of $205,000 was made to further the brother's business activity, with a lot owned by Mrs. Nixon and assessed at $13,000 serving as collateral.

The inference placed by the Democrats upon the transaction was that the security given by the family was negligible for so large a loan, and therefore the corporation, or other unknown persons, probably hoped to benefit in other ways, possibly through government contracts, by its association with the Nixons. Prompted by questions from the press, Brown often posed a rhetorical question in his speeches, wondering when Nixon would give "the people" a "full explanation" of the conditions surrounding the loan.[19]

No issue in the campaign so agitated the Republican candidate. Nixon repeatedly denied any knowledge of the details of the transaction. In addition to the needling by Brown, an organization entitled Citizens for Honesty in Politics sponsored a leaflet on *Questions Nixon Won't Answer About the $205,000 Hughes Tool Company Loan.* Answers suggesting "a deal" and worse were supplied to five basic queries:

1. Why did Hughes Tool Co., a major defense contractor, lend $205,000 to the Nixon family to finance a chain of drive-in restaurants selling Nixon-burgers? . . .
2. Why were dummies and phony names used in the Hughes loan? . . .
3. Why did Nixon's man LIE about the Hughes loan? . . .
4. How did Nixon's family get $205,000 loan with property assessed at only $13,000 for security? . . .
5. Why won't Nixon answer reporters' questions about the Hughes Tool Loan of $205,000?[20]

The constant reiteration of these and similar questions can only be interpreted as a concerted attempt to throw suspicion on Nixon's character and to indict the integrity of his family, friends, and political associates.

A second major campaign issue employed by Democratic sympathizers represented an organized effort to impeach Nixon's views on civil liberties. Unnumbered thousands of "throw away broadsides" were peddled at public meetings of minority groups; often the audience would find these papers in their seats when they entered the building. Misrepresentation, quotation out of context, linkage, and other propaganda devices were utilized to "prove" that Nixon harbored racial bias, minority group bias, and antiunion sentiments.

One of the most reprehensible of these was a legal-sized sheet distributed by "Independent Voters of California" entitled: "Do You Want This Kind of Governor in California?" The word SHAME and a large arrow, red superimposed upon black, slashed across the page. The script purports to be the reproduction of a portion of a property deed to a house purchased by the Nixons in Washington, D.C., on July 5, 1951. The red arrow points to a paragraph containing a restrictive covenant passage, preventing the buyer from disposing of his property to Armenians, Jews, Hebrews, Persians, Syrians, or Negroes.[21] The leaflet was circulated widely in Negro and Jewish districts in southern California. The lethal impact of this literature brought a rebuttal from the Republicans entitled "Dick Nixon Speaks Out on Restrictive Covenants," stating that Supreme Court decisions rendered in May 1948 invalidated any such agreements and that this fact was known to Nixon when he signed the deeds on July 5, 1951, and February 13, 1957.[22]

Democratic sympathizers were especially active among old-age groups. Handbills were made of extracts taken from publications by the California League of Senior Citizens and the Citizens Committee for Old Age Pensions, all portraying Nixon as hostile to the principles of social security. Typical phrases in this category: "Your Pension is in Jeopardy"; "Are You a Chiseler?"; "Don't Risk Your Social Security"; "Richard Nixon Says Your Pension Check is a 'Handout.' He promises to slash $27 million a year from your welfare program."[23]

One of the most unconscionable propaganda tracts in the entire campaign attempted to link Nixon to alleged corruption charged against his running mate, San Francisco's Mayor George Christopher, candidate for lieutenant governor. Entitled "The Real Christopher of San Francisco," the story appeared in volume one, number one, of *The Californian*, edited by one Burton H. Wolfe, characterized as a one-time reporter for the San Francisco Bureau of Hearst International News Service.[24]

The cover of this thirty-one page pamphlet carried two pictures, one a conventional view of the mayor speaking over KCBS, the other purported to represent Christopher in prison clothes as "Convict No. 2366, Marin County, 2-2-40." The caption read: "Which is the TRUE picture of Richard Nixon's Running Mate?" One page is devoted to what appears to be a facsimile of a San Francisco municipal court record citing the candidate's alleged criminal conviction on a charge of selling "unmerchantable cream." The text as a whole is a tortured interpretation of selected evidence carrying a series of charges including arrest for violation of a state law prohibiting secret rebates from milk producers; the violations having occurred between 1939-1940, while Christopher was in the dairy business. By innuendo he was cited as a draft dodger and disloyal to his party for having changed his registration from Republican (1930) to Progressive (1932) to Democrat (1936) and back to Republican.

Nixon was the subject of a biographical treatment laced with distortions published by the "Committee to Reelect Governor Brown." The three-volume *Nixonpedia*, subtitled "Richard M. Nixon—Handcuffed to a Negative Image 1947-1960," attacked the former vice-president's voting record and ridiculed the allegation that his executive experience had contributed to his qualifications for the presidency.[25] Typical commentary on the voting record included: on housing and rent issues he voted for special treatment of selected groups including both individuals and corporations; and in the area of immigration legislation, he supported laws discriminating against Polish Catholics and Jews. In the matter of expertise, under the title "Exposing the Myth of Nixon's Executive Experience," Nixon was charged with duplicity in constantly disclaiming that his brief trips abroad made him a specialist in international policy, but subsequently making categorical statements criticizing past or proposed policy decisions.

Nixon was particularly bitter about what he alleged was unfair treatment in relation to his television broadcasts. In the eyes of impartial observers, his demeanor was very serious, often belligerent, sometimes complaining, and rarely reflected genuine lightheartedness or good humor. Although expressing satisfaction with the impact of the TV sessions, he repeatedly complained that "professional hatchetmen," presumably Democrats, executed a calculated attempt to exploit his telethons with "seven lies that are being used in a statewide attempt to scare the voters with a phony chamber of horrors." An analysis by his staff of the subject matter of 4,400 telephoned questions during the first 6 telethons purportedly revealed the opposition's plan to frighten segments of the electorate by alleging that if he were elected, the former vice-president would follow certain policies inimical to their interests. Some examples of "inspired questions," themes, and target groups were: union labor, by right-to-work laws; old people, by abolition of pensions; defense workers, by loss of state contracts; the blind, by abolishing public assistance; parents and teachers, with dictatorship of local school systems; news media, with supression of the press; and career workers, with dismissal from their jobs.

The Democrats developed a technique of sending in "loaded" questions to Nixon telethons and then claiming that they had not been answered. On Nixon's May thirtieth broadcast Roger Kent, Democratic vice-chairman for northern California, submitted twelve questions and then offered a one thousand dollar reward per answer for proof that any one had been answered directly. The subjects related to the purchase of Nixon's house, possible support from Jimmy Hoffa, endorsement of the John Birch congressmen, and so forth.[26]

Several episodes in Nixon's political past were exhumed and refurbished as half-myth and half-truth, becoming significant campaign issues. The former Vice-President and Chief Justice Earl Warren had not been on good terms since Nixon allegedly deserted the former governor's "favorite son" delegation at the 1952 Republican national convention. Nixon's early interest in the Eisenhower candidacy and subsequent election to the vice-presidency alienated both Warren and Senator William F. Knowland. During the course of his gubernatorial campaign Nixon occasionally castigated the John Birch Society for its condemnation of Eisenhower, but remained strangely silent on that organization's plans to impeach the chief justice.

As though tilting in the lists for family honor, attorney Earl Warren, Jr., changed his registration from Republican to Democrat and campaigned vigorously for Brown. His presence on the Democratic side prompted the frequent repetition of Nixon's alleged traitorous abandonment of his delegation pledge. Nixon denied the insinuation and was promptly contradicted by both former Senator Knowland, who had chaired the delegation in 1952, and its secretary, Mrs. Patricia Connich Crawford, the latter remarking that "Mr. Nixon's efforts to undercut Mr. Warren were obvious."[27]

With almost intuitive prescience regarding the rough nature of the campaign which his candidacy in California would engender, Nixon announced in January that he had not "come back to my home state to allow a bunch of political assassins to smear me and my family. When they attack my integrity, I am going to hit back very, very hard." He did not await the start of the campaign, however, before he was quoted in the press with reference to his plans to "clobber Brown."

The most interesting single issue in the campaign, and in several respects the most important in terms of the dynamics of electioneering, was the utilization by Nixon forces of the "soft-on-communism" theme. Once Nixon decided to legitimize the communist issue, it was exploited on three different levels of campaign activity: the pronouncements of the candidate, the contributions of official and semiofficial Republican party spokesmen, and the uninhibited ful-minations of unofficial and occasionally repudiated "friends" of the Republi-can cause. As in Republican campaigns of the past, there were a variety of Democratic culprits and a wide range of levels of alleged culpability. The Democratic candidate, his associates, the leadership of particular support groups such as the labor unions and the CDC, and the designated party "left wing" served as targets. The degree of assumed guilt ranged from the total in-volvement of the treasonous card carrier, through the pink shade of socialist inclination, to the extreme vulnerability of the witless dupe.

Nixon chose to separate the candidate from his party in this context and implied that Brown was the ingenuous captive of the left wing of the CDC. At no time did Nixon publicly call Brown a Communist; on the contrary, he pro-tested that the governor was "as much against communism as I am." However, the former vice-president claimed that he was better qualified to deal with the menace than was the governor. He attacked the Brown administration with fail-ure to pass a single anti-Communist bill during the preceding four years, with the inescapable implication that there was urgent need for such legislative ac-tion. He repeatedly called upon Brown to repudiate resolutions of the CDC made in earlier years, implying that the governor embraced the views of "ex-tremists" within the organization. In part, Nixon may have hoped that by forc-ing Brown into a vigorous position against the CDC, the governor would lose the support of that effective grass-roots organization. On the other hand, if Brown said nothing, he could be criticized for "softness" on the CDC. With luck, Nixon might have it both ways, and to some extent he did. In addition, he alleged that Brown had displayed "incredible ignorance" by permitting eight identifiable "subversives" to speak at state-supported institutions. Nixon thereby inadvertently became embroiled with the regents and the president of the University of California over the issue of academic freedom.

When the insinuations and innuendo of Nixon's speeches began to excite the electorate and found support in pro-Republican campaign literature, Brown suggested that they "remove this ugly and divisive kind of material from the campaign." Nixon retorted that "it would be a mockery of the American system to remove one of the most crucial areas of concern from public debate."

If any additional evidence of the significance of the "soft-on-communism" theme to the Republican party was needed, it was provided by a "model," two-thousand-word resolution prepared by representatives of the party's Los Angeles County Central Committee for general distribution to all other county committees in the state. In it Brown was indicted for his "subservience to the dominance of the extreme left." Its utility was somewhat impaired when, by misadventure, a stray copy fell into the possession of Roger Kent, northern

California vice-chairman of the Democratic state central committee, who promptly labeled the contents a personal vilification of Brown and a campaign of "smear, fear and scare" against his party.

The Communist issue in California politics opens up a veritable Pandora's Box of right-wing activity which exceeds the realm of credulity; the resulting excesses in extremism elicit revulsion among the genuine conservatives in both parties. In the 1962 campaign the smear literature against Brown followed a readily discernible pattern. The *theme* was that the California Democratic Council was dominated by its left wing and that Brown was a captive of the CDC. The alleged *proof* was a series of resolutions sponsored by the extremists in the organization in recent years relating to such matters as: abolition of the House Un-American Activities Committee; admission of Red China into the UN; unilateral disarmament; and elimination of loyalty oaths. The propaganda vehicles included the notorious booklet, *California Dynasty of Communism*; a four-page pamphlet, *Pat Brown and the CDC*; a questionnaire prepared by the Anti-Communist Voters League entitled, "Evaluation of Candidates on the Issue of Communism"; and an "opinion poll" under the title, "Communication of Extreme Importance to California Democrats," authored by an organization called the Committee for Preservation of the Democratic Party in California.

California Dynasty of Communism (the first letters of the title spelling CDC for California Democratic Council), or "The Little Red Book" as it soon became known, was probably the most controversial single piece of propaganda in the campaign. A thirty-three-page booklet with a red cover, it represented the issues of an extremist publication known as *Heads Up* (volume 2, numbers one, two, and three).[28] The author was a self-styled FBI counterspy named Karl Prussion.

One of each of three chapters is devoted to Attorney General Stanley Mosk, State Comptroller Alan Cranston, and Governor Brown, and the material is in the character-assassination, guilt-by-association, and linkage-with-communism category. Mosk is characterized as "this astute, opportunistic, slithering, political charlatan" with a record which "reveals him to be a collaborator, appeaser and consistent supporter of communist objectives." Cranston is labeled the "father of red-organized and controlled California Democratic Clubs." It was alleged that "Cranston's Red Objectives pass at Fresno Convention" and the CDC adopted the "entire platform of the Communist Party."

Brown is charged with a "record of collaborating with and appeasing Communists." A picture of Brown bowing with hands pressed together imitating the welcoming gesture of a young woman visitor from Laos was cropped to give the impression that the governor was bowing to a picture of Kruschev on the opposite page; the caption: "Premier Kruschev, we who admire you, we who

III BROWN IS A RED APPEASER . . . . .

*"PREMIER KHRUSHCHEV, WE
WHO ADMIRE YOU, WE WHO
RESPECT YOU, WELCOME
YOU TO CALIFORNIA."*

— *P. Brown*

Governor Pat Brown, over the years, has established an unchallengeable record of collaborating with and appeasing communists from "top to bottom."

"Premier Khrushchev, we who admire you, we who respect you, welcome you to California."

These are the words of greeting by Pat Brown, the red-appeasing Governor of our great State to Dictator Khrushchev, who rules an empire built of mountains of human skeletons and rivers of blood. Hitler, by comparison, was a Boy Scout!

Brown continued his eulogizing representatives of Communist tyranny on May 8, 1962 by sending a telegram in which he honored Astronaut Titov at a reception arranged by the American Russian Institute, of which Dr. Holland Roberts and Michael Shepovalov (clearly identified communists) are Directors. The telegram was read in a Cheshire-cat manner to a multitude of communists, their sympathizers and red liberals by none other than Holland Roberts, communist international emissary.

BROWN LAUDS COMMUNIST FRONT AND RED PUBLICATION

On the bottom of the conspiracy, Governor Brown's picture appeared on the front page of the official communist organ for Leninist work among the farmers, THE FARM REPORTER; this was their 20th anniversary edition, published in 1961. A letter from Governor Brown to the Farm Legislative and Research Committee,

. . . . . FROM TOP TO BOTTOM

"WHEN WE SPIT IN THE FACE OF AN AMERICAN, HE THINKS IT'S DEW."

— N. Khrushchev

an official communist organization for work among farmers, appeared below his photograph. He highly commended this Red organization and its press (THE FARM REPORTER) for the superb work they have been doing on behalf of the farmers of America.

Pettis Perry, Chairman of the Farm Commission of the Communist Party, in July, 1951, at a closed meeting of the hierarchy of the conspiracy made the following statement: "Along with the question of building the Party, we must build all of the left and Marxist press. In California we have the **Farm Reporter**. This should be built into a mass publication. It would be most helpful in advancing our work among the farmers." (Political Affairs, July, 1951)

The editors of this Red propaganda sheet and the leaders of the Farm Legislative and Research Committee are: Mr. Davis, Mr. Reich, and Mrs. McDonald, all three clearly identified as hardcore dedicated communists, loyal to the Soviet Union.

BROWN AND THE NATIONAL LAWYERS GUILD

The National Lawyers Guild was cited as a communist front as far back as 1944. The Governor is a past vice-president of the San Francisco Chapter of the National Lawyers Guild. He left the organization in 1946 because, he said, of its being declared respect you, welcome you to California." The text continues: "These are the words of greeting by Pat Brown, the red-appeasing Governor . . . to Dictator Khrushchev, who rules an empire built of mountains of human skeletons and rivers of blood."

Brown retorted that "the fakery and distortion of these pamphlets is the filthiest campaigning I have seen in twenty years of public life." Nixon characterized the Little Red Book as "disgraceful." The FBI announced that Prussion had never been an employee of the organization and in an October thirtieth press conference the author admitted that he had been neither an employee nor an agent, but had offered information "voluntarily" from time to time over a twelve-year period.

The four-page brochure, *Pat Brown and the CDC*, may be classed as official Republican campaign literature since it was prepared by Democrats for Nixon, an adjunct of the Nixon campaign organization.[29] The two inside pages contained four quotations carefully selected from CDC literature placed in juxtaposition to four equally carefully cropped pictures of Brown. Under the caption "Pat Brown says" were four quotations taken out of context, presumably reflecting the governor's personal endorsement of the extremist policy positions of the CDC. All of the cropped pictures were "faked" out of context. One originally represented Brown applauding the little crippled "poster girl of the year" being introduced to state capitol officials in the fund drive for victims of paralysis.

In an attempt to discover "which candidates for National and State office are best qualified to formulate and pursue policies that will reverse the Communist imperialist onslaught against the United States," the Anti-Communist Voters League posed 13 questions to 287 candidates for elective office and published the resultant "Evaluations" in a 16-page pamphlet entitled *Evaluation of Candidates on the Issue of Communism*.[30] The questionnaires were sent before the primary with a follow-up mailing to nonrespondents before the general election. They covered such subjects as "loyalty oaths, admission of Red China to the United Nations, continuation of the House Committee on Un-American Activities, a firm stand on Berlin and Cuba, and the use of tax supported buildings for subversive purposes."

The evaluations were made in four categories: "*Approved* (sufficiently qualified on the Communist issue); *Not Endorsed* (qualifications . . . do not measure up to the standard that is demanded for victory in the cold war); *Opposed* (approach . . . would tend to weaken the hands of government); and *Doubtful* (candidate refused to answer; . . . record is either nil, or inconclusive)." The basis of the evaluations included the voting record of incumbents on issues pertaining to communism, public statements in the press, and pledges in campaign literature, as well as answers to the questions. The results as published and mailed to an indeterminate number of registered voters were: *Approved*, 125 Republicans and 27 Democrats; *Doubtful*, 63 Democrats and 12 Republicans; *Opposed*, 25 Democrats and 0 Republicans; *Failed to Endorse*, 25 Democrats and 3 Republicans.

The questions dealt with issues upon which the California Democratic Council had passed resolutions in recent years. The Democratic State Central Committee viewed the project, however, as an attempt to trap unwary candidates into making policy statements which might be construed to equate past CDC policy with current party campaign positions. Any such identity would serve the purposes of the Republican party in saddling the Democrats with past and present views of the most liberal fringe element within the CDC; moreover, cooperation with the project would imply erroneously that the CDC speaks for the Democratic party. Democratic candidates were warned not to participate in the poll. Among the leading candidates, only Stanley Mosk replied, and drew a stinging rebuke from the Communist *People's World* for his views.

On October thirty-first, retired Vice-Admiral Roland N. Smoot, executive director of the organization, issued an endorsement of Nixon. Brown was censured for his belated disavowal of the "flagrantly Communist line" of the 1960 CDC Convention resolutions; of "his failure to proceed with . . . fervor against infiltration itself"; and for his denial that any Communist had appeared on any state college campus during his term of office. Brown's "opposed" rating by the organization supposedly indicated a "lack of understanding of the Communist menace."

One of the most controversial ventures of the official Republican organization was a "Communication of Extreme Importance to California Democrats" issued by a Committee for the Preservation of the Democratic Party in California. The committee was a "paper organization" apparently created by the Nixon staff operating from addresses in both San Francisco and Los Angeles. A press release by a San Francisco public relations firm on the committee's letterhead, dated October twelfth, began with the clarion call, "Left-wing forces are moving to capture the Democratic Party in California." The accompanying letter stated that fifty thousand copies of a double-carded "poll" were going to registered Democrats with "as many more as we find it possible to reach." The message was placed on two attached 5½ by 8½ post cards, one containing a letter to the Democratic voter and the other a poll card to be detached and returned (postpaid) with the answers to a series of questions.[31]

The letter links the CDC with the Communist conspiracy, under a salutation to "Dear Fellow Democrats" and the slogan "Let's Not Deliver California to the CDC!" The poll questions attempt to determine whether the respondent is favorable to positions taken by the ultraliberal element of the organization. With the anonymous quotation, "If we refuse to ban Communists from the Democratic party—it means we welcome them" as a guideline, the voter is expected to answer four banks of questions. The first group represents eight alleged policy statements "the CDC leadership viewpoint favors." The second asks for a "yes" or "no" answer to the question: "Can California afford to have a Governor . . . indebted to the CDC," and is embellished with quotations of approbation by Brown. The third suggests courses of action with unacceptable alternatives: "Support a Republican candidate rather than sell out the party. . . ." Finally, the voter was directed to express a preference among the candidates for the six statewide elective offices. Not only were the questions "loaded" in respect to eliciting desired responses such as "allowing subversives the freedom of college campuses" and "foreign aid to countries with Communist governments," but the publication of "results" of the poll offered a double-barreled impact upon the public.

The Democrats claimed "foul" in respect to several other Republican maneuvers whose sponsorship as between the official organization and mere "sympathizers" was beclouded. Late in August pink-colored auto bumper stickers suddenly appeared in profusion carrying the inscription "Is Brown Pink?" The Republican party disclaimed any involvement with this stunt. A week before the election, the Democrats for Nixon supported the Republican candidate's repeated charges that Brown had surrounded himself in Sacramento with hacks by placing two-column advertisements in the press entitled, "The Men Around Brown: Californians Deserve Better."[32] Thirteen individuals were named including four related to the governor; allegations included such comments as: "indicted by federal grand jury for 19 counts of embezzlement" and "charged with violation of the Hatch Act." In the San Francisco Bay area the Citizen's Fact Finding Committee on Governor Brown distributed rather widely a four-page leaflet asking and glibly answering such questions as: "Is . . . Brown soft on Communism?" Finally, an abortive attempt by a group designated as "Free Democrats" was made to draft a Democratic rival to compete with Brown's candidacy.

Why did Nixon adopt the Communist issue which had proven ineffective in the 1958 and 1960 campaigns? There were apparently a number of compelling reasons. The primary campaign had not produced a really effective point of attack on Brown, and some new approach was needed to excite the voters; the Communist charges struck fire in Nixon's public appearances. Shell supporters demonstrated little enthusiasm for the Nixon candidacy and the John Birch Society nurtured some antipathy. The Democratic party had skillfully pinned the "soft on Birchism" label on Nixon, and the Communist issue spanned party lines, appealing to all conservatives. Finally, Republican strategists apparently concluded that the only group whose sensibilities could be outraged at the calculated decision to employ the issue would be the "old guard" of unregenerate and irredeemable Democrats who have nursed a deep and abiding resentment against Richard Nixon and Murray Chotiner since the Voorhis campaign in 1946 and the Douglas campaign of 1950. Even former United States Senator William F. Knowland, although endorsing Nixon in the columns of the *Oakland Tribune* which he edits, rebuked him on the issue: "We deem absolutely fantastic the claim that Governor Brown is soft on Communism."

In retrospect, it is possible the Democrats actually gained more from the Nixon attack on Brown than did the Republican candidate himself. The issue was clearly a synthetic one as far as the allegation that any immediate Communist threat to the state was concerned, and neither Brown as a practicing Catholic nor his administration was vulnerable in the eyes of the electorate. The "old Nixon" image was revived, instead of that of a positive new force on the state scene.

Without doubt, one of the genuine hallmarks of the entire campaign was the changed role of the press of the state. Overwhelmingly Republican in editorial policy and often blatantly partisan in the presentation of political news during elections, the press achieved a degree of fairness in the treatment of both parties not experienced in California in this generation. Preparing to meet the competition of the western edition of the *New York Times*, the major dailies in the state and particularly the *Los Angeles Times* gained stature in the world of journalism and kudos from leaders in each party for thoroughness and professional objectivity in reporting. It is entirely possible that from the depths of his disappointment, Richard Nixon's bitter denunciation of the press at his "last" news conference was a true measure of the extent to which the major newspapers have achieved political maturity in California.

An interesting innovation in this campaign was the desire of some citizens in both parties for the organization of a state Fair Campaign Practices Committee (FCPC). After several months of negotiation, principally for the services of individuals of unassailable integrity, partisan identification, and yet acceptable to both parties, a committee was appointed on October 15, 1962, under the aegis of the national organization. Membership was divided equally between the two major parties, each represented by a cochairman and three other members. Six of the eight members were attorneys (one a law associate of Richard Nixon's), one a newspaperman, and the other an academician; two were drawn from the San Francisco Bay area, a similar number from Los Angeles, and the remaining four afforded geographic distribution representing the communities of San Diego, Santa Barbara, Fresno, and Sacramento. All names were approved by the state leadership of each party.[33]

The committee work was expedited by procedural guidelines provided by the national organization.[34] The seven-point *Code of Fair Campaign Practices* signed by the principal candidates was amplified by some thirty explanatory and interpretive phrases keyed into descriptions of as many specific illustrations of violations of the code, which were culled from past elections. Complaints were to be filed only by the national committeemen and state chairman of the major parties. In the interest of saving time, travel problems, and expenses, telephonic conferences (tie-lines) were accepted in lieu of face-to-face meetings. Finally, State Attorney General Stanley K. Mosk, himself a candidate for reelection, offered to designate a lawyer (or lawyers) chosen by a majority of the committee as special assistant attorney general to investigate any legal question bearing on the state election law. This procedure had been used successfully in the state of New York.

The committee received an official complaint supported by exhibits from each major party indicting the opposition for a series of violations of the code. The Democratic complaint was filed on October 25, 1962, by state Vice-chairman Roger Kent of northern California on behalf of the Democratic State Central Committee, with the approval of National Committeewoman Elizabeth Rudel Gatov. It was acted upon the next day and a statement was given to the press for immediate release in ample time to influence the electorate. The Republican complaint was filed by Nixon's campaign manager, H. R. Haldeman, and although dated October thirty-first, did not reach the individual committeemen at their homes until Saturday, November third, only two days before the election. It is interesting to note, however, that the essential contents of the document were released to the press two days earlier by State Chairman Casper Weinberger, so that a highly partisan version was in print twenty-four hours before the official complaint reached the committee!

In a series of nine exhibits of booklets, pamphlets, photos of cropped pictures side by side with the originals, news stories, and press releases, the Democrats purported to find a "skillfully planned and massively conducted campaign to smear . . . Brown as a left-winger, a pro-Communist, and a red appeaser." Moreover, the complaint alleged that the Republican party organization and its leaders were involved in the design and execution of the plan.

Affidavits were submitted by persons who had purchased the Prussion booklet, *California Dynasty of Communism*, in Republican campaign headquarters. Charges were made that Republican officials admitted sponsoring the *Pat Brown and the CDC* pamphlet; that the double postcard questionnaire violated three provisions of the Elections Code relating to literature identification; and that the cost of the "Free Democrats" movement to draft a write-in candidate opposing Brown was so great that no source of funds other than those available to an organized party could have been utilized for the purpose.

The press release of November first, announcing the findings of the FCPC of California, mentioned only three exhibits. The Prussion booklet was characterized as "highly unethical," "an unwarranted and vicious attack," and "extremely offensive." The committee also pointed out that both Nixon and Republican spokesmen had denounced the brochure and denied any involvement in its publication. The two-way post-card poll was "disaffirmed" on grounds that it violated the state Election Code. The leaflet by the Citizen's Fact-Finding Committee was branded a "vicious" attack on Governor Brown and condemned for both its content and its undisclosed sponsorship.

Governor Brown immediately attempted to exploit the FCPC statement by claiming that the group had "put the seal of Bad Housekeeping" on the Nixon campaign. The committee responded the following day with another press release reiterating the fact that the ruling was based upon content and anonymity of source and emphasizing that no evidence was found involving either the Republican gubernatorial candidate or his organization. The FCPC also took occasion to label "misleading" the use of statements by President Kennedy on the principle of reapportionment, which had been placed upon billboards in such a manner as to indicate specific approval of Proposition 23 on California Senate reapportionment.

The timing and press handling of the Republican complaint raises a question relating to that party's concept of the role which the FCPC should play in the campaign. In a four-page statement, the first page was devoted to a reprint of the *Code* with Brown's name typed at the bottom. The remaining pages were citations of alleged violations committed by Brown, each of the twelve infractions classified under one of the seven stipulated principles of the *Code*. The charges may be summarized as follows: (1) a radio commercial falsely identified the Prussion publication as connected with the Nixon campaign and was in error in labeling the pictures in the Brown-CDC pamphlet as false; (2) a television film made by Brown to show the accomplishments of his administration made false claims; (3) a letter signed by one John J. Keller of the Republican Committee to reelect Governor Brown and sent to citizens of Polish ancestry claiming that Nixon supported discriminatory immigration laws was in error and that Keller was a registered Democrat; (4) Brown and George McLain, pension group leader and a Democratic campaign vice-chairman, repeatedly and erroneously alleged that Nixon advocated a reduction of benefits for the elderly; (5) Brown encouraged his supporters to circulate libelous copy alleging that Nixon or his family acted improperly in connection with the Hughes Tool Company loan; (6) the California Democratic Council had ordered one thousand copies of the Prussion booklet and Brown had continually insisted that the Nixon organization issued it; (7) Democratic State Chairman Eugene Wyman charged on television that Nixon had called Harry Truman a traitor and Brown failed to correct him; and (8) "Mr. Brown has stated repeatedly . . . that Mr. Nixon has accused him of being 'soft on Communism.' This is a lie."

There appeared to be no thematic approach to the Republican analysis of Democratic violations of the code, except perhaps that the attack was centered more upon the alleged misbehavior of Brown personally. Some emphasis was placed upon Democratic charges stigmatizing Nixon's attitude toward civil liberties and minority groups. Several of the charges, such as those criticizing the background of commercial television shorts, seem somewhat trivial. It is a reasonable assumption that, had time to process the material permitted, the FCPC would have cited the Democrats for insistence that the Prussion booklet was officially inspired and for the malicious content in the Hughes-loan and Nixon-trust-deed leaflets.

The experience of the committee was inconclusive, although its mere existence was a tribute to the perseverance of men of good will in both parties who served on the committee. It served as a demonstration of the crusading spirit of Chairman Charles P. Taft and Bruce L. Felknor, executive director of the national organization of the Fair Campaign Practices Committee. Several circumstances militated against the role that the committee was fully capable of playing on behalf of political fair play. The committee lacked the authority and capability of searching out and apprehending questionable practices and literature. Both parties seemed reluctant to utilize its services, while resort to court suits proved to be unusually effective. The greatest sanction of the FCPC rested with censure by public opinion, and the parties could nullify this weapon by delay in filing complaints; it is probable that parties were fearful of appealing to the committee because of possible retaliation. In at least one instance, a brazen attempt was made to use the committee's decision as a political weapon.

Court action is assuming an increasingly important role in smear campaigning in California. Political litigation may be viewed objectively as a technique rather than as a search for justice, since such cases originate before an election and almost without exception are dropped immediately thereafter. During the brief interim, each party has its day posing as the injured innocent, pointing the finger of accusation at a licentious opponent.

There is an important tactical advantage to be gained by flooding the electorate with vicious propaganda just before the end of the campaign. Since denial or retaliation is impracticable, the principle value of a court suit is to try to prevent the wide dissemination of such literature. The pattern of legal action has assumed a relatively fixed format: (a) filing of a complaint requesting a restraining order or injunction temporarily preventing the circulation of the offending materials; (b) a libel suit claiming monetary damages for defamation of character, ranging from two hundred thousand to two million dollars; (c) naming one or more national committeemen, the cochairman of the state party, and the state central committee as defendants; and (d) occasionally singling out a particular individual or group as codefendants in order to draw attention to their roles on behalf of the opposition party.

California has had an "election disclosure law" on the statute books since the reform era of 1901 prohibiting the publication and dissemination of anonymously authored campaign materials.[35] Several sections of the *California Elections Code* relate to the distribution of circulars, pamphlets, letters or posters, and campaign literature, but the emphasis for legal action rests upon the anonymity of the source. Apparently questions relating to the content of the text are left to suit under the libel laws of the *Civil Code.* The prevailing regulations make it a misdemeanor to write or cause to be written materials "designed to injure or defeat any candidate for nomination or election to any public office by reflecting upon his personal character or political action," unless the name and address of the printer is conspicuously displayed along with either the name and address of the chairman and secretary of the originating organization (or similar identification of two officers), or the name and residence address (including street number) of some voter of the state who assumes responsibility for the publication. Approximately the same restrictions govern the distribution of literature promoting the passage or defeat of a ballot measure. Further stipulations are that campaign material is not a privileged communication, nor will the printer's union label or identifying code number satisfy the regulations relating to anonymity. Windshield stickers and bumper strips, which abound in profusion in California, are excepted from the disclosure law. Otherwise, conviction of violation of these provisions is punishable by a one-thousand-dollar fine or one year in the county jail, or both.

A recent augmentation of the *Code* declares it unlawful for a candidate or a committee to misrepresent, either verbally or in writing, alleged support from a qualified political party with which the candidate is not affiliated. This particular restraint upon the candidate prevents the use of misleading nomenclature such as "county," "county committee," or "central committee" in such a manner as to infer endorsement from the county or state central committee with reference to an opposition party. It is possible, however, for a candidate to enlist support from a committee constituted of legitimate members of the opposite party.

During the 1962 and 1963 sessions of the state legislature, the *Election Code* was amended in an attempt to control the problem of endorsement by party and nonparty groups. The question of official party endorsement before and during the primary election had been raised when several party officers and county committees had indulged in the practice. The law is clear on this point stating that the governing bodies of the parties "shall not endorse, support or oppose any candidate for nomination by that party for partisan office in the direct primary election." Moreover, the county committee was given the power to remove any member who affiliates with, or registers as a member of, another party, or who publicly advocates that the public should not vote for the nominee of his own party, or who otherwise opposes his party's candidate.

One particular source of confusion of party identity is the plethora of ad hoc political groups which preempt their own or a rival party name in whole or in part, giving the distinct impression that their literature has the party's official blessing. The law on this point requires such a group to print on its literature and campaign publications a "Notice to Voters," reading: "The endorsement herein is by an unofficial political group. Official organizations of the ———— Party are prohibited by law from endorsing candidates in primary elections." The same provision applies to post cards and must be rendered orally on radio and television.

There were several violations of the *Elections Code* cited in court actions during the 1962 election, where the disclosure law was tested. On October twenty-ninth, representatives of the Democratic party obtained a temporary restraining order in the Superior Court in Los Angeles from Judge Kenneth N. Chantry preventing the distribution of Prussion's notorious *California Dynasty of Communism*. The technical grounds for the order were the alleged failure to comply with the law governing identity of the printer and publisher. The complaint was reinforced with a five-hundred-thousand-dollar libel suit against the author for insinuating a close connection between Democratic leaders and the Communist conspiracy.

Several interesting sidelights resulted from this maneuver. One was a statement by the author in the booklet that he would "welcome the opportunity to present in a court of law the evidence in his possession"; he also issued an open invitation for "legal action." Prussion's attorney was an acknowledged sympathizer with the John Birch Society and newly elected president of the Los Angeles County Young Republicans, Robert A. Gaston. The attorney offered to paste stickers on the booklet containing the necessary information to provide clearance for distribution, thus by implication denying the alleged libelous nature of the charges. On November second, the American Civil Liberties Union (of southern California), which had been pilloried by Prussion as "the armor plate of the Communist conspiracy," joined in his defense, pleading freedom of the press. Republican leaders vehemently denied having become involved with the booklet in any manner. State Chairman Casper Weinberger termed the content "scurrilous" and insisted that the Democrats were printing and distributing it "solely for the purpose of enabling them to make another false charge against Republicans." Finally, Jud Leetham, Los Angeles County Republican Central Committee chairman, who had been singled out as a defendant in the action for allegedly distributing the pamphlet, retaliated with a six-hundred-thousand-dollar claim against the Democratic State Central Committee, charging that an attempt was being made to destroy his professional reputation. Mr. Leetham had, in fact, written a letter to Republican campaign workers within his jurisdiction dated October fifteenth stating: "If this booklet is being stocked as a service in any Republican headquarters or facility, it is requested that it be discontinued at once." In the seven-page communication he denied passing a value judgment upon the contents on the theory that the court decision would prevail in respect to the legitimacy of the booklet as campaign material. He further pointed out that there was "scant justification for the Party undertaking the promotion of a position for which we do not have adequate verification."

The Democratic party obtained a second court order in San Francisco from Superior Court Judge Byron Arnold on October twenty-ninth, temporarily interrupting the distribution of the questionnaire, sponsored by the Committee for the Preservation of the Democratic Party in California. Five hundred thousand of the double post cards allegedly casting aspersions upon the loyalty of the Democratic party members had been printed and some fifty thousand mailed, but half of the remainder were in post offices and elsewhere. Attorneys for the committee admitted that their clients had not obtained permission from the Democratic party to use its name, but attempted to argue the case on the basis of free speech. The cards carried an address in San Francisco and another in Los Angeles, but no person, printer, or publisher could be identified.

In a third successful Superior Court action instituted on October thirtieth in Los Angeles, the Democrats named Murray Chotiner, a principal Nixon advisor, along with others as defendants in a suit involving the production and distribution of the allegedly libelous and anonymously authored and printed four-page pamphlet, *Pat Brown and the CDC*. Sponsorship of the publication was credited to a "Democrats for Nixon" committee, and Chotiner allegedly boasted that one million copies were to have been distributed before election day. Along with the restraining order, the complaint requested five hundred thousand dollars for libel damages.

The Republican party failed to act upon two major Democratic campaign pieces, the *Nixonpedia* and the purple "pseudo-biography" of Mayor Christopher. A veritable flood of broadsides and fliers purporting to prove Nixon's addiction to discrimination against the entire spate of civil liberties was loosed at minority group meetings, mostly in the southern California area. The party hierarchy was moved to take retaliatory measures, accusing the Democrats of "peddling smears in the Negro and Jewish sections of Los Angeles." On November second, Nixon's campaign manager, H. R. Haldeman, sought a restraining order from Judge Chantry, halting the distribution of two of the more flagrant leaflets: *Want This Kind of Governor in California?* relating to a restrictive covenant contained in a housing deed signed by Nixon and *Questions Nixon Won't Answer About the $205,000 Hughes Tool Company Loan to the Nixon Family.* The Democratic leaders who had spearheaded that party's own court action were named as defendants along with two ad hoc groups: Independent Voters of California and Citizens for Honesty in Politics. In addition to charges that the content of the leaflets was false and misleading, Haldeman demanded two million dollars damages against the Democratic State Central Committee.

Perhaps the most interesting legal action resulting from the 1962 election involved Richard Nixon's policy of nonendorsement of candidates for federal office. The issue became a cause célèbre in an acrimonious, litigous contest in the Twenty-seventh Congressional District race between the incumbent and John Birch Society member Edgar W. Hiestand, and his Democratic challenger, Everett G. Burkhalter.[36]

Seizing upon Nixon's dilemma of being unable to endorse any Republican congressional candidate without including three members of the John Birch Society, Burkhalter claimed that Hiestand did not have Nixon's support. He alleged specifically that Nixon had called his opponent "a Republican handicap." On October ninth, Hiestand filed a two-hundred-thousand-dollar libel suit in Superior Court against his opponent and two supporting organizations, the Burkhalter for Congress Committee and Republican Volunteers for Burkhalter. In the same action Hiestand was successful in obtaining a temporary restraining order against the distribution of two of his opponent's publications: *The 27th District Democrat* and *The Republican Review.* The offending statements related Hiestand to the opinions of leaders of the John Birch Society, particularly concerning General Eisenhower, and to the list of 227 bills introduced during the past 5 sessions of Congress, none of which allegedly became law. A corollary issue was the possible misrepresentation of Republican support for Burkhalter in the *Republican Review.* Within three weeks Burkhalter countered with a two-hundred-thousand-dollar libel suit against Hiestand charging that his opponent had employed false statements in obtaining the restraining order.

During the course of the litigation the court instructed Nixon to give a deposition on November fifth to Burkhalter's attorney answering the question: "Do you, Richard M. Nixon, endorse Edgar W. Hiestand for election to the United States House of Representatives from the 27th Congressional District in California?" Nixon replied that he would not endorse any candidate for federal office. In a statewide telethon the evening before, however, Nixon was quoted as having remarked that "he wouldn't endorse Mr. Burkhalter for dog catcher." The following Monday he was sued for slander, being charged with insulting and abusive conduct and with having subjected Mr. Burkhalter to contempt and public ridicule. The congressman asked for $5,200 damages.

These various suits were eventually dismissed, but Superior Judge MacIntyre Faries upheld the restraining order affecting the distribution of the Burkhalter literature. Since Judge Faries spent a lifetime in politics before ascending to the bench, including many years as a distinguished Republican national committeeman, his views are of particular interest. In an eight-page document, which he characterized as "a cursory memorandum of some thinking of the undersigned which he feels to be pertinent," the judge expressed the view that those who are professionally political in their occupation are under some obligation to compete fairly. Since the tort of unfair competition has not frequently been applied to political activity, the principle was somewhat novel and was challenged by the counsel for the defendant. At any rate, the judge felt that some of the innuendoes in Burkhalter's campaign literature were not warranted, at least by the facts presented to the court. He also enjoined the defendants to refrain from using the name "Republican" or "G.O.P." in such a manner as to imply that they had the support of the official apparatus of the Republican party in California.[37]

Many complex problems are encountered in the area of political campaign literature evaluation, such as source, motivation, cost, distribution, total voter impact, and the relation of the entire operation to the campaign, the party system, and the political process in a democracy. Ascertainment of the motivation of individuals who create and utilize smear literature is itself an unsolved problem; party victory alone is obviously only a partial explanation. The application of any given set of ethical standards to a series of intentional misrepresentations and unfounded allegations is fraught with hazards of misunderstanding. About the only safe conclusion is that neither of our major political parties has a monopoly on morality; the breaches of the legal and ethical code seem to fall rather evenly in each camp.

Viewing the situation in California objectively, certain hypotheses may be ventured relating the various actors on the political state with questionable political practices:

1. *The candidate.* The public expectations of the candidate force him to play the role of a leader protecting the public interest in a righteous cause. Due in part to the weakness of party discipline and the practical necessity of appealing to the broad middle of the ideological road, his contribution is the identification and legitimatization of an issue through usage. His own demeanor may reflect an attempt to achieve a "statesmanlike level" of public responsibility, but his official and unofficial adherents may exploit the same issue on a series of descending levels of moral and ethical integrity.

The candidate eschews the crude tactic of name calling per se in favor of the more subtle technique of innuendo and linkage. Thus he preserves the illusion that he is taking "the high road" of responsibility and fair play, while in fact he carefully nurtures an issue through the campaign, which his adherents may exploit at will and in any chosen manner within the law. Brown kept the Hughes Tool Loan issue alive with its obvious implications of moral turpitude, while Nixon monitored the soft-on-communism issue with the equally plain inference of impeached loyalty. Brown never, of course, called Nixon a crook, nor did Nixon ever refer to Brown as a Communist, but both made certain that the semantic door was left wide open for their less scrupulous supporters.

2. *The official party organization.* The great bulk of campaign material emanates from this source and by most objective standards may be classed as unobjectionable. Measured by their own criteria of fairness applicable to opposition performance, however, each party produces some materials in the smear category, or in the classification of intentional misrepresentation. Two cases reported to the California Fair Practices Campaign Committee may suffice as illustrations. The Democrats produced a series of television commercials praising the accomplishments of the Brown administration. Several of these, including the one on water development, were staged before backgrounds of dams, parks, and public buildings belonging to previous administrations. The backdrop for the water program, for instance, was the Mulholland Spillway, completed when Brown was eight years of age!

The Republican party on the other hand produced the notorious pamphlet *Pat Brown and the CDC*, with its cropped, "faked" pictures and carefully selected quotations out of context. Only a court restraining order nipped a plan to flood the state with hundreds of thousands of copies.

One significant unknown in the equation of party involvement with scurrilous campaign tactics is the degree to which sympathetic partisan groups, operating under less legal restraint, are "cued-in" by party officials and professional campaign firms on exploitable vulnerabilities of the opposition candidates as well as the official strategic and tactical decisions of the campaign. Any fair evaluation of the 1962 election would indicate that the massive, coordinated Republican attack on Brown through alleged domination by the left wing of the CDC, and the similar indictment of Nixon's alleged discriminatory views on civil rights for racial and religious minorities, involved some degree of collaboration between party officers, leaders of auxiliary groups, and producers of smear literature.

3. *Auxiliaries to the parties.* Cross-filing forced each party to create auxiliaries to perform essential political services such as preprimary endorsements and the manufacturing of political ammunition. The California Republican Assembly and the California Democratic Council are "two-hatted" organizations with party personnel serving in both structures. Other auxiliaries include Republican and Democratic "Associates," women's organizations, and the youth groups.

A great deal of issue and candidate research is accomplished at this level and some of the product is beyond the pale of respectability. In the 1958 campaign, for instance, "Compare the Record" fly sheets contrasting biographical data of opposition candidates in the areas of patriotism, family, education, and experience were credited to the "research Committee, Los Angeles Federation of Republican Women." By a process of careful selection, emphasis, and omission, the opposition candidate was made to appear unpatriotic, and so forth.

4. *Sympathetically affiliated, nonparty groups.* Both California parties are frequently victimized in a campaign by groups pursuing their own political ends. Such groups will practically cannibalize a legitimate partisan issue by indulging in vicious extremism, which plays into the hands of the enemy.

For almost a generation the Communist party, particularly through the *People's World*, planted the kiss of death upon Democratic issues or candidates, either by open endorsement or Marxist rationalization of means and ends. Republicans enjoyed an extended field day quoting communist sources to capitalize on the fortuitous concurrence between Communists and liberal Democrats concerning some issues of public policy such as the abolition of the House Un-American Activities Committee. The obvious irrational inference was that fortuitous concurrence on principle or conviction meant that Democrats "followed the Commie line."

The relationship between the John Birch Society and the Republican party is in hot dispute on all echelons of party activity, and little, if any, research has yet been done on the connection between extremist Republican literature and the Birchers. Certainly the organization offers the Democrats the same opportunity to victimize the conservative wing of the Republican party as the Communists have given the Republicans to exploit the liberal wing of the Democratic party. Both the Birchers and the Communists are activist political groups and their schemes and plans constitute a natural source for extremist literature.

5. *Ad hoc groups constituted for a single campaign.* It is legal in California for either party to harbor dissident elements which organize to support a candidate in an opposing party as long as the titles of such groups do not employ nomenclature such as "county or state committee" which would imply official representation of their own party organization. On the other hand, each election brings a spate of "morning glory" or "boiler room" political operations constituted with or without party sponsorship for the duration of a campaign, or perhaps, only to execute a single project. Their titles are intentionally misleading, their sources of income unknown, although public relations firms are believed to finance many of these ventures, operating under a cloak of anonymity. Examples during the 1962 campaign were: Committee for the Preservation of the Democratic Party (R), Citizens for Honesty in Politics (D), Citizens Fact Finding Committee for Governor Brown (R), and the Independent Voters of California (D). All of these groups produced literature cited either in court orders or before the Fair Campaign Practices Committee, or both.

6. *Professional political campaign firms.* Probably no single potential source of spurious campaign literature will bare closer scrutiny than professional political public relations firms working for a substantial retainer. California probably leads the nation in these propaganda-for-pay agencies whose longevity in the trade is contingent upon victory at the polls. The sums of money changing hands in the transactions between candidates, parties, and the business community is staggering. In 1956, Proposition 4, a measure on oil conservation tagged "The battle between the million dollar and the billion dollar corporations," cost opponents and proponents an acknowledged total of approximately five million dollars.

7. *Individuals operating independently.* The last group defied further categorization except to point out that some radio and television commentators and newspaper columnists peddle rumors and half truths which form part of the smear lexicon of any campaign. During the 1962 campaign one television commentator in Los Angeles became so blatantly partisan that the Democratic party submitted tapes of his broadcasts to the FCC and won an order allocating fifteen minutes of prime air time in the nightly program for rebuttal.

A few other problems may be stated in terms of questions. First, *motivation*: what is the quid pro quo for stooping to conquer by becoming a mudslinger? Is it a question of principle, no matter how misguided? Or material gain in dollars and cents, or an avaricious hunger for power? Or perhaps merely psychological therapy for a diseased personality?

What are the channels for distribution of smear literature? Where do the mailing lists come from? Who selects the human targets? What is the voter impact of a smear campaign? Why doesn't some pollster test the three greatest myths in California politics: that the Republicans believe that most Democrats are Communist sympathizers; that the Democrats believe that most Republicans are neo-Fascists; and finally the myth of the professional politician in both parties that smear literature really wins or loses an election?

Several hypotheses relating to smear literature in California await scientific testing:

1. The sense of responsibility for what is said and done is highest in the deportment of the candidate and decreases in each succeeding lower echelon to the relatively irresponsible behavior of ad hoc groups and the "loners."

2. The degree of venality in the content of smear literature is greatest in the product of other-directed, peripheral groups and individuals.

3. Anonymity is the greatest ally of the political smear artist.

4. What are the ethical connotations of the dichotomy of means and ends as applied to campaigning in California?

5. Parties have little or no control over the activities of self-appointed allies who make common cause with their issues and candidates.

6. Despite the juvenile game that the American voter plays in siding with the "good guys against the bad guys," neither the Republican nor Democratic parties have a monopoly on political ethics or morality; both are equally culpable in respect to tolerating and using smear literature.

7. Politicians as a group are neither more nor less honest than other members of the social community; they are creatures of their time and their behavior reflects the ethical standards of the cultural mores.

8. California regulations, to the degree that they do control predatory political behavior, might be improved in three ways: by better enforcement of the present full disclosure laws including insistence on bringing violators to trial; by tightening of the libel laws by withdrawing the common granting of conditional privilege during political campaigns and lessening the distinction between political injury and injury to personal reputation in political damage suits; and, to the degree that it is possible, by emulating the British system of electioneering by introducing the principal-agent relationship between candidate, campaign managers, party officials, and even auxiliary groups speaking in the name of the party.

9. Since many political scientists insist upon defining politics as a struggle for power, perhaps the whole question of smears, morality, and ethics is merely an esoteric exercise in intellectual frustration.

NOTES

1. For an analysis of the 1958 gubernatorial campaign, see Totton J. Anderson, "The 1958 Election in California," *Western Political Quarterly*, 12 (March 1959), 276-300. For the 1962 campaign, see Totton J. Anderson and Eugene C. Lee, "The 1962 Election in California," *ibid.*, 16 (June 1963), 396-420. The author acknowledges with appreciation the permission of the editors of the *Quarterly* and of his coauthor of the latter article to utilize some materials contained in the articles cited.

2. For a description of the major developments in contemporary California politics: Totton J. Anderson, "California: Enigmatic Eldorado of National Politics," in Frank H. Jonas (ed.), *Politics in the American West* (Salt Lake City: University of Utah Press, 1969), pp. 73-123.

3. Joseph P. Kamp, "Meet the Man Who Plans to Rule America" (New York: Headlines, 1958). This brilliant news-beat was credited to W. H. Lawrence, in a story appearing in the *New York Times*, September 14, 1958.

4. Kamp, "Meet the Man," p. 16. Joseph P. Kamp has long been identified as an extremist, right-wing pamphleteer. A report upon his activities has been made for the Anti-defamation League by Arnold Forster entitled *A Measure of Freedom* (Garden City: Doubleday and Co., 1950).

5. *Los Angeles Mirror News*, September 15, 1958. Nixon did repudiate the Kamp pamphlet.

6. *Los Angeles Times*, October 19, 20, and 25, 1958.

7. Citing Senator John F. Kennedy's speech on Brown's behalf, a leaflet entitled "To the People of California" stated: "A Roman Catholic in the White House is the Pope for President." (Material arranged by Raywood Frazier and published by Heritage Manor, Inc., P.O. Box 75673, Sanford Station, Los Angeles.) A pamphlet entitled "Shadows Over Our Schools" by Frank S. Mead, published by Heritage Manor, is in the same vein. I. W. Paden of 11314 Leffingwell, Norwalk, Connecticut, wrote and circulated an undated, open letter to Pat Brown using a similar theme.

8. "Brown Bans the Bible," California Christian Citizen's Association, 1860 W. 95th St., Los Angeles (n.d.).

9. "Arguments in Favor of Initiative Proposition No. 16," *Proposed Amendments to Constitution Propositions and Proposed Laws* (Sacramento: California State Printing Office, 1958), pp. 21-22. The opposing group was named Citizens United Against Taxing Schools.

10. California poll taken September 4, 1958, and data made available from IBM cards supplied through the courtesy of Marvin Field. These findings are tentative since the sample was relatively small.

11. *Los Angeles Examiner*, November 1, 1958. James G. Law and William V. Thompson were listed as cochairmen and the address as 609 So. Grand Ave., Los Angeles.

12. *Human Events*, Vol. XV, No. 40 (October 6, 1958), published at 408 First Street, SE, Washington, D.C.

13. *Los Angeles Times*, November 1, 1958, and *Sacramento Bee*, November 3, 1958. The news dispatches did not report whether Hinckley specified the time and place at which Brown's remarks were delivered.

14. *Los Angeles Times*, October 25, 1958.

15. Committee for Constitutional Government, 202 East 44th Street, New York, in *Wall*

Street Journal, September 22 and October 6 and 14, 1958. Comparable advertisements attacking Proposition 18 but not mentioning Reuther were placed in the metropolitan press by an organization entitled Dollars for Voluntary Unionism, 4536 Wilshire Blvd., Los Angeles. One, entitled "Why are the Union Bosses so Afraid of Proposition 18?" appeared in the *Los Angeles Times*, September 28, 1958.

16. *Los Angeles Times*, October 29, 1958. One of the "adopted authors" sanctioned the letter in Los Angeles ex post facto. Democratic leaders charged a clear violation of the *Elections Code*. A similar Knight project in Long Beach came to a humorous end. Between seventy thousand and one hundred thousand envelopes, carrying the return address of the Democratic party headquarters, were mistakenly delivered by the printer to that address and Democratic party workers refused to relinquish them to Republican headquarters on the supposition that a fraud was being committed.

17. Knight advisers decided almost immediately that the pamphlet was creating an adverse impression and made a valiant effort to destroy all copies that could be retrieved.

18. Two examples of this type of literature: the contrast between Hillings (R) and Mosk (D) in the attorney general race and Trenham (R) and Richards (D) in the state senatorial contest in Los Angeles County. The latter was "Prepared by Research Committee, Los Angeles County Federation of Republican Women," 914 South Olive St., Los Angeles, California.

19. One of the best summaries of the "Hughes Loan" story was written by Gladwin Hill in the *New York Times*, October 7, 1962.

20. Citizens for Honesty in Politics, Carl Strand, 2421 Durant, Berkeley, chairman, and James Aruesen, 2125 Lyan Ave., Belmont, secretary-treasurer.

21. Distributed by Independent Voters of California, 8563 So. Broadway, Los Angeles, Calif., R. Grady (chairman). In a telegram to the Fair Campaign Practices Committee, H. R. Haldeman, Nixon's campaign manager, protested that the address was a Brown headquarters.

22. Republican Research Center, 315 West 9th St., Los Angeles.

23. The League's literature carried several addresses including: Chester Wood, regional director, 1138 East 7th St., Long Beach, Calif., and 1031 S. Grand Ave., Los Angeles, Calif. A flier announcing a League rally advertised, "Learn About the Plot to Force the Elderly off Pension Rolls"; a "Postal-Gram" signed by George McLain, chairman of the League claimed, "If the elderly fail to turn out on Election Day to vote for Brown—and Nixon is elected—the old, the blind and the physically disabled will be forced with a desperate fight just to retain what they have." In another flier distributed by the Citizen's Committee is the statement, "Nixon says there are too many 'chiselers' among the elderly; . . . Don't risk your security."

24. Summer 1962 (San Francisco: Western Independent Publications, 1005 Market St., San Francisco 3, 1962), 31 pages.

25. The Committee to Re-elect Governor Brown, *Nixonpedia*, 3 vols., 505 Market St., San Francisco, and 456 Subway Terminal Bldg., 417 S. Hill St., Los Angeles, 1962.

26. The single confrontation of the two gubernatorial candidates was held October first before the United Press International Editors and Publishers Conference in San Francisco. Roughly the same rules prevailed which governed the 1960 Kennedy-Nixon debates. Both candidates parried some embarrassing questions. It remained for Nixon to break the agreed-upon format by asking a direct question of the governor regarding his endorsement of two assemblymen who "helped lead the riots against the House Un-American Activities Committee" in San Francisco in 1960. Brown reaffirmed his confidence in the two legislators, and accused Nixon of "deliberate slander" and "character assassination," pointing out that they had not been present during the demonstrations.

27. *New York Times*, October 20, 1962.

28. Karl Prussion, *California Dynasty of Communism, Heads Up* (P.O. Box 913, Los Altos, Calif., 1962), 33 pages. The booklet carries a "challenge" on page one: "Karl Prussion will welcome the opportunity to present in a court of law the evidence in his possession regarding the charges made in this issue. He therefore invites legal action by any or all of those named herein." Note: *Democratic State Central Committee* v. *Karl Prussion.* Case No. 806883 at Los Angeles County Superior Court, November 1962.

29. Democrats for Nixon, *Pat Brown and the CDC* (Z. Wayne Griffin, 3908 Wilshire Blvd., Los Angeles 5, and Merritt K. Ruddock, 525 Market St., San Francisco 5, California, 1962), 4 pages.

30. Anti-Communist Voters League, 739 No. Highland, Los Angeles 38, Calif., 16 pages.

31. The press release carried the address Ed Fitzharris and Associates, 607 Market St., San Francisco, and the letter is signed by one William Marlin, executive secretary, with the double address, Central Consular Bldg., 607 Market St., San Francisco, and National Oil Bldg., 609 S. Grand, Los Angeles, Calif. The "Committee's" address: Crocker Anglo Bank, One Montgomery St., San Francisco, Calif.

32. *Los Angeles Herald-Examiner*, November 2, 1962. This was another Democrats-for-Nixon promotion; a tie-in with the Nixon campaign organization. Z. Wayne Griffin, 3908 Wilshire Blvd., Los Angeles 5, and Merritt K. Roddock, 525 Market St., San Francisco 5, Calif.

33. Members of the California FCPC were: Democrats, Cochairman Paul Veblen, executive director of the Santa Barbara *News-Press* (Santa Barbara); W. D. Henderson, legislative advocate (Fresno); Professor Eugene C. Lee, assistant director, Institute of Governmental Studies, University of California (Berkeley); James C. Sheppard, attorney (Los Angeles); and Republicans, Cochairman H. Connor Templeton, member, Stock Exchange firm (Sacramento); Henry Duque, partner in firm for which Nixon was legal counsel (Los Angeles); Richard E. Guggenhime (San Francisco) and Leon Scales (San Diego), both lawyers. The chairman of the national organization was Charles P. Taft; the executive secretary, Bruce L. Felknor.

34. Several of these: *Fair Play in Politics*, a twenty-four-page booklet describing "Campaign Tactics in Actual Use"; the FCPC *Code*; a *Report* entitled "The State-by-State Study of Smear: 1960" in the form of a sixteen-page pamphlet; and a "Voter's Check List" of twelve common techniques of misrepresentation in political campaigning, each illustrated with an appropriate cartoon (in folder format). The committee's address: 45 East 65th St., New York 21, New York.

35. The applicable sections of the *Elections Code*: Division 8, Ch. 3, Art. 2, Sec. 12047-12057. The status of the "election disclosure law" was put in legal limbo on January 9, 1964, when the Third District Court of Appeals ruled in effect that the statute violated freedom of speech and was therefore unconstitutional. The court held that

> in the context of political association and communication, anonymity is an essential ingredient of free expression, protected against all but the rock-bottom minimum of governmental interference. No less than censorship, forced disclosure may have the practical effect of an advance restraint on expression.

References to the *Code* reflect the status of regulations in effect at the time of the 1962 election.

In the case of *Walter Nelson* v. *George Cannon*, the latter in the capacity of campaign manager for one Ray Chism, candidate in a supervisorial race in El Dorado County, was accused of writing and circulating an anonymous letter in favor of his client. Chism won the 1962 race as an incumbent. Subsequently his defeated opponent, Walter Nelson, charged Cannon with authorship of the letter. Cannon pleaded innocent and moved for dismissal, challenging the law. He then sought a writ of prohibition in Superior Court which was denied. The District Attorney of El Dorado County asked for a rehearing of the decision.

36. *Edgar G. Hiestand* v. *Everett G. Burkhalter, et al.* Order of Presiding Judge MacIntyre Faries. November 5, 1962. Case 805673. Dismissed 3 April 63. Related cases: *Everett Burkhalter* v. *Edgar Hiestand* (C806891), dismissed 15 April 63; *Everett Burkhalter* v. *Richard Nixon* (C807312), dismissed 10 December 62.

37. One of the most interesting general discussions of the legal implications of "defamation" is Dix W. Noel, "Defamation of Public Officers and Candidates," *Columbia Law Review* 49 (November 1949), 875-903. An analysis of questionable campaign materials in California campaigns may be found in Peter R. Leigh, "The Legal and Political Implications of the Utilization of Campaign Literature in California Elections" (Master's thesis, University of Southern California, 1964). See also Edward L. Miller, "Political Libel," 33 *Southern California Law Review* (1959).

POLITICS AND
MORALITY — APART ?

W ALTER Eli Quigley is aptly called "the artist" in Professor Frank Jonas' chapters on that peripatetic Minnesota dynamiter. He was an artist who led his generation in the capacity to take tiny bits and pieces of truth and fashion them into a mosaic of persuasive power and seeming consistency. The picture thus presented of the target candidate was a portrait of an evil and dangerous man, and for all the verisimilitude of its ingredients, it had no real relation to the actual life and record of the man under attack.

Quigley prided himself on sticking to facts as the basis of these weird compositions. He viewed his work as libel proof, and so it was. He thought of himself as a skilled practitioner who was not himself dishonest, but here his analysis was simply self-serving.

If Walter Quigley was not a consummate political liar, then he was an even more dangerous threat to the political system: a political psychopath, unable to comprehend the moral and ethical limits in which less alienated men find they must operate.

Quigley's field of operation was that crazy quilt of open space between and among the strictures and prohibitions of the law. No one could prove that he was unfairly or unlawfully demolishing the careers he hired himself out to ruin. Thus he was the archetype of the political defamer, able to present a subtly or blatantly false impression, always lethal, yet able to prove the accuracy of every ingredient.

V. O. Key observed that most smears are lies, nothing more, nothing less. Quigley saw himself as a dynamiter rather than as a liar, and certainly not as a smear artist. Yet the view was as self-deceptive as his product was deceptive to others. It was entirely sophistic; if he painted lies with a brush dipped in facts, that fact did not make him less a liar.

Quigley's understandable passion for self-justification seems superficially to have been supported in at least one regard. He was not a last-minute bomber, but preferred to plant and ignite his charges early in the campaign so they could become current conversation from one end of the victim's state to the other. The standard smear artist waits until the last few days of the campaign to plant his fabrications, when there is no time for the abused candidate to seek out the facts of a rebuttal and get them into circulation.

But the master dynamiter did not prefer early release out of scruple. His reasons were entirely based on what he saw as the effectiveness of his arguments. And they were supported by the cynical knowledge that a pattern of deception woven carefully enough could be made public early and would indeed spread and feed on itself, making quite enough voters angry or perplexed to have the desired effect. Quigley's atypical timing did not make him more honest than other political smearers, but simply more brazen and cynical.

It is very well for the scholar or historian to suspend moral judgment while he is compiling the record of a dishonest election campaign. But it must be remembered that it is this very suspension of moral judgment which the dishonest politician asks of the voter, and practices himself.

"We knew he wasn't a Communist but we had to get him out of office." Here is the perennial, standard disclaimer of all moral responsibility for destructive and reprehensible actions. When the voter does suspend moral judgment he accepts the doctrine that there is no room for morality in politics. And accepting that doctrine degrades his government, his political society, and the voter himself as a participant in that society.

Viscount Morley put it succinctly: "Those who would treat politics and morality apart will never understand the one or the other." The observation remains as true as it was in Morley's day, but because the penalties for political failure are higher today, it is more important in the second half of this century than in the preceding one.

Political pros who came early or late to the conclusion that they would do anything to win are the source of much of the trouble examined in this book. Some primitive societies interpret "sin" as getting caught violating a taboo, and the dishonest pros celebrated here might fare better in such societies than in our own. However, the often spectacular dirty work of the professional probably is dwarfed in volume by more numerous but more drab deceptions by well-meaning but inept amateurs. Deliberate and highly professional smear sheets like the output of Walter Quigley are outnumbered at least two-to-one in the files of the Fair Campaign Practices Committee by the handiwork of the home craftsman.

Rarely are these amateur productions as sensational in effect as was one of them: the Stalin leaflet of the 1958 Arizona campaign. The motivations that impel amateurs into the arena of political propaganda, however, often enough are quite comparable to those that motivated that bizarre anti-Goldwater episode. Frank Goldberg was outraged at the unrestrained appetite of the Pulliam press to have it both ways, or every possible way, to depict the Arizona senator as a hero of the age, and any opposition as knaves.

Capably set forth, the points behind the Stalin cartoon could have been devastating, virtually impossible to refute, and proof against the legal punishment that awaited Goldberg and his friend Anderson. The misadventure argues for leaving political literature to canny professionals, just as the other illustrations between these covers speak of the need for *honest* pros.

One can understand Goldberg's thirst for retaliation and exposure of the transparent and unscrupled eagerness of the Pulliam newspapers to elect Goldwater. But one need not condone the fashion in which he did it. One may accept his contention that he was unaware of the identification requirement of federal law without denying the validity and the social utility of the requirement.

The angry shock with which the Pulliam papers learned of the Stalin leaflet would be funny were it not for the absence of perspective it reveals. When a participant in a political dialogue elects to do "anything to win," he should never be startled to find that the opposition has made or is making a similar decision.

Stanley Kelley, Jr., the perceptive and distinguished Princeton political scientist, has noted the oversimplification with which politicians often present issues, and he cautions against ascribing the phenomenon to cynicism. He observes that politicians themselves often tend to see issues in oversimplified terms.

So also with some politically oriented newspapers, clearly including those published by Eugene Pulliam. Goldwater, larger than life and pure white; McFarland, also outsize, but all black. In this way it was possible for any Goldwater "support"–Communist-oriented labor figures or not–to be seen by the *Arizona Republic* as all-wise and good. Further, therefore, it was possible for the Pulliam press to see damning Goldwater with faint praise as unqualified praise. So also it became not only acceptable but specifically honorable journalism to depict McFarland's bona fide labor supporter Al Green as a jailbird. There was no need to highlight the circumstances of his jailing for union activity. That his offense was quite a different matter from theft, kidnapping, murder, or some other more heinous crime was not so important to the paper. Any lurid cause for his arrest could be supplied by the imagination of the reader, to which the newspaper's account gave full rein and an invitation.

The role attributed to the press and the role it actually plays in American elections often are quite different things. The presidential campaign of 1952 saw the Democrats condemning a monolithic, one-party press which favored

Eisenhower and ignored Stevenson. Twelve years later Goldwater chafed at the press as arrayed all but solidly against him. Usually the press has betrayed a Republican bias in its ownership and editorial policy and some Democratic bias in its news and opinion columns. Perhaps more damage is done by a bland rehearsal of statistics and statements under the guise of objectivity, and for fear of giving free rein to bias, than by actual slanting of news stories and headlines. The case of the Arizona Senate campaign of 1958, and the Pulliam papers, is quite different. There do remain a few newspapers where the "fact" diet of the subscriber is rigidly controlled by management. The Manchester (N.H.) *Union-Leader* comes readily to mind. Fortunately, however, such instances are rare.

If the colorful career of Walter Quigley illumines for us the craft of the political smear artist, and the curious affair of the Stalin cartoon in Arizona shows the confusion amateurs can sow, it remains for the California capers of 1958 and 1962 to enrich the tapestry by introducing an important thread. This is the work of the zealot, whose comprehension of politics is limited and whose participation in politics is rare. To be sure, anti-Communist zealots do speckle many of the pages devoted to Quigley and his assorted prey, but it is in California, and southern California in particular, that there exists the largest and most richly varied crop of zealots in America today, and probably in political history.

Professor Totton Anderson, from the vantage point of a campus surrounded by Los Angeles County, brings perspective to our consideration of the interaction among political pros, smear artists, amateurs, and zealots. The state's political history reflects the climate and dreamy here-is-Utopia quality that has populated California with people who came for a two-week visit and elected to stay. Whereas, until the admission of Alaska to the Union, Texas was always the biggest, California was always the most. Unlike the Lone Star State, which was the biggest simply by being there, the Golden State had to perform to win its distinction. From a brawling frontier it was completely civilized and operated—by the railroads. Hiram Johnson wrested control from the railroads and turned over a monstrous burden of reform-oriented freedom from politics to a rootless and scantily informed public. Democrats populated the state and with spectacular docility enshrined a permanent Republican government. Republicans turned from baiting and cutting would-be Democratic politicians to predacious attacks on one another, and with characteristic abandon the state went Democratic.

When newspapers called the California campaign of 1958 "the dirtiest in the 108-year history of the state," they exhausted an image they might have saved for 1962, whose elections were the dirtiest in the 112-year history of the state.

The anti-Catholicism displayed in the 1958 private-school-tax issue was vented not only for the merits of the issue but also as a dry run for the awful possibility that in 1960 a Catholic might run for the presidency of the United States. It demonstrated the zealot in action. The eager readers of tracts like those described by Professor Anderson believed devoutly that the Pope's agent was about to gobble up their freedom. Many of the authors of this scare material believed so, too. So they rushed to the lists to do battle for the Lord—white, Anglo-Saxon, and Protestant, like themselves.

They failed to fend off Papal Agent Pat Brown in 1958. In 1960 their denial of the California electoral vote to Papal Agent Kennedy did not avail. So by 1962 many of these troops were ready to work for a new god, anti-Communism. Anti-Communism had become a way of life in California before McCarthyism entered the language. Its exploitation for election campaign purposes had been brought to a high degree of polish by the Nixon-Chotiner axis, and it is not surprising that in 1962, when Nixon sought to rehabilitate his political career on his own home ground, the spectre of the Kremlin should be raised and waved over Pat Brown. To California's Republican liberals and moderates and conservatives and reactionaries had been added a horde of glandular rightists who needed a massive Communist conspiracy to explain the social and political misadventures of modern history. Thus when Casper Weinberger and Jud Leetham sought to have Karl Prussion's lurid red pamphlet removed from party headquarters staffed by these avid volunteers, all they managed to do was win for themselves more enmity and suspicion from the rightists.

The left orientation of much of the California Democratic Council, and the ardent, far-out left extremism of some of its activists, had quietly disturbed many California Democrats for years. For this reason, it was perhaps inevitable that pamphlet efforts to paint the CDC as a Communist phalanx and Pat Brown as its dupe or captive would bulk heavily on the political horizon. The pros knew Pat Brown was no Communist; they needed to get him out of office. The zealots knew he was a Communist and therefore *they* had to get him out. California style, they went all out. They went too far.

Going too far to damn a public figure, painting him so utterly black (or red) as to defy belief, is where political dynamiting is most likely to fall apart. This was the principal flaw of the effort to make a pro-Communist out of Senator James E. Murray in Montana's 1954 campaign.

Perhaps the relative blatancy of all these campaigns reflects the celebrated direct-action, rough-and-ready character of the West. None of these dynamiting efforts had the subtlety, the delicacy of innuendo, of perhaps the most famous modern-day smear effort in America—the Tydings-Browder composite photograph used in Maryland in 1950 to defeat conservative Democratic Senator Millard Tydings. The Maryland campaign of 1950 was basically responsible for the subsequent development of the Fair Campaign Practices Committee. The prescription for such a citizens' effort appeared in the final report of the Senate elections subcommittee that investigated the Maryland contest. The fact that the Fair Campaign Committee came into existence in 1954, an election year that was, if possible, even dirtier than that of 1950, is a gentle irony. Yet the Committee had to start somewhere, and it could hardly have come into existence at a time more opportune to observe the full range of dishonest and scurrilous electioneering.

Republicans and uninvolved citizens, which latter is to say deficient citizens, may be disturbed by the incidence of complaints against the Republicans implied in this volume. But the fact is that on the pro-Communist issue the Democrats have been maligned often and unjustly, and dishonestly (we knew he wasn't a Communist; we had to get him out of office), for two decades. It is only natural—in human terms it is inevitable—that Democrats and liberals generally should smart at and bitterly resent this epoch of calumny. It is as natural that they should strike back at the first opportunity. The opportunity is offered now by the existence of a radical right, which under the guise of conservatism would work a revolution as profound and radical as that of the most ardent Maoist, and hardly less bloody. ("Our cross hairs are on the backs of your necks," the Minutemen cautioned the liberals a few years ago. "Don't impeach him, hang him," some of their confreres urged of Earl Warren.)

If the temptation of the liberals to sully the Republican image with the epithet *Bircher* and worse is irresistible, it is neither rational nor admirable, nor more soundly based than the slings and arrows which the liberals suffered all those years. But it must be understood.

Understanding is the end which I think this book serves admirably. Only the scratchy and uncomfortable details of the scandals and smears and slanders of some of America's more disgraceful election campaigns of present memory can give the reader anything akin to an emotional comprehension of the vicissitudes which some of the nation's most distinguished public servants have borne, sometimes philosophically, sometimes bitterly and in frustrated rage.

Such understanding in the long run can help not only to see in recent history the causes of new excesses, but to attack the new smears at their roots.

The deepest root is the fact that politicians as a class are neither better nor worse, stronger nor weaker, wiser nor stupider, than the population at large. Proportionately as many of them are mercenary, or dishonest, or opportunistic, or short-sighted, or overly emotional, or implacably zealous, as are the citizens they serve and whose votes they seek.

Here is a study involving a handful of smear artists, and only a few more candidates for public trust, as traducers and traduced. The import for the nation of these cases is larger: the number of American citizens who accepted or rejected the spurious arguments advanced by the mortal men celebrated in this volume.

BIBLIOGRAPHY

Allyn, Paul [pseud.], and Joseph Greene [pseud.]. *See How They Run: The Making of a Congressman.* Philadelphia: Chilton, 1964.

Anderson, Totton J. "Extremism in California Politics: The Brown-Knowland and the Brown-Nixon Campaigns Compared," *Western Political Quarterly,* 16 (1963), 371-72.

————. "The 1958 Election in California," *Western Political Quarterly*, 12 (1959), 276-300.

Anderson, Totton J., and Eugene C. Lee. "The 1962 Election in California," *Western Political Quarterly*, 16 (1963), 396-420.

Anderson, Walt. *Campaigns: Cases in Political Conflict.* Pacific Palisades, Calif.: Goodyear Publishing Co., 1970.

Baus, Herbert M., and William B. Ross. *Politics Battle Plan.* New York: Macmillan Co., 1968.

Bone, Hugh A. *Smear Politics: An Analysis of 1940 Campaign Literature.* Washington, D.C.: Public Affairs Press, 1941.

Bousliman, George. "The 1954 Campaign of Senator James E. Murray." M.A. thesis, University of Montana, 1964.

Burdick, Eugene. *The 480.* New York: McGraw-Hill, 1964.

Cannon, Lou. *Ronnie and Jesse: A Political Odyssey.* Garden City: Doubleday and Co., 1969.

Costikyan, Edward N. *Behind Closed Doors: Politics in the Public Interest.* New York: Harcourt, Brace and World, 1966.

Felknor, Bruce L. *Dirty Politics.* New York: W. W. Norton and Co., 1966.

————. *Fair Play in Politics.* New York: Fair Campaign Practices Committee, 1960.

————. *State-by-State Studies of Smear*, 1956, 1958, 1960, 1962, 1964. New York: Fair Campaign Practices Committee.

———. *You Are They*. New York: M.W. Lads, 1964.

Glick, Edward M. "Strategy and Tactics of the Party in Power in the 1958 Campaign." Ph.D. dissertation, Ohio State University, 1960.

Hansen, Gerald Edwin. "The Conservative Movement in Utah after World War II." Ph.D. dissertation, University of Missouri, 1962.

Hill, Gladwin. *Dancing Bear: An Inside Look at California Politics.* Cleveland: World Publishing Co., 1968.

Jonas, Frank H. "The Art of Political Dynamiting," *Western Political Quarterly*, 10 (1957), 374-91.

———. "The Mormon Church and Political Dynamiting in the 1950 Election in Utah," *Proceedings*, Utah Academy of Sciences, Arts, and Letters, 40 (1963), 94-110.

———. "The 1950 Elections in Utah," *Western Political Quarterly*, 4 (1951), 81-91.

———. "Political Dynamiting," *Proceedings*, Utah Academy of Sciences, Arts, and Letters, 33 (1956), 135-47.

———. "Political Slander in Election Campaigns," *Western Political Quarterly*, 16 supp. (1963), 15-20.

———. *The Story of a Political Hoax*. Salt Lake City: University of Utah, Institute of Government, 1966.

Kelley, Stanley, Jr. *Political Campaigning: Problems in Creating an Informed Electorate.* Washington, D.C.: Brookings Institution, 1960.

———. *Professional Public Relations and Political Power.* Baltimore: Johns Hopkins Press, 1956.

Kelly, Joseph. "A Study of the Defeat of Senator Burton K. Wheeler in the 1946 Democratic Primary Election." M.A. thesis, University of Montana, 1959.

Leuthold, David A. *Electioneering in a Democracy: Campaigns for Congress.* New York: John Wiley and Sons, 1968.

Mayer, Martin. *Madison Avenue, USA*. New York: Simon and Schuster, Pocket Books, 1959; originally published by Harper and Brothers, 1958.

McCaffrey, Maurice. *Advertising Wins Elections.* Minneapolis: Gilbert, 1962.

Meyer, D. Swing. *The Winning Candidate: How to Defeat Your Political Opponent.* New York: James H. Heineman, 1966.

New Methodology: The Study of Political Strategy and Tactics. Washington, D.C.: American Institute for Political Communication, 1967.

Novak, Robert D. *The Agony of the G.O.P.* New York: Macmillan Co., 1965.

Parkinson, Hank. *Winning Your Campaign: A Nuts-and-Bolts Guide to Political Victory.* Englewood Cliffs: Prentice-Hall, 1970.

Payne, Thomas. "The 1954 Election in Montana," *Western Political Quarterly*, 7 (1954), 610-613.

Phillips, Herbert L. *Big Wayward Girl: An Informal Political History of California.* Garden City: Doubleday and Co., 1968.

Polsby, Nelson W., and Aaron B. Wildavsky. *Presidential Elections: Strategies of American Electoral Politics.* 2d. ed. New York: Charles Scribner's Sons, 1968.

Pool, Ithiel de Sola, and Robert P. Abelson. "The Simulmatics Project," *Public Opinion Quarterly*, 25 (1961), 167-83.

Pool, Ithiel de Sola, Robert P. Abelson, and Samuel L. Popkin. *Candidates, Issues, and Strategies: A Computer Simulation of the 1960 Presidential Election.* Cambridge, Mass.: M.I.T. Press, 1964.

The Republican Campaign Plan. Washington, D.C.: Republican National Committee, 1958.

Rice, Ross. R. "The 1958 Election in Arizona," *Western Political Quarterly*, 12 (1959), 266-75.

Shadegg, Stephen. *Barry Goldwater: Freedom Is His Flight Plan.* New York: Fleet Publishing Corp., 1962.

———. *How to Win an Election: The Art of Political Victory.* New York: Taplinger Publishing Co., 1964.

———. *What Happened to Goldwater? The Inside Story of the 1964 Republican Campaign.* New York: Holt, Rinehart and Winston, 1965.

Taft, Charles P., and Bruce L. Felknor. *Prejudice and Politics.* New York: Antidefamation League of B'nai B'rith, 1960.

White, F. Clifton. *Suite 3505: The Story of the Draft Goldwater Movement.* New Rochelle, N.Y.: Arlington House, 1967.

White, Theodore H. *The Making of the President, 1960.* New York: Atheneum Publishers, 1961.

———. *The Making of the President, 1964.* New York: Atheneum Publishers, 1965.

CONTRIBUTORS

TOTTON J. ANDERSON is Professor of Political Science (from 1947), a former chairman of the Department of Political Science and Associate Dean of the College of Letters, Arts and Sciences, University of Southern California. He received his A.B. and M.A. degrees from the University of California (Berkeley) and his Ph.D. from the University of Southern California. He was a teaching fellow at the University of California and registrar and dean at Ventura College, 1935-47. During World War II he served in the U.S. Army Air Corps in the European Theater of Operations. He was separated in the rank of Lieutenant Colonel; in 1954 he was promoted to Colonel, U.S. Air Force Reserve, and served as an Intelligence Staff Officer, USAFR. He has served as president of the Western Political Science Association; as Associate Director of the National Center for Education in Politics, New York; and as Director of the Southern California-Arizona Citizenship Clearing House. He is now serving as a member on the Board of Trustees of the Coro Foundation, San Francisco, as Chairman of the Executive Committee of the California Legislative Intern Program, Sacramento, and on the Executive Committee of the California State Constitution Revision Commission. He has recently served on the Mayor's Advisory Commission on Community Development (Los Angeles), and is a sometime member of the Reserve Officer Advisement Board to the Commandant, Air ROTC, Air University, Alabama. He is co-author of *Politics in the American West* (1969), *Introduction to Political Science* (1967), *Bibliography on Western Politics* (1958), and *Problems of Democratic Society; Readings and Study Outlines* (1941). He has contributed to *Cooperation and Conflict: Readings in American Federalism* (1969), *Collier's Encyclopedia, The Western Political Quarterly, The Annals of the American Academy of Political and Social Science*, the *World Affairs Interpreter*, the *Social Science Review* (Los Angeles), and the University of Southern California *Law Review*.

R. JOHN EYRE is Associate Professor of Government, Chairman of the Department of Government, and Director of the Government Research Institute at Idaho State University. He received his B.A. degree from the University of Utah, his M.A. from the University of New Mexico and his Ph.D. from the University of Colorado. He held research and teaching assistantships at the University of Colorado and taught courses in political science at the Colorado Springs and Denver campuses of that institution. During 1960, as a Citizenship Clearing House fellow, he served as assistant to the Chairman of the Democratic State Central Committee in Colorado and subsequently was elected state president of the Young Democrats in the Centennial State. He was director of the Boulder regional office of the Foreign Policy Association from 1961 to 1967. He has been president of the Colorado Council of Adult Education (1964-65), and has served on the Board of Adjustments of the City of Pocatello and on the Advisory Council to the Committee on Election Laws of the Idaho Legislature. He is co-author of *The Colorado Preprimary System*, and has written chapters and/or articles in *Readings in Colorado Governmental Politics*, *Idaho Government and Politics*, *The Journal of the Idaho Academy of Science*, and *Rendezvous: A Journal of Arts and Letters* as well as reports and monographs based on field research conducted in Idaho.

BRUCE L. FELKNOR attended the University of Wisconsin, 1939-41. He was a visiting lecturer at Hamilton College in 1966. At the present time he is assistant to the publisher and chairman of the board of the Encyclopedia Britannica, Inc. His long association with the Fair Campaign Practices Committee, Inc. from 1956 to 1966 has qualified his writings on campaign propaganda and techniques. In public relations work he has been associated with Market Relations Network, Inc., Foote, Cone and Belding, Inc., Ford Motor Company, International Telephone and Telegraph Corporation, and American Airlines. He has been a radio officer in the Air Transport Command and the Merchant Marine. He has also participated actively in a number of civic and religious groups. His publications include: *Dirty Politics* (1966), *Fair Play in Politics* (1960), *Prejudice and Politics* (1960), *State-by-State Smear Study* (1956, 1958, 1960, 1962), and *You Are They* (1964).

FRANK H. JONAS is Professor of Political Science at the University of Utah. He received the B.S. and M.A. degrees from the University of Utah, and the Ph.D. from the University of Washington and holds certificates of achievement from the University of Berlin and the Hochschule fuer Politik in Germany (1931). After holding teaching and research fellowships at the University of Washington, he served subsequently on the staffs of the following universities:

Idaho State, Southern California, New Mexico, Utah State, and, in summer sessions, Illinois and Vanderbilt. He held the Chester W. Nimitz Chair of Social and Political Philosophy at the Naval War College in Newport, Rhode Island (1960-61). From 1943 to 1945 he served in the U.S. Army Signal Corps; he spent 1951-53 in Germany as a Press Scrutiny Officer, Cultural Exchange Officer and Information Specialist in HICOG, United States Department of State; and in 1958 he was a guest exchange professor of the Federal Republic of Germany. Professor Jonas was a member of Utah's first Legislative Council (1947-49); chairman of the Veterans' Council, Utah State Department of Veterans' Affairs (1948-51); and a consultant in personnel administration at Hill Air Force Base, USAF, Ogden, Utah (1951). He has served as president of the Western Political Science Association (1964-65) and of the University of Utah Education Association (1965-67). He has been a member of the UEA Political Action Committee (1964) and the Salt Lake County Planning Council (1963), and is now on the Salt Lake County Welfare Board. Beginning his writings in local politics with "Utah: Sagebrush Democracy," in *Rocky Mountain Politics* (1940), he has produced over fifty articles on local and regional politics, has edited and contributed to *Western Politics* (1961) and *Politics in the American West* (1969), and has written the following monographs: *Western Politics and the 1956 Elections*, *Bibliography on Western Politics*, *Western Politics and the 1958 Elections*, and *Western Politics and the 1962 Elections*. His most recent monograph is *The Story of a Political Hoax*.

THOMAS PAYNE is Professor of Political Science at the University of Montana. He was born in Fulton, Missouri, where he graduated from Westminister College in 1941. After serving in the Army Air Force (1942-46), he was discharged as a First Lieutenant and entered the University of Chicago from which he received his Ph.D. in 1951. He was instructor in political science at the University of Tennessee from 1948 to 1950. He has been a member of the University of Montana faculty since 1951. From 1958 to 1964, he served as a member of the Board of Trustees of the Missoula Elementary School District, and was chairman of the Board from 1962 to 1964. He has contributed articles to the *Western Political Quarterly* and other professional journals and a chapter to *Presidential Nominating Politics*; he is co-author of *Service and Security: Municipal Retirement in Tennessee*. He has also contributed to such regional studies in government and politics as *Bibliography on Western Politics* and *The States in the Pacific Northwest*. He has served as a member of the Board of Editors of the *Western Political Quarterly*, and was President of the Pacific Northwest Political Science Association, 1964-65. He was Chairman of the Department of Political Science at the University of Montana from 1959 to 1966.

INDEX

Al Green Advises Arizona Demos In Goldwa'

(Continued from Page 1)

ern Conference of Teamsters and former administrative assistant to the notorious Dave Beck; Edward Dean Woodward, Mountain States teamster representative f r o m Colorado; and Carl J. Windschanz and Jack J. Williams, officers of large Los Angeles teamster locals.

THE FOURSOME was picked up at the Sky Riders Hotel at Sky Harbor Airport here by the car of Bill Waggoner, Phoenix business agent for transport and local delivery drivers. Their meeting in downtown Phoenix lasted from about 9:30 a.m. to 1:15 p.m. They left town by air the same day.

A check of Green's movements shows he was registered at the Adams Hotel in Phoenix or the Santa Rita Hotel in Tucson for 13 days in February. In May, he was registered at the Adams for nine days. In July, he was registered at the Adams or Santa Rita for 26 days.

In August, he was registered ? the Adams or Santa Rita for days. In September, he wa tered at the Adams or S' for 28 days. He was ' both hotels again t'

IN TUCSON

homes of t' active ir fairs. tact' tr

SEN. GOLDWATER